Accounting Best Practices

Sixth Edition

Steven M. Bragg

WILEY

John Wiley & Sons, Inc.

Published by John Wiley & Sons, Inc., Hoboken, New Jersey.

Published simultaneously in Canada.

For general information on our other products and services, or technical support, please contact our Customer Care Department within the United States at 800-762-2974, outside the United States at 317-572-3993 or fax 317-572-4002.

Wiley also publishes its books in a variety of electronic formats. Some content that appears in print may not be available in electronic books.

For more information about Wiley products, visit our Web site at www.wiley.com.

Library of Congress Cataloging-in-Publication Data:

ISBN: 978-0-470-56165-2

Printed in the United States of America

10 9 8 7 6 5 4 3 2 1

About the Author

Steven Bragg, CPA, has been the chief financial officer or controller of four companies, as well as a consulting manager at Ernst & Young and auditor at Deloitte & Touche. He received a master's degree in finance from Bentley College, an MBA from Babson College, and a bachelor's degree in economics from the University of Maine. He has been the two-time president of the Colorado Mountain Club and is an avid alpine skier, mountain biker, and certified master diver. Mr. Bragg resides in Centennial, Colorado. He has written the following books published by John Wiley & Sons:

Accounting and Finance for Your Small Business

Accounting Best Practices

Accounting Control Best Practices

Accounting Policies and Procedures Manual

Billing and Collections Best Practices

Business Ratios and Formulas

Controller's Guide to Costing

Controller's Guide to Planning and Controlling Operations

Controller's Guide: Roles and Responsibilities for the New Controller

Controllership

Cost Accounting

Essentials of Payroll

Fast Close

Financial Analysis

GAAP Guide

GAAP Policies and Procedures Manual

Inventory Accounting

Inventory Best Practices

Just-in-Time Accounting

Managing Explosive Corporate Growth

Mergers and Acquisitions

Outsourcing

Payroll Accounting
Payroll Best Practices
Revenue Recognition
Running a Public Company
Sales and Operations for Your Small Business
The Controller's Function
The New CFO Financial Leadership Manual
The Ultimate Accountants' Reference
Treasury Management

Free On-Line Resources
by Steve Bragg

Steve issues an accounting best practices podcast, and posts many other accounting materials at accountingtools.com.

Contents

Preface

The accounting department is a cost center. It does not directly generate revenues, but, rather, provides a fixed set of services to the rest of the company, and is asked to do so at the lowest possible cost. Consequently, the accounting staff is called on to process transactions, write reports, create new processes, or investigate old ones—while doing so as an ever-shrinking proportion of total corporate expenses.

This cost-based environment is a very difficult one for most accountants, for their training is primarily in accounting rules and regulations, rather than in how to run a very specialized department in a cost-effective manner. They find a few ideas for improvements from attending seminars or perusing accounting or management magazines, but there is no centralized source of information for them to consult that itemizes a wide array of possible improvements. Hence the need for the sixth edition of *Accounting Best Practices*, which contains 406 accounting best practices, of which 57 are new to this edition.

This book is compiled from the author's lengthy experience in setting up and operating a number of accounting departments, as well as by providing consulting services to other companies. Accordingly, it contains a blend of best practices from a wide variety of accounting environments, ranging from small partnerships to multibillion-dollar corporations. This means that not all of the best practices described within these pages will be useful in every situation—some are designed to provide quick and inexpensive, incremental improvements, while others are groundbreaking events requiring six-figure investments (or more) and months of installation time. Consequently, each chapter includes a table that notes the ease, duration, and cost of implementation for every best practice within it. These tables separate best practices into a number of subcategories, and also contain a reference number that is useful for locating the main text for each best practice within the chapter. Also, a selection of best practices have an "Author's Choice" graphic posted next to them. These best practices are ones the author has found to be particularly effective in improving accounting operations. All best practices are also noted in summary form in Appendix A.

Although this book is the central source of best practices information for the accountant, there are several other books available that specialize in smaller niches within the accounting area. Each of these books contains many additional best practices not found in *Accounting Best Practices*. These include the author's *Inventory Best Practices* (John Wiley & Sons, 2004), *Billing and Collections Best Practices* (John Wiley & Sons, 2005), *Payroll Best Practices* (John Wiley & Sons, 2005), and *Fast Close*, 2nd Edition (John Wiley & Sons, 2009).

STEVEN M. BRAGG
Centennial, Colorado
November 2009

Chapter 1

Introduction

A chief executive officer (CEO) spends months deciding on a corporate strategy. The plan probably includes a mix of changes in products, customers, and markets, as well as demands for increased efficiencies or information in a number of existing areas. The CEO then hands off the plan to a group of managers who are quite capable of implementing many of the changes, but who scratch their heads over how to squeeze greater efficiencies or information out of existing departments in order to meet their strategic goals. This is where best practices come into play.

A best practice is really *any* improvement over existing systems, though some consultants prefer to confine the definition to those few high-end and very advanced improvements that have been successfully installed by a few world-class companies. This book uses the broader definition of any improvement over existing systems, since the vast majority of companies are in no position, in terms of either technological capabilities, monetary resources, or management skill, to make use of truly world-class best practices. Using this wider definition, a best practice can be anything that increases the existing level of efficiency, such as switching to blanket purchase orders, signature stamps, and procurement cards to streamline the accounts payable function. It can also lead to improved levels of reporting for use by other parts of the company, such as activity-based costing, target costing, or direct costing reports in the costing function. Further, it can reduce the number of transaction errors, by such means as automated employee expense reports, automated bank account deductions, or a simplified commission calculation system. By implementing a plethora of best practices, a company can greatly improve its level of efficiency and information reporting, which fits nicely into the requirements of most strategic plans.

One can go further than describing best practices as an excellent *contributor* to the fulfillment of a company's strategy, and even state that a strategy does not have much chance of success *unless* best practices are involved. The reason is that best practices have such a large impact on overall efficiencies, they unleash a large number of excess people who can then work on other strategic issues, as well as reduce a company's cash requirements, releasing more cash for investment in strategic targets. In addition, some best practices link company functions more closely together, resulting in better overall functionality—this is a singular improvement when a company is in the throes of changes caused by strategy shifts. Further, best practices can operate quite well in the *absence* of a strategic plan. For example, any department manager can install a variety of best practices with no approval or oversight from above, resulting in a multitude of beneficial changes. Thus, best practices are a linchpin of the successful corporate strategy, and can also lead to improvements even if they are not part of a grand strategic vision.

The scope of this book does not encompass all of the best practices that a company should consider, only those used by the accounting department. This area is especially susceptible to improvement through best practices, since it is heavily procedure-driven. When there are many procedures, there are many opportunities to enhance the multitude of procedure steps through automation, simplification, elimination of tasks, error-proofing, and outsourcing. Thus, of all the corporate functions, this is the one that reacts best to treatment through best practices.

Chapter 2 covers a variety of issues related to the implementation of best practices, such as differentiating between incremental and reengineering changes, circumstances under which best practices are most likely to succeed, and how to plan and proceed with these implementations. Most important, there is a discussion of the multitude of reasons why a best practice implementation can fail, which is excellent reading prior to embarking on a new project, in order to be aware of all possible pitfalls. The chapter ends with a brief review of the impact of best practices on employees. This chapter is fundamental to the book, for it serves as the groundwork on which the remaining chapters are built. For example, if you are interested in modifying the general ledger account structure for use by an activity-based costing system, it is necessary to first review the implementation chapter to see how any programming, software package, or interdepartmental issues might impact the project.

Chapters 3 through 18 each describe a cluster of best practices, with a functional area itemized under each chapter. For example, Chapter 9 covers a variety of improvements to a company's commission calculation and payment systems, while Chapter 18 is strictly concerned with a variety of payroll-streamlining issues related to the collection of employee time information, processing it into payments, and distributing those payments. Chapter 14 is a catchall chapter. It covers a variety of general best practices that do not fit easily into other, more specific chapters. Examples of these best practices are the use of process-centering, on-line reporting, and creating a contract-terms database. Chapters 3 through 18 are the heart of the book since they contain information related to over 400 best practices.

For Chapters 3 through 18, there is an exhibit near the beginning that shows the general level of implementation cost and duration for each of the best practices in the chapter. This information gives the reader a good idea of which best practices to search for and read through, in case these criteria are a strong consideration. For each chapter, there are a number of sections, each one describing a best practice. There is a brief description of the problems it can fix, as well as notes on how it can be implemented, and any problems one may encounter while doing so. Each chapter concludes with a section that describes the impact of a recommended mix of best practices on the functional area being covered. This last section almost always includes a graphical representation of how certain best practices impact specific activities. Not all the best practices in each chapter are included in this graphic, since some are mutually exclusive. This chapter layout is designed to give the reader a quick overview of the best practices that are most likely to make a significant impact on a functional area of the accounting department.

Appendix A lists all of the best practices in each of the preceding chapters. This list allows the reader to quickly find a potentially useful best practice. It is then a simple matter to refer back to the main text to obtain more information about each item.

This book is designed to assist anyone who needs to either improve the efficiency of the accounting department, reduce its error rates, or provide better information to other parts of a company. The best practices noted on the following pages will greatly assist in attaining this goal, which may be part of a grand strategic vision or simply a desire by an accounting manager to improve the department. The layout of the book is extremely practical: to list as many best practices as possible, to assist the reader in finding the most suitable ones, and to describe any implementation problems that may arise. In short, this is the perfect do-it-yourself fix-it book for the manager who likes to tinker with the accounting department.

Chapter 2

How to Use Best Practices

This chapter is about implementing best practices. It begins by describing the various kinds of best practices and goes on to cover those situations where they are most likely to be installed successfully. The key components of a successful best practice installation are also noted. When planning to add a best practice, it is also useful to know the ways in which the implementation can fail, so there is a lengthy list of reasons for failure. Finally, there is a brief discussion of the impact of change on employees and the organization. Only by carefully considering all of these issues in advance can one hope to achieve a successful best practice implementation that will result in increased levels of efficiency in the accounting department.

Types of Best Practices

This section describes the two main types of best practices, each one requiring considerably different implementation approaches.

The first type of best practice is an incremental one. This usually involves either a small modification to an existing procedure or a replacement of a procedure that is so minor in effect that it has only a minimal impact on the organization, or indeed on the person who performs the procedure. The increased level of efficiency contributed by a single best practice of this type is moderate at best, but this type is also the easiest to install, since there is little resistance from the organization. An example of this type of best practice is using a signature stamp to sign checks (see Chapter 3); it is simple, cuts a modest amount of time from the check preparation process, and there will be no complaints about its use. However, only when this type of best practice is used in large numbers is there a significant increase in the level of efficiency of accounting operations.

The second type of best practice involves a considerable degree of reengineering. This requires the complete reorganization or replacement of an existing function. The level of change is massive, resulting in employees either being laid off or receiving vastly different job descriptions. The level of efficiency improvement can be several times greater than the old method it is replacing. However, the level of risk matches the reward, for this type of best practice meets with enormous resistance and consequently is at great risk of failure. An example of this type of best practice is eliminating the accounts payable department in favor of

5

having the receiving staff approve all payments at the receiving dock (see Chapter 3); it involves the elimination of many jobs and is an entirely new approach to paying suppliers. A single best practice implementation of this sort can reap major improvements in the level of accounting efficiency.

Thus, given the considerable number and size of the differences between the incremental and reengineering best practices, it is necessary to first determine into which category a best practice falls before designing a plan for implementing it. Given the difficulty of implementation for a reengineering project, it may even be necessary to delay implementation or intersperse a series of such projects with easier incremental projects in order to allow employees to recover from the reengineering projects.

The Most Fertile Ground for Best Practices

Before installing any best practice, it is useful to review the existing environment to see if there is a reasonable chance for the implementation to succeed. The following bullet points note the best environments in which best practices not only can be installed, but also have a fair chance of continuing to succeed:

- *If benchmarking shows a problem.* Some organizations regularly compare their performance levels against those of other companies, especially those with a reputation for having extremely high levels of performance. If there is a significant difference in the performance levels of these other organizations and the company doing the benchmarking, this can serve as a reminder that continuous change is necessary in order to survive. If management sees and heeds this warning, the environment in which best practices will be accepted is greatly improved.

- *If management has a change orientation.* Some managers have a seemingly genetic disposition toward change. If an accounting department has such a person in charge, there will certainly be a drive toward many changes. If anything, this type of person can go too far, implementing too many projects with not enough preparation, resulting in a confused operations group whose newly revised systems may take a considerable amount of time to untangle. The presence of a detail-oriented second-in-command is very helpful for preserving order and channeling the energies of such a manager into the most productive directions.

- *If the company is experiencing poor financial results.* If there is a significant loss, or a trend in that direction, this serves as a wake-up call to management, which, in turn, results in the creation of a multitude of best practices projects. In this case, the situation may even go too far, with so many improvement projects going on at once that there are not enough resources to go around, resulting in the ultimate completion of few, if any, of the best practices.

- *If there is new management.* Most people who are newly installed as managers of either the accounting department or (better yet) the entire organization want to make changes in order to leave their marks on the organization. Though this can involve less effective practice items like organizational changes or a new strategic direction, it is possible that there will be a renewed focus on efficiency that will result in the implementation of new best practices.

In short, as long as there is a willingness by management to change and a good reason for doing so, then there is fertile ground for the implementation of a multitude of best practices.

Planning for Best Practices

A critical issue for the success of any best practices implementation project is an adequate degree of advance planning. The following bullet points describe the key components of a typical best practices implementation plan:

- *Capacity requirements.* Any project plan must account for the amount of capacity needed to ensure success. Capacity can include the number of people, computers, or floor space that is needed. For example, if the project team requires 20 people, then there must be a planning item to find and equip a sufficient amount of space for this group. Also, a project that requires a considerable amount of programming time should reserve that time in advance with the programming staff to ensure that the programming is completed on time. Further, the management team must have a sufficient amount of time available to properly oversee the project team's activities. If any of these issues are not addressed in advance, there can be a major impact on the success of the implementation.

- *Common change calendar.* If there are many best practices being implemented at the same time, there is a high risk that resources scheduled for one project will not be available for other projects. For example, a key software developer may receive independent requests from multiple project teams to develop software, and cannot satisfy all the requests. To avoid this, one should use a single change calendar, so that planned changes can be seen in the context of other changes being planned. The calendar should be examined for conflicts every time a change is made to it, and also be made available for general review, so that all project teams can consult it whenever needed.

- *Contingencies.* Murphy's Law always applies, so there should be contingencies built into the project plan. For example, if the project team is being set up in a new building, there is always a chance that phone lines will not be installed in time. To guard against this possibility, there should be an additional project step to obtain some cellular phones, which will supply the team's communications needs until the phone lines can be installed.

- *Dependencies.* The steps required to complete a project must be properly sequenced so that any bottleneck steps are clearly defined and have sufficient resources allocated to them to ensure that they are completed on time. For example, a project planning person cannot set up the plan if there is no project planning software available and loaded into the computer. Consequently, this step must be completed before the planning task can commence.

- *Funding requirements.* Any project requires some funding, such as the purchase of equipment for the project team or software licenses or employee training. Consequently, the project plan must include the dates on which funding is expected, so that dependent tasks involving the expenditure of those funds can be properly planned.

- *Review points.* For all but the smallest projects, there must be control points at which the project manager has a formal review meeting with those people who are responsible for certain deliverables. These review points must be built into the plan, along with a sufficient amount of time for follow-up meetings to resolve any issues that may arise during the initial review meetings.

- *Risk levels.* Some best practices, especially those involving a large proportion of reengineering activities, run a considerable risk of failure. In these cases, it is necessary to conduct a careful review of what will happen if the project fails. For example, can the existing system be reinstituted if the new system does not work? What if funding runs out? What if management support for the project falters? What if the level of technology is too advanced for the company to support? The answers to these questions may result in additional project steps to safeguard the project, or to at least back it up with a contingency plan in case the project cannot reach a successful conclusion.

- *Total time required.* All of the previous planning steps are influenced by one of the most important considerations of all—how much time is allocated to the project. Though there may be some play in the final project due date, it is always unacceptable to let a project run too long, since it ties up the time of project team members and will probably accumulate extra costs until it is completed. Consequently, the project team must continually revise the existing project plan to account for new contingencies and problems as they arise, given the overriding restriction of the amount of time available.

The elements of planning that have just been described will all go for naught if there is not an additional linkage to corporate strategy at the highest levels. The reason is that although an implementation may be completely successful, it may not make any difference, and even be rendered unusable, if corporate strategy calls for a shift that will render the best practice obsolete. For example, a fine new centralized accounts payable facility for the use of all corporate divisions is not of much use if the general corporate direction is to spin off or sell all of those divisions. Thus, proper integration of low-level best practices planning with high-level corporate planning is required to ensure that the correct projects are completed.

Given the large number of issues to resolve in order to give an implementation project a reasonable chance of success, it is apparent that the presence of a manager who is very experienced in the intricacies of project planning is a key component of an effective project team. Consequently, the acquisition of such a person should be one of the first steps to include in a project plan.

This section described in general terms the key components of a project plan that must be considered in order to foresee where problems may arise in the course of an implementation. We now proceed to a discussion of the impact of time on the success of a best practices implementation.

Timing of Best Practices

The timing of a best practice implementation, the time it takes to complete it, and the pacing of installations have a major impact on the likelihood of success.

The timing of an implementation project is critical. For example, an installation that comes at the same time as a major deliverable in another area will receive scant attention from the person who is most responsible for using the best practice, since it takes a distant second place to the deliverable. Also, any project that comes on the heels of a disastrous implementation will not be expected to succeed, though this problem can be overcome by targeting a quick and easy project that results in a rapid success—and that overcomes the stigma of the earlier failure. Further, proper implementation timing must take into account other project implementations going on elsewhere in the company or even in the same department, so there is no conflict over project resources. Only by carefully considering these issues prior to scheduling a project will a best practice implementation not be impacted by timing issues.

In addition to timing, the *time* required to complete a project is of major importance. A quick project brings with it the aura of success, a reputation for completion, and a much better chance of being allowed to take on a more difficult and expensive project. Alternatively, a project that impacts lots of departments or people, or that involves the liberal application of cutting-edge technology, runs a major risk of running for a long time; and the longer the project, the greater the risk that something will go wrong, objections will arise, or that funding will run out. Thus, close attention to project duration will increase the odds of success.

Also, the concept of *pacing* is important. This means that a best practices implementation will be more likely to succeed if only a certain number of implementations are scheduled for a specific area. For example, if corporate management wants to install several dozen different types of best practices in five different departments, the best implementation approach is to install one best practice in a single department and then move on to a different department. By doing so, the staff of each department has a chance to assimilate a single best practice, which involves staff training, adjustments to policies and procedures, and modifications of work schedules. Otherwise, if they are bombarded with multiple best practices at the same time or one after another, there is more likelihood that all of the best practices will fail or at least not achieve high levels of performance for some time. In addition, the staff may rebel at the constant stream of changes and refuse to cooperate with further implementations.

Implementing Best Practices

The actual implementation of any best practice requires a great degree of careful planning, as noted earlier. However, planning is not enough. The implementation process itself requires a number of key components in order to ensure a successful conclusion. This section discusses those components.

One of the first implementation steps for all but the simplest best practice improvements is to study and flowchart the existing system about to be improved. By doing so, one can ascertain any unusual requirements that are not readily apparent and that must be included in the planning for the upcoming implementation. Though some reengineering efforts do not spend much time on this task, on the grounds that the entire system is about to be replaced, the same issue still applies—there are usually special requirements, unique to any company, that must be addressed in any new system. Accordingly, nearly all implementation projects must include this critical step.

Another issue is the cost-benefit analysis. This is a compilation of all the costs required to both install and maintain a best practice, which is offset against the benefits of doing so. These costs must include project team payroll and related expenses, outside services, programming costs, training, travel, and capital expenditures. This step is worth a great deal of attention, for a wise manager will not undertake a new project, no matter how cutting-edge and high-profile it may be, if there is not a sound analysis in place that clearly shows the benefit of moving forward with it.

Another cost-benefit analysis consideration is that the installation of a cluster of interconnected best practices can result in an exceptionally large payback. For example, if a payroll department employed a paymaster to distribute paychecks, it might find that it could not eliminate this position solely through the use of direct deposit, because unbanked employees could not take advantage of electronic payments; instead, only by also implementing paycards for the unbanked employees could the company switch entirely away from manual payments, thereby allowing it to actually eliminate the paymaster position and maximize its savings. A second consideration is that some existing processes will not achieve high levels of efficiency improvement if only a single link in the process is replaced with a best practice; instead, a wholesale process replacement is needed in order to achieve maximum profit enhancement. However, when considering the installation of best practice clusters, be aware that this can have an adverse impact on employees, whose morale may suffer from having been burdened with an unending stream of best practices projects. Sometimes, spreading out implementation projects over time, with scheduled breaks, will result in more complete success of individual projects, thereby resulting in a better overall impact on the success of a cluster of improvements—it just takes longer to complete.

Yet another implementation issue is the use of new technology. Though there may be new devices or software on the market that can clearly improve the efficiency of a company's operations, and perhaps even make a demonstrative impact on a company's competitive situation, it still may be more prudent to wait until the technology has been tested in the marketplace for a short time before proceeding with an implementation. This is a particular problem if there is only one supplier offering the technology, especially if that supplier is a small one or with inadequate funding, with the attendant risk of going out of business. In most cases, the prudent manager will elect to use technology that has proven itself in the marketplace, rather than using the most cutting-edge applications.

Of great importance to most best practice implementations is system testing. Any new application, unless it is astoundingly simple, carries with it the risk of failure. This risk must be tested repeatedly to ensure that it will not occur under actual use. The type of testing can take a variety of forms. One is volume testing, to ensure that a large number of employees using the system at the same time will not result in failure. Another is feature testing, in which test transactions that test the boundaries of the possible information to be used are run through the system. Yet another possibility is recovery testing—bringing down a computer system suddenly to see how easy it is to restart the system. All of these approaches, or others, depending on the type of best practice, should be completed before unleashing a new application on employees.

One of the last implementation steps before firing up a new best practice is to provide training to employees in how to run the new system. This must be done as late as possible, since employee retention of this information will dwindle rapidly if not reinforced by actual practice. In addition, this training should be hands-on whenever possible, since employees retain the most information when training is conducted in this manner. It is important to identify in advance all possible users of a new system for training, since a few untrained employees can result in the failure of a new best practice.

A key element of any training class is procedures. These must be completed, reviewed, and be made available for employee use not only at the time of training, but also at all times thereafter, which requires a good manager to oversee the procedure creation and distribution phases. Procedure-writing is a special skill that may require the hiring of technical writers, interviewers, and systems analysts to ensure that procedures are properly crafted. The input of users into the accuracy of all procedures is also an integral step in this process.

Even after the new system has been installed, it is necessary to conduct a post-implementation review. This analysis determines if the cost savings or efficiency improvements are in the expected range, what problems arose during the implementation that should be avoided during future projects, and what issues are still unresolved from the current implementation. This last point is particularly important, for many managers do not follow through completely on all the stray implementation issues, which inevitably arise after a new system is put in place. Only by carefully listing these issues and working through them will the employees using the new system be completely satisfied with how a best practice has been installed.

An issue that arises during all phases of a project implementation is communications. Since there may be a wide range of activities going on, many of them dependent on each other, it is important that the status of all project steps be continually communicated to the entire project team, as well as to all affected employees. By doing so, a project manager can avoid such gaffes as having one task proceed without knowing that, due to changes elsewhere in the project, the entire task has been rendered unnecessary. These communications should not just be limited to project plan updates, but should also include all meeting minutes in which changes are decided on, documented, and approved by team leaders. By paying attention to this important item at every step of an implementation, the entire process will be completed much more smoothly.

As described in this section, a successful best practice implementation nearly always includes a review of the current system, a cost-benefit analysis, responsible use of new technology, system testing, training, and a post-implementation review, with a generous dash of communications at every step.

Best Practice Duplication

It can be a particularly difficult challenge to duplicate a successful best practice when opening a new company facility, especially if expansion is contemplated in many locations over a short time period. The difficulty with best practice duplication is that employees in the new locations are typically given a brief overview of a best practice and told to "go do it." Under this scenario, they have only a sketchy idea of what they are supposed to do, and so create a process that varies in some key details from the baseline situation. To make matters worse, managers at the new location may feel that they can create a better best practice from the start, and so create something that differs in key respects from the baseline. For both reasons, the incidence of best practice duplication failure is high.

To avoid these problems, a company should first be certain that it has accumulated all possible knowledge about a functioning best practice—the forms, policies, procedures, equipment, and special knowledge required to make it work properly—and then transfer this information into a concise document that can be shared with new locations. Second, a roving team of expert users must be commissioned to visit all new company locations and personally install the new systems, thereby ensuring that the proper level of experience with a best practice is brought to bear on a duplication activity. Finally, a company should transfer the practitioners of best practices to new locations on a semipermanent basis to ensure that the necessary knowledge required to make a best practice effective over the long term remains on-site. By taking these steps, a company can increase its odds of spreading best practices throughout all of its locations.

A special issue is the tendency of a new company location to attempt to enhance a copied best practice at the earliest opportunity. This tendency frequently arises from the belief that one can always improve upon something that was created elsewhere. However, these changes may negatively impact other parts of the company's systems, resulting in an overall reduction in performance. Consequently, it is better to insist that new locations duplicate a best practice in all respects and use it to match the performance levels of the baseline location before they are allowed to make any changes to it. By doing so, the new location must take the time to fully utilize the best practice and learn its intricacies before they can modify it.

Why Best Practices Fail

There is a lengthy list of reasons why a best practice installation may not succeed, as noted in the following bullet points. The various reasons for failure can be grouped into a relatively small cluster of primary reasons. The first is lack of planning, which can include inadequate budgeting for time, money, or personnel. Another is the lack of cooperation by other entities, such as the programming staff or other departments that will be impacted by any changes. The final, and most important, problem is that there is little or no effort made to prepare the organization for change. This last item tends to build up over time as more and more best practices are implemented, eventually resulting in the total resistance by the organization to any further change. At its root, this problem involves a fundamental lack of communication, especially to those people who are most impacted by change. When a single implementation is completed without informing all employees of the change, this may be tolerated, but a continuous stream of them will encourage a revolt. In alphabetical order, the various causes of failure are noted as follows:

- *Alterations to packaged software.* A very common cause of failure is that a best practice requires changes to a software package provided by a software supplier; after the changes are made, the company finds that the newest release of the software contains features that it must have and so it updates the software—wiping out the programming changes that were made to accommodate the best practice. This problem can also arise even if there is only a custom interface between the packaged software and some other application needed for a best practice, because a software upgrade may alter the data accessed through the interface. Thus, alterations to packaged software are doomed to failure unless there is absolutely no way that the company will ever update the software package.

- *Custom programming.* A major cause of implementation failure is that the programming required to make it a reality either does not have the requested specifications, costs more than expected, arrives too late, is unreliable—or all of the above! Since many best practices are closely linked to the latest advances in technology, this is an increasingly common cause of failure. To keep from being a victim of programming problems, one should never attempt to implement the most "bleeding-edge" technology, because it is the most subject to failure. Instead, wait for some other company to work out all of the bugs and make it a reliable concept, and then proceed with the implementation. Also, it is useful to interview other people who have gone through a complete installation to see what tips they can give that will result in a smoother implementation. Finally, one should always interview any other employees who have had programming work done for them by the in-house staff. If the results of these previous efforts were not acceptable, it may be better to look outside of the company for more competent programming assistance.

- *Inadequate preparation of the organization.* Communication is the key to a successful implementation. Alternatively, no communication keeps an organization from understanding what is happening; this increases the rumors about a project, builds resistance to it, and reduces the level of cooperation that people are likely to give to it. Avoiding this issue requires a considerable amount of up-front communication about the intentions and likely impact of any project, with that communication targeted not just at the impacted managers, but also at all impacted employees, and to some extent even the corporation or department as a whole.

- *Intransigent personnel.* A major cause of failure is the employee who either refuses to use a best practice or who actively tries to sabotage it. This type of person may have a vested interest in using the old system, does not like change in general, or has a personality clash with someone on the implementation team. In any of these cases, the person must be won over through good communication (especially if the employee is in a controlling position) or removed to a position that has no impact on the project. If neither of these actions is successful, the project will almost certainly fail.

- *Lack of control points.* One of the best ways to maintain control over any project is to set up regular review meetings, as well as additional meetings to review the situation when preset milestone targets are reached. These meetings are designed to see how a project is progressing, to discuss any problems that have occurred or are anticipated, and to determine how current or potential problems can best be avoided. Without the benefit of these regular meetings, it is much more likely that unexpected problems will arise, or that existing ones will be exacerbated.

- *Lack of funding.* A project can be canceled either because it has a significant cost overrun that exceeds the original funding request or because it was initiated without any funding request in the first place. Either approach results in failure. Besides the obvious platitude of "don't go over budget," the best way to avoid this problem is to build a cushion into the original funding request that should see the project through, barring any unusually large extra expenditures.

- *Lack of planning.* A critical aspect of any project is the planning that goes into it. If there is no plan, there is no way to determine the cost, number of employees, or time requirements, nor is there any formal review of the inherent project risks. Without this formal planning process, a project is very likely to hit a snag or be stopped cold at some point prior to its timely completion. On the contrary, using proper planning results in a smooth implementation process that builds a good reputation for the project manager and thereby leads to more funding for additional projects.

- *Lack of post-implementation review.* Though it is not a criterion for the successful implementation of any single project, a missing post-implementation review can cause the failure of later projects. For example, if such a review reveals that a project was completed in spite of the inadequate project planning skills of a specific manager, it might be best to use a different person in the future for new projects, thereby increasing his or her chances of success.

- *Lack of success in earlier efforts.* If a manager builds a reputation for not successfully completing best practices projects, it becomes increasingly difficult to complete new ones. The problem is that no one believes that a new effort will succeed and so there is little commitment to doing it. Also, upper management is much less willing to allocate funds to a manager who has not developed a proven track record for successful implementations. The best way out of this jam is to assign a different manager to an implementation project, one with a proven track record of success.

- *Lack of testing.* A major problem for the implementation of especially large and complex projects, especially those involving programming, is that they are rushed into production without a thorough testing process to discover and correct all bugs that might interfere with or freeze the orderly conduct of work in the areas they are designed to improve. There is nothing more dangerous than to install a wonderful new system in a critical area of the company, only to see that critical function fail completely due to a problem that could have been discovered in a proper testing program. It is always worthwhile to build some extra time into a project budget for an adequate amount of testing.

- *Lack of top management support.* If a project requires a large amount of funding or the cooperation of multiple departments, it is critical to have the complete support of the top management team. If not, any required funding may not be allocated, while there is also a strong possibility that any objecting departments will be able to sidetrack it easily. This is an especially common problem when the project has no clear project sponsor at all—without a senior-level manager to drive it, a project will sputter along and eventually fade away without coming anywhere near completion.

- *Relying on other departments.* As soon as another department's cooperation becomes a necessary component of a best practice installation, the chances of success drop markedly. The odds become even smaller if multiple departments are involved. The main reason is that there is now an extra manager involved, who may not have the commitment of the accounting manager to make the implementation a success. In addition, the staff of the other department may influence their manager not to help out, while there may also be a problem with the other department not having a sufficient amount of funding to complete its share of the work. For example, an accounting department can benefit greatly at period-end if the warehouse is using cycle-counting to keep inventory accuracy levels high, since there is no need for a physical inventory count. However, if the warehouse does not have the extra staff available to count inventory, the work will not be done, no matter how badly the accounting staff wants to implement this best practice.

- *Too many changes in a short time.* An organization will rebel against too much change if it is clustered into a short time frame. The reason is that change is unsettling, especially when it involves a large part of people's job descriptions, so that nearly everything they do is altered. This can result in direct employee resistance to further change, sabotaging new projects, a work slowdown, or (quite likely) the departure of the most disgruntled workers. This problem is best solved by planning for lapses between implementation projects to let the employees settle down. The best way to accomplish this lag between changes without really slowing down the overall schedule of implementation is to shift projects around in the accounting department, so that no functional area is on the receiving end of two consecutive projects.

The primary reason for listing all of these causes of failure is not to discourage the reader from ever attempting a best practice installation. On the contrary, this allows one to prepare for and avoid all roadblocks on the path to ultimate implementation success.

A useful approach for dealing with many of the problems spotlighted in this section is to use a rapid-results initiative (RRI). An RRI is a mini-project intended to create results similar to a full-scale best practices project, but for a more limited area and within a very short time period. By undertaking an RRI, the project team can spot problems faster than would be the case with a major initiative, and then transfer its findings to the main project, thereby increasing the chances of success for the main project. In short, an RRI is designed to locate and correct pitfalls that could otherwise cause major problems for a full-scale best practices implementation.

Another approach to avoiding best practice failure is to spend a considerable amount of time examining logical deficiencies in a proposed best practice. Since the person proposing a best practice installation is more likely to be blind to its possible downsides, it is better to have another person review the proposal for these deficiencies; better yet, have a subject-matter expert examine the proposal for problems. When a project will involve other departments, including the staffs of those departments in the logical deficiencies review will inherently work to gain their acceptance if their issues can be overcome as part of the implementation process.

The Impact of Best Practices on Employees

The impact of best practices on employees is significant. In the short run, there is an overwhelming feeling of discontent, because any kind of change makes employees nervous about what the impact will be on their jobs. Admittedly, a primary purpose of using best practices is to reduce the payroll expense in the accounting department, or at least to handle an increased workload with the same number of employees. Consequently, employees have a reason to be concerned.

There are several ways to deal with employee concerns. One is to create a standard policy of rolling all displaced employees onto a project team that will be used to implement even more best practices. This approach tends to attract the best employees to the project team, but also has the disadvantage of eventually displacing so many employees that there are too many people staffing the implementation team. The opposite approach is to be up-front about projected changes to employee jobs and to give a generous amount of both notice and severance pay to those people who will be displaced. Given the realities of paying extra money to departing employees and the need for well-staffed implementation teams, the recommended approach is somewhere in the middle—to retain a few of the best employees to run new projects, which reduces the amount of severance that must be paid out to departing employees.

The other problem, which is more of a long-run issue, is communications. Even after the initial round of layoffs, there will be a continued emphasis on constantly improving the accounting department's processes. These changes cannot take place in a vacuum. Instead, the implementation team must carefully research the costs and benefits of each prospective best practice, discuss the issue with those employees who are most knowledgeable about how any changes will impact the organization as a whole, and rely to a considerable extent on their advice in regard to whether there should be any implementation at all, and if so, how the best practice should be modified to fit the organization's particular circumstances. Only by making the maximum use of employees' knowledge and by paying close attention to their opinions and fears can an implementation team continually succeed in installing a series of best practices.

Thus, communication is the key—both in handling employee departures in the short term, while the accounting department is reducing its staffing levels to match greater levels of efficiency, and in the long run, when employee cooperation is crucial to continued success.

Summary

This chapter has given an overview of the situations in which best practices implementations are most likely to succeed, what factors are most important to the success or failure of an implementation, and how to successfully create and follow through on an implementation project. By following the recommendations made in this chapter, not only those regarding how to implement, but also those regarding what *not* to do, a manager will have a much higher chance of success. With this information in hand, one can now confidently peruse the remaining chapters, which are full of best practices. The reader will be able to select those practices having the best chance of a successful implementation, based on the specific circumstances pertaining to each manager, such as the funding, time available, and any obstacles, such as entrenched employees or a corporate intransigence pertaining to new projects.

Chapter 3

Accounts Payable Best Practices

The accounts payable function is the most labor-intensive of all the accounting functions and is therefore an excellent source of labor savings if the correct best practices can be implemented. The basic process in most companies is to receive three types of information from three sources—an invoice from the supplier, a purchase order from the purchasing department, and a proof of receipt from the receiving department. The accounts payable staff then matches all three documents to ensure that a prospective payment is authorized and that the underlying goods have been received, and then pays the bill. The process is labor-intensive—partially because there is such a large amount of matching to do, but also because the three documents almost never match. Either the purchase order quantities or prices do not match what the supplier is charging or else the amount received does not match the quantities on the other two documents. Because of these inaccuracies, the amount of labor required to issue a payment can be extraordinarily high.

The best practices in this chapter fall into a few main categories, most of them designed to reduce the matching work. One category attempts to consolidate the number of invoices arriving from suppliers, thereby shrinking the paperwork from this source—typical best practices in this area are using procurement cards and shrinking the number of suppliers. Another category tries to reduce or eliminate the number of receiving documents. Typical best practices in this area are substituting occasional audits for ongoing matching of receiving documents, as well as directly entering receipts into the computer system. Finally, another category reduces the number of purchase orders that must be matched. Typical best practices in this area include using blanket purchase orders and automating three-way matching. Other solutions to the matching problem involve going away from the traditional matching process entirely, by using payments based solely on proof of receipt. It is not possible to use all of these best practices together, since some are mutually exclusive—one must be careful in choosing the correct best practices.

Lastly, a number of best practices focus on the overall accounts payable process, attempting to either shrink or automate the number of steps required before a company issues payment to a supplier. Examples of best practices in this area include using a signature stamp and switching to wire transfers.

The number of best practices in the accounts payable area indicates that this function is ripe for improvements. However, some best practices require a large investment of money or time, as noted in the chart in the next section, so the person doing the improving should verify that resources are available before embarking on an implementation.

Implementation Issues for Accounts Payable Best Practices

This section notes a number of issues related to the implementation of each best practice. The reader should peruse Exhibit 3.1 to ensure that the effort required to install a best practice is in agreement with the available constraints. For example, automating expense reporting is listed as requiring a long implementation period and being moderately expensive (all because of the programming required). If the reader has a large staff of traveling employees who constantly submit expense reports, this may be a viable option, despite the projected implementation barriers. However, if only a few expense reports are submitted, then perhaps this is a best practice that should be passed over in favor of more practical opportunities.

Exhibit 3.1 lists all of the best practices in this chapter. Next to the best practices are ratings for estimates of the cost to completely install each best practice. The last column shows the duration of implementation, which can be an issue for anyone looking for quick results. Any large programming projects are assumed to have long implementation durations.

One should be careful to not just select "quick hits" from Exhibit 3.1. Though these best practices are certainly worth the effort of installing, it is important to remember that some of the most difficult items on the list can have the largest payback. Accordingly, it is best to review the list in detail and assemble a set of best practices that provide for a combination of quick and easy victories, while also allowing for solid, long-term improvements that will impact the accounts payable function's levels of efficiency and effectiveness.

3–1 Pay Based on Receiving Approval Only   ✔ *Author's Choice*

The accounts payable process is one of the most convoluted of all the processes that a company can adopt, irrespective of the department. First, it requires the collection of information from multiple departments—purchase orders from the purchasing department, invoices from suppliers, and receiving documents from the receiving department. The process then involves matching these documents, which almost always contain exceptions, and then tracking down someone either to approve exceptions or to at least sign the checks, which must then be mailed to suppliers. The key to success in this area is to thoroughly reengineer the entire process by eliminating the paperwork, the multiple sources of information, and the additional approvals. The only best practice that truly addresses the underlying problems of the accounts payable process is paying based on receipt.

Exhibit 3.1 Summary of Accounts Payable Best Practices

	Best Practice	Cost	Install Time
Approvals			
3–1	Pay based on receiving approval only	$$$	⏰⏰
3–2	Reduce required approvals	$	⏰
3–3	Use negative assurance for invoice approvals	$	⏰
Credit Cards			
3–4	Use procurement cards	$	⏰
3–5	Use a ghost card	$	⏰
3–6	Negotiate procurement card rebates	$	⏰
Documents			
3–7	Route all invoices directly to accounts payable	$	⏰
3–8	Split payables processing based on discounts	$	⏰
3–9	Adopt a standard invoice numbering convention	$	⏰
3–10	Automate three-way matching	$$$	⏰⏰
3–11	Digitize accounts payable documents	$$	⏰⏰
3–12	Directly enter receipts into computer	$$	⏰⏰
3–13	Fax transmission of accounts payable documents	$	⏰
3–14	Have suppliers include their supplier numbers on invoices	$	⏰⏰
3–15	Receive billings through electronic data interchange	$$$	⏰⏰⏰
3–16	Request that suppliers enter invoices through a Web site	$$	⏰⏰
3–17	Shift incoming billings to an EDI data-entry supplier	$$	⏰⏰
Expense Reports			
3–18	Audit expense reports	$	⏰
3–19	Automate expense reporting	$$	⏰⏰⏰
3–20	Eliminate cash advances for employee travel	$	⏰
3–21	Link corporate travel policies to automated expense reporting system	$$$	⏰⏰⏰

(continues)

Exhibit 3.1 *(Continued)*

	Best Practice	Cost	Install Time
Management			
3–22	Centralize the accounts payable function	💵💵💵	⏰⏰⏰
3–23	Store late fees in a separate general ledger account	💵	⏰
3–24	Issue standard account code list	💵	⏰⏰
3–25	Link supplier requests to the accounts payable database	💵💵💵	⏰⏰
3–26	Implement a reverse lockbox	💵	⏰⏰
3–27	Outsource the accounts payable function	💵	⏰⏰
3–28	Shrink the supplier base	💵💵	⏰⏰⏰
3–29	Withhold first payment until W-9 form is received	💵	⏰
3–30	Verify taxpayer ID numbers	💵	⏰
Payments			
3–31	Automate payments for repetitive processing	💵	⏰
3–32	Install a payment factory	💵💵💵	⏰⏰⏰
3–33	Eliminate manual checks	💵	⏰
3–34	Increase the frequency of check runs	💵	⏰
3–35	Have regularly scheduled check signing meetings	💵	⏰
3–36	Implement positive pay	💵	⏰
3–37	Incorporate copy protection features into checks	💵	⏰
3–38	Avoid acronym payees on checks	💵	⏰
3–39	Use the universal payment identification code	💵	⏰
3–40	Revise payment terms for electronic payments	💵	⏰
3–41	Install advanced ACH debit blocking	💵	⏰
3–42	Use signature stamp	💵	⏰

Exhibit 3.1 *(Continued)*

	Best Practice	*Cost*	*Install Time*
Purchasing			
3–43	Notify purchasing of lower invoiced prices or terms	💵	⏰
3–44	Create direct purchase interfaces to suppliers	💵💵	⏰⏰
3–45	Create online purchasing catalog	💵💵💵	⏰⏰⏰
3–46	Install a low-cost spend management system	💵💵	⏰⏰
3–47	Use blanket purchase orders	💵	⏰⏰
Suppliers			
3–48	Issue a welcome packet to new suppliers	💵	⏰
3–49	Clean up the supplier master file	💵	⏰⏰
3–50	Adopt a supplier naming procedure	💵	⏰
3–51	Assign payables staff to specific suppliers	💵	⏰
3–52	Create different supplier accounts for different terms	💵	⏰
3–53	Ignore supplier invoices and pay from statements	💵	⏰
3–54	Review supplier statements for open credits	💵	⏰
3–55	Issue standard adjustment letters to suppliers	💵	⏰

To pay based on receipt, one must first do away with the concept of having an accounts payable staff that performs the traditional matching process. Instead, the receiving staff checks to see if there is a purchase order at the time of receipt. If there is, the computer system automatically pays the supplier. Sounds simple? It is not. A company must have several features installed before the concept will function properly. The main issue is having a computer terminal at the receiving dock. When a supplier shipment arrives, a receiving person takes the purchase order number and quantity received from the shipping documentation and punches it into the computer. The computer system checks against an on-line database of open purchase orders to see if the shipment was authorized. If so, the system automatically schedules a payment to the supplier based on the purchase order price, which can be sent by wire transfer. If the purchase order number is not in the database, or if there is no purchase order number at all, the shipment is rejected at the

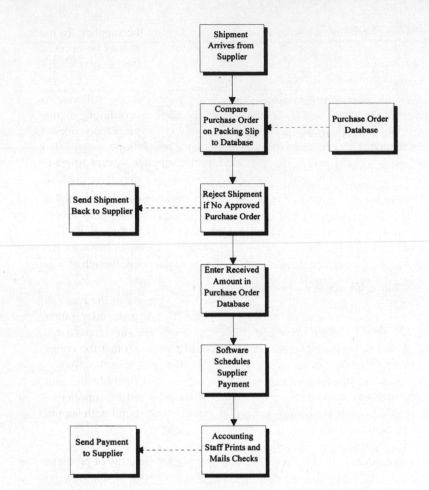

Exhibit 3.2 The Process Flow for Payment Based on Receiving Approval

receiving dock. Note that the accounts payable staff takes no part whatsoever in this process—everything has been shifted to a simple step at the receiving location. The process is shown graphically in Exhibit 3.2.

Before laying off the entire accounts payable staff and acquiring such a system, there are several problems to overcome. They are as follows:

- *Train suppliers.* Every supplier who sends anything to a company must be trained to include the purchase order number, the company's part number, and the quantity shipped on the shipping documentation, so this information can be punched into the computer at the receiving location. The information can be encoded as bar codes to make the data-entry task easier for the receiving employees. Training a supplier may be difficult, especially if the company only purchases a small quantity of goods from the supplier. To make it worthwhile for the supplier to go to this extra effort, it may be necessary to concentrate purchases with a smaller number of suppliers to give each one a significant volume of orders.

- *Alter the accounting system.* The traditional accounting software is not designed to allow approvals at the receiving dock. Accordingly, a company will have to reprogram the system to allow the reengineered process to be performed. This can be an exceptionally major undertaking, especially if the software is constantly being upgraded by the supplier—every upgrade will wipe out any custom programming that the company may have created.

- *Prepare for miscellaneous payments.* The accounts payable department will not really go away because there will always be stray supplier invoices of various kinds arriving for payment that cannot possibly go through the receiving dock, such as subscription payments, utility bills, and repair invoices. Accordingly, the old payments system must still be maintained, though at a greatly reduced level, to handle these items.

- *Pay without a supplier invoice.* One of the key aspects of the reengineered process is paying based on the information in the purchase order, rather than the information in the supplier's invoice. To do so, one must have a database of all the tax rates that every supplier would charge, so that the company's computer system can automatically include these taxes in the invoice payments. Also, there will sometimes be discrepancies between the purchase order prices and quantities paid, versus those expected by suppliers, so an accounts payable staff must be kept on hand to correspond with suppliers to reconcile these issues.

The preceding bullet points reveal that there are a wide array of problems that must first be overcome before the dramatic improvements of this new process can be realized. However, for a company with a large accounts payable staff, this can be a highly rewarding system to install, for the savings realized can be the elimination of the majority of the accounts payable department.

Cost: 💵💵💵   Installation time: 🕐🕐

3–2 Reduce Required Approvals   ✔*Author's Choice*

The accounts payable process is typically a long one. Part of the problem is that many accounting systems require a manager's signature (or those of several managers!) on a supplier invoice before it can be paid. Though it is reasonable to have such a requirement if there is no purchase order for the invoice, many systems require the signature even if there is already a purchase order (which is, in effect, a form of prior approval). Also, most accounting systems require a manager's signature on unapproved invoices, no matter how small the invoice may be. The result of these common approval procedures is that the accounts payable staff delivers invoices to managers for signatures and then waits until the documents are returned before proceeding further with the payment process. If the manager is not available to sign an invoice, then it sits; if the manager loses the invoice (a common occurrence), the invoice is never paid, resulting in an angry supplier who must send a fresh copy of the invoice for a second pass through the dangerous shoals of the company's approval process. This is a clearly inefficient process, both lengthy and likely to annoy suppliers. What can be done?

A superb best practice for any company to implement is to limit approvals to a single event or document and, wherever possible, to limit this approval to a period prior to the receipt of the supplier invoice. For example, an authorized signature on a purchase order should be sufficient overall approval to pay an invoice. After all, if the signature was good enough to authorize the initial purchase of the item or service, shouldn't the same signature be sufficient approval for the payment of the supplier's bill? In addition, by shifting the approval to the purchase order, we avoid having the accounts payable staff track down someone after the supplier's invoice has been received, which effectively chops time from the overall accounts payable process. Another variation is to use a signature on the purchase requisition, which comes before the purchase order. As long as either document is signed by an authorized person and sent to the accounts payable staff in advance, it does not matter which document is used as authorization. The key is to use a single authorization, before the supplier sends an invoice.

One reason why so many companies require multiple approvals, both at the time of purchasing and at the time of payment, is that they do not have a sufficient degree of control over the authorization process. For example, there may not be any real check of authorization signatures when purchase requisitions are converted into purchase orders, nor might there be any required signature when purchase orders are issued to suppliers. In addition, the signature stamp used to sign checks may not be properly controlled. In all these cases, if there were tight control over the authorization used, there would only be a need for a single authorization. For example, there should be an audit of all purchase orders to ensure that every one of them has been signed, that every signature is by an authorized person, and that the person signing is authorized to purchase what was ordered. This level of control requires continual internal audits to ensure that the control point is working, as well as continual follow-up and training of employees so that they know precisely how the control system is supposed to work. Only by instituting this degree of control over authorizations can a company reduce the number of approvals to a minimum.

Using tight control over approvals that are given early in the accounts payable process results in a shorter processing cycle and fewer delays.

Cost: **Installation time:** 🕰

3–3 Use Negative Assurance for Invoice Approvals ✔*Author's Choice*

One of the most significant problems for the accounts payable staff is the continuing delay in receiving approvals of supplier invoices from authorized employees throughout the company. Invoices tend to sit on employee desks as low-priority items, resulting in constant reminders by the accounting staff to turn in documents, as well as late payments and missed early-payment discounts.

This universal problem can be avoided through the use of negative assurance. Under this approval system, invoice copies are sent to authorizing employees, and are automatically paid when due unless the employees tell the accounts payable staff *not* to issue payment. By focusing only on those invoices that may be incorrect, the accounting staff can process the vast majority of all submitted invoices without cajoling anyone to submit an approved document.

The process can be streamlined even further by digitizing an incoming invoice and e-mailing it to the authorizing employee. By doing so, employees can be reached even when they are off-site, as long as they check their e-mail on a regular basis. By linking these transmissions to workflow software, the accounting staff can designate how long an invoice can wait in a recipient's e-mail box before it is automatically routed to another authorized person, thereby ensuring that *someone* will see every invoice and raise a red flag if a potential problem exists.

Cost: **Installation time:**

3–4 Use Procurement Cards ✔*Author's Choice*

Consider the number of work steps required to process a payment to a supplier: receiving paperwork, sorting and matching it, entering data into a computer, routing invoices through the organization for approvals, expediting those invoices that have early-payment discounts, creating month-end accruals, setting up files on new suppliers in the computer and the filing system, processing checks, obtaining check signatures, mailing payments, and filing away check copies. Now consider how many purchases are so small that the cost of all these activities exceeds the cost of the purchase. In many instances, one-quarter or more of all payment transactions fall into this category.

The answer to this problem is not to find a more efficient way to process the supplier invoices, but to change the way in which these items or services are purchased. Instead of using a purchase order or check to purchase something, one should instead use a procurement card. A procurement card, also known as a purchasing card, is simply a credit card with a few extra features. The card is issued to those people who make frequent purchases, with instructions to keep on making the same purchases, but to do so with the card. This eliminates the multitude of supplier invoices by consolidating them all into a single monthly credit card statement.

As there is always a risk of having a user purchase extraneous items with a credit card, including cash advances or excessively expensive purchases, the procurement card adds a few features to control precisely what is purchased. For example, it can have a limitation on the total daily amount purchased, the total amount purchased per transaction, or the total purchased per month. It may also limit purchases to a specific store or to only those stores that fall into a specific Standard Industry Classification (SIC code) category, such as a plumbing supply store and nothing else. These built-in controls effectively reduce the risk that procurement cards will be misused.

Once the credit card statement arrives, it may be too jumbled, with hundreds of purchases, to determine the expense accounts to which all the items are to be charged. To help matters, a company can specify how the credit card statement is to be sorted by the credit card processing company; it can list expenses by the location of each purchase, by SIC code, or by dollar amount, as well as by date. It is even possible to receive an electronic transmission of the credit card statement so that a company can do its own sorting of expenses. The purchasing limitations and expense statement changes are the key differences between a regular credit card and a procurement card.

Another feature provided by those entities that offer procurement cards is "Level II" data; this includes a supplier's minority supplier status, incorporated status, and its tax identification number. Another option to look into when reviewing the procurement card option is the existence of "Level III" reporting, which includes such line-item details as quantities, product codes, product descriptions, and freight and duty costs—in short, the bulk of the information needed to maintain a detailed knowledge of exactly what is being bought with a company's procurement cards. Most major national suppliers of credit cards can supply Level II or Level III data.

Though this best practice may appear to be nirvana to many organizations, the following issues must be carefully considered in order to ensure that the program operates properly:

- *Card misuse.* When procurement cards are handed out to a large number of employees, there is always the risk that someone will abuse the privilege and use up valuable company funds on incorrect or excessive purchases. There are several ways to either prevent this problem or to reduce its impact. One approach is to hand out the procurement cards only to the purchasing staff, who can use them to pay for items for which they would otherwise issue a purchase order; however, this does not address the large quantity of very small purchases that other employees may make, so a better approach is a gradual rollout of procurement cards to those employees who have shown a continuing pattern of making small purchases. Also, the characteristics of the procurement card itself can be altered, either by limiting the dollar amount of purchases per transaction, per time period, or even per department. One can also restrict the number of usages per day. An additional method for avoiding employee misuse of procurement cards is to have them sign an agreement describing the sanctions that will be imposed when the cards are misused, which may include termination. Some mix of these solutions can mitigate the risk of procurement card abuse.

- *Spending on special items.* The use of a procurement card can actually interfere with existing internal procedures for the purchase of some items, rendering those systems less efficient. For example, an automated materials planning system for the inventory can issue purchase orders to suppliers with no manual intervention; adding inventory items to this situation that were purchased through a different methodology can interfere with the integrity of the database, requiring more manual reconciliation of inventory quantities. Thus, procurement cards are not always a good idea when buying inventory items. Also, capital purchases typically have to go through a detailed review and approval process before they are acquired; since a procurement card offers an easy way to buy smaller capital items, it represents a simple way to bypass the approval process. Thus, they are not a good choice for capital purchases.

- *Dealing with users of the old system.* Some employees will not take to the new procurement card approach, if only because they are used to the old system. This can cause headaches for both the purchasing and accounting departments, since they must deal with both the old system and the new one in combination. It may be impossible to completely eliminate the old purchase order system in some cases (if only because of company politics), so a good alternative is to charge to those departments using the old system the fully burdened cost of each transaction that does not use a procurement card. Since this burdened cost, which includes the cost of all the processing steps noted at the beginning of this section, can easily exceed $100 per transaction, it becomes a very effective way to shift usage toward the procurement card solution.

- *Summarizing general ledger accounts.* The summary statements that are received from the credit card processor will not contain as many expense line items as are probably already contained within a company's general ledger (which tends to slice-and-dice expenses down into many categories). For example, the card statements may only categorize by shop supplies, office supplies, and shipping supplies. If so, then it is best to alter the general ledger accounts to match the categories being reported through the procurement cards. This may also require changes to the budgeting system, which probably mirrors the accounts used in the general ledger.

- *Purchases from unapproved suppliers.* A company may have negotiated favorable prices from a few select suppliers in exchange for making all of its purchases for certain items from them. It is a simple matter to ensure that purchases are made through these suppliers when the purchasing department is placed in direct control of the buying process. However, once purchases are put in the hands of anyone with a procurement card, it is much less likely that the same level of discipline will occur. Instead, purchases will be made from a much larger group of suppliers. Though not an easy issue to control, the holders of procurement cards can at least be issued a "preferred supplier yellow pages," which lists those suppliers from whom they should be buying. Their adherence to this list can be tracked by comparing actual purchases to the yellow pages list and giving them feedback about the issue.

- *Paying sales and use taxes.* Occasionally, a state sales tax auditor will arrive on a company's doorstep, demanding to see documentation that proves it has paid a sales tax on all items purchased. This is not easy to do when procurement cards are used, not only because there may be a multitude of poorly organized supplier receipts, but also because the sales tax noted on a credit card payment slip only shows the grand total sales tax paid, rather than the sales tax for each item purchased; this is an important issue, for some items are exempt from taxation, which will result in a total sales tax that appears to be too low in comparison to the total dollar amount of items purchased. One way to alleviate this problem is to obtain sales tax exemption certificates from all states with which a company does business; employees then present the sales tax exemption number whenever they make purchases, so that there is no doubt at all—no sales taxes have been paid. Then the accounting staff can calculate the grand total for the use tax (which is the same thing as the sales tax, except that the purchaser pays it to the state, rather than to the seller) to pay, and forward this to the appropriate taxing authority. An alternative is to "double bag" tax payments, which means that the company pays the full use tax on all procurement card purchases, without bothering to spend the time figuring out which sales taxes have already been paid. This is a safe approach from a tax audit perspective, and may not involve much additional cost if the total of all procurement card purchases is small. Yet another alternative is the reverse—to ignore the entire sales tax issue, and only confront it when audited; this decision is usually based on the level of risk tolerance of the controller or chief financial officer.

Though the problems noted here must be addressed, one must understand the significance of the advantages of using procurement cards in order to see why the problems are minor in relation to the possible benefits. Here are the main attractions of this best practice:

- *Extend payment period.* The payables staff can contact a supplier, just before an invoice is due for payment, and see if the supplier will accept payment of the invoice with a procurement card. By doing so, the company has just extended its payment interval (depending on the cutoff period for the procurement card), since it can now wait an additional period until the monthly procurement card statement arrives before making a payment.

- *Fewer accounting transactions.* Some of the accounts payable staff may be redirected to other tasks, because the number of transactions will drop considerably.

- *Fewer invoice reviews and signatures.* Managers no longer have to review a considerable number of invoices for payment approval, nor do they have to sign so many checks addressed to suppliers.

- *No cash advances.* Whenever an employee asks for a cash advance, the accounting staff must create a manual check for that person, record it in the accounting records, and ensure that it is paid back by the employee. This can be a very time-consuming process in proportion to the generally meager advances given to employees. A credit card can avoid this entire process, because employees can go to an automated teller machine and withdraw cash, which will appear in the next monthly card statement from the issuing bank—no check issuances required. Of course, this benefit only applies if those employees needing cash advances are the same ones with access to a procurement card.

- *Fewer petty-cash transactions.* If employees have procurement cards, they will no longer feel compelled to buy items with their own cash and then ask for a reimbursement from the company's petty-cash fund.

- *Fewer purchasing transactions.* A whole range of purchasing activities are reduced in volume, including contacting suppliers for quotes, creating and mailing purchase orders, resolving invoicing differences, and closing out orders.

- *Reduced supplier list.* The number of active vendors in the purchasing database can be greatly reduced, which allows the buying staff to focus on better relations with the remaining ones on the list.

- *Reduced mailroom volume.* Even the mailroom will experience a drop in volume, since there will be far fewer incoming supplier invoices and outgoing company checks.

A procurement card is easy to implement (just hand it out to employees), though one should keep a significant difficulty in mind: The banks that issue credit cards must expend extra labor to set up a procurement card for a company, since each one must be custom-designed. Consequently, they prefer to issue procurement cards only to those companies that can show a significant volume of credit card business—usually at least $1 million per year. This volume limitation makes it difficult for a smaller company to use procurement cards. This problem can be partially avoided by using a group of supplier-specific credit cards. For example, a company can sign up for a credit card with its office supply store, another with its building materials store, and another with its electrical supplies store. This results in a somewhat larger number of credit card statements per month, but they are already sorted by supplier, so they are essentially a "poor man's procurement card."

Cost: 🪙   **Installation time:** ⏰

3–5 Use a Ghost Card

Most companies have their employees make purchases with various types of credit cards, for which they are reimbursed by the company. This approach reduces the risk of liability for excessive purchases made by employees, though employees are put at risk of not being reimbursed in a timely manner for possibly substantial company-related charges. A common alternative is to issue individual company-sponsored purchasing cards to selected employees, who are authorized to make a variety of purchases within certain restrictive limits.

The trouble in both cases is that employees may circumvent centralized purchasing rules, which prevents the company from taking advantage of bulk pricing deals with a small number of preferred suppliers. Also, in the case of company-sponsored cards, a relatively high level of control is generally applied, so that they are given to only a small minority of employees, thereby making it more difficult to roll out the comprehensive use of credit cards for small-dollar purchases. Finally, purchases with these cards may be applicable to a variety of departments, requiring a detailed and sometimes difficult month-end reconciliation to determine which purchases are to be charged to each department.

An alternative that resolves some of these issues is the *ghost card*. A ghost card does not involve the use of an actual card. Instead, each department is given its own ghost card number, with which it can make a variety of purchases that will be charged back to that department. By centralizing such purchases with a single account number, payment processing is made considerably easier. Also, since the company is directly responsible for all purchases made with the ghost card, it will be billed by the card provider in a timely and predictable manner (as opposed to the use of personal cards, where expenses may not appear until several months later).

Another use for the ghost card is to provide it to preferred suppliers for ongoing use, with each supplier being given a unique ghost card number; the suppliers automatically charge it when purchases are made by employees. This greatly streamlines the more common approach of charging the plastic card of whichever company employee shows up to make a purchase.

Another advantage of the ghost card is that some suppliers are now providing direct input of charge information into corporate ERP systems, so that purchases can be charged directly to the correct department with no manual data entry needed.

Cost: 💵   **Installation time:** ⏰

3–6 Negotiate Procurement Card Rebates

If a company has shifted a large part of its purchases to procurement cards, then this represents a significant revenue source for procurement card companies. Once a company has built up a sufficient volume of procurement card business, it is in a position to negotiate for better terms with its procurement card supplier. One of the best such deals is to obtain a rebate percentage that is tied to the volume of payments made with a specific procurement card.

This best practice is not available for smaller procurement card programs, but if a company can surpass about $5 million per year in card purchases, then it can bargain for a small rebate percentage that can increase as its purchases increase. Initial rebates are extremely small, but can reach 0.5 percent for very large procurement card programs.

Cost: **Installation time:** 🕰

3–7 Route All Invoices Directly to Accounts Payable

The accounts payable department is constantly faced with supplier complaints that they are not being paid on time, usually because the payables staff has never received the supplier's invoice. Instead, suppliers send invoices directly to the person who originally ordered from the supplier, and this person has never forwarded the invoice to accounts payable. This is a particular problem when the person placing the order does so with a verbal order, so there is no written record of the approval—suppliers know this could be a problem, so they send the invoice directly to the person placing the order, in hopes of having him approve it on the spot.

To avoid this missing invoice conundrum, remind suppliers to always send all invoices directly to the accounts payable department, which can then immediately log them into the payables computer system for timely payment. Suppliers should always include on an invoice either the authorizing purchase order number or the name of the person who authorized the order, so the payables staff can then process the related invoice approval. If suppliers persist in sending invoices elsewhere than to the accounts payable department, then the payables staff should log in these invoices as they arrive from elsewhere in the company, and have the accounting manager contact his or counterpart in the supplier's billing department to discuss the issue. If necessary, the problem can be escalated through higher levels of management. An alternative approach is to send these invoices back to the supplier (without first logging them in), with a note regarding the proper delivery procedure, so that the supplier is forced to address the invoice properly in order to be paid. Yet another approach is to instruct the mailroom staff to forward all incoming supplier invoices directly to the accounts payable department, even if they are addressed to someone elsewhere in the organization.

Cost: 💵   **Installation time:** 🕰

3–8 Split Payables Processing Based on Discounts

When a supplier offers an early payment discount, the terms offered are nearly always so advantageous that the payables staff must pay early. However, these invoices tend to be lost amidst the sea of invoices that arrive in the mail every day, resulting in late processing and therefore no discount taken.

To avoid this problem, examine invoices for discounts at the point of receipt, and set aside all invoices offering early payment discounts. This batch of invoices can then follow a higher-speed processing track that uses expedited data entry and approvals. If these invoices are processed manually, use negative approvals (will be paid unless the approver says otherwise) to ensure that early payment is not delayed by a late approval.

If all invoices are digitized at the point of receipt, these invoices can be flagged with a special index code. If prioritized invoices are being approved with a work flow management system, then set them up to be bounced to a different person for approval if they are not approved within a very short time frame by the primary approver.

Cost: **Installation time:**

3–9 Adopt a Standard Invoice Numbering Convention

A major cause of duplicate payments is multiple copies of the same supplier invoice being entered in the computer system, but with slight variations on the invoice number that keep the computer from flagging them as duplicate invoices. This is an especially common problem when suppliers issue invoices with leading zeros, since one data entry clerk may enter the zeros, while another may ignore them. It also common for employee expense reports and a variety of utility billings, since these documents have no invoice number. It also happens when an original invoice is not paid on time, so the supplier floods the company with extra copies of the invoice, hoping that one of the copies will eventually be paid.

There is no perfect solution to this problem, but the basic approach is to adopt a standard invoice numbering convention for the data entry staff to follow, thereby introducing some consistency into this aspect of invoice data entry. It can include some of the following rules:

- *Drop leading zeros.* It is also possible to reverse this rule and *always* use leading zeros, but the extra characters may overflow the computer field for invoice numbers.
- *Use the packing slip number.* If the invoice contains no invoice number and it is related to a physical delivery, then there should be a packing slip that accompanied the delivery. If so, enter the packing slip number as the invoice number. If a duplicate invoice arrives, it must still be matched to the packing slip before payment is approved, so the packing slip number will be flagged by the computer as a duplicate invoice number.
- *Use an alternate document identifier.* If an invoice contains no invoice number but does have other tracking numbers, such as an internal indexing number or a job number, then use this number instead.

- *Use invoice date.* A less foolproof alternative is to use the invoice date. This approach can still result in duplicate payments, because suppliers may legitimately issue more than one invoice on the same day, resulting in such coding variations as MMDDYY-2 to signify that an invoice is the second one received that has the same invoice date. If this alternative must be used, then at least require that dates always be entered using the same format every time, such as MMDDYY or MMDDYYYY.

- *Avoid all punctuation and spaces.* Some invoice numbers include slashes, spaces, or dashes, which should be avoided. It is especially common for some systems to add "-IN" to the end of an invoice number, in order to signify that this number is related to an invoice. If so, drop both the dash and the "IN" from the invoice number.

The numbering convention should specify what type of alternate identifier to use if there are several options available; otherwise, the data entry staff may enter a different number, resulting in a possible duplicate payment.

Cost: Installation time:

3–10 Automate Three-Way Matching

The three-way matching process is a manual one at most companies; that is, a clerk matches a supplier invoice to a company purchase order and a receiving document in order to ensure that the correct quantities (and costs) ordered are the same ones received and billed. This is a painfully slow and inefficient process, given the large number of documents involved, as well as the startling number of exceptions that nearly always arise.

There are two ways to solve the problem. One is to dispense with three-way matching entirely, which requires considerable reengineering of the accounts payable process, as well as retraining of the receiving staff and even of suppliers. This process was described in detail in the "Pay Based on Receiving Approval Only" section earlier in this chapter. Though the most elegant solution, it also requires the most work to implement.

The second solution requires some software changes that may already be available in the existing software package, with minimal changes to employee procedures, while still resulting in efficiency improvements (though not on the scale of the first solution). This best practice involves keeping the matching process in its current form, but using the computer system to perform the matching work. In order to automate three-way matching, all three documents must be entered into the computer system. This is easy for purchase orders, since most companies already enter purchase orders directly into the computer in order to track purchase orders through the manufacturing system. The next-easiest document to enter is the receiving document, which can be either a bill of lading or a packing slip. To do so, there should be a computer terminal at the receiving dock that is linked to the main accounting database so that all information entered at the dock is centrally stored. Finally, the supplier invoice must be entered into the computer system—line by line. It is common enough to enter the supplier's invoice number and dollar amount into the computer system, but automated matching requires the complete entry of all line items, quantities, and costs into the system, which can be a considerable chore. Once this information is in the accounting database, the computer system automatically matches the three documents (usually using the purchase order number as the index), compares all line items, and presents a summary of the matched documents to the accounting staff, showing any variances between the matched documents. The accounting staff can then scan the information and decide if the variances require further analysis or if they can be paid as is. This best practice automates an existing manual process without a large number of changes.

When deciding to use this best practice, it is useful to compare the savings from eliminating manual matching to the added cost of keying all the documents into the central database. There may also be an expense associated with installing the matching software in the system, though it is usually an integral part of the more advanced accounting packages. Low-end accounting packages do not normally contain the automated matching feature.

Cost: **Installation time:**

3–11 Digitize Accounts Payable Documents

When accounting files are sent to the archives at the end of the year, the portion taken up by the accounts payable documents usually exceeds that of all other documents combined. For some companies with voluminous accounts payable files, it is a major expense to remove all the paperwork, box it up and identify it, and ship it off to a warehouse, from which it must be recalled occasionally for various tasks. Digitizing the documents is a means of avoiding the expense of archiving.

Digitizing a document means that it is laid on a scanner that converts the document image into an electronic image stored in the computer database, which can be recalled by anyone with access to the database. To digitize a document, there should be a high-speed scanner available that is linked to a computer network. Documents are fed into the scanner and assigned one or more index numbers or codes, so that it will be easy to recall the correct documents from storage. For example, a document can be indexed by its purchase order number, date, or supplier number. A combination of several indexes is the best approach, since one can still recall a document, even if one does not remember the first index number. The document images are usually stored on an optical disk since it can hold enormous amounts of storage space (and digitized documents take up a lot of computer storage space). There will probably be many optical disks to provide a sufficient amount of storage, so the disks are usually stored in a "jukebox," which gives the user access to all the data on all the storage disks. Users can then call up the images from any terminal that is linked to the network where the information is stored.

There are additional advantages to using digitization of documents. Besides the reduced archiving costs, it is also possible to nearly eliminate the time needed to access documents. With a traditional archiving system, older documents must be requested from a warehousing facility that may require several days to deliver. Even in-house documents may require several minutes to an hour to locate. If customer service is important, and that service is linked to providing rapid access to data, then digitizing documents allows a company to instantly satisfy customer requests for documents by searching the computer files for them, no matter how old the documents may be. Another advantage to using digitization is that it avoids having to take out and replace files. Whenever someone removes a file and later returns it, there is a risk that the file will be misplaced. Every time a file is misplaced, it will be time-consuming to find it again. By accessing documents through a computer network, there is no need to take out or replace the document—it is always sitting in the same storage location in the computer, and cannot be lost. Yet another advantage is that multiple users can access the same file at the same time. Since it is a digital image, there is no reason why the computer cannot potentially distribute a copy of the digital document to everyone who asks for it, even if they all do so at the same time. A final advantage to digitization is that it can be used to send an electronic file to a manager requesting an electronic approval before a payment will be made. This approach keeps the digital document from being lost during the approval process (a common problem when paper documents are used for approvals), while instantly moving a digital approval through the computer network, which also speeds up the transfer of approval information. In short, there are a variety of good reasons for digitizing accounts payable documents, besides the most common one of eliminating archiving costs.

Though this best practice may seem like an ideal way to avoid lost files, reduce archiving costs, shrink document search times, and allow for remote payment approvals, there is one problem with it that bars most small companies from installing it. The main issue is cost. The price of a high-speed scanner, computer, and optical storage jukebox can easily exceed the cost savings from all the advantages of this approach. The most cost-effective situations for digital storage are when there is either a very high storage cost that can be eliminated (especially common in high-rent accounting facilities where storage space is at a premium) or the volume of transactions is so high that there is no practical alternative to storing, filing, and moving all the paperwork. Consequently, digitizing accounts payable documents is normally limited to larger companies or those with expensive storage facilities.

Cost: 💵💵   **Installation time:** ⏰⏰⏰

3–12 Directly Enter Receipts into Computer   ✔ *Author's Choice*

One portion of the accounts payable matching process is to physically match some evidence of receipt, usually a packing slip or bill of lading, to a supplier invoice, thereby proving that the goods being paid for were actually received. The receiving documentation usually wends its way to the accounts payable staff over a period of several days, and may be lost on the way. Once it arrives, the information may not agree with the quantities being billed by the supplier. Consequently, the matching of receiving documentation tends to be either delayed, missing, or cause for extra reconciliation work by the accounting staff.

There are several solutions to the receiving paperwork problem. Two are outlined in other sections of this chapter. One is using fully automated matching of all accounts payable documents, which requires the input of all paperwork into the computer—receiving information, the supplier invoice, and the purchase order—so that the computer can automatically match the documents. This requires complicated software that not all computer systems may have available. It is described further in the "Automate Three-Way Matching" section. Another solution is to have the receiving staff approve purchase orders for payment based on what has just been received. This is a more radical approach that is extremely efficient but that requires a complete redesign of the accounts payable process. This section describes a less monumental change that can usually be implemented by most accounting systems.

The alternative approach is to enter receipts directly into the computer system, rather than forwarding receiving documents to the accounting department for manual matching to the supplier invoice. This approach has the advantage of instant communication of receipts to the accounting staff, since an entry into the accounting database at the receiving dock will be instantly transmitted to the accounting staff. The accounting software can then compare received amounts to the purchase order (which is usually entered into the computer already). All that is left for the accounting staff to do at this point is to enter the purchase order number listed on the supplier's invoice into the computer to see what quantity has been received and how much has not yet been paid. By taking this approach, the bulk of the accounts payable matching process is eliminated.

Before implementing this best practice, there are a few issues to review. One is that the receiving staff must be properly trained in how to enter receipts into the computer. If they are not, receipts information will be inaccurate, probably resulting in the accounts payable staff going back to manual matching, since it is the only way to ensure that invoices are accurately paid. Another issue is ensuring that the existing accounting software allows the receiving personnel to enter receipts information. This is a standard feature on most accounting software packages. However, some software packages do not use the information once it is entered, so it is important to see if the software will match receipts to purchase orders, showing any variances that may arise. If these issues can be overcome, then it is reasonable for companies of any size or complexity to implement the direct entry of receiving information into the computer at the receiving dock.

Cost: 💵💵   **Installation time:** ⏰⏰

3–13 Fax Transmission of Accounts Payable Documents

A centralized accounts payable department may have some difficulty receiving documents from outlying locations or suppliers in time to take early payment discounts. For example, a supplier invoice may be sent to the wrong location, from which it must be mailed to the accounts payable location, or a bill of lading must be forwarded. In either case, the time delay involved may be so long that there is no way to take an early payment discount.

The best way to avoid this problem is to find an alternative method for transmitting documents (with all due respect to the Postal Service). Though one approach is to enter all information directly into the accounting database from any location (see the "Directly Enter Receipts into Computer" section earlier in this chapter), many companies cannot afford an enterprisewide computer system that makes such an approach feasible. A simpler approach is to fax all documents to the accounts payable facility. To do so, there should be a separate fax machine that only handles incoming accounts payable documents; by setting aside a machine for this purpose, it guarantees that the fax machine will not be tied up by outgoing fax transmissions. Also, since it is only used for one purpose, it is unlikely that incoming faxes will be mistakenly taken to other departments. To make this system work even better, the accounting manager should look into getting a fax rerouting capability that sends incoming faxes to an electronic mailbox if the fax machine is busy, with transmission occurring as soon as the fax machine is available to receive new incoming transmissions. This service is inexpensive and ensures that all documents sent are received.

There are few disadvantages to this best practice. It requires a separate phone line for the fax machine, a fax rerouting capability that is nothing more than a voice mailbox for faxes, and a fax machine. However, none of these requirements are expensive. Also, there is a slight risk that some faxes will not be sent correctly or will be lost in transmission. In these cases, it may be possible to generate a custom report from the accounting software that lists all missing documents needed to process various accounts payable transactions. The accounting staff can use this report to fax out requests to subsidiaries for missing documents, so that anything that was lost on the first transmission attempt can be sent again. On the whole, this is an easy best practice to implement for those organizations that use centralized processing of accounts payable for multiple company locations.

Cost: 💵   **Installation time:** ⏰

3–14 Have Suppliers Include Their Supplier Numbers on Invoices

The typical vendor database includes listings for thousands of suppliers. Every time an invoice arrives from a supplier, the accounts payable staff must scroll through the list to determine the vendor code for each one. If there are similar names for different suppliers, or multiple locations for the same one, it is quite likely that the resulting check payments will go astray, leading to lots of extra time to sort through who should have been paid. This basic problem can be partially resolved by having suppliers include the supplier number, as created by the company's accounting system, on their invoices. The easiest way to do so is to mail out a change-of-address form to all suppliers, listing the same company address, but also noting as part of the address an "accounts payable code" that includes the supplier number. Suppliers will gladly add this line to the mailing address to which they send their invoices, since they think it is a routing code that will expedite payment to them (which, in a way, it will). Some follow-up may be necessary to ensure that all suppliers adopt this extra address line. Even if not all of the suppliers elect to make the change, there will still be an increase in efficiency caused by those that have done so.

There are two problems with this approach. One is that the change of address mailing cannot be a bulk mailing of the same letter, since each letter must include the supplier code that is unique to each recipient. This will call for a mail merge software application that can create a separate and unique letter for each recipient. The other problem is that new suppliers (i.e., those arriving *after* the bulk mailing) must be given a supplier code at the time they are first set up on the system. This may require a special phone call to the supplier's accounts payable department to ensure that the code is added to their address file, or else a periodic mailing to all new suppliers that specifies their supplier codes.

     Cost: 🖋   **Installation time:** ⏰ ⏰

3–15 Receive Billings through Electronic Data Interchange

Many of the larger companies, especially those in the retailing industry, have been using electronic data interchange (EDI) for some time. This section describes what EDI is, how it works, why more companies should use it, and why so many do not.

EDI involves the transfer of electronic documents between companies. These documents are sent in strictly defined formats, of which there are over a hundred, one for each type of standard company transaction, including a supplier billing. These formats tend to be very large and complex because they are designed for use by multiple industries; most companies only need to fill out a small portion of each EDI message. Once completed, an EDI message is transmitted to the recipient. This can be done directly, but it usually goes to a third-party provider who maintains a mainframe computer that receives messages from a number of subscribing companies. The message recipient dials into its electronic mailbox at the third-party's mainframe (usually several times a day) to pick up any EDI messages. The recipient then enters each EDI message into its own system for further processing. The reader may notice that a company could achieve the same rapid transfer of information by sending a fax with the same information. This is true, but if properly installed, EDI allows for a greater degree of automation by linking directly into a company's computer system. For example, a paper-based fax must be rekeyed into the recipient's computer system, whereas an EDI message is in a standardized electronic format and so can be run through an automatic conversion program that enters the data into the recipient's computer system with no manual data-entry work at all. This feature gives EDI a distinct advantage over a fax transmission.

Larger companies use EDI most frequently because it allows them to automatically process large quantities of transactions with no manual data-entry work, which can be important when there are hundreds of thousands of transactions flowing through the system. When data are entered by hand, there is a potential for errors in the keypunching, which probably means that there will be hundreds or thousands of manmade errors to correct in these larger companies, just given the volumes of data that must be entered. Thus, EDI allows them to avoid not only the expense of data entry, but also the expense of tracking down and fixing data-entry errors.

If EDI makes a company so efficient, why are only the largest companies using it? The answer is simple: It is expensive to implement and only the largest transaction volumes will offset the cost of the initial setup. For example, if a company wants to receive all of its accounts payable billings by EDI, it must first contact each supplier and persuade it to send EDI transmissions, set up procedures between the two companies for doing so, and then test the system before "going live." In addition, the true labor savings will only be realized if the incoming EDI messages are automatically entered into the recipient's computer system, which calls for the customized programming of an automated interface between the EDI system and the recipient's computer system—this can be an expensive undertaking. Most suppliers will not want to participate in this system unless there are significant transaction volumes between them and the company—why go to the trouble for a small customer? In short, EDI is not catching on in smaller companies because of the expense and effort of installing the system, plus the difficulty of forcing suppliers to participate. Though larger companies may convince their direct trading partners to use EDI, this best practice will only spread through the ranks of smaller companies with the greatest difficulty.

Cost: 💵💵💵   Installation time: 🕐🕐🕐

3–16 Request That Suppliers Enter Invoices through a Web Site

A company may be experiencing some difficulty in persuading its suppliers to switch over to the transmission of invoices by EDI, which would allow it to automatically process all incoming invoices without any data rekeying. A typical complaint when this request is made is that special EDI software must be purchased and stored in a separate computer, while someone must be trained, not only in how to use the software, but also in how to reformat the invoicing data into the format used by the EDI transaction. This problem can be partially avoided by having suppliers access a Web site where they can conduct the data entry.

By having suppliers enter data into a Web site instead of through an EDI transaction, it can avoid the need for any special software that is stored on an in-house computer. A Web site merely requires Internet access, which is commonly available through most computers. Once the data have been entered at the Web site, a company can shift the data to an automated EDI transaction processing program that will convert data into an EDI format and transmit the information to the company's accounting system. Thus, suppliers can use either EDI or Web-based data entry to send invoices to a company, which will process them both in EDI format.

There are some costs associated with this best practice. One is that the company may have to use special discounts or early payments to convince suppliers to use the Web site, rather than simply mailing in their invoices. Also, the Web site must be constructed and maintained, while other software must be created that converts the incoming transactions into EDI format and then ports the resulting data to the accounting system for further processing. Consequently, this can be a relatively expensive option to implement, and so may only be useful for those organizations experiencing a large volume of transactions.

Cost: 💵💵   **Installation time:** ⏰⏰

3–17 Shift Incoming Billings to an EDI Data-Entry Supplier

A company may have the best intentions for improving its accounts payable process, but cannot shift to a fully automated system because its suppliers refuse to send invoices in EDI format. Consequently, the company has no opportunity to automatically shift incoming EDI messages into the accounts payable system, automatically process them, and automatically send out an automated clearinghouse payment. In short, the company is stuck with a manual data entry front end to the accounts payable process. This is a particular problem when a company is so small that its suppliers see no reason to shift over to EDI transactions just for its benefit. This issue can be surmounted by sending the incoming invoices to an EDI supplier that is willing to keypunch the invoices into an EDI format.

To do so, a company can either have suppliers mail all invoices to a lockbox that is accessed by the EDI supplier, or it can remail the invoices to the EDI supplier. This supplier (really just a "body shop" that keypunches data) will reenter the invoice information into an EDI format and transmit it to the company, which can then process the invoices in a highly automated manner. Though this may seem like an expensive way to handle invoice processing, it will allow an accounts payable department to eliminate virtually all of its data-entry positions. The disadvantages to this approach are a slight increase in costs over what it would take to process the invoices in-house, as well as a time delay while the invoices are remailed to the supplier (which may have an impact on the timing of payments back to suppliers).

A variation on this approach is to arrange with an Internet-based bill presentment service to handle this function. For example, one can tell suppliers to send their invoices to companies such as StatusFactory or Paytrust, which scan the bills into their computer systems and then send an e-mail to the company, notifying the accounting department when a payment is due. The accounting staff can then access the on-line databases of these bill presentment services and pay for all bills electronically from one central location.

Cost: Installation time:

3–18 Audit Expense Reports   ✔*Author's Choice*

A labor-intensive task for the accounts payable employees involves carefully reviewing every line item on employee expense reports, comparing everything to the company policy for allowable travel or entertainment expenses, and then contacting employees regarding inconsistencies prior to issuing a check. For a large company with many traveling employees, this can be an extraordinarily labor-intensive task. Furthermore, most employees create accurate expense reports, so the labor expended by the accounts payable staff is rarely equal to the cost savings all the review work generates. To make the situation more unbearable for employees, the expense reviews take so long to complete that there can be a serious delay before an employee receives payment for a check—especially if the expense report is rejected due to reporting failures by the employee, resulting in the expense report moving back and forth several times between the employee and the accounting department before it is paid. When there is so much document travel time, it is also common for the expense report to be "lost in the shuffle," meaning that the employee may have to create the expense report all over again and resubmit it. All of these factors result in an inefficient process in the accounting department and lots of angry employees who are waiting for reimbursement.

The solution to this problem is to replace a total review of all expense reports with an occasional audit. This approach involves taking a sample of many employees' expense reports every few months and comparing the reported amounts to the company travel and entertainment policy to see if there are any exceptions. If the exceptions are significant, it may be necessary to follow up with additional reviews of the expense reports of the same employees to investigate possible abuse. The audit usually results in a list of common expense reporting problems, as well as the names of employees who are abusing the expense reporting system. There are several solutions to ongoing expense reporting problems:

- *Employee education.* It may be necessary to periodically reissue the company policy on travel and entertainment, with follow-up calls to specific abusers to reinforce the policy. This advance work keeps problems from showing up on expense reports.

- *Flag employees for continual audits.* If some employees simply cannot create a correct expense report, they can be listed for ongoing audits to ensure that every report they create is reviewed for accuracy.

- *Flag employees for complete reviews by the accounts payable staff.* Some employees may be so inept at issuing proper expense reports that their reports must be totally reviewed prior to reimbursement. These problem employees can be flagged during the audits.

The audit work is usually carried out by the internal audit department, rather than the accounts payable personnel, since the internal auditors are appropriately experienced in this sort of review work.

The following bullet points include some in-depth audit techniques that the internal auditors can use to ensure that all submitted claims on expense reports are valid:

- See if a boarding pass is included as supporting detail for airfare. A receipt for a flight is not sufficient, since the employee could have booked a flight and then canceled it.

- See if a final grade document or course certificate is included as supporting detail for a training class. A receipt for a training class payment is not sufficient, since the employee could have canceled the class and obtained a refund.

- If an employee submits a receipt for a group, such as for a block of hotel rooms, multiple airfares, or a group dinner, then review the expense reports submitted by the other employees in the group to see if they have also submitted expenses for the same things.

- Look for multiple receipts from the same store that have a date and time stamp that are very close together. This could mean that an employee waits for other customers to buy items from the store, and then asks them for the receipt.

If any expenses look questionable, obtain the employee's credit card statements for the expense report period under review, as well as for the following month, to see if charged receipts actually appear on the statements, and if any refunds appear in the following month.

When using this best practice, there can be a concern that employee reporting abuses will go unnoticed until an auditor finds a problem after the fact. This is a legitimate concern. However, when the audit staff selects expense reports for review, they should stratify the sample of reports so that there is a preponderance of very expensive expense reports in the sample, which means that any potentially exorbitant abuses will have a greater chance of being discovered. Though these discoveries will be after the fact, when employees have already been paid, the company can still seek reimbursement, especially if the employees are still on the payroll, so that adjustments can be taken from their paychecks. However, if employees have already left the company, any overpayments probably cannot be reimbursed.

In short, replacing a total review of all expense reports with an occasional audit can significantly reduce the workload of the accounts payable staff, though there is some risk that employee reporting abuses will result in large overpayments prior to discovery.

Cost: **Installation time:** 🕰

3–19 Automate Expense Reporting

One of the tasks of the accounts payable staff is to check carefully all of the expenses reported in an employee's expense report to ensure that all expenses are valid and have the correct supporting documentation. This can be a major task if there are many expense reports. This will be the case if a company is a large one or has a large proportion of personnel who travel, which is common if a company is in the consulting or sales fields. Luckily, some companies have found a way to get around all of this review work.

A best practice that nearly eliminates the expense report review work of the accounts payable staff is to create a "smart" computer program that walks an employee through the expense reporting process, flagging problem expenses as soon as they are entered and requiring back-up receipts for only selected items. The system is highly customized, since the review rules will vary by company. For example, one company may have a policy of requiring back-up for all meals, whereas another company may automatically hand out a *per diem* meals payment and will not care about meals receipts. Such variations in expense reporting policies will inevitably result in an automated expense reporting system that is closely tailored to each company's needs; such a system should probably be programmed in-house, which is a very expensive undertaking. Due to the high level of expense, this best practice will only pay for itself if it offsets a great deal of accounts payable work, so there should be a very large number of expense reports being submitted before anyone tries to implement the concept. These software packages are quite expensive. A package that is hosted on the Internet, with a dedicated line to the customer, could cost as little as $35,000, while a full-blown installation at a large company could cost as much as $500,000.

The logical flow of automated expense reporting is noted in the following process. The key issue here is that all employees must have direct access to the program so it can respond to their expense entries as soon as they make them. This requires online access by anyone who will use the program, which means that every user not only must have access to a computer or terminal, but probably also have a modem or access to a broadband linkage. One must consider these hardware costs as well as the previously noted software costs before implementing this best practice. The processing steps are as follows:

1. The user accesses an online expense reporting form that is linked to the central expense reporting software and database.

2. The user enters expenses by date and category.

3. The software reviews all expenses as entered and flags those that are not allowable. It rejects these and notifies the user, along with an explanation.

4. The software reviews all remaining expenses and decides which items require a back-up receipt.

5. The user prints out a transmittal form detailing all required receipts and that also contains a unique transmittal number that is linked to the expense report that was just entered into the computer.

6. Upon completion by the user, the electronic expense report is routed by e-mail to the user's supervisor, who electronically approves or rejects the report. If rejected, the supervisor can note the problem on the expense report, which is then routed back to the user for resubmission.

7. The user attaches all receipts to the transmittal form and mails it to the accounts payable department.

8. When the accounts payable department receives the transmittal form and receipts, it verifies that all receipts are included and that the expense report has been approved by the supervisor, and then approves the entire package.

9. Upon approval by the accounts payable staff, the expense report is immediately paid by wire transfer to the bank account of the user.

10. The transmittal form and receipts are filed.

These detailed steps are shown in graphical form in Exhibit 3.3. Though there appear to be more steps in the automated process than there are in a traditional process, the extra steps are automatic or much simpler. The overall result is far less processing time, as well as a significant reduction in the time needed before an employee is paid.

The solution just noted is for an automated employee expense reporting system that is entirely custom programmed. However, many organizations do not process a sufficient number of employee expense reports to justify the cost of all the programming time that is required to create the system. For these organizations,

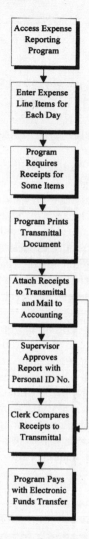

Exhibit 3.3 The Automated Expense Reporting Process

a good alternative is to purchase an automated expense reporting software package. These packages are entirely self-contained and do an effective job of processing employee expense reports, but they do not provide direct linkages to the rest of a company's accounting system. For this, a custom-designed interface module is still required. A Web-based expense reporting package is especially useful, since employees in outlying locations or who are traveling can use the system at any location where they can access the Internet; moreover, it requires no software installation on anyone's computers. Also, Web-based software can be updated easily, whereas client-server systems require updates on individual user computers.

Further, if someone steals an employee's computer, there is no time or expense information stored on it, since this information is submitted directly through the Internet to a different storage location.

Cost: 💵💵   **Installation time:** ⏰⏰⏰

3–20 Eliminate Cash Advances for Employee Travel

Many employees with few funds on hand will come to the accounts payable department asking for cash advances so they can go on company-mandated trips. By doing so, the department may be handing over more cash than the employee really needs, which can make it difficult to collect any unspent cash. In addition, employees who have already been paid for their expenditures have no incentive to submit an expense report, especially when the report may reveal that they must pay some of the original advance back to the company. The usual result is a prolonged process of asking employees for expense reports, while the amount of the original advance remains, incorrectly, on the accounting books as a prepaid asset.

This problem is eliminated by denying cash travel advances. However, this is much easier said than done. In reality, many employees simply cannot afford to be out-of-pocket on any company-related expenses. If so, the company can purchase many of their expenses for them, such as airline tickets. Also, such an employee can travel with another employee who has the financial wherewithal to absorb cash expenditures for both employees. As a last resort, the company can also issue company credit cards to employees, though this raises the risk of having the cards used for noncompany purchases. Through some combination of these actions, a company can reduce its reliance on cash advances to employees.

Cost: 💵   **Installation time:** ⏰

3–21 Link Corporate Travel Policies to an Automated Expense Reporting System

The typical set of travel policies used by a company is quite detailed—thou shalt not charge to the company the cost of movies, clothing, first-class upgrades, and so on. However, the overburdened accounts payable staff has little time to review expense reports for these items, much less to then create variance reports and send them out to the violating employees and their supervisors. An additional problem is that corporate travel policies change with some regularity, which makes it difficult for the accounts payable staff to even know which policies are still valid. A further problem arises when a company reimburses its employees based on the per diem rates listed in the Federal Travel Regulation. This document is used by the federal government to determine a reasonable cost of living at each of over 100 cities throughout the country; given the frequency of change in these numbers (at least quarterly), it becomes very labor-intensive to determine which payments to make to employees. However, these problems can be eliminated by converting the travel policies into rules that can be used by a computer to automatically spot problems with expense reports that have been submitted through an automated expense reporting system.

For example, input from a corporate travel card into an automated expense reporting system can tell if an airfare is for a first-class seat, which may be prohibited by company travel policy. If the first-class purchase can be set up as a flagged field, then the computer system can automatically spot this issue and either note it on a report or (more proactively) send an e-mail to the appropriate person, who makes note of the issue. Examples of other rule violations are to verify that the correct airline was used (since there may be a bulk-purchase agreement in place) and that restaurant bills were actually incurred during the period spanned by a business trip (rather than before or after, which would be suspicious). However, this sort of early-warning system can be quite expensive to create. There are no standard software packages that perform this task, so the programming staff must be called on to convert policies into rules that can be understood by the computer system, and then set up an interface between the rules database and the expense report database that will spot rule violations. In short, this can be an expensive option to install, and so should only be considered if there is a clear likelihood that there will be significant resulting cost savings.

Cost: 💵💵💵   **Installation time:** ⏰⏰⏰

3–22 Centralize the Accounts Payable Function

A company with many subsidiaries or locations usually has a separate accounts payable function located in each facility. This can be inefficient for several reasons. First, the accounting staff at each location requires a supervisor, so the sum total of supervisors at all the locations can be substantial. Second, there can be problems with suppliers sending invoices to the wrong locations. This is a particular problem when the subsidiaries all have the same or similar names, since it is difficult for a supplier to figure out which location is the correct one to which a bill should be sent. The problem is exacerbated if a supplier ships to several company locations and then must issue a separate invoice to each location, since it is confusing to issue billings when not only the company names are identical, but also the goods shipped to all of them. Third, the many accounts payable departments all require training and auditing to ensure that they all process payments in the same manner. If a company does not do this, it is likely that discounts will not be taken or that payments will be made without proper authorization. Finally, there is a lack of control when the accounts payable function is widely distributed.

Local management can interfere with the payable process to make payments to themselves or to entities they control, while still giving the appearance of good local controls. All of these problems can be either eliminated or mitigated by using a central accounts payable facility.

A centralized accounts payable facility does not have to be near any other company locations. It pays all supplier invoices, using a single computer system and a single accounting database, and operates under the control of a small, unified group of managers. It has multiple advantages. First, there are far fewer managers, since there is only one group of people to control. Second, there are no problems with supplier invoices and related information disappearing, because all invoices are sent to the one processing location. If a supplier incorrectly sends paperwork to the wrong location, all facilities know where it must be forwarded, so the documents always arrive at the correct point (though they may take a roundabout route to get there). Third, all accounts payable activities can be easily monitored and corrected, since the auditing personnel only have to review one facility. Finally, there is better control over the process, since the accounts payable function is divorced from local control; there is no way for a local manager to influence payments. All of these advantages have a single result—lower cost, primarily through an overall reduction in the number of personnel. It has been proven many times that a single, centralized accounts payable function is considerably cheaper than a dispersed function.

Despite all these advantages, some companies balk at centralizing because of protests by local managers. They claim that some payments must be made locally, because some payments are cash-on-delivery, in cash, or require such short payment intervals that the central facility cannot respond in time. They are correct. However, this is such a small proportion of the bills at most facilities that a local plant can get by with a few checks per month, which are drawn on a separate bank account in which the company keeps a very small cash reserve. By limiting the size of local payments, a company can limit its exposure to any unwarranted local payments. By meeting local management demands partway, a company can still centralize the bulk of its payments while continuing to allow some local flexibility. This is a very good best practice to implement if a company has multiple locations.

Cost: 💵💵💵   Installation time: 🕰🕰🕰

3–23 Store Late Fees in a Separate General Ledger Account

An inefficient accounts payable process, or one that loses track of supplier invoices, will inevitably incur late fees charged by suppliers. When this happens, the fee is generally recorded in the same expense account to which the rest of a supplier invoice is charged. As a result, the inefficiency of the accounting department is passed through to the department that originally ordered the goods or services from the supplier, even though it is not the originating department's fault.

A more responsible approach is to record late fees in a separate general ledger account that is charged to the accounting department. By summarizing all late fees in a single account, management can also see if late payments are a significant expense for the company—information that would be impossible to locate under the old system.

The prime difficulty with this best practice is that the accounting staff does not like to document its own failures, and so might "accidentally" charge late fees to other accounts. Accordingly, have the internal audit department periodically test the payables recording system to ensure that late fees are being stored in the correct account.

Cost:    **Installation time:**

3–24 Issue Standard Account Code List

Accounts payable can be a difficult area in which to replace employees while still experiencing high levels of productivity. The problem is caused by the time it takes a new person to learn the accounts to which invoices should be coded. Even when experienced accounts payable clerks are hired, they still must memorize the account codes, which will slow them down considerably. Even an experienced, long-term employee may occasionally misdirect a supplier invoice to the wrong account, so some solution is necessary to resolve the issue.

The easiest way to resolve the problem is to reduce the chart of accounts (which can be a very lengthy document) down to a single page of key accounts to which invoices are to be coded. Most invoices can be applied to a very small number of accounts, so this is usually a very viable option. When the shortened list is posted at each accounts payable clerk's desk, it becomes a simple reference tool for finding the correct account, which improves productivity while reducing the error rate.

A more sophisticated way to resolve the problem is to encode the accounting software with an account number for each supplier. Under this method, the clerk does not have to worry about the account to which anything should be coded because the computer already contains the information. However, there are two problems with this approach. One is that some software packages do not contain this information, and expensive programming is necessary to install it. Second, the account code may change, depending on what the supplier is billing. Given the trend toward supplier consolidation, it is increasingly likely that a company will go to one supplier for a wide range of products and services, so that several account codes may apply to a single supplier.

A simple list of approved account codes is an easy way to improve the productivity and reduce the error rate of the accounts payable staff, especially that of new employees.

Cost: **Installation time:**

3-25 Link Supplier Requests to the Accounts Payable Database

A significant task for an accounts payable person, especially one working for a company that pays its bills late, is to answer payment queries from suppliers. They want to know when their invoices were paid, the amount of the payments, and the check numbers that were issued. For a company that is seriously delinquent in its payments, this can be a full-time job for the accounting staff, which is also a clear loss of productive time.

A recent innovation that largely eliminates verbal responses to suppliers is to have suppliers call a phone number that links them to a keypad-activated inquiry system that will answer their most common questions. For example, they can enter the company's purchase order number, their invoice number, or the supplier's name; the system will then respond with the specific payments made, the date on which the check was cut, and the check number. The system can even be extended to list the date on which payments are scheduled to be made.

However, there are some issues to consider before installing an automated supplier response system. One issue is that this is a very recent innovation and most suppliers will not be used to it—they want to talk to a person and will deluge the company's operator to voice this opinion. To quell this type of response, the system should include an option to exit the automated system and contact a person. This allows the more technologically versed suppliers to use the automated system, while other users can still talk to an employee. This option is also necessary for those cases where there are unusual circumstances. For example, a company may not be paying due to a lack of receiving documentation, or because the quantity billed was incorrect. It is better to discuss these problems with a person instead of a computer, since special actions may need to be taken to resolve the situation. The other problem is the cost of the installation. It requires an interface computer that links to the main accounting computer system, as well as modem access and software, to translate supplier requests into inquiries that the accounting database can answer. These costs can be considerable, especially when there are expected to be many callers and many requests for information. The price range typically starts at $20,000 for the smallest installations and can be many times higher for large systems. Nonetheless, this is a good approach for companies that feel they can bring about a major efficiency improvement by routing suppliers straight to the accounts payable database for information.

An alternative to having suppliers access accounts payable information through a phone connection is to do so through an Internet site. This approach is somewhat more flexible than a voice-activated system that is generally limited to a few simple status messages. Instead, a Web page can itemize the exact status of each payable item, assign a code to it that explains the reasons for any delays, and note the name of the contact person in the accounts payable department who is responsible for processing the supplier invoice. It can also list any missing information that is delaying payment, such as a purchase order number or bank account number for the supplier, which can be entered by the supplier directly into the Web site, and which will be automatically loaded into the accounting database to assist in the completion of processing. The Web page may even list the name of the person who is responsible for approving the invoice, as well as this person's contact information. A company may not want to add this last piece of information, since it can greatly increase the volume of phone calls to these people, who will in turn bother the accounts payable staff about payment—something that it is trying to avoid through the use of this Web site.

Cost: 🏦🏦🏦   **Installation time:** ⏰⏰

3–26 Implement a Reverse Lockbox

Banks have offered lockbox services for many years, where a company's customers send their payments directly to the bank, which deposits them on behalf of the company. A few of the larger banks also offer a similar outbound payment service, called a *reverse lockbox,* where they pay suppliers on behalf of the company. Under this approach, suppliers send their invoices to the bank rather than the company, either by mail or by entering the invoices electronically through a Web site. If arriving by mail, the bank images the invoices and converts them to an electronic file that it exports to the company's accounts payable system. Up to this point, the reverse lockbox takes advantage of the regular lockbox capabilities of most banks, which is the high-speed imaging of paper documents.

A more advanced reverse lockbox solution adds business rules that allow the bank to automatically pay suppliers if dollar amounts are below a certain level and suppliers are on a preapproved list. This can include a three-way match of supplier invoices with company purchase orders and receiving reports, and payment of the invoices if the matching amounts fall within certain business rules (which may vary by spending category). All invoices not meeting the business rules are presented to the company via Web browser for approval prior to payment.

After payments are made, the bank updates the company's accounting system to show the reduction in payable liability and cash balance.

This is a useful option for those public companies looking for a way to reduce the volume of work needed to comply with the control requirements of section 404 of the Sarbanes-Oxley Act. By shifting the bulk of the payables process to a bank, the myriad of payables controls are now the responsibility of the bank to maintain.

Thus, the reverse lockbox solution applies a very high level of automation to the payables process, while also reducing the administrative burden associated with payables controls.

Cost: 🏦   **Installation time:** ⏰⏰

3–27 Outsource the Accounts Payable Function

Many controllers do not want to waste time managing such a mundane function as accounts payable. It does not directly contribute to the mission of any company, nor does it impact customer service. In short, it is a baseline clerical function that merely takes up management time with no particular payback. By off-loading this function to a supplier who specializes in accounts payable processing, a controller can reduce the management time devoted to this functional area and allocate more time to other more profitable company functions.

Besides reduced management time, it can also be less expensive to outsource to a qualified supplier. A well-run supplier has an excellent knowledge of accounts payable best practices and uses that knowledge to drastically cut the processing effort needed. This is an especially attractive option for those companies that are in difficult financial circumstances and that would prefer to pay just a per-transaction fee, rather than an entire staff. This essentially converts a large fixed cost to a variable cost that will not be incurred if there are no transactions to process.

Outsourcing accounts payable usually means that the entire company staff devoted to this work will be shifted to the supplier who is taking over the work, though it is also possible that the supplier will not need these people, or will "cherry-pick" only the most qualified. If the latter is the case, then the controller should meet with the staff to honestly appraise their future prospects with the supplier or to provide outplacement counseling. The supplier should also be available at these meetings to answer any employee questions, as well as to enroll employees in supplier benefit plans and to convert them to the supplier's payroll system.

Besides the staff conversion, the controller must also determine how to manage the supplier. This is not a case of handing the work to the supplier and then paying the supplier's bills—on the contrary, some oversight will always be necessary to handle any problems that may arise, such as complaints from suppliers that are not being paid, verifications that discounts are being taken, and approvals of all payments prior to payment. These activities are most commonly handled at the level of an assistant controller, though the controller may manage the supplier directly if the transaction volume is minimal. In all cases, some continuing oversight by the remaining accounting staff is necessary.

One should also consider the degree and form of ongoing interaction with the supplier necessary to ensure that accounts payable are processed correctly. For example, if a company has a fully integrated accounting and manufacturing software package, it will be impossible for the supplier to process accounts payable on its own accounting software, because these transactions must be completed on the company's software package. The best way to resolve this problem is to give the supplier remote access to the company's computer system, so that it can process accounts payable as though it were an on-site service. However, this arrangement will require an extra expenditure to train the supplier's employees in how to use the system. Another option is to have the supplier perform only the most mundane accounts payable tasks, such as matching documents, and leave any data-entry or check-cutting work to the in-house staff. This option eliminates the worst drudge work from the function, while still allowing for greater control over it. Yet another variation is to allow the supplier to cut checks in payment of accounts payable, though this reduces some company control over cash flows. The best way to resolve the problem is to have company management approve check runs before they are printed and mailed. Clearly, there are a variety of approaches to the extent to which the accounts payable function can be outsourced.

Cost: Installation time: 🕰 🕰 🕰

3–28 Shrink the Supplier Base

Part of the job of the accounts payable staff is to maintain a complete and accurate database of suppliers, which typically includes address and payment information. If data are entered incorrectly, the accounting staff is usually notified by a supplier that has not received a payment (because it was sent to the wrong address), has been paid the wrong amount (because of an incorrect early payment discount rate), or has been paid at the wrong time (because of an incorrect due date). This type of problem is inevitable in even the best-run company and will require some time to research and fix. However, the problem is greatly exacerbated in a company that has many suppliers, because there are so many chances for the supplier information to be incorrect. Another problem with having many suppliers is that there is typically little control over adding new suppliers (after all, that is how there came to be so many suppliers in the first place!). The accounting staff must deal constantly with adding new data to the supplier database, consolidating supplier records that have been entered multiple times, and (especially) making a multitude of small payments to a plethora of suppliers. Wouldn't it be much easier if there were just fewer suppliers?

This is a best practice—reducing the number of suppliers. It is much easier to maintain accurate data in a relatively small number of supplier records, while there are few new suppliers to add to the database. In addition, the volume of purchases from the smaller number of suppliers tends to be larger, so there are typically fewer, larger invoices that can be keypunched more easily into the accounting database and paid with fewer, larger checks. Essentially, shrinking the supplier database reduces a variety of data-entry tasks.

Unfortunately, shrinking the number of suppliers is not easy. The first problem is that the accounting staff must convince the purchasing staff to adopt a supplier reduction strategy, which the purchasing staff may not be so eager to pursue, especially if they prefer the strategy of sourcing parts from multiple suppliers. In addition, company employees may be in the habit of buying from any supplier they want, which can require a considerable amount of retraining before they are willing to buy from a much shorter list of approved suppliers. The effort required to reduce the number of suppliers is frequently far in excess of the productivity gains realized by the accounts payable staff, so most controllers do not pursue this best practice unless there is already either an active supplier reduction campaign in place, or else the head of the purchasing department appears to be amenable to the idea. Even then, a supplier reduction strategy does not take place overnight. On the contrary, it can take years to effect a massive cutback in the supplier base. Accordingly, this strategy should only be adopted when there is multidepartmental support for the idea as well as a long implementation timeline.

Cost: 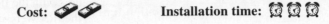   **Installation time:**

3–29 Withhold First Payment until W-9 Form Is Received

Within one month after the calendar year is complete, the accounts payable department must issue completed 1099 forms to a variety of business entities, detailing how much money the company paid them during the year. The IRS uses its copy of this information to ensure that the revenue reported by the recipients is correct. The trouble for the issuing company is that many potential recipients do not want to report income to the government, and so will refuse to fill out a W-9 form or to supply a taxpayer identification number to the company. Thus, completing 1099 forms by the IRS-mandated due date can be a substantial problem.

A simple way to avoid this issue is to withhold payment of a company's first payment to a supplier until it completes and submits a W-9 form to the company. By doing so, the accounts payable staff avoids the year-end hassle of determining who receives a 1099 form. This step does add work to the check-processing function, but eliminates so much more work when the 1099 forms are issued that the extra labor is worth it. This best practice can put the accounts payable staff under some pressure from the materials management department if that group is trying to obtain rapid delivery of crucial parts from a new supplier who wants payment in advance. In most other instances, there will be little in-house opposition to this system.

Cost: **Installation time:**

3–30 Verify Taxpayer Identification Numbers

When a company issues Form 1099 annual reports to the IRS, there will inevitably be some rejections by the IRS because the taxpayer identification number (TIN) listed on the form does not match the company name that the IRS has in its files. The IRS issues rejections on a backup withholding notice, stating that the company has filed Forms 1099 with erroneous TIN information.

Before sending out the 1099 annual report to the IRS, the accounting staff can verify TIN numbers against IRS records, using its TIN matching program.

This program is accessible over the Internet and is available in two varieties. The first is interactive TIN matching, which accepts up to 25 payee TIN/Name combinations on-screen. The second version is bulk TIN matching, which allows up to 100,000 payee TIN/Name combinations to be matched via a text file submission. For both versions, there is no limit to the number of submissions that a user can submit per day.

The TIN matching program is accessible only by an "authorized payer," which the IRS defines as one who has filed information returns with the IRS in at least one of the past two tax years. Sign-up is available on the IRS Web site.

Cost: Installation time:

3–31 Automate Payments for Repetitive Invoicing

The typical company has a small proportion of invoices that arrive at regular intervals and are for the same amount, month after month. Examples of such payments are rent invoices or lease payments. These payments usually go through the typical accounts payable matching process, including searches for approval documents, before they are paid. However, it is possible to utilize their repetitive nature to create a more efficient subprocess within the accounts payable area.

The simple best practice that streamlines repetitive supplier invoices is to create a payment schedule to bypass the approval process and automatically issue a check in a prespecified amount and on a prespecified date. This can be done by creating a table of repetitive payments in the accounting computer system; but there is no reason why the programming expense cannot be avoided by just listing the payments on a piece of paper and posting it in the accounts payable area. In either case, there is no need to look for approvals, so there is less labor required of the accounts payable staff. However, there are two problems. First, the repetitive payment schedule must note the termination date of each payment, so that checks are not inadvertently issued after the final payment date. These payments can be time-consuming when the supplier returns them, if the company even notices the overpayment at all. Second, the repetitive payments may change from time to time, so the schedule must note both the dates when payment amounts change and the amounts of the changes. For example, rental payments frequently contain preset escalation clauses, which must be recognized by the repetitive payment schedule.

An especially fine use for repetitive invoicing is the remittance of garnishments to various courts on behalf of employees. In the case of child support payments, these garnishments may go on for years, and usually in the same amount through the entire period (unless the court orders that a different amount be withheld from time to time). Repetitive invoicing is quite useful here, because a company is liable to the court to make these payments, and can be subject to onerous penalties if it does not do so. By shifting the burden of making this payment to the computer system, there is less risk of not making the payment.

Automating repetitive payments that occur in the same amounts and on the same dates is a good way to remove the approval step from the accounts payable process, though this improvement typically only covers a small percentage of the total workload of the accounts payable staff.

Cost: 💵   Installation time: ⏰

3–32 Install a Payment Factory

In a typical accounts payable environment, a company allows its subsidiaries to manage their own payables processes, payments, and banking relationships. The result is higher transaction costs and banking fees, since each location uses its own staff and has little transaction volume with which to negotiate reduced banking fees.

An improvement on this situation is the payment factory, which is a centralized payables and payment processing center. It is essentially a subset of an enterprise resources planning (ERP) system, specifically targeted at payables. It features complex software with many interfaces, since it must handle incoming payment information in many data formats, work-flow management of payment approvals, a rules engine to determine the lowest-cost method of payment, and links to multiple banking systems.

Key payment factory benefits include a stronger negotiating position with the company's fewer remaining banks, better visibility into funding needs and liquidity management, and improved control over payment timing.

The payment factory is especially effective when the payables systems of multinational subsidiaries are centralized, since cross-border banking fees can be significantly reduced. For example, it can automatically offset payments due between company subsidiaries, resulting in smaller cash transfers and similarly reduced foreign exchange charges, wiring costs, and lifting fees (a fee charged by the bank receiving a payment), while also routing payments through in-country accounts to avoid these international fees.

There are several problems with payment factories—the seven-figure cost of the software, gaining the cooperation of the various subsidiaries who will no longer have direct control over their payment systems, and different banking relationships.

How can you adapt the payment factory to a low-budget situation? First, centralize your accounts payable operations. Second, minimize the number of banking relationships. Third, try outsourcing the foreign exchange operations with one of your remaining banks.

Cost: 💵💵💵   Installation time: ⏰⏰⏰

3–33 Eliminate Manual Checks

The accounts payable process can be streamlined through the use of many best practices that are listed in this chapter; however, a common recurring problem is those payments that go around the entire preplanned payable process. These are the inevitable payments that are sudden and unplanned and that must be handled immediately. Examples are payments for pizza deliveries, flowers for bereaved employees, or cash-on-delivery payments. In all of these cases, the accounting staff must drop what it is doing, create a manual check, get it signed, and enter the information on the check into the computer system. To make matters worse, due to the rush basis of the payment, it is common for the accounting person to forget to make the entry into the computer system, which throws off the bank reconciliation work at the end of the month, which creates still more work to track down and fix the problem. In short, issuing manual checks significantly worsens the efficiency of the accounts payable staff.

One can use three methods to reduce the number of manual checks. The first method is to cut off the inflow of check requests, while the second is (paradoxically) to automate the cutting of manual checks. The first approach is a hard one, since it requires tallying the manual checks that were cut each month and following up with the check requesters to see if there might be a more orderly manner of making requests in the future, thereby allowing more checks to be issued through the normal accounts payable process. Unfortunately, this practice requires so much time communicating with the check requesters that the lost time will overtake the resulting time savings by the accounting staff from writing fewer manual checks. The second, and better, approach, is to preset a printer with check stock so that anyone can request a check at any time, and an accounting person can immediately sit down at a computer terminal, enter the check information, and have it print out at once. This approach has the unique benefit of avoiding any trouble with not reentering information into the computer system, since it is being entered there in the first place (which avoids any future problems with the bank reconciliation). It tends to take slightly longer to create a check in this manner, but the overall time savings are greater.

A third alternative is to make the process of creating a manual check so difficult that requesters will avoid this approach. For example, the request may require the signature of a senior manager or multiple approving signatures. In addition, the accounting department could charge an exorbitant amount for this service to the requesting department on the corporate financial statements. Further, a report itemizing all manual check requests can be sent to senior management each month, highlighting who is bothering the accounting staff with these items. Any combination of these actions should reduce the use of manual checks.

Cost: **Installation time:**

3–34 Increase the Frequency of Check Runs

The issuance of a manual check involves a great deal of extra work for the accounts payable staff, because they must perform a number of tasks that are normally spread over a much larger number of checks in the typical check run, plus handle the manual logging of the check into the computer system. If they forget to enter the manual check, then even more time is lost during the bank reconciliation process, when the check will appear as an exception, and must be investigated and reconciled.

One way to reduce the number of manual checks is to investigate how many of the checks could have been included in the normal check run if there had been more frequently scheduled check runs. For example, if check runs are performed only on Fridays and a check request appears on Monday, could the person demanding the check wait a few days until a midweek check run, or would he still require an immediate payment? In many cases, adding one or two check runs per week will be more cost-effective than issuing a large quantity of manual checks. The correct solution will vary by company, depending on the volume and nature of each manual check request.

An alternative approach is to shift the date on which check runs are completed, rather than increase their frequency. For example, what if most manual checks are demanded by the sales staff, who return from out-of-state sales trips on Fridays and want to be paid the following Monday? The solution may be shifting the standard check run to the end of the day on Monday, in order to eliminate these manual payments.

Yet another alternative is to offer electronic payments if those requiring payments can wait until the standard pay date. Since an electronic payment clears the bank much faster than a check, this can be an inducement for those requesting checks to wait until the normally scheduled pay date.

Cost: **Installation time:** 🕑

3–35 Have Regularly Scheduled Check-Signing Meetings

If company management insists on signing all checks, as opposed to the use of signature stamps, then the accounts payable staff must either track down these people and loom threateningly over them while they sign the checks, or else meekly leave piles of checks on their desks and hope to receive the completed checks back within not too many weeks. Either approach is unacceptable, since the first puts the accounting staff in the uncomfortable position of forcing managers to interrupt their workdays in order to sign checks, while the latter approach interferes with the timely distribution of checks to suppliers and employees.

A good way to resolve this difficulty is to arrange for regularly scheduled check-signing meetings, preferably immediately after scheduled check runs. By doing so, managers will have already blocked out time for this work and will feel less compelled to drop other work to complete their signing duties. Also, it means that the accountant delivering the checks can sit and amicably discuss issues with the check signer, such as queries about the reason for some payments, while also presenting issues on behalf of the accounting department. Because of the increased level of communication available under this approach, it is not unusual for an assistant controller to deliver the checks, rather than an accounting clerk.

Cost: Installation time: 🕐

3–36 Implement Positive Pay

Depending on the types of antifraud features used on a company's check stock, it may not be that difficult to alter the payable amount of a check. Consider using positive pay to prevent such altered checks from being cashed. Under this approach, the issuing company creates a file containing the check number, date, and amount of all checks it issues each day and forwards the file to its bank. The bank then compares the check information in this file to checks being presented for payment and refuses to accept any checks containing different information. This approach is considered the most effective way to keep fraudulently altered checks from being cashed. Some banks offer a more advanced positive pay system, where a company can review the digital images of exception items online and enter a pay or return decision on the spot.

An improvement on the basic positive pay concept is for banks to also offer positive pay that includes the name of the payee, which keeps anyone from cashing a company check on which the payee name has been altered.

For those companies that do not want to spend time issuing a check file to the bank whenever they issue checks, reverse positive pay is the solution. Under this approach, the bank creates a file containing information about all checks presented during the day, and sends it to the issuing company. Ideally, the company reviews the file and approves only those checks for which it has matching information. In reality, the bank can wait only a short time for the company to review the file, and then accepts all checks if it is not otherwise notified by the company—which makes this a weaker control than positive pay.

There are a few problems with positive pay:

- If the payables clerk forgets to send the file of new checks to the bank after each check run, then every check in that run will be refused by the bank.
- If the payables clerk forgets to include stop payments, voided checks, and manual checks in the file, checks may be cleared that the company did not intend to have clear, and vice versa.
- If the bank only updates its files with new incoming positive pay information during an overnight batch process, then anyone taking a check directly from

the company to the bank to be deposited at once may find that the check will be rejected.

Despite these problems, positive pay is a useful fraud deterrent for many companies.

Cost: 🪙   **Installation time:** 🕐

3–37 Incorporate Copy Protection Features into Checks

Though rare, check counterfeiters occasionally either modify a check created by a company or create an entirely new one, resulting in significant losses to the company. There are a number of check protection features available that one can incorporate into the company check stock in order to thwart the efforts of counterfeiters. As a general rule, always add more security features to a check, because they compound the difficulty of replicating or altering the check. Here are some of the features that can be ordered from the check printer:

- *"Void" image.* When a check is copied, the word "Void" appears multiple times on the copied version of the check. This makes it impossible for a counterfeiter to create clean color copies of a check.
- *Microprinting border.* Text can be added along the edges of a check using very small fonts, so they are only visible as text when magnified. When copied, they appear as a line, with no discernible wording visible. This is a less obvious way to deter the efforts of someone attempting to color-copy a check.
- *Modified background in dollar space.* A set of wavy lines can be designed into the check, in the area where the dollar amount is printed on the check. By doing so, counterfeiters will have a very difficult time erasing existing dollar amounts without visibly damaging the background.
- *Watermark.* A watermark can be added to a check that is only visible when seen from an angle and that is impossible to duplicate when a check is run through a copier. This technique is most effective when the check contains a warning not to accept the check unless the watermark can be seen.
- *Chemical sensitivity.* The check stock is sensitive to a wide array of chemicals, which will discolor the check when it is subjected to a chemical wash.
- *Copy void endorsement.* If anyone attempts to photocopy the endorsement on the back of a check, the word *void* will also appear in the photocopy.
- *Endorsement warning.* The endorsement box on the back of the check contains a message stating that the check contains an authentication feature and how to view it.
- *Fluorescent ink.* When exposed to ultraviolet light, wording appears that authenticates the validity of the check. This feature can be enhanced with

the use of fluorescent fibers that are integrated into the check stock and also appear under fluorescent light.

- *Integrated Fourdrinier watermark.* This is a watermark that is pressed into the check stock at the paper mill and is visible from either side of the check.

- *Laid lines.* Lines of varying widths and spacing are printed on the back of the check, which makes it difficult to make alterations to the check by cutting and pasting.

- *Prismatic printing.* The background of the check includes subtle gradations of color that are difficult to reproduce on a color copier.

- *Thermochromatic ink.* This is a heat-sensitive type of ink that is used within an authentication seal on the back of a check. When rubbed, it reveals the seal.

- *Warning banner.* This is a banner on the check, advising the user of various security features of the check, and to review these features before accepting the check.

Cost: **Installation time:** 🕐

3–38 Avoid Acronym Payees on Checks

When a company enters an acronym for a payee name on a check, there is a heightened risk that someone could fraudulently alter the acronym, so that the check can be paid to a different entity. For example, someone could easily add a single letter to the acronym on a check made payable to the NAC (National Arts Center), changing it to NACM (National Association for Credit Managers).

To avoid this type of fraud, always fully spell out the name of the payee on a check. Since a computerized accounting system draws the payee name from the vendor master file, this may require a review of that file to ascertain if any acronyms are currently being used.

Cost: 💵   **Installation time:** 🕐

3–39 Use the Universal Payment Identification Code

Companies frequently avoid giving out their bank account information on the grounds that it can be used to debit their account without approval, or because they change bank accounts with sufficient frequency to require constant notifications to those customers making electronic payments. These issues can be avoided by using the universal payment identification code (UPIC).

The UPIC is a banking address used to receive electronic credit payments. It is a unique number that is assigned to a company's bank account, and is essentially a mask for the real account number. It is combined with a universal routing/transit (URT) number, which routes all incoming payment information for the associated UPIC to the Clearing House Payments Company, which in turn translates this information into the company's actual bank account information for payment purposes.

With the UPIC, only ACH credits can be initiated, with all debits blocked. Given this high level of security, a company can print its UPIC on invoices or display it on the Internet with no fear that the information will be used to extract money from its account. Of course, this feature is already available through debit blocking, but the next feature is truly unique.

The company keeps the same UPIC even if it changes bank accounts within the same bank, changes banking relationships entirely, or if its bank is involved in a merger. To do so, the company merely links its new bank account number to the existing UPIC.

Finally, the UPIC also protects a company from someone's using the number to create fraudulent checks or demand drafts, because the UPIC cannot be used to clear a paper item.

A UPIC can be obtained only through a participating bank. To see if your bank offers the UPIC, access *www.upic.com/companies/obtain.php* and type in the name of your financial institution and you will be contacted with the necessary information.

Cost:    Installation time: 🕰

3–40   Revise Payment Terms for Electronic Payments

When a company pays with checks, it cuts a check on the negotiated due date, which reaches the customer after a few days of mail float; they cash it, and another two or three days pass before the check clears. This results in an average total float of perhaps five days.

If the company switches to electronic payments, then the entire float vanishes, so the cost to the issuing company has increased by the five days of interest income that the company did not earn on the funds during the float period. In addition, the company must pay a fee to process the electronic transaction. Offsetting this lost income and processing fee is the cost savings from not having to process paper checks, which includes the cost of the checks and the bank's check processing fee. Be sure to include in these costs only the *incremental* savings from not creating a check (e.g., if the check signer no longer has to sign checks, is the company actually saving money by then terminating the check signer (!), or does this person merely work on other tasks?). Thus, it is probable that the company's actual incremental cost reduction is the cost of the check and the bank's check processing fee, and nothing else.

After netting the lost interest income, electronic payment fee, and reduced processing cost, the company may still be losing money through the issuance of electronic payments. If so, consider negotiating slightly longer payment terms with suppliers to offset the increased cost. Of course, if the accounting department's long-term strategy is to convert entirely to electronic payments, irrespective of cost, then it may not be useful to attempt a payment term renegotiation, since some suppliers may opt to still receive check payments.

Cost:    Installation time: 🕑

3–41 Install Advanced ACH Debit Blocking

Banks have offered debit blocking for many years; this keeps unauthorized parties from extracting funds from a company's bank account with an ACH debit transaction. Unfortunately, some ACH debits are legitimate, and are also rejected by the debit block.

More advanced debit blocking options are now available that allow for fine-tuning of the use of debit blocking. They are as follows:

1. Block all debit transactions.
2. Enter broad screening criteria.
3. Enter specific instructions to accept only the following items:
   - Accept one-time debits.
   - Limit the number of times a recurring debit can post.
   - Limit the time period over which an authorization is accepted.
   - Specify a fixed, variable, or maximum debit dollar limit.

Also, if debits do not match the screening criteria, they can be sent to the company in an unauthorized transaction report. An authorized person can then review this report and contact the bank to authorize the acceptance or rejection of specific debits.

Banks offer many variations on these advanced debit blocking features, so contact your bank to determine what is available.

Cost:    Installation time: 🕑

3–42 Use Signature Stamp   ✔ *Author's Choice*

One of the most common delay points in the accounts payable process is when an accounting clerk must go in search of someone to sign checks. If there is only one person who is so authorized, and who is not always available, it can keep any checks from being issued at all. The situation grows worse when multiple signatures are required for larger checks. On top of these delays, it is also common for the check-signers to require back-up documents for each check being signed, which requires a considerable extra effort by the accounting staff, not only to clip the correct documents to each check, but also to unclip the documents after the checks are signed and file them away in the appropriate files (which also increases the risk that the documents will be filed in the wrong place). This is an exceptional waste of time, since it does not add a whit of value to the process.

The solution to the multitude of inefficiencies related to check-signing is to get rid of the check-signers completely. Instead of assuming that there must be a complete review of all checks prior to signing, one must get management used to the idea of installing approvals earlier in the process, thus eliminating approval at the point of signing. Once management is comfortable with this idea, it is a simple matter of complying with bank regulations, which require a signature on each "check"—this is now a matter of finding the easiest way to place a signature on checks, rather than an approval process. Check-stamping can be accomplished most simply by creating a signature stamp from the signature of an authorized check-signer, which requires that someone stamp all checks by hand. A more efficient, though more complicated, approach is to digitize an authorized signature and incorporate it into the check-printing program, so that the signature is automatically affixed to each check with no manual intervention. Under this later approach, removable memory cards contain the fonts, company logos and signatures used for check printing, and are inserted into a special check printer for the duration of each check run.

The only problem with a signature stamp is that it can be misused to sign unauthorized checks or legal documents. This problem can be avoided by locking it up in the company safe and severely limiting access to the safe. Removable memory cards are more secure, but must still be locked when not in use. It may also be necessary to lock up check stock, thereby making it doubly difficult for anyone to issue an unauthorized signed check.

By using a signature stamp, one can eliminate the time wasted to find a check-signer, while also avoiding the work required to attach back-up documents to checks and then file these documents subsequent to review. This is one of the easiest best practices to implement and should be one of the first ones that a controller should institute.

Cost: **Installation time:**

3–43 Notify Purchasing of Lower Invoiced Prices or Terms

The payables staff is supposed to compare the prices on a supplier's invoice to the authorized prices on the originating purchase order to ensure that the price on the supplier's invoice is no higher than the authorized price. However, what should the payables staff do in the rare cases when the invoiced price is *lower* than the purchase order price?

The payables staff should post the lower of the two figures into the payables system as the one to be paid. In addition, they should notify the purchasing staff when these lower prices are charged, so their next purchase orders will incorporate the lower price. In addition, if other invoice terms, such as the early payment discount or payment duration, change in the company's favor, then the payables staff should also forward this information to the purchasing department.

Cost: **Installation time:** 🕰️

3–44 Create Direct Purchase Interfaces to Suppliers

A common practice when purchasing is to issue a separate purchase order to a supplier whenever a company wants to buy additional items. One solution to this problem is to consolidate all the purchase orders into a single large one that covers a long time period, which is called a blanket purchase order. This best practice is described later in this chapter in the "Use Blanket Purchase Orders" section. Though an excellent approach, it is sometimes possible to eliminate the purchase order entirely by using a direct purchase interface to a supplier.

This best practice involves creating a computer or fax linkage to a supplier, so that employees can order supplies directly from the supplier. By doing so, the purchasing staff does not have to become involved in any purchases and the accounts payable staff does not have to match any purchase orders to supplier invoices, thereby saving time in two departments. Though a clear efficiency improvement, this approach must be used with care because it eliminates some control over purchases. Accordingly, it is usually only used for the purchase of small-dollar items that are bought on a repetitive basis. Good examples of suppliers that might be used for this approach are office or maintenance supply vendors. In these cases, a company can create a standard form that only includes certain products. Employees are allowed to fill out the form with any quantity they want (within reason) and fax or mail it to the supplier, which uses it as authorization to send goods to the company. A more advanced version of this format is to set up the form on e-mail or on an electronic form directly linked to a supplier's customer orders database, for instant electronic transmission to the supplier. This latter approach is faster and may allow a supplier to directly input an order into its computer system, eliminating keypunching errors. By using a preset form for ordering, a company can effectively curtail purchases to a few preselected items that do not require further control.

The accounting staff will know in advance that any billings from the suppliers to which employees send orders directly do not require purchase order matching, and so they will expend less effort on paperwork prior to releasing a payment— just match the supplier's invoice to receiving documents to prove that the billed items were really received. Though this is not an approach that can be applied to all purchases, given the inherent lack of control, it can be used in a few cases, resulting in increased accounts payable processing efficiency.

Cost: **Installation time:** 🕰️🕰️

3–45 Create Online Purchasing Catalog

The typical purchasing process involves the creation of a purchase requisition by whomever needs to buy something; this is used by the purchasing staff to search for the lowest price offered by a supplier, at which point a purchase order is issued to the appropriate supplier. The accounting department then has to match the receiving documentation to the purchase order and supplier invoice before generating a payment. This cumbersome process is being dismantled in many instances through the use of an online purchasing catalog.

When a user buys through an online catalog, he or she scrolls through a list of standard products that have been compiled by the purchasing staff, and selects the appropriate item. This automatically places an order on an electronic purchase order, on which is noted the number of the blanket purchase order that has already been negotiated with the supplier from which the item is being bought. The computer system then sends either an electronic or paper-based order to the supplier, which fills the order. Upon receipt, the receiving department checks off the item in the online system, which flags the accounting system to make a payment to the supplier.

This online catalog approach has the exceptional benefit of significantly reducing the workload of the purchasing and accounting staffs, to the point where they are simply monitoring the flow of transactions, rather than directly creating them. It also channels the flow of purchases through a small set of preapproved suppliers, so there is little chance that a new supplier will be foisted on the purchasing staff by an employee. However, there are also downsides to this approach. The required software is a major programming project that will be quite expensive to create. Also, the time required to set up blanket purchase orders with a number of suppliers will be very time consuming, requiring a long lead time to complete the project. Finally, it cannot be used for inventory purchases, since these are driven by production requirements rather than employee needs. Nonetheless, a large corporation can experience a dramatic decline in the amount of manual procurement transactions by implementing an online purchasing catalog.

Cost: 💵💵💵   Installation time: ⏰⏰⏰

3–46 Install a Low-Cost Spend Management System

Spend management systems look like a great way to save money. Using these systems, companies can analyze their expenditures in a number of ways—by commodity, supplier, business unit, and so on. They then summarize this information for centralized procurement negotiations with suppliers, thereby reducing costs. Spend management suppliers, such as Ariba, Emptoris, and Ketera Technologies, add contract management capabilities and even set up electronic supplier catalogs, so that users can conduct on-line ordering with a predefined set of suppliers. They also impose better controls over spending, since their systems require access passwords, approval cycles, contract compliance alerts, and supplier performance measurements.

The problem is that these systems are extremely expensive to install and maintain—costs start at $1 million and rapidly head north from there. So, what can a smaller business do to emulate a spend management system? Here are some suggestions:

- *Identify unauthorized purchases with exception reports.* The reason for centralizing procurement contracts is to negotiate lower prices in exchange for higher purchasing volumes, so anyone purchasing from an unauthorized supplier is reducing a company's ability to reduce its costs. To identify these people, create a table of approved suppliers and match it against the vendor ledger for each period, yielding a report that lists how much was spent with various unauthorized suppliers. It is also useful to record in an empty purchasing or payables field the name of the requisitioning person, who can then be tracked down and admonished for incorrect purchasing practices.

- *Impose a penalty system.* People resist centralization, especially when it involves eliminating their favorite suppliers. Though penalties may be considered a coercive approach to solving the problem, the imposition of a graduated penalty scale will rapidly eliminate unauthorized spending. For example, a department may incur a $100 penalty for one unauthorized expenditure, $1,000 for the next, and $10,000 for the next.

- *Restrict procurement cards to specific suppliers.* If there is a procurement card system in place, it may be possible to restrict purchases to specific suppliers, thereby achieving centralized purchasing without any central oversight of the process. If there is no procurement card system, then consider obtaining a credit card from each designated supplier, and restrict purchases to those cards.

- *Require officer-level approval of all contracts.* Department and division managers love to retain control over supplier relationships by negotiating their own deals with local suppliers. By enforcing a corporatewide policy that all purchasing contracts be countersigned by a corporate officer, contract copies can be collected in one place for easier examination by a central purchasing staff.

- *Add granularity to the chart of accounts.* To gain a better knowledge of costs, consider altering the chart of accounts to subdivide expenses by individual department, and then go a step further by adding subcodes that track costs at an additional level of detail. For example, if the existing account code is 5020 for the travel expense account, and the revised code is 5020-01 to track travel costs for just the engineering department, then consider adding a set of subcodes, such as 5020-01-XX, to track more detailed expenditures within the travel category, such as airfare (code 5020-01-01), hotels (code 5020-01-02), and rental cars (code 5020-01-03). This approach requires careful definition of spending categories and can result in data entry errors if there are too many subcategories of expenses. Also, it will not be of much use if reports cannot be created to properly interpret and present this extra level of expense information.

These suggestions will not result in a seamless in-house spend management system. However, they will yield somewhat greater control over expenses and more visibility into the nature of a company's expenditures.

Cost: 💵💵   **Installation time:** ⏰⏰

3–47 Use Blanket Purchase Orders

One of the most time-consuming parts of the accounts payable process is matching supplier invoices to purchase orders to ensure that all payments have been authorized. This task is a difficult one if there are a multitude of supplier purchase orders. In the typical company, there are hundreds if not thousands of open purchase orders at any time; it is standard practice to issue a separate purchase order every time an item is purchased. However, by shrinking the number of purchase orders to be matched, one can reduce the workload of the accounts payable staff.

A best practice that vastly reduces the number of purchase orders is blanket purchase orders. These are long-term purchase orders, typically extending for a one-year time period, which cover all of the expected purchases from a supplier for that entire time period. By using blanket purchase orders, the accounts payable staff can continually match to the same purchase orders for the entire year, reducing the number of purchase orders that must be kept on hand.

This best practice is a simple one to implement from the accounting perspective. There is no change in the way the accounting staff stores or matches blanket purchase orders. They will continue to staple the purchase order to the invoice and move it on for further processing. The only difference is that because the amounts on the blanket purchase orders are so large, they will hardly ever be equaled by a single supplier delivery. The accounting clerk must instead make a facsimile of each purchase order and staple the copy to the supplier invoice. This is a minor change and will be easily accepted by the accounting staff when they see that, in exchange, the volume of purchase orders has dropped significantly.

Though this seems like a best practice that should be implemented at once due to the obvious benefits, one should consider the problem of working with an extra department to ensure that the new system works. The problem with a blanket purchase order is that it cannot be implemented without the cooperation of the purchasing staff and the suppliers. To ensure that blanket purchase orders are used, one must discuss the benefits of the system with the purchasing manager (who will see a significant decline in paperwork as a result of using blanket purchase orders). The purchasing manager *must* buy into the concept because this is the person who must in turn sell the concept to suppliers. Another problem is that a typical company has so many suppliers that it takes a substantial amount of time to implement blanket purchase order agreements with all of them. Instead, it is frequently easier to either pare down the number of suppliers or just implement blanket purchase orders with the 20 percent of suppliers with which a company typically does 80 percent of its business. Either approach will allow a company to enter into blanket purchase orders with suppliers that will substantially reduce the total number of blanket purchase orders.

Cost: Installation time:

3–48   Issue a Welcome Packet to New Suppliers

When a company gains a new supplier, it rarely bothers to inform the supplier about its payables processing rules. As a result, the supplier uses its standard billing procedures by default, and is rightfully surprised if those procedures do not mesh with the company's payables system, resulting in delayed payments.

The solution is to create a welcome packet for new suppliers. At a minimum, this should contain a W-9 form and a note that no payments will be made to the supplier until the form is properly completed and returned to the company. However, the welcome packet can contain a great deal more information that will assist in the development of smoothly interlocked billing and payable systems between the supplier and the company. For example, the welcome packet can include the following additional information:

- *Mailing address.* The welcome packet should clearly state where all supplier invoices are to be mailed. This is especially important if the company digitizes all incoming invoices, because these invoices must first be routed through a high-volume scanning operation that is usually fed from a single mailing address.

- *Purchasing reference.* Most companies want to see an authorizing purchase order number posted prominently on an invoice, so they can easily research the payment authorization. If invoices are not supported by a purchase order, then specify in the welcome packet the procedure suppliers are to follow in regard to the identification of the authorizing party on the invoice.

- *Payment frequency.* If the company only processes check payments once a week, then say so—suppliers need to know which day of the week payments are made, which will prevent them from calling the payables staff to ask when their checks will be cut.

- *Access codes.* If the company has an online payables query system, make sure that suppliers are fully informed about how to use it, and give them user identification and passwords as part of the welcome packet, so they are fully outfitted to use the system.

- *Evaluated receipts instructions.* If the company has an evaluated receipts system, (e.g., it pays suppliers based on quantities received rather than on invoices received), the welcome packet should specify exactly what purchase order information is to be included with each delivery, including the encoding of this information on bar coding and radio frequency identification (RFID) tags.

If suppliers habitually ignore the instructions contained within the welcome packet, then remind them that failure to follow the rules may result in delayed payments, or result in a lower score on any supplier scorecard system that the company may use.

Cost: 💵   **Installation time:** ⏰

3–49 Clean Up the Supplier Master File

A company with even a modest number of suppliers will gradually build up a considerable number of errors in its vendor master file, which can result in several problems. First, a supplier with a missing tax identification number could be a problem when annual 1099 forms are delivered. Also, if a supplier has multiple records in the database, the same invoice may be entered against each supplier name, resulting in multiple payments of the same invoice. Here is how to clean up the file:

1. Each quarter, print a report listing, for each active supplier, every field in the vendor master file. Use the accounting software's report writer to avoid printing any fields not currently in use. Once printed, any empty fields will be easily observable. In particular, look for missing taxpayer identification numbers and tax codes.

2. Print several variations on a duplicate names report in order to spot duplicate vendor records. One version is sorted by supplier name, another by supplier address, and yet another by taxpayer identification number (TIN). Once a duplication is spotted, figure out which one is not being used and flag it as archived.

3. Run a report listing all suppliers with whom the company has done no business in the past year (or two years, depending on company policy). Flag them as archived in order to remove them from the current vendor master file.

4. Print a report listing all suppliers added to the file since the last review date. Then go to the *www.irs.gov* Web site and click on its link to sign up for e-services. This allows the company to access the IRS's TIN verification program online. Then use the IRS site to verify the TIN of all the new suppliers. Contact suppliers if their TINs are incorrect, and update the vendor master file with this information.

Cost: 💵   **Installation time:** ⏰ ⏰

3–50 Adopt a Supplier Naming Procedure

As just noted in the last best practice, the supplier master file can become clogged with multiple records for the same supplier, which can lead to duplicate payments. To reduce the amount of master file review and consolidation, always use a standard supplier naming convention to reduce the incidence of duplicate supplier names.

The supplier naming procedure requires the payables staff to follow precisely the same approach every time it must convert a supplier name into a supplier identification number in the supplier master file. Here are some possible ways to compress a supplier name into an identification code:

- First, strip out all spaces and punctuation marks from the supplier name.
- Next, eliminate all symbols from the supplier name, such as "&," "@," and apostrophes.
- Next, use the letters in the stripped-down supplier name, starting on the left, and proceed to the right for a predetermined number of spaces. Then add a multidigit code at the end of this truncated name, starting at (for example) "001" and ascending by one digit for each additional name that begins with the same letters.

For example, a company truncates after 12 letters and then adds a three-number code to the end. If a supplier's name is Abercrombie & Arbuthnot, then its supplier code will now be ABERCROMBIEA001. If the company does business with another supplier named Abercrombie & Arrow, then its supplier code will be ABERCROMBIEA002.

Cost: **Installation time:** 🕰

3–51 Assign Payables Staff to Specific Suppliers

When suppliers call a company to check on the status of payments, the clerical staff must research the information prior to giving a response. This can require a substantial amount of clerical time, and can also yield differing replies to suppliers if they call the company several times, resulting in supplier frustration. In addition, incoming supplier invoices may contain special provisions that require a detailed knowledge of the underlying purchasing contracts; otherwise, payments may be recorded improperly.

A simple way to avoid all these problems is to assign supplier accounts to specific accounts payable staff. By doing so, the accounting staff can individually concentrate their attention on a smaller group of suppliers, allowing them to learn how each one presents invoices for payment and how their payment transactions should be recorded. In addition, because of their increased knowledge level, they can provide answers to supplier questions more quickly and with greater accuracy.

This best practice is not a useful solution for very small companies, since there may be only one payables staff person available. It also presents problems for suppliers if their assigned staff person is not available, so the accounting manager should consider assigning a back-up person to each account.

Cost: Installation time: 🕰

3–52 Create Different Supplier Accounts for Different Terms

Suppliers occasionally require different payment terms for different products or services. For example, one product must be paid for within 30 days, while another can be paid for sooner in exchange for an early payment discount. If so, the accounts payable staff will have a hard time differentiating between the different terms, resulting in errors that require yet more work to correct.

A possible solution is to create different computer master files for each set of terms. By doing so, supplier invoices can be assigned to the appropriate supplier account, resulting in accurate payment processing. However, this best practice still requires knowing to which account a supplier invoice should be assigned. This problem can be resolved by forcing the issue back to the supplier and having it enter the correct supplier code on all submitted invoices, depending upon the type of transaction submitted.

Cost: 💵   Installation time: 🕰

3–53 Ignore Supplier Invoices and Pay from Statements

Many suppliers provide frequent deliveries and services, each one for small amounts of money. They tend to send large volumes of invoices, which can inundate the accounts payable staff. Also, given the high volume of invoices received, it is quite possible that some invoices will mistakenly be paid twice, especially if there are no invoice numbers that the computer system can check for duplicate payments.

One solution to these high-volume, low-cost invoices is to throw them all away; then, when the suppliers send the usual month-end statement of invoices outstanding, just record the statement in the computer system, using the statement date as the invoice number, and issue a single payment from that document. This also works well for the supplier, which receives just one check instead of many. The only problem with this approach occurs when the underlying invoices would normally be charged to different departments, which would require one to see the content of those invoices. However, in most cases, these invoices are so small that an incorrect or missing expense allocation would have little impact on departmental financial statements.

Cost: 💵   Installation time: 🕰

3–54 Review Supplier Statements for Open Credits

A company may deal with a supplier over many years, and over that time it will occasionally return products or protest incorrect billings that result in credits being granted by the supplier. The trouble is that the supplier may not send formal notice of the credit to the company, so the accounts payable staff has no idea that there is a credit available that it can use to offset other billings issued by the supplier.

The solution is to request that a formal statement of outstanding invoices and credits be sent to the company by every major supplier at least once a year. These statements should identify all open credits, for which the accounts payable staff can either request repayment or use as offsets to new billings. The key elements in this best practice are (1) to monitor which suppliers refuse to send a statement, so that follow-up action can be taken, and (2) proper review of the statements by the accounts payable staff, which may not want to spend the extra time on this chore.

Cost:    **Installation time:**

3–55 Issue Standard Adjustment Letters to Suppliers

When the accounts payable staff have a valid reason for making a deduction from a payment to a supplier, this can result in a prolonged series of complaints from the supplier as to why a short payment was made. The adjustment will appear on the next monthly statement of unpaid invoices from the supplier, and will likely end with a series of irate collection calls. At some point, the accounting staff may feel that the cost savings from taking the deduction were not worth the effort required to convince the supplier of the reasoning behind the adjustment.

This issue can be solved to some extent by checking off a box on a standard adjustment letter and mailing the letter to the supplier. The letter should note the invoice number that is at issue, as well as a series of common problems that caused the short payment to be made. The accounting staff can quickly check off the appropriate box and mail it out, using far less time than would be required to construct a formal, customized letter of notification. The letter should contain space for a free-form written description of the issue, in case it is a unique one not covered by any of the standard explanations already listed on the letter.

Cost: **Installation time:**

Total Impact of Best Practices on the Accounts Payable Function

The preceding list of accounts payable best practices is too voluminous and overlapping for a company to install all of them—in fact, there is no need to do so. If a small number of the most radical changes are implemented, such as using the receiving personnel to approve payments to suppliers, many of the other practices are rendered ineffective. Accordingly, this section does not attempt to describe the impact of all the best practices. Instead, it assumes that all of the changes requiring considerable reengineering *are* implemented, since they have the most impact on the efficiency and effectiveness of the department. This leaves a much smaller number of additional best practices to be tacked on to make a truly world-class accounts payable function.

As just noted, the most important and far-reaching item to install is approval of payment at the receiving dock by the receiving staff. This best practice negates a number of incremental improvements to the accounts payable function, such as automated three-way matching and digitizing accounts payable documents. Once that improvement is made, the remaining best practices for the new accounts payable functions are primarily those that deal with special payment situations that will not be routed through the receiving dock. For example, expense reports and repetitive payments should be automated. The number of payments can also be reduced by using procurement cards and ghost cards to consolidate the number of billings received, while blanket purchase orders are useful for shrinking the number of purchase orders in the system. Suppliers can also be linked directly to the accounts payable database to see if payments have been made, which avoids any regular need for the suppliers to talk to the staff. When taken together, the accounts payable function is transformed into a small group of highly computer-literate employees who monitor ongoing automated transactions to ensure that all processing is proceeding in accordance with expectations. There is very little paper-processing, nor is there much need to correspond with suppliers. This is the accounts payable function of the future. The combination of these best practices is noted in Exhibit 3.4.

Though the system advocated in this exhibit is certainly the most efficient one of all the combinations of best practices presented in this section, it is important to note that it is not for everyone. It requires substantial implementation time and cost; accordingly, it may not be practicable for smaller companies that are operating on a limited budget. In these cases, other combinations of best practices can be used to create a system that is somewhat less efficient, but at a much lower cost.

Summary

This chapter itemized a number of best practices that can be used to vastly streamline the accounts payable function, one of the most labor-intensive accounting functions. Of all the functional areas, this is the one that can yield the most impressive productivity gains with the use of best practices.

One can select a series of small and simple changes, such as using signature stamps and auditing expense reports, to make incremental improvements in the accounts payable process. However, this is an area where massive gains are possible if a controller is willing to completely restructure the traditional accounts payable processing approach. To this end, the most important best practice listed in

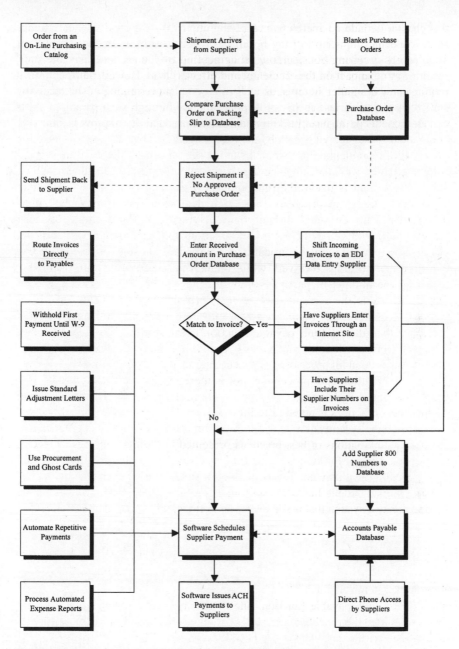

Exhibit 3.4 An Accounts Payable Function That Uses Best Practices

this chapter is that of paying upon receiving approval—the receiving staff authorizes payment simply by looking up all items received in an online database of open purchase orders. No further work is required by the accounts payable staff, resulting in a major reduction in the accounting workload. However, this approach requires new computer systems, as well as a complete retraining of the receiving staff regarding their role in paying suppliers. Only through such paradigm shifts can an accounts payable staff achieve sensational productivity improvements.

Chapter 4

Billing Best Practices

This chapter covers the best practices that can be used to create a more efficient billing operation. The best practices fall into three main categories. One group covers the need for more accurate information that is used to create an invoice. These items focus on the stream of information going from the shipping department to the invoicing staff, with a particular emphasis on rooting out any missing or incorrect information. The next group of best practices covers the efficiency of the invoicing operation itself, eliminating month-end statements and using a smaller number of multipart invoice forms. The final group focuses on changing the method of invoice delivery to the customer, such as using electronic data interchange or allowing the delivery person to create the invoice at the point of delivery. When taken as a whole, these best practices result in an invoicing operation that is remarkably error-free, issues invoices as soon as products are shipped, and ensures that customers receive invoices almost at once.

Implementation Issues for Billing Best Practices

The best practices in this chapter comprise a broad mix of issues that are easily put in place and others that are much more challenging to implement, depending on a company's specific circumstances. This section contains a table (Exhibit 4.1) that lists the best practices and then describes the cost and duration of implementation for each one. The most difficult ones are those requiring extra computer programming to achieve, as well as those that require the cooperative efforts of other departments. The easiest ones can generally be achieved within the accounting department and with no additional capital or personnel costs of note.

Some of the most difficult implementation jobs result in the greatest improvements in the performance of the billing function. Accordingly, it is best to alternate easy implementations with more difficult ones so that there is a constant stream of successes, some of which represent significant advances in efficiency. Also, by including an occasional "quick-hit" implementation, a controller can point toward a continuing stream of successes, which is useful when trying to obtain funds for more best practices–related projects.

The remainder of this chapter describes the best practices that were itemized in Exhibit 4.1. Each description includes the benefits and problems associated with each best practice, as well as any implementation problems to be aware of.

Exhibit 4.1 Summary of Billing Best Practices

	Best Practice	*Cost*	*Install Time*
Invoice Delivery			
4–1	Avoid missed billings	💵	🕐
4–2	Add carrier route codes to billing addresses	💵💵	🕐🕐
4–3	Mark envelopes with "Address Correction Requested"	💵	🕐
4–4	Do early billing of recurring invoices	💵	🕐
4–5	Issue electronic invoices through the Internet	💵💵	🕐🕐
4–6	Issue single, summarized invoice each period	💵💵	🕐🕐
4–7	Print separate invoices for each line item	💵	🕐
4–8	Transmit transactions via electronic data interchange	💵💵💵	🕐🕐🕐
Invoice Error Checking			
4–9	Enhance the invoice layout	💵	🕐
4–10	Add receipt signature to invoice	💵	🕐
4–11	Automatically check errors during invoice data entry	💵💵	🕐🕐🕐
4–12	Proofread invoices	💵	🕐
4–13	Have delivery person create the invoice	💵💵💵	🕐🕐🕐
4–14	Computerize the shipping log	💵💵	🕐🕐
4–15	Track exceptions between the shipping log and invoice register	💵	🕐🕐
Invoicing Efficiency			
4–16	Eliminate month-end statements	💵	🕐
4–17	Reduce number of parts in multipart invoices	💵	🕐
4–18	Replace intercompany invoicing with operating transactions	💵	🕐🕐
4–19	Improve shipping charge revenue	💵	🕐

The descriptions should be sufficient for the reader to form a knowledgeable opinion regarding the need to implement one or more of these best practices, depending on the specific operations of the reader's organization.

4–1 Avoid Missed Billings

One of the most serious billing problems is when shipments are made or services delivered, and no billing is issued at all. For a variety of reasons, there are holes in the sales process that allow documentation of sales to never reach the billing department. Depending on the number of times this happens, the amount of lost profits can be quite large. Here are some techniques for minimizing missed billings:

- *Orders not entered through standard system.* The sales staff sometimes walks a customer order around the order entry department and straight to the warehouse, just to ensure that a delivery takes place as soon as possible (or worse, they hand-carry it to the customer, so there is also no shipping record). When this happens, there is no record of a customer order in the computer system, so there is no indicator of an unbilled order that would normally flag some form of investigation by the accounting manager. The only solution is to require everyone at every step of the order fulfillment process to force anyone circumventing the system to return to the order entry department, where the order will be properly entered into the system.

- *Billable hours changed after the fact.* Employees have a habit of going back into the timekeeping system and altering their billable hours after the billing period has closed. This problem can be avoided entirely by locking down access to timekeeping periods in the previous month, so that no changes can be made.

- *Late timesheet entry.* Begin reminding the staff starting on Monday to ensure that they have entered their hours in the timekeeping system for the preceding week. Each reminder is escalated, first to the human resources manager, then to the local supervisor, and then to the company president. This approach is far better than waiting until month-end to remind people, because they tend to forget what they did if too much time has passed.

- *Automated reminders.* Have the timekeeping system automatically send email reminders to anyone whose timesheet has not yet been entered.

- *Shipping notices stuck together.* This one sounds trivial, but have you ever seen glue or gum sticking multiple shipping notices together? Alternatively, they may be mistakenly clipped or stapled together, so the shipping notices on the bottom of the stack are never seen by the billing staff, and so are never billed. To avoid this, consider having a second billing clerk skim through the daily batch of shipping notices from the shipping dock, and compare them to the daily invoice run to see if any shipping notices were missed by the first billing clerk.

- *Formalize sample shipment authorizations.* Most shipping logs contain entries for the shipment of free samples, which are usually authorized by the marketing department. If the accounting staff is regularly reviewing the shipping log to ensure that all shipments are billed, these special deliveries require a considerable amount of investigation to verify. To reduce the work level, require the marketing department to issue a sales order through the normal order entry system for all free deliveries, so the accounting staff can more easily trace the authorizing documentation.

- *What about customer on-site pickups?* The standard system for invoicing assumes that the shipping dock sends a shipping notice to the billing staff, which triggers an invoice. But what if the customer shows up to take delivery? This is easy enough for a retail establishment, but can cause fits for a company whose systems are designed for freight deliveries to customers. If the solution is manual handling of each case, then the odds of not billing a customer pickup are extremely high. The solution is to direct customers making their own pickups to the shipping dock, so that the shipping personnel (who are the most experienced in documenting shipments) will handle the "delivery" to the customer and can be relied on to fill out the usual paperwork and forward it to the billing staff in the normal manner.

Cost: **Installation time:**

4–2 Add Carrier Route Codes to Billing Addresses

For those organizations that issue large quantities of small-dollar invoices, the cost of mailing is a substantial portion of the total cost of doing business. For these organizations, a lower-cost approach to mailing an invoice must be found. One alternative is to include a carrier route code in the address field for each customer. This information is used by the postal service to more easily sort incoming mail pieces by carrier route. In exchange for this information, the postal service allows a small reduction in the cost of each item mailed. At the time of this writing, the difference between the standard price for an automated letter-size mailing and one that includes the carrier route code is about three cents (for the most recent rates, go to *www.usps.com*). This difference is sufficiently large that a billing manager who processes thousands of invoices per year should certainly consider it as a potential way to save costs.

To implement this best practice, one must obtain the route codes from the postal service on either a monthly or bimonthly basis. They are available on tape, CD-ROM, cartridge, or hard copy. The company's customer address files must be updated with the latest carrier route information, as specified in the postal service's Domestic Mail Manual. To determine the exact format of the file, one can download a sample file from the postal service's Web site. These steps obviously require some effort on a continuing basis, so one must carefully determine the cost-benefit associated with this best practice before implementing it. Realistically, only a very large mailing operation will save money through this approach.

Cost: **Installation time:** 🕑 🕑

4–3 Mark Envelopes with "Address Correction Requested"

Customers move to new locations all the time, and sometimes they do not notify their suppliers of this change. When this happens, the collection process can be significantly delayed while the collections team tracks down new addresses and re-mails invoices.

A simple best practice to circumvent this problem is to mark the words "Address Correction Requested" on each envelope mailed. If the customer has moved and filed a forwarding address with the Postal Service, the Postal Service will forward the mail to the new address and also notify the company of the new address, which can then be updated in the customer address file at once. The Postal Service will charge a small fee for this notification service.

If for some reason the company does not want its mail to be forwarded, it can instead mark envelopes with the words "Address Correction Requested—Do Not Forward." This will result in not only the return of the mail but also a notice of the forwarding address.

Cost: 💵   **Installation time:** 🕑

4–4 Do Early Billing of Recurring Invoices   ✔ *Author's Choice*

There are many situations in which a company knows the exact amount of a customer billing well before the date on which the invoice is to be sent. For example, a subscription is for the preset amount, as is a contractual obligation, such as a rent payment. In these cases, it makes sense to create the invoice and deliver it to the customer one or two weeks in advance of the date when it is actually due. By doing so, the invoice has more time to be routed through the receiving organization, passing through the mailroom, accounting staff, authorized signatory, and back to the accounts payable staff for payment. This makes it much more likely that the invoice will be paid on time, which improves cash flow and reduces a company's investment in accounts receivable.

The main difficulty with advance billings is that the date of the invoice should be shifted forward to the accounting period in which the invoice is supposed to be billed. Otherwise, the revenue will be recognized too early, which distorts the financial statements. Shifting the accounting period forward is not difficult for most accounting software systems, but the controller must remember to shift back to the current period after the invoice processing has been completed; otherwise, all other current transactions that are subsequently entered will be recorded in the next accounting period, rather than the current one.

Cost: **Installation time:** 🕐

4–5 Issue Electronic Invoices through the Internet

The traditional invoicing process is extraordinarily wasteful in terms of the effort and time that goes into creating and issuing an invoice. It must be created and inserted into an invoice printing batch, which, in turn, requires the use of a customized invoice with prepositioned fields and logos, plus a review of the printed invoices, stuffing into envelopes, affixing postage, and mailing. Even then, there is a risk that the invoice will be lost in the mail, either due to a problem at the post office or because the recipient's address has changed. Further, there are delays at the receiving company, while the mailroom sorts through the mail and delivers it internally (sometimes to the wrong person).

Some of these problems can be avoided through the use of e-mailed billings that are delivered through the Internet. There are several ways to do this. The least-recommended approach is to post the invoices on a company's own Web site. This means that customers can access the company's credit card payment system at the same time they access their invoices, which results in accounts receivable that are collected with inordinate speed. However, this approach requires customers to access the company's Web site in order to find their invoices, which they are not likely to do (especially because this will result in their immediate use of funds to pay for the invoice). In addition, this requires an interface between the accounting database and the Web site, so that invoices are posted regularly to the Web site. Further, there may be a need to create user identification numbers and passwords, so that they can access their invoices. Also, if customers forget their access codes, there must be an internal customer service function that can assist them with this information, which involves additional personnel costs to maintain.

A better approach is to "push" electronic invoices to customers by email. This requires the collection of an email address from each customer at the time an order is taken (or verification of an existing one when a reorder occurs). This address is then attached to an electronic invoice form that is generated, instead of a paper-based invoice, and issued to the customer over the Internet. It is then available to the customer a few moments later, allowing for immediate payment (possibly) or at least a quick perusal of the invoice and a return of information to the company regarding any problems discovered by the customer. This approach greatly reduces the time required to get invoicing information to the customer.

There are several problems with Internet invoicing that one must be aware of. First, some customers change their email addresses with some regularity, so there is a chance that invoices will be sent to an old address, and therefore never accessed. Also, there is some risk that customers will accidentally erase an incoming electronic invoice without reviewing it. Furthermore, this approach leaves no paper record of the invoice at the company, just a computer record; this is a problem for those organizations where the collections effort is primarily based on paper files, rather than ready access to the accounting database.

Some of the problems with emailed invoices can be addressed through the careful analysis of which customers reliably pay their invoices by this means and (more importantly) which do not. If there is a consistent problem with payment by some customers, they can be flagged in the accounting database and a traditional paper-based invoice can be created for them. Alternatively, the same invoices can be continually reissued every week or two by email. This is a zero-cost option, since there are no mailing or printing costs. When using this approach, the entire file of unpaid invoices can be reissued electronically to customers. However, to avoid multiple payments for the same invoices, it may be useful to alter the format of these secondary issuances, so that they are clearly labeled as reminder invoices. An alternative format is to cluster all unpaid invoices for each customer into an electronic statement of unpaid invoices, which can be issued at regular intervals.

A final variation on the use of electronic invoices through the Internet is the use of a consolidator. This is an entity that maintains a Web site that allows a company's customers to access not only their billings, but those of their other suppliers, too. This approach has the distinct advantage of allowing customers to pay a number of different bills at the same time, without switching to a number of different Web sites in order to do so.

A company that wishes to have its invoices posted on a consolidator Web site must create a data file that reformats the invoice information into the format needed by the consolidator, and then send this file over the Internet to the consolidator, which then posts the information. Customers then access their invoices in a summary format, which are clustered together for all of their suppliers, and either accept or reject them for payment; if there is a problem, customers can access greater levels of detail for each invoice, and usually access an email account that will be sent to the company's customer service department.

The cost of this service varies considerably by consolidator, with some charging the customer, some the company, and some charging both. It is best to refer to the fee schedule of each one to determine the precise amounts. The fees charged to a company are not excessive, and should not get in the way of adopting this option.

The main problem with using a consolidator is that not all customers will want to use the one to which the company prefers to send its invoicing information, since they may have already set up payment plans with many of their other suppliers through different consolidators. Accordingly, a company may find itself issuing invoice files to a large number of consolidators, which presents additional work for the person reformatting the invoice file.

Cost: 💵💵   **Installation time:** ⏰⏰

4–6 Issue Single, Summarized Invoices Each Period

Some companies make a business out of selling small quantities of products in small batches, which necessitates a very large quantity of invoices. For example, a company that sells nails in batches of an ounce per sale will issue 16 more invoices than one that sells nails in batches of no less than one pound. If the cost of issuing an invoice is as little as $1 (and it is usually much more), then the price at which the nails were sold will probably be far less than the cost of issuing the associated invoices. Clearly, companies that must issue enormous numbers of invoices in this manner will find that their administrative costs are excessive.

A way out of this dilemma is to group all sales for a specified time period, such as a month, and then issue a single invoice that covers all of the sales during that period. This approach is similar to the invoicing method used by credit card companies, which congregate all sales for a full month and then issue a single billing. By using this best practice, a company can eliminate a very large proportion of its total invoice volume.

There are some issues to consider before using this best practice. One is that this approach is obviously most suitable for companies that issue large quantities of low-dollar invoices. Conversely, it is *not* a reasonable approach if invoice volume is low and dollar volumes are high. If a billing is for a large amount of money, it makes little sense to wait until the end of the month to issue an invoice, since this only delays the time period before the customer will pay for it. Another issue is that the existing accounting software may not support this feature. If not, a company must go through the added expense of custom-programming to group a series of shipments or sales into a single invoice. Another problem may be customers—they are accustomed to receiving a single invoice for each shipment, with a separate purchase order authorizing each invoice, and they will not know what to do when a single, summary-level invoice arrives in the mail. The best way to resolve this problem is to make it an option for customers to accept summary-level invoices, rather than unexpectedly springing it on them with no warning and requiring their use of it. By taking the time to explain the reason for the single invoice and how it can benefit customers, too (with less paperwork for them to sort through), the customer acceptance rate should be quite high. The final problem with this method is that it takes longer to bring cash in to pay for shipped goods, since some shipments may be sent out at the beginning of a month, but not billed until the end of the month. To avoid this problem, a company can impose a shorter due date in which customers must pay, though customers rarely receive this well. Instead, it is best to carefully analyze the interest cost of the large amount of committed working capital to the reduced cost of invoicing; if there is a clear benefit despite the added cost, then this best practice should be implemented.

In short, issuing a single invoice to customers each period makes a great deal of sense for those companies that ship many small-dollar orders. Companies that deal with large-dollar orders should probably leave this best practice alone, since there is an added working capital cost associated with its use.

Cost: 　　　　　　Installation time: 🕰 🕰

4–7 Print Separate Invoices for Each Line Item

When an accounting department issues an invoice containing a large number of line items, it is more likely that the recipient will have an issue with one or more of the line items, and will hold payment on the entire invoice while those line items are resolved. Though this may not be a significant issue when an invoice is relatively small, it is a large issue indeed when the invoice has a large dollar total, and holding the entire invoice will have a serious impact on the amount of accounts receivable outstanding.

One way to avoid this problem is to split large invoices into separate ones, with each invoice containing just one line item. By doing so, it is more likely that some invoices will be paid at once, while other ones for which there are issues will be delayed. This can have a significant positive impact on a company's investment in accounts receivable.

The only complaint that arises from this approach is that customers can be buried under quite a large pile of invoices. This can be ameliorated by clustering all of the invoices in a single envelope, rather than sending a dozen separately mailed invoices on the same day. Also, it may be prudent to cluster small-dollar line items on the same invoice, since this will cut down on the number of invoices issued, while not having a significant impact on the overall receivable balance if these invoices are put on hold.

Cost: 💵　　　　　　Installation time: 🕰

4–8 Transmit Transactions via Electronic Data Interchange

Sending an invoice to a customer requires some labor, cost, and time, but does not guarantee that the invoice will be paid. For example, someone must print out an invoice, separate the copy that goes to the customer, stuff it in an envelope and mail it, which may then take several days to reach the customer, be routed through its mailroom, reach the accounts payable department, and be entered into the customer's computer system (where the data may be scrambled due to keypunching errors). The invoice may even be lost at the customer site and never be entered into its computer system for payment at all.

To avoid all of these issues, a company can use electronic data interchange (EDI). Under this approach, a company's computer system automatically issues an electronic invoice that is set up in a standard format (as defined by an international standard-setting organization) and transmits it to a third-party mainframe computer, where it is left in an electronic mailbox. The customer's computer automatically polls this mailbox several times a day and extracts the electronic invoice format. Once received, the format is automatically translated into the invoice format used by the recipient's computer and stored in the accounting system's database for payment. At no time does anyone have to manually handle the data, which eliminates the risk of lost or erroneous invoicing data. This is an excellent approach for those companies that can afford to invest in setting up EDI with their customers, since it fully automates a number of invoicing steps, resulting in a high degree of efficiency and reliability.

There are several problems with EDI that keep most smaller companies from using it, especially if they have many low-volume customer accounts. The main problem is that it takes some time and persuasion to get a customer to agree to use EDI as the basis for receiving invoices. This may take several trips to each customer, including time to send trial transmissions to the customer's computer to ensure that the system works properly. To do this with a large number of low-volume customers is not cost-effective, so the practice is generally confined to companies with high-volume customers, involving a great many invoices, so that the investment by both parties pays off fairly quickly. The other problem is that the most efficient EDI systems require some automation. A standard EDI system requires one to manually enter all transactions, as well as manually extract them from the EDI mailbox and keypunch them into the receiving computer. To fully automate the system, a company must have its software engineers program an interface between the accounting computer system and the EDI system, which can be an expensive undertaking. Without the interface, an EDI system is really nothing more than a fancy fax machine. Thus, installing a fully operational EDI system is usually limited to transactions with high-volume customers and requires a considerable programming expense to achieve full automation.

Cost: 💵💵💵   Installation time: ⏰⏰⏰

4–9 Enhance the Invoice Layout

Many companies lose sight of a simple philosophical issue involving the invoice— it is for the customer's sole use, not theirs. This means that the company should not clutter up the invoice with excess information that the customer does not need, nor make the invoice layout so difficult to read that the customer's accounting staff cannot enter the invoice into its computer system without a great deal of perusal. The usual result is incorrect or delayed payments.

The solution is to simplify the format and general presentation of the invoice in order to make it as simple as possible for the recipient to understand. Here are some examples of proper invoice structure:

- *Eliminate graphics and shading.* Fancy images may look pretty, but if the customer is trying to scan the invoice into a document imaging system, this may result in an unreadable gray blob. Even if information is only being manually translated from the invoice to the customer's computer system, invoice graphics will still be a distraction, and could interfere with data entry.

- *Present the invoice number as clearly as possible.* Many companies put their own tracking number or document index number next to the invoice number. Customers frequently mix up these numbers, and enter the wrong number in their computer systems in place of the invoice number. If document tracking numbers must be included on an invoice, then at least keep them out of the upper right corner of the document, which is where customers expect to see the invoice number. Better yet, convert the tracking number to a bar code, which customers cannot read.

- *List the early payment or late payment amount well away from the invoice total.* If all these different payment totals are clustered together, it is too easy for the customer's payables staff to enter the wrong one as the payable amount.

- *Clearly show contact information.* If there is a problem with an invoice, the customer does not want to use the White Pages to locate your headquarters. Do them a large favor and clearly show the accounting department's phone number on the invoice. Also, make sure that someone in the accounting department checks the voice mail for this phone number every day, in order to provide better customer service.

Cost: 🖋   **Installation time:** ⏰

4–10 Add Receipt Signature to Invoice

There may be cases where customers demand proof of their receipt of a delivery from the company before they will pay its invoice. Normally, this proof is generated internally by the customer through the use of a receiving log or the forwarding of bill of lading information to the accounting department. However, there are cases where there is a paperwork disconnect between the customer's accounting and receiving functions, so that some company invoices are not paid for long periods of time, while the customer scrambles to find evidence of receipt.

This problem can be reduced by using either FedEx or United Parcel Service to make deliveries, since both organizations post receipt signatures on their Web sites. One can then copy the signature images out of the Web sites and paste them directly into an invoice, thereby providing proof of receipt to the customer on the invoice. If necessary, the billing staff can also add the delivery reference number used by either United Parcel Service or FedEx to the invoice. Either the customer or the company can then go straight to the Web sites of either package delivery company to obtain further evidence of the time and place of delivery of the package in question. This approach has the distinct advantage of consolidating both the billing and receiving information for a delivery on one piece of paper. The downside is that the invoice cannot be issued until the delivery has been received by the customer, rather than being sent when the package leaves the company's premises. Also, one must always use either of these package delivery companies in order to have access to the signature information, when there may be less expensive shipping options available.

Cost: **Installation time:** 🕰

4–11 Automatically Check Errors during Invoice Data Entry

Errors during the data-entry phase of creating an invoice can result in a variety of downstream problems. For example, an incorrect billing address on an invoice means that the customer will never receive it, which means that the collections staff must send a new invoice copy. Also, if the quantity, product description, or price is entered incorrectly, the customer may have a good reason for not paying the bill. If this happens, the collections staff will have to get involved to work out the reason for nonpayment and negotiate extra payments (if possible) by customers. All of these problems are exceptions and require very large amounts of time to research and fix.

A very useful best practice is to prevent as many data-entry problems in advance as possible by using computerized data-checking methods. For example, a field for zip codes can only accept five-digit or nine-digit numbers, which prevents the entry of numbers of an unusual length. The field can also be tied to a file of all cities and states, so that entering a zip code automatically fills in the city and state fields. Also, prices of unusual length can be automatically rejected, or prices can be automatically called up from a file that is linked to a product number. Similarly, product descriptions can be automatically entered if the product number is entered. An example of a "smart" data-entry system is one that flags part numbers that are being entered for an existing customer for the first time. The computer can check the part number entered against a file of items previously ordered by a customer and see if there is a chance that the part being ordered might not be the correct one. There can also be required fields that must have a valid entry or else the invoice cannot be processed; a good example is the customer purchase order number field, which is required by many customers, or else they will not pay the invoice. By including these automatic error-checking and expert systems into the data-entry software, it is possible to reduce the number of data-entry errors.

The main problem with creating automatic error-checking is that it can be a significant programming project. There may be a dozen different error-checking protocols linked to the invoice data-entry screen, and each one is a separate programming project. Also, if a company purchased its software from a third party, it is common for the company to periodically install software updates issued by the supplier, which would wipe out any programming changes made in the interim. Accordingly, it is best to apply these error-checking routines only to custom-programmed accounting systems. An alternative is to use error-checking as a criterion for the purchase of new packaged software, if a company is in the market for a new accounting system. In either of these cases, having automatic error-checking is a worthy addition to an accounting system.

Cost:  Installation time: 🕐 🕐 🕐

4–12 Proofread Invoices

Some invoices are so complex—involving the entry of purchase order numbers, many line items, price discounts and other credits—that it is difficult to create a perfect invoice. This is a particular problem when employee expenses are sent to a customer for reimbursement and the submitted expenses are incomplete or inaccurate. When sent to the customer, the customer ends up being the proof-reader and rejects the invoice until the company goes through more delays and eventually issues an accurate invoice. The time delay can be substantial.

The solution is to assign a second person to be the invoice proofreader. This person does not create the invoice, and so can provide a more independent view of invoice accuracy. Since this can introduce some delay into the invoice-creation process, proofreading could be limited to only the larger invoices, or to invoices sent to those customers most apt to comb through invoices looking for mistakes.

Proofreading is of particular concern when an invoice is being prepared in a foreign language. If incorrectly written to the point of being incomprehensible or at least misunderstood by the recipient, then this can cause major delays in pay-ment. A solution is to have one person create the initial translation, and then have a second person review the translation. Ideally, one person would be a bilingual English-speaking native, and the other person would be a bilingual foreign trans-lator from the country where the invoice is to be sent. This provides different views of the same text.

Cost: Installation time: 🕐

4–13 Have Delivery Person Create the Invoice

Many companies have difficulty with their customers when the company bills for the quantity that it believes it shipped to the customer, but the customer argues that it received a different quantity and only pays for the amount it believes it has received. This problem results in the invoicing staff having to issue credits after the fact in order to reconcile the amount of cash received from customers to the amounts billed to them. The amount of work required in these cases to match the amounts billed to the amounts paid is usually greatly in excess of the dollar amounts involved and has a profound impact on the efficiency of the billing staff.

New technology makes it possible for some companies to completely bypass this problem. If a company has its own delivery staff, it can equip them with portable computers and printers and have them issue invoices at the point of receipt, using the quantities counted by the customer as the appropriate amount to invoice. A flowchart of the procedure is shown in Exhibit 4.2. To begin, the shipping staff determines the amount to be shipped to a customer and enters this amount into

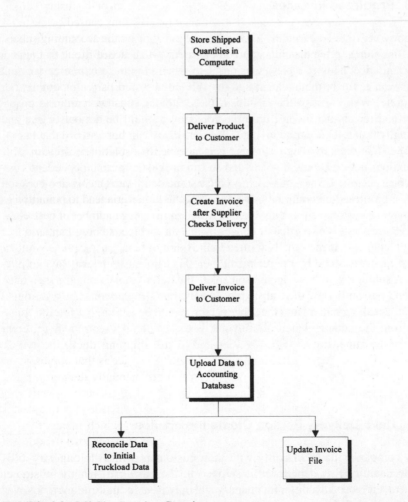

Exhibit 4.2 Off-Site Invoice Creation

the main accounting database. The amount in a specific truckload is downloaded into the portable computer of the delivery person, who then brings the truckload of goods to the customer. The customer counts the amount received. The delivery person calls up the amount of the delivery on the screen of the portable computer, enters the quantities that the customer agrees has been received, and prints out and delivers an invoice (which may be on a diskette or compact disc if the customer has a compatible computer system that can receive invoice data in this fashion). The delivery person then returns to the company and uploads all invoicing information from the portable computer to the main accounting database, which records the invoices and notes any variances between the amounts shipped and the amounts received by customers (which will be investigated if the variances are significant). It is also possible to upload information at the customer site, either by dialing up the accounting database through a local phone connection or by using cellular phone access. This process is capable of eliminating problems caused by customer disputes over delivered quantities, resulting in less work for the accounting staff.

Though a technologically elegant solution, this best practice is one that applies to only a small number of companies that meet some very specific criteria. First, a company must make deliveries with its own staff; a third-party delivery service will not perform the on-site invoicing function. Next, this solution requires a good knowledge of computer systems to implement. There must be not only a qualified and knowledgeable in-house computer system department, but also one that has the budget to create such a system. Also, this is an expensive solution to implement (if only because every driver must be furnished with a computer and printer), so there must be a clear trade-off between the implementation and capital cost of the system and benefits from reduced accounting staff labor. These criteria tend to point toward only larger companies that make frequent deliveries to a large number of customers. Smaller firms will not find that this is a cost-effective practice to install and use.

Cost: 💵💵💵   Installation time: 🕐🕐🕐

4–14 Computerize the Shipping Log

For a company with no computer linkage to the shipping dock, the typical sequence of events leading up to the creation of an invoice is that copies of the packing slip and the initial customer order form are manually delivered to the accounting department from the shipping dock; then the accounting staff uses this information to create an invoice. Unfortunately, this manual transfer of information can sometimes lead to missing documents, which means that the accounting department does not create an invoice and sales are lost. In addition, this system can be a slow one—if the shipping department is a long way away from the accounting department, perhaps in a different city, it may be several days before the invoice can be created, which increases the time period before a customer will receive the invoice and pay it. Finally, there is a problem with data entry, because the accounting staff must manually reenter some or all of the customer information before creating an invoice (depending on the amount of data already entered into the computer system by the order-entry department). Any additional data entry brings up the risk of incorrect information being entered on an invoice, which may result in collection problems, especially if the data-entry error related to an incorrect shipment quantity.

The solution is to provide for the direct entry of shipping information by the shipping staff at the shipping location. By doing so, there is no longer any time delay in issuing invoices, nor is there a risk that the accounting staff will incorrectly enter shipping information into an invoice. There is still a risk that the shipping staff will incorrectly enter information, but this is less likely because they are the ones who shipped the product and they are most familiar with shipping quantities and other related information. For this system to function properly, there must be a computer terminal in the shipping area that is directly linked to the accounting database. In addition, the shipping staff must be properly trained in how to enter a shipment into the computer. There should also be a continuing internal audit review of the accuracy of the data entered at this location, to ensure that the procedure is handled correctly. Finally, the accounting software should have a data input screen that allows the shipping staff to enter shipping information. These tend to be minor problems at most companies, since there is usually a computer terminal already in or near the shipping area, and most accounting packages are already set up to handle the direct entry of shipping information; some even do so automatically as soon as the shipping staff creates a bill of lading or packing slip through the computer system. In short, unless there are very antiquated systems on hand or a poorly trained or unreliable shipping staff, it is not normally a very difficult issue to have the shipping employees directly enter shipping information into the accounting system, which can then be used to immediately create and issue invoices.

Cost: 💵💵   **Installation time:** ⏰⏰

4–15 Track Exceptions between the Shipping Log and Invoice Register

If a company relies on the manual transfer of shipping information from the shipping dock to the accounting department, it is likely that some shipments are never billed, resulting in a permanent loss of revenue. This situation arises because information can be lost on its way from the shipping dock; it can be mixed with other paperwork, put into the wrong bin, given to the wrong person, or any number of other variations. In even the best-run companies, there is a strong chance that, from time to time, a shipment will not be invoiced. If the shipment in question is a high-dollar one, the cost of the missing transaction can be considerable and may make it worthwhile to take steps to remedy the situation.

Fortunately, the solution is not a very expensive one. To avoid any missing invoices, one must continually compare the shipping log maintained by the shipping department with the invoice register maintained by the accounting department. Any shipment listed on the shipping log that has not been invoiced must be investigated at once. There may be good reasons for a shipment that is not invoiced, such as the delivery of a free sample, but the investigation must still be completed to ensure that there are no problems. If a problem is uncovered, it is not enough to just issue the missing invoice. One must also determine the reason why the paperwork for the shipment never reached the accounting department and fix the underlying problem. Only by taking this extra step can a company keep from having a continual problem with its invoicing. Any company using a manual transfer of information between these two departments should always track exceptions between the shipping log and invoice register.

It is also possible to avoid the entire problem by having the shipping department record all shipments directly into the accounting database, as described in the preceding section, "Computerize the Shipping Log." By using this approach, there is no manual transfer of information, so there is no exception tracking to perform. It is also possible to have the shipping department not only enter shipments into the computer, but also print out invoices in the shipping department for delivery with the shipments. This approach was also described earlier, in the section "Delivery Person Creates the Invoice." However, if the shipping area does not have the level of computerization or training to use either of these more advanced best practices, a periodic comparison of the shipping log to the invoice register is mandatory, in order to avoid not billing customers for shipments to them.

Cost: 💵   **Installation time:** ⏰ ⏰

4–16 Eliminate Month-End Statements

The employees in charge of printing and issuing invoices each day have another document that they print and issue each month, the month-end statement. This is a listing of all open invoices that customers have not yet paid. Though it seems like a good idea to tell customers what they still owe, the reality of the situation is that most customers throw away their statements without reading them. The reason is that the person receiving a statement, the accounts payable clerk, does not have time to research strange invoices that appear on a supplier's statement, nor is it likely that this person will call the supplier to request a copy of a missing invoice. Instead, it is easier to wait for a contact from the supplier, asking about a specific invoice. By waiting, the onus of doing some work falls on the supplier instead of the accounts payable person, which is a preferable shifting of the workload from the latter person to the former.

The simple approach to eliminating this problem is to stop printing statements. By doing so, one can avoid not only the time and effort of printing the statements, but also eliminate the cost of the special form used to print the statements, as well as the cost of stuffing them in envelopes and mailing them. Though it is possible that the collections staff may complain that this collection tool is being taken away from them, it is at best a poor method for bringing in errant accounts receivable, and does little to reduce the workload of the collections personnel. Thus, eliminating the periodic issuance of statements to customers is an easy way to shift the accounting staff away from a nonvalue-added activity, which gives them time to pursue other more meaningful activities.

Cost: Installation time: 🕰

4–17 Reduce Number of Parts in Multipart Invoices
✔ Author's Choice

Some invoices have the thickness of a small magazine when they are printed because they have so many parts. The top copy (or even the top two copies) usually goes to the customer, while another one goes into a file that is sorted alphabetically; another goes into a file for invoices that is sorted by invoice number, and yet another copy may go to a different department, such as customer service, so that they will have an additional copy on hand in case a customer calls with a question. This plethora of invoice copies causes several problems. One is that the printer is much more likely to jam if the number of invoice copies running through it is too thick. Another much more serious problem is that each of those copies must be filed away. The alphabetical copy is probably a necessary one, since all of the shipping documentation is attached to it, but there is no excuse for filing invoices in numerical order; they can be found just as easily by calling them up in the computer. A final problem is that multipart forms are more expensive.

The best practice that avoids this problem is to reduce the number of invoice copies. Only one copy should go to the customer, and one copy should be retained. That is two copies, not the four or five that some companies use. By reducing the number of copies, there is much less chance that the printer will jam, and the cost of the invoices can be substantially reduced. The biggest cost saving, however, is of the filing time that has been eliminated, which can be many hours per month, depending on the volume of invoices created.

The biggest objection to reducing the number of invoice copies is from those parts of the company accustomed to using them. This group is rarely the accounting department, which must do the work of filing the extra copies, but rather other departments that have an occasional need to look at them. The best way to overcome these objections is to educate the dissenters in advance regarding the required filing time needed to keep extra copies, so they understand that the cost of additional filing does not match the benefit of their occasional need for the invoices. Another option is to give these people read-only access to invoices in the accounting computer system, so they can call up invoice information on their computers, rather than looking for it manually in an invoice binder. The combination of these two approaches usually eliminates any opposition to reducing the number of invoice copies, allowing the accounting staff to achieve extra efficiencies.

Cost: 💵   Installation time: ⏰

4–18 Replace Intercompany Invoicing with Operating Transactions

Those companies with subsidiaries will find some difficulty at the end of the fiscal year, because they must back out all sales between subsidiaries, which are not, according to accounting rules, true sales. The most common way to record product shipments between locations is to issue an invoice to another subsidiary, which pays it as though it is from an independently owned organization. At the end of the year, the accounting staff must then determine the margin on all sales to subsidiaries (which can be a lengthy undertaking) and create a journal entry to reverse out the margin. This is clearly not a value-added activity, and reducing it to the minimum gives the accounting staff more time to deal with other issues.

A best practice that multiple-subsidiary companies can use is to avoid using invoices when shipping between company-owned facilities. Instead, there are two ways to record the transactions. The first and easiest approach is to record any inventory transfers as a simple movement of inventory between warehouse locations in the computer system. This approach is only possible if a company uses a single enterprisewide database of information to control activities in all company locations. If such a system is in place, a shipping clerk can simply record a delivery as being moved from one warehouse to another, or as being in transit to another warehouse, where it will be recorded as having been received as soon as it arrives at that location. The other possibility is to accumulate all material transfers in a log and create a journal entry at the end of each reporting period (or sooner, such as daily) to record inventory as having been shifted to a different company location. This second approach requires more manual labor and is more subject to error than the first approach, but can be used even if there is no enterprisewide computer system for all locations. In either case, there is no need to create an invoice, nor does the accounting staff have to worry about backing out the profit on sales to company subsidiaries.

Cost: 💵   Installation time: ⏰ ⏰

4–19 Improve Shipping Charge Revenue

A standard component of many customer invoices is the shipping charge, which may include a hefty profit percentage. Part of the billing process requires the accounting staff to separately calculate this shipping charge and include it in each invoice. Since the accounting staff sometimes forgets to include this line item, companies suffer revenue leakage and correspondingly reduced profits.

The best way to ensure that shipping charges are always billed is to make their inclusion in an invoice completely unavoidable. Here are some ways to do so:

- *Default template.* Create a default invoicing template in the accounting software that includes a prelisted shipping line item, as well as a default shipping charge. A problem is that the billing staff may use the default shipping charge every time.

- *Summary price.* Roll the freight charge into the product price, and offer "free" shipping. Though this approach ensures that shipping will always be charged, the company may not be able to compete on a price basis against competitors who offer lower initial prices and then add a shipping charge.

- *Use a "freight" sales tax.* If shipping is charged as a standard percentage of sales, consider setting up a "freight" sales tax authority in the accounting software that will automatically include a shipping charge as part of the sales tax calculation. Since customers may protest the unusually high "sales tax" line item, consider changing the title of this line to "sales tax and freight charge," if the software will allow it.

- *Add footer to shipping document.* The warehouse sends a completed pick list or sales order to the billing staff, containing notice of which items can be billed; whatever document is used, consider altering its format with a footer line item, containing a reminder (in bold) to include the shipping charge.

The above approaches represent the simplest, most automated ways to ensure that shipping charges are added to every invoice. Other approaches with higher error rates or costs are the use of billing checklists (tend to be ignored), regular retraining of billing staff (high labor costs), and auditing of issued invoices with follow-up training of any billing staff with high error rates (high labor costs).

Cost: **Installation time:** 🕰️

Total Impact of Best Practices on the Billing Function

This section describes a set of best practices that, when integrated into the billings function, results in significant efficiency improvements. The best practices presented here are a subset of the complete list presented earlier in this chapter, in Exhibit 4.1. This listing, as diagrammed in Exhibit 4.3, eliminates several best practices that are mutually exclusive. For example, if a company uses a computerized shipping log to create invoices, there is no need to use another best practice, such as tracking variances between invoices created and the paper-based shipping

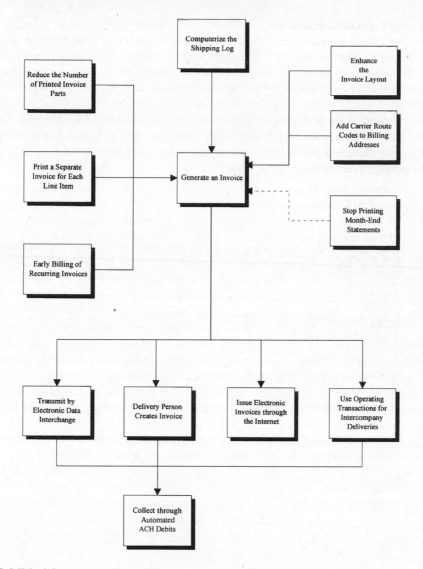

Exhibit 4.3 Impact of Best Practices on the Billing Function

log. When these types of conflicts arise, only the most advanced best practice is assumed to be used. As a result, the best practices shown in Exhibit 4.3 note that a company should always directly link its shipping dock with the accounting database by having all shipments automatically invoiced as soon as the shipping staff puts a delivery on an outbound truck. The printed invoice should use a minimum number of copies, avoiding several downstream steps to file them. The invoicing function should also avoid the use of month-end statements. Finally, a company has a variety of invoice-delivery options to choose from, ranging from EDI transmissions to point-of-delivery invoicing, or even the complete elimination of invoices by using automated ACH debits from customer bank accounts. The exact invoicing method or combination of methods chosen will depend on the special circumstances and requirements of each company.

If some of the best practices noted in Exhibit 4.3 cannot be completed for any reason, some lesser combination of best practices will still result in efficiency improvements, though not to as great a degree as would be possible if the entire set of improvements were implemented.

Summary

This chapter focused on improving the speed and accuracy of invoice preparation and delivery. There are several ways to achieve these goals. One is to increase the accuracy of invoicing information reaching the accounting department, which calls for changes in the shipping department, as well as the method for transferring shipping information to the accounting department.

Another set of methods involve how invoices are transmitted to customers. New technologies allow one to do so electronically or at the point of delivery, so that customers receive more accurate invoices more quickly than ever before. Finally, invoices can be completely eliminated in a limited number of cases, resulting in direct cash transfers from customer bank accounts to the company. When used together, these best practices result in a significant improvement in the efficiency of the billing function.

For more information about billing best practices, please refer to *Billing and Collections Best Practices* by the author (John Wiley & Sons, 2005).

Chapter 5

Budgeting Best Practices

Many companies find the budgeting process to be excruciatingly slow and painful, requiring many months of continual effort before a reasonable budget document is completed. Once it is done, they wonder why the company went to all the effort, since no one makes a strong effort to follow it. This chapter addresses both problems. There are a variety of best practices focusing on creating and implementing a budget model, ranging from defining capacity levels and step-costing points to using activity-based budgeting. These are designed not only to make the budgeting process simpler, but also to result in a better budget that closely reflects management's expectations regarding operations in the upcoming budget period. In addition, there are several best practices that can improve a company's usage of the budget, so that it is closely integrated into daily operations.

This chapter begins with an overview of implementation issues for all of the best practices, followed by a discussion of individual best practices, each one being presented in a separate section. The chapter finishes with a review of how these best practices will change a company's budgeting operations.

Implementation Issues for Budgeting Best Practices

With few exceptions, improvements to the budgeting system are easy to implement and can be done rapidly, with a minimum of fuss. The cost and duration are noted in Exhibit 5.1. The reason is that most changes are to the budgeting model and procedures, neither of which are under the control of anyone but the accounting department, and neither of which need, unlike humans, some explanation and cooperation. Accordingly, one can assume a rapid implementation process that can mostly be completed during the current budget cycle, resulting in immediate and rapid improvement in the entire process.

There are only three best practices requiring a considerable amount of implementation effort. One is linking the budget to the purchase order system, since this usually requires some custom programming. The second is switching to an activity-based budget model, since this approach requires a complete revamping of the budget model, as well as a new chart of accounts to reflect the changes. The third is the installation of budgeting and planning software, which is particularly difficult for multilocation companies. Also, online budget updating and video conferencing have a moderate associated expense, since they require modem access

Exhibit 5.1 Summary of Budgeting Best Practices

	Best Practice	Cost	Install Time
Budget Assumptions			
5–1	Link the budget to key business drivers	💵	⏰
5–2	Clearly define all assumptions	💵	⏰
5–3	Clearly define all capacity levels	💵	⏰
5–4	Establish project ranking criteria	💵	⏰
5–5	Apply throughput analysis to capital budgeting	💵	⏰⏰
5–6	Establish the upper limit of available funding	💵	⏰
5–7	Identify step-costing change points	💵	⏰
5–8	Budget for attrition	💵	⏰
Budget Models			
5–9	Budget by groups of staff positions	💵	⏰
5–10	Create a summarized budget model for use by upper management	💵	⏰
5–11	Include a working capital analysis	💵	⏰
5–12	Use activity-based budgeting	💵💵	⏰⏰⏰
5–13	Incorporate target costing into the budgeting process	💵	⏰
5–14	Link a bonus sliding scale to the budget	💵	⏰
5–15	Use flex budgeting	💵	⏰⏰
5–16	Incorporate risk analysis into budget modeling	💵	⏰⏰
Budget Management			
5–17	Automatically link the budget to purchase orders	💵💵💵	⏰⏰⏰
5–18	Issue a budget procedure and timetable	💵	⏰
5–19	Preload budget line items	💵	⏰⏰
5–20	Adopt two-stage capital budgeting	💵	⏰
5–21	Purchase budgeting and planning software	💵💵💵	⏰⏰⏰
5–22	Reduce the number of accounts	💵	⏰⏰⏰
5–23	Revise budgets on a quarterly basis	💵	⏰⏰
5–24	Simplify the budget model	💵	⏰
5–25	Use online budget updating	💵💵	⏰⏰

(in the first case) and video conferencing equipment (in the latter case). With these exceptions, one can expect best practice implementations in this area to be an easy chore, resulting in quick improvements.

5–1 Link the Budget to Key Business Drivers

In many businesses, the budgeting process has acquired a reputation for a great deal of political infighting, because managers push very hard to ensure that their capital and department budget requests are approved before those of other managers, while also obtaining the lowest possible performance goals for the upcoming year. Thus, it appears that the budget is driven by the most politically astute and well-connected managers.

A much better approach is to link the budget to the overall corporate strategy, as represented by a set of key business drivers. By doing so, it is much more difficult for managers to twist the budget in their favor, when doing so clearly undermines the corporate strategy. For example, a car company's president may have concluded that the use of alternative fuels is the company's best hope for survival, so key business drivers for this strategy will be the development of an engine that can handle multiple fuels, a hybrid car, and the creation of a hydrogen-powered fuel cell. With all available funding going into these targeted activities, it will become painfully obvious if someone attempts to divert funding into the development of a low-fuel economy sport-utility vehicle.

The incorporation of business drivers into the budgeting process also tends to reduce the time period required to complete the budget, since less time is spent on political battles and budgeting minutia.

The main problem with this approach is that managers can simply shift their political maneuvering into altering the company strategy to best serve their personal objectives. It takes a strong company president to overcome this maneuvering and ensure that the correct strategy and related business drivers are selected.

Cost: **Installation time:**

5–2 Clearly Define All Assumptions

When the budget model is first presented to senior management, the person doing the presenting is deluged with questions about what assumptions are used in the model. Examples of assumptions that can cause problems are tax rate percentages, sales growth rates (especially by product line, since some of those lines may be exceedingly mature), capacity levels (see the next section), cost-of-goods-sold margins, commission rates, and medical insurance rates per person. Upper management wants to make sure that all assumptions are reasonable before they spend a great deal of their time reviewing the presented information. If there are specious assumptions, they will probably kick the budget back and demand changes before they will agree to look at it.

The best way around this problem is to list all key assumptions either right at the top of the budget model or else in clearly noted spots on each page. It is also helpful to note how these assumptions have changed from previous years, either by providing this information in a commentary or by showing prior year information in an extra column in the budget. By providing this information as clearly as possible, there will be fewer questions for the budgeting team to answer.

An even better approach is to tie as many of these assumptions into the budget model as possible, so that a change to an assumption will result in an immediate ripple effect through the budget. For example, changing a tax rate assumption will immediately alter the tax expense in the budget, while altering the medical expense per person will have a similar impact on personnel costs. Linking assumptions to the budget allows one to make nearly instantaneous changes to a budget with minimal effort.

Cost: **Installation time:** 🕐

5–3 Clearly Define All Capacity Levels

When creating a budget that contains major increases in revenues, a common problem is failing to reflect this change in the rest of the budget, resulting in an inadequate amount of staffpower, machinery, or facilities to handle the added growth. For example, a planned increase in revenue requires a corresponding increase in the number of sales staff who are responsible for bringing in the sales, not to mention a time lag before the new sales personnel can be reasonably expected to acquire new sales. Similarly, new sales at a production facility may result in machine utilization levels that are too high to maintain—has anyone thought of adding machinery purchases to the budget? This problem can be turned around and dealt with from the point of view of planned expense reductions, too—if the percentage of direct labor is budgeted to decline due to the use of automation, has anyone included the cost of the automation in the budget, and has a suitable time lag been built into the plan to account for the ramp-up time needed to implement the automation? Some of these problems are present in all but the best budget models.

The best practice that resolves this issue is the definition of capacity levels in the budget model. This can take the form of a table in the budget, such as the one shown in Exhibit 5.2. This example notes the capacity levels for staffpower, such as a specific number of shipments per warehouse worker, sales per salesperson, and new product releases per engineer. It is very important to list these capacity levels for previous years in the same table, providing a frame of reference that tells the reader if the assumed capacity levels in this year's budget are attainable. Also, consider including another comparison column in the table that shows the capacity levels of competitors or of best practice companies, against which

Exhibit 5.2 Capacity Assumptions Table

Employee Description	Capacity/Person in 2009	Capacity/Person in 2010
Computer Help Desk	1 per 250 Computer Users	1 per 238 Computer Users
Engineer	1 per 5 Engineering Change Requests/Month	1 per 4.8 Engineering Change Requests/Month
Machine Operator	1 per 2 Presses	1 per 1.7 Presses
Salesperson	1 per $1,200,000 Sales	1 per $1,174,000 Sales
Shipper	1 per 12 Truck Ships/Day	1 per 9 Truck Ships/Day

the company has benchmarked its activities. By using this informational layout, one can easily tell if more or less resources are needed to attain the revenue and expense goals in a budget.

Cost: **Installation time:** 🕰

5–4 Establish Project Ranking Criteria

When it comes time for the annual budget process, the accounting staff is usually inundated with a flood of requests for funding capital projects. These are sometimes pet projects, others are for repairs or replacements, and still others are entirely new business propositions. The trouble is that a great deal of time is spent in sorting through them to see which ones are viable. Further, after the remaining ones are put in the budget, capital constraints typically lead to some of them being thrown back out. As a result, capital projects can be a bottleneck during the formation of the budget.

One can reduce this bottleneck by establishing project ranking criteria in advance and distributing this information to anyone who may be submitting a capital request. These criteria should itemize how funds will be allocated. For example, any project with a return on capital that exceeds a target level is a top priority; next in line may be any project needed to bring a company in line with government regulations, and so on. Once they see the criteria, budget participants may voluntarily eliminate some of their own requests. In addition, if the capital expenditure request form accompanies the ranking criteria, applicants can fill out all the information the accounting staff needs to sort through the various projects, making the accountant's jobs much easier. This method not only eliminates some of the least probable capital projects up front, but also does a better job of categorizing those that are left.

Cost: 💵   **Installation time:** 🕰

5–5 Apply Throughput Analysis to
Capital Budgeting   ✔*Author's Choice*

The traditional capital budgeting approach involves having the management team review a series of unrelated requests from throughout the company, each one asking for funding for various projects. Management decides whether to fund each request based on the discounted cash flows projected for each one. If there are not sufficient funds available for all requests having positive discounted cash flows, then those with the largest cash flows or highest percentage returns are usually accepted first, until the funds run out.

There are several problems with this type of capital budgeting. First and most important, there is no consideration of how each requested project fits into the entire system of production. Instead, most requests involve the local optimization of specific work centers that may not contribute to the total throughput of the company. Second, there is no consideration of the constrained resource, so managers cannot tell which funding requests will result in an improvement to the efficiency of that operation. Third, managers tend to engage in a great deal of speculation regarding the budgeted cash flows resulting from their requests, resulting in inaccurate discounted cash flow projections. Since many requests involve unverifiable cash flow estimates, it is impossible to discern which projects are better than others.

A greater reliance on throughput accounting concepts eliminates most of these problems. First, the priority for funding should be placed squarely on any projects that can improve the capacity of the constrained resource, based on a comparison of the incremental additional throughput created to the incremental operating expenses and investment incurred.

Second, any investment requests not involving the constrained resource should be subject to an intensive critical review, likely resulting in their rejection. Since they do not impact the constrained resource, these investments cannot impact system throughput in any way, so their sole remaining justification must be the reduction of operating expenses or the mitigation of some type of risk.

The one exception to investing in nonconstraint resources is when there is so little excess capacity in a work center that it has difficulty recovering from downtime. This can be a major problem if the lack of capacity constantly causes holes in the inventory buffer and places the constrained resource in danger of running out of work. In this case, a good investment alternative is to invest in a sufficient amount of additional sprint capacity to ensure that the system can rapidly recover from a reasonable level of downtime. If managers are applying for a capital investment based on this reasoning, they should attach a chart to the proposal that shows the capacity level at which the targeted resource has been operating over the past few months, as well as the severity of holes in the buffer caused by that operation.

At what point should a company invest in more of the constrained resource? In many cases, the company has specifically designated a resource to be its constraint because it is so expensive to add additional capacity, so this decision is not to be taken lightly. The decision process is to review the impact on the incremental change in throughput caused by the added investment, less any changes in operating expenses. Because this type of investment represents a considerable step-cost (where costs and/or the investment will jump considerably as a result of the decision), management must usually make its decision based on the perceived level of long-term throughput changes, rather than smaller expected short-term throughput increases.

Cost: Installation time: 🕰 🕰

5–6 Establish the Upper Limit of Available Funding

Too many budgeting processes take an inordinate amount of time to complete because management goes through too many iterations while deciding on how much money it has to spend. For example, the initial budget model may include funding for a new facility, an acquisition, or a distribution to stockholders. However, once management determines that the amount of available funding is not sufficient, they must recast the budget in order to arrive at a much smaller total expenditure. This plays havoc with the accounting staff, who must coordinate all the budgeting changes, modify the model, and reissue it.

The answer is to determine the amount of available funding as early in the process as possible. For example, the amount of fixed assets, inventory, and accounts receivable currently on hand can be extrapolated into the next year to determine the total amount of borrowing base that is likely to be available for borrowing purposes. Also, one can inquire of senior management if there is any likelihood of making a public offering of shares or of making a bond placement in the near future; this option is most unlikely for smaller companies, while larger ones may be constrained by established policies regarding the suitable debt-to-equity ratio that management is not allowed to exceed. Finally, the company may spin off cash from continuing operations; a review of current margin levels and cash flows can be used to determine the level of funds originating from this source. When all of these sources are put together, management usually finds that there is far less money available than they had wished for, which keeps them from developing overblown budgets that cannot possibly succeed.

The only issue with this approach is that some managers like to produce budgets that represent flights of fancy and do not appreciate having the extra information regarding funding, since it brings them back to reality rather abruptly. When these unique personalities are in management, it is best to use a great deal of tact when presenting funding information. A good variation is to present a range of funding amounts, along with the percentage chance of having each amount available, plus the likely interest rate that the company will have to pay in order to obtain the funds. By showing a probable interest rate, management will then understand that extra tiers of funding will only be available at a greater cost, since the company's credit risk rises as it borrows more money. This form of presentation is an effective way to increase management's understanding of funding availability.

Cost: 💵   **Installation time:** ⏰

5–7 Identify Step-Costing Change Points   ✔*Author's Choice*

A typical problem for anyone constructing a budget is to determine when step-costing points occur. A step-cost is a block of additional expenses that must be added when a certain level of activity is reached. For example, machinery can only operate at a reasonable capacity level, perhaps 75 percent, before another machine must be added to cope with more work, even if that workload will only fill the machine at a very low level of capacity. The same principle applies to adding personnel or building space. In all cases, there is a considerable added expense that must be incurred in one large block. If the expense is sufficiently large, it can play havoc with the total level of expenses. Or, in the case of a really large capital purchase, it may leave no room for other capital purchases for the next year. Accordingly, it is necessary to keep close track of step-cost change points.

The best way to determine when an increase in step-costs will occur is to create a table of activity measures that directly relates to each step-cost. For example, a new shipping person is needed for every 135 pallets of product shipped per day. By relating sales for the next year to the number of pallet loads of shipments, one can reasonably predict when an additional shipper is needed. Similarly, if a piece of production machinery will support $1 million of sales, it is an easy matter to extrapolate this relationship based on expected sales to determine when additional machine purchases must be made. However, keep in mind that step-costs can be delayed by using new work methods, which can alter these relationships. For example, an automated shrink-wrapping machine can substantially increase the number of pallets that a single shipper can handle in a day, while a good preventive maintenance routine can reduce the amount of machine downtime, thereby increasing utilization rates and delaying the need for more production equipment. When these changes are added to the budget, it becomes necessary to change the relationship between the activity levels and step-costs, possibly with the relationships varying over the course of the budgeted period, as more work methods are implemented.

Thus, identifying step-costing change points is necessary to understand when new costs will be added to a budget, but one must also account for alterations in the relationship between the underlying activity measures that cause the step-costs to occur.

Cost: 💵   **Installation time:** ⏰

5–8 Budget for Attrition

One problem with budget models is trying to anticipate the number of employees who will leave the company during the budget year, which is expressed as a general reduction in the wage expense. One option is to budget for no departures, which results in the maximum possible wage expense, and one that the budget preparer knows in advance is unlikely to occur. Another possibility is to attempt to predict exactly who is leaving, and when, which is subject to an extraordinary degree of error.

An alternative approach is to incorporate into the budget an attrition percentage that is based on the company's historical experience. This is the only alternative that has some justifiable basis. It tends to be more accurate in larger companies, since averages work better across several thousand employees than just a few dozen or hundred. To derive a reasonable attrition percentage, review the attrition for the past year and strip out those departures caused by one-time events, such as the closure of a facility. Also, if the job market is tightening and the company employs mostly skilled positions, then assume that the replacement interval for positions will be longer, which results in a higher attrition percentage.

Since the timing of attrition is nearly impossible to predict, it is easier to apply the same percentage across the entire year. It may be more inaccurate earlier in the year, but the average level of attrition should move closer to the anticipated level by the end of the year.

Cost: 💵 **Installation time:** ⏰

5–9 Budget by Groups of Staff Positions ✔*Author's Choice*

The payroll portion of the budget model can be an excessively long one because every person in the company is listed on it. In particular, many accountants have difficulty avoiding a complete listing of *all* people who are not categorized as direct labor. As a result, this portion of the budget becomes an unwieldy cluster of information, requiring a long time to read, as well as a considerable amount of updating work to keep track of everyone's pay levels.

A simple best practice is to summarize these positions by title, ensuring that there are far fewer line items, so the budget becomes much easier to update and review. To do so, one must summarize the pay levels of everyone with the same job title and post the average pay rate in the model. For those people who object that they can no longer determine who is summarized into which category, one can either issue a separate list that identifies the title of each person in the company or else insert the initials of all the people with each job title next to the summary-level description in the budget (a difficult proposition when there are many people with the same title!). The only real problem is in those companies where there is no record of the job titles of employees. In this case, it may be sufficient to summarize all payroll for each department into a single line item in the budget, with an average pay rate for the entire group; this approach completely avoids the problem of determining pay by title. Any of these variations will result in a simplified payroll section of the budget, while still retaining a high degree of accuracy.

Cost: 💵   **Installation time:** ⏰

5–10 Create a Summarized Budget Model for Use by Upper Management

The full budget model used by the accounting staff is a large one, with separate pages for the balance sheet, income statement, cash flow, capital expenditures, and each department, not to mention additional subsets of this information for each subsidiary. The full budget for a small company should run about 20 pages, while one for a multilocation corporation can easily run into the hundreds of pages. This presents a problem for senior management when it wants to conduct what-if analysis work with the budget. For example, the president of the company may want to know what would happen to profits if there were 1 percent less direct labor, or if materials costs changed due to an increase in inflation. Given the size of the model, a senior manager's only way to get this information is to request that a budget analyst access the budget model, make the changes, and send the results back. This can take days for one request to be completed, which is a problem when the manager may want to model dozens of changes. Waiting for the results of all possible variations on the manager's requests may require months. During the budget period, there is not enough time to process all of these requests, which leads to delays in completing the budget and frustration on the part of senior management.

The solution is to create a small, summarized version of the full budget model for use by the senior management team. By doing so, these managers can play with all possible what-if variations on the budget on their own computers, without waiting for someone in the accounting department to process these changes for them, saving a large amount of time. To create this model, one should interview senior managers to see what kinds of variables they will want to alter. These will not vary much from year to year, unless there are drastic changes in the business, so once the variables are identified, they can be listed in the front of the model for easy access by the managers. For example, the variables can include the direct labor and materials percentages, the inflation rate, average pay raise, average employee benefit percentage, seasonality percentage for revenues, changes in revenues, and the tax and interest rates. The remainder of the budget should be shrunken down to the point where there is only a single expense line item for each department and the smallest possible number of revenue line items.

The goal should be to keep the summarized budget model down to just a couple of pages. Also, to keep the data in this model fresh, one can either give data a direct computer link to the main budget model, automatically extracting the most current data from the real budget, or else manually extract the information and retype it into the manager's budget model (which is a much easier proposition, and avoids any special programming). Creating this model may take a few extra weeks, but will be greatly appreciated by senior management.

The only problem with this budget model is that senior managers may not know how to use it or the computer on which it runs. If so, training is necessary, which may be difficult to fit into a manager's busy schedule. A good alternative is to train each manager's executive assistant, who can process any changes to the budget model that the manager wishes to make.

Cost: 💵   **Installation time:** ⏰

5–11 Include a Working Capital Analysis

All too many companies have found that their budgets are entirely unworkable because they have not accounted for the added cash required for working capital. This is a particular problem for those organizations forecasting extremely high rates of growth. They do not realize that they must have funds in advance to pay for the staff and materials required to produce products, as well as to fund the considerable increases in accounts receivable that will occur. Because of this, a company finds that its sales take off, as per the budget, while cash reserves rapidly dry up, resulting in a cash-starved organization that must scramble to find more cash to keep it growing. More times than not, a promising start is hamstrung because of lack of anticipation of working capital needs.

Clearly, the budget must account for working capital. There should be an extra page devoted to it in the budget, or it can be included in the cash flow page. In either case, the budget should make an assumption regarding the amount of inventory, accounts payable, and accounts receivable that will occur as sales go up; for example, there may be inventory turns of 12 per year, accounts receivable turns of 9, and accounts payable turns of 10. These turnover figures must then be built into the working capital formulas to determine how much extra cash will be needed as sales increase. An alternative approach is to assume that all working capital changes will be cleared in one month; for example, accounts payable will be paid in precisely one month, and accounts receivable paid by customers in the same period. This simpler approach is the one most commonly found in budgets, though it is not quite as accurate as the first method. The importance of accurate working capital forecasting cannot be overstated, especially for a cash-strapped company.

Cost: 💵   **Installation time:** ⏰

5–12 Use Activity-Based Budgeting

For many organizations, the existing budgeting system simply does not yield adequate results. Management can fiddle with the numbers all they want, but working within the existing structure of revenues by product line and expenses by department is so rigid that there is little room for improving operating results. Only by using outlandish assumptions, such as inordinate price increases or cost reductions, can any reasonable profit improvement be attained. As the new budget year progresses and everyone realizes that those absurd assumptions are not attainable, some of the blame is put on the budgeting process, resulting in a loss of credibility. This problem is especially common in old, established industries, where competition is high and low profits are the norm.

Activity-based budgeting is the best solution for companies in this quandary. To use it, the existing budget model must either be scrapped or used alongside a new model, which pools all costs into cost centers, assigns these costs to activities, and charges the activities to products and customers. By using this new approach, one can see much more clearly the products on which a company really makes (or does not make) money, and margins on all customers, based on the services they demand from the company. With this better information, management can target cost reductions in those areas where there is little return on the money invested, while targeting expense increases if there is a corresponding increase in margin.

The biggest problem with activity-based budgeting is that it requires an entirely new budget model, as well as a new chart of accounts in which to store the budget information. Both of these changes are significant and require months (and sometimes years) of careful planning and implementation. The reason for all the planning is that all accounting information systems are designed to feed information into the existing chart of accounts, so these systems must be modified to accumulate data in the manner required for the activity-based budgeting system instead. One way around this problem is to keep the old budgeting model and continue to account for it through the chart of accounts in the traditional manner, manually maintaining the new budgeting model to one side and reporting on actual results with a separate system. Though certainly more labor-intensive, this approach can be implemented at once and requires very little change in the existing accounting systems.

Cost: 💵💵   Installation time: 🕐 🕐 🕐

5–13 Incorporate Target Costing into the Budgeting Process

Target costing is the process of setting a target cost for a new product design and requiring the product design team to either meet the cost target or abandon the project if it cannot do so. The accounting department's sole involvement in this process is typically the inclusion of a cost accountant on the design team who monitors the team's ongoing progress in meeting its cost goals.

The problem with this level of accounting involvement is that there is no linkage to the corporate budgeting process, so there is likely to be a reduced level of budgeting accuracy for the cost of goods sold. To improve the situation, require the participating cost accountants to forward status reports to the budgeting staff for the current status of all product design projects for which target costing is used. This has the following positive impacts on the budgeting process:

- The preliminary budget can be adjusted continually to reflect the go/no-go status of each design project. Thus, if the decision is made to eliminate a prospective product, its related revenues and costs can be immediately removed from the budget model.

- The budgeted cost of goods sold for each product can be adjusted to match the estimated final cost of each new product design.

To incorporate this target costing information into the budgeting process, the budget model must already itemize revenues and costs at the individual product level. However, if the current budget model only aggregates revenues and costs at the product line level, one can at least incorporate into the model (in percentage terms) the general impact expected from a target costing program.

Cost: **Installation time:** 🕙

5–14 Link a Bonus Sliding Scale to the Budget

A reasonably progressive budgeting model will include a direct link into the corporate bonus plan, with staff being paid bonuses based on their achievement of certain goals. Although the intention is good—to create incentives to achieve the budget—it actually tends to create more problems than it solves.

One problem is that, if employees realize that they will fall short of their bonus targets, they will be more likely to hoard their resources or possible sales for the next period, when they will have a better opportunity to achieve better performance and be paid a bonus. The result is wild swings in corporate performance from period to period as employees cycle through the hoard-to-splurge cycle.

Another problem is that if the bonus target cannot be attained by normal means, employees will stretch or break the accounting rules in a variety of ways to achieve the target. By doing so, a low level of ethics is introduced into the company, while also likely saddling the company with a variety of accounting problems that must be addressed in future periods.

The solution is to link the budget to a sliding performance scale that contains no "hard" performance goals. The best example of the sliding bonus scale is what it is *not*—there are no specific goals at which the bonus target suddenly increases in size. Instead, the bonus is a constant percentage of the goal, such as 1 percent of sales or 5 percent of net after-tax profits. Also, there should be no upper boundary to the sliding scale, which would present employees with the disincentive to stop performing once they have reached a maximum bonus level. Similarly, there should theoretically be no lower limit to the bonus either, though it is more common to see a baseline level that is derived from the corporate breakeven point, on the grounds that employees must at least ensure that the company does not lose money. The sliding-scale approach also makes it much easier to budget for the bonus expense at various activity levels, rather than trying to budget for the more common all-or-nothing bonus payment.

Cost: **Installation time:** 🕰

5–15 Use Flex Budgeting

Perhaps the single most tedious part of updating a budget is altering the myriad expense line items every time someone makes a change to the estimated revenue level. Revenue is far and away the most commonly tweaked number in a budget, so the underlying expenses have to be recast to be in proportion to the changed revenue levels a multitude of times. This is a major chore not only for the accounting staff maintaining the budget, but also for those managers who must be contacted about changes to the expense levels they had previously authorized.

A recasting of the budget model will largely eliminate this problem. Instead of making changes to the expense line item for every expense in the budget, it is much easier to set up each one as either a flexible expense account or one that is fixed within a broad range of revenue levels. If it is fixed, there is no need for change, unless there is an enormous alteration in budgeted revenue levels. However, many other expenses will vary directly with revenue; in these cases, it is possible to revise the budget formulas so that they are listed as percentages of the monthly revenue level. By making these formula alterations, it becomes an easy matter to adjust revenue and see a swath of expense changes ripple through the budget model—with no manual intervention whatsoever. This best practice can reduce budget maintenance work to a fraction of the amount formerly needed.

Though the flex budget discussion has centered on tying expenses to specific revenue levels, it is also possible, and probably more accurate, to tie some expenses to other levels of activity. For example, telephone usage or office expenses should be linked more properly to the number of budgeted employees, while utility costs can be tied either to square footage used or the number of machines in operation. Thus, one can link expenses to a number of activity measures in a flex budget.

Cost: **Installation time:** 🕰 🕰

5–16 Incorporate Risk Analysis into Budget Modeling

Most budgets include only a single scenario, where a single mix of assumptions culminate in a single estimate of revenue and expenses. Examples of key assumptions are the inflation rate, the price of energy, the impact of a lawsuit, and the entry into the market of a low-priced competitor. Usually, these assumptions are based on what actually happened during the preceding year. Unfortunately, reality can diverge sharply from an assumption, resulting in an extremely inaccurate budget model.

Though it is impossible to predetermine every possible variation in assumptions, the budget model can at least be structured so that a wide range of assumption values can be entered into it, to see what impact they will have on the company's financial results. This type of risk analysis calls for the use of a flex budget, as described in a preceding best practice, since a flex budget will automatically change many of its numerical values as a result of a change in an assumption.

To the extent possible, try to cluster all assumptions on a single page of the budget model, where they will be more readily accessible for modeling and viewing activities. Once all risk analysis has been conducted with the budget model, include the results of this experimentation in a separate budget report, and forward it to the management team for review. Managers can use it to determine if further action is needed to mitigate the impact of changes in certain assumptions.

Cost: Installation time: 🕰️ 🕰️

5–17 Automatically Link the Budget to Purchase Orders

A budget is not of much use if it is not tightly linked to company operations. It is common for a company to spend an inordinate amount of time constructing a fine budget and then struggle with how to force the company to live by it. When this happens, the people who participated in creating the budget wonder why they spent time on it and will certainly be less willing to do so in the future. In this instance, the budget is seen as a mere formality.

To avoid the problem, one can link the budget to purchase orders. Under this method, the budget is loaded into the purchasing database used by the purchasing staff to create purchase orders. Whenever they enter a new purchase order into the computer system, they must include the account number to which the expense is charged; the system then compares the total year-to-date or period-to-date expense for this item to the budgeted amount and either issues a warning for an overbudget expenditure or rejects it. By using this best practice, one can be assured of keeping expenditures within budgeted levels.

However, there are some issues to deal with when using this system. One is that there may be necessary reasons for making an expenditure, such as an emergency purchase of some kind that must be made in order to keep the facility

Exhibit 5.3 Budget versus Actual Report

Description	Spent Year-to-Date	Full Year Budget	Budget Remaining
Auto	$ 42,000	$ 80,000	$ 38,000
Building Repairs	100,100	150,000	49,900
Insurance	53,000	55,000	2,000
Interest Expense	12,000	24,000	12,000
Maintenance	39,000	41,000	2,000
Office Supplies	5,000	7,000	2,000
Telephones	14,000	20,000	6,000
Travel	18,500	19,000	500
Utilities	21,000	30,000	9,000

running. In this case, it may be useful to allow a manager to override the system with a special password. Also, some managers may be caught unawares toward the end of the year—if they have spent an inordinate amount earlier in the year, they will have no funding available at all for the last few weeks or months of the year. In this situation, it is best to forewarn managers over the course of the year by issuing a simple report, such as the one shown in Exhibit 5.3, that lists each expense item, the year-to-date amount spent, the full-year budget, and the amount left to spend. This information allows managers to know the exact amount available for their use and generally avoids the problem of people running out of money at the end of the year.

Cost: 💵💵💵   Installation time: 🕰🕰🕰

5–18 Issue a Budget Procedure and Timetable
✔*Author's Choice*

The typical budget dies a lingering death. It is not issued on time, nor is the first issuance likely to be the last one. Instead, there are a multitude of last-minute changes that force the budget process to continue into the next year. As a result, the budget may not be usable as a basis of comparison for new year results for several months.

The best solution is to issue a tightly structured budget procedure to the organization, along with an accompanying timetable, that specifies when all activities will occur, who will complete them, and when a deliverable is due back at the budget manager's office. By laying out the process in this manner and following up closely on all due dates, it is possible to issue a complete budget on time, every time. A good budget procedure should include the following steps, at a minimum:

- *Benchmarking comparison.* Though rarely used in a budget, it is extremely useful to conduct a benchmarking comparison of corporate performance against those of "best in class" companies, and to provide this information with the budget packages that go out to all departments, so that they can set expectations for improvements in their areas. This task can be completed well in advance of the regular budget process.
- *Revenue budget.* The first part of the budget process is always a determination by the sales staff of what they think they can sell in the upcoming year. Without this information, the remainder of the budget is impossible to construct. This portion must be completed and returned before any other steps can be completed.
- *Materials budget.* The purchasing department uses the revenue budget to determine its purchasing volumes, which is necessary for forecasting materials costs based on purchase volumes.
- *Automation budget.* The industrial engineering staff must determine what automation it plans to add to the production floor in order to eliminate direct labor and improve efficiencies. The timing of when these changes will be completed has a major impact on when to budget changes in labor and efficiencies into the forthcoming budget.
- *Personnel budget.* There must be a separate budget that outlines all the staff positions needed, their average pay rates, and the associated payroll burden. This number will vary based on the revenue volumes that were previously determined, not to mention any automation projects.
- *Capital budget.* The automation budget will feed into the capital budget, since these projects usually require a considerable amount of funding. There may be other capital projects that do not run through the engineering department, such as for office equipment, so this budget is not normally completed until all departments have submitted their budgets.
- *Departmental budget.* Each department must note its expected expenditures, as well as personnel requirements.
- *Cash flow budget.* After all the previous budgets are returned, the accounting staff loads them into the budget model, which determines any resulting profits or losses, working capital changes, and capital requirements, all of which feed into the cash flow budget.
- *Funding and investments budget.* The cash flow budget feeds into the funding and investments budget. This one is used by the chief financial officer, who determines either the sources and cost of funds (if cash is needed) or where it is to be invested and the expected returns from doing so (if there-will be a

cash surplus). The results of this budget will also feed back into the interest expense and investment income line items elsewhere in the budget.

- *Employee performance budget.* Finally, after the budget is completed, the human resources manager uses it to create an employee performance budget that links pay levels and bonus payments to the performance levels noted elsewhere in the budget, such as completing automation projects or attaining budgeted sales levels.

Also, some companies may want to include an acquisitions budget, which is closely linked to the funding and investments budget, since this activity will have a major impact on cash flows.

The preceding list of budget modules makes it obvious that the budget process flows in a very specific sequence, with one part of the budget being used as a basis for the next part. The budget procedure and timetable must be built around this budget flow; specific dates of completion for one piece of the budget tie into the start date of the next part of the budget that requires information from the first part. It is wise to include a buffer of a few days between the completion date of one part and the start of the next, so that inevitable completion troubles can still be ironed out, leaving sufficient time to complete the overall budget by the targeted date. Do not be surprised if the timetable is not accurate in the first year it is used, since it is difficult to estimate completion times. Just be sure to note actual completion dates in the first year and adjust the timetable accordingly in the following year. Only by constant adjustment over a long period of time will the budget procedure and timetable become fine-tuned tools for the efficient and orderly completion of the budget.

Cost: **Installation time:**

5–19 Preload Budget Line Items

The traditional way to create budgets at the department level is to send each department manager a copy of the year-to-date department financials, and a blank budget form for the next year, with a detailed procedure for how to fill out the budget form for every line item in the department's budget. By doing so, department managers are taken away from their operational duties for an extended period of time, while they read through the procedure and make a series of educated guesses about what their revenues and expenses will be for the upcoming year. The considerable amount of time taken up by budgeting activities is one of the main reasons why the budgeting cycle is roundly detested by many managers.

This level of aversion can be mitigated by having the accounting staff preload many of the budget line items. Most expenses are relatively fixed from year to year, or are easily linked to key drivers, such as head count. Consequently, the accounting staff can probably arrive at more accurate budget numbers than a department manager for most line items. This approach leaves only a few of the larger and more variable accounts for managers to enter in the budget form. In some cases where a department is anticipating no major changes for the next budget year, it may even be possible for the accounting staff to create the entire department budget, so the department manager only has to make revisions to it. However, total preloading tends to shift responsibility (and blame) from the department managers to the accounting department, and so should only be used with caution.

Procedurally, the accounting staff should negotiate with each manager the number of budget line items they are to fill out, and the basis upon which they are to arrive at their numbers. The basis used could be the previous year's numbers multiplied by the current inflation rate, or a set dollar amount per department employee. Once this agreement is set up, it can usually be rolled forward over multiple years with little subsequent change.

Cost: 💵   **Installation time:** ⏰ ⏰

5–20 Adopt Two-Stage Capital Budgeting

The average operations manager does not have a degree in finance, and does not want one. And yet, part of the capital budgeting process requires them to fill out a funds application that requires justification based on such discounted cash flow models as net present value or an internal rate of return, as well as cash flow modeling during each year of the proposed project. The typical manager will require a great deal of time to complete this application, and there is a significant risk that it will not be completed correctly, given the low expertise level of the user.

A better approach is to split the capital budgeting procedure in two—only expensive capital requests are still required to follow a comprehensive application process, while lower-cost ones can follow a simplified application process that is easier for managers to complete. The more comprehensive approach will still be needed for the 20 percent of capital requests that require about 80 percent of all funding, leaving the simplified approach for all remaining requests, which should be about four out of every five requests.

A simplified capital request should not require a discounted cash flow analysis; a simplified matrix showing when cash expenditures are anticipated should form the core of the financial analysis. Also, those managers still required to wade through the more comprehensive application form should receive some help—the accounting manager can assign a budgeting specialist to each manager who is filling out this form and assist the manager with the creation of a discounted cash modeling part of the application. This assistant can also review the application for mistakes, which will reduce the number of iterations to which the application is likely to be subjected.

Cost: 💵   **Installation time:** ⏰

5–21 Purchase Budgeting and Planning Software

The vast majority of businesses create and maintain their budgets using an electronic spreadsheet such as Excel. Though this approach works fine for small
organizations, it is quite unwieldy for large ones. The trouble is that individual
departments create their own budget models using formats that vary from the
one used by the budgeting department. When the budgeting staff receives these
models from the various departments, they must manually reinput the information into a master spreadsheet, which is quite labor-intensive. Also, when any
significant variable is added to the model, all related formulas must be manually
altered and then tested to ensure that the model still operates properly. Further, it
is difficult to track which department has submitted budget information or when
it made its last update. For these reasons, larger companies have considerable difficulty using spreadsheets as the basis for a budgeting system.

The solution is to purchase budgeting and planning (B&P) software. This
software maintains a central database of budgeting information that is automatically updated when users enter information. They can enter information in
a variety of ways—via dial-up modem, through a local or wide area network, or
the Internet (depending on what software is purchased). The software can also
be maintained off-site by an application service provider (ASP). In addition, the
software generates templates for data-entry use by each department, as well as
issuing all pro forma financial reports at the press of a button. The better systems
also have workflow management capabilities that reveal who has not yet submitted a budget. Variance analysis tools issue warnings to the budgeting staff
when submitted budgeting information exceeds predetermined levels or when
other preset rules are violated. A variety of other capabilities are available, such
as automatically calculating line-of-credit projections, designing what-if scenarios, determining inventory requirements based on sales and turnover levels, and
conducting ratio analysis.

These are complex software systems that require customized installation, so
one should expect to pay more than $100,000 for the larger systems. A pay-as-you-
go ASP solution will be significantly less expensive in the short term, and may be a
better solution if a company wants to see how the system works before investing in
an in-house installation.

A more advanced version of budgeting and planning software is called business performance management (BPM) software. A BPM system is usually layered
on top of a company's data warehouse and is useful for measuring the performance
of an entire organization, and then connecting the analysis to budgets and forecasts.
Though separate software packages are available for both budgeting and performance measurement, the BPM systems are capable of seamlessly connecting the
two areas, resulting in less software maintenance and the elimination of data inconsistencies among multiple systems.

Cost: 💵💵💵   Installation time: ⏰⏰⏰

5–22 Reduce the Number of Accounts

Some budget models are astoundingly complex because there are so many account line items in which to record budgeting information. This is nearly always the fault of the controller, who has allowed the chart of accounts to grow to an excessive degree. Once there are too many accounts in the general ledger, it becomes obligatory to budget for the contents of each one. This presents the dual problems of adding new lines to the budget every year, and of forcing managers to do extra analysis to determine the budgeted amounts for the upcoming year.

The solution is to eliminate as many accounts as possible from the chart of accounts. This takes a long time, since one must be careful to shift account balances to surviving accounts, verify that inactivated accounts are not used for some special purpose, and confirm that there will be no impact on the resulting financial reports. Given the intricacies of eliminating accounts, it is usually best to do so in small groups of just a few per month, with an overall reduction in the number of accounts taking as long as a year to complete. Once this is done, it is a simple matter to eliminate the same accounts from the budget.

Another approach that is not only quicker, but also bypasses the need for a lengthy reduction in the chart of accounts, is to eliminate the accounts in the budget model, but to keep them in the actual chart of accounts. This option will result in no budget in the upcoming budget period for those accounts that have been excluded from the budget model, so it is only useful for those accounts with very small balances. Thus, this is only good for a few accounts and is not as definitive a solution as eliminating accounts from the chart of accounts for good.

Cost: 💵   Installation time: 🕐 🕐 🕐

5–23 Revise Budgets on a Quarterly Basis

Most organizations create new budgets just once a year. By doing so, they make estimates of sales volume for a number of months into the future that are extremely difficult to meet, and then build a "house of cards" of projected expenses and capital purchases that are justified by these weak sales numbers. Because of the difficulty of estimating sales, managers tend to err on the conservative side, estimating revenues that are too low. Furthermore, when the budget year has been completed, the management team tends to waste time arguing about why actual performance did not meet the expectations set within the budget. Finally, any unexpected changes in the business during the year, such as an acquisition or the elimination of a product, will not be included in the budget, so all budget-versus-actual analyses will be off by the amount of these changes, rendering the analyses worthless.

One can incrementally revise budgets on a quarterly or even a monthly basis in order to avoid these problems. By doing so, all key revenue and related expense or capital decisions can be revised to reflect short-term changes in the business, making the budget a much more relevant document.

The difficulty with this best practice is the greatly increased number of required budgeting iterations. Since this is generally considered to be a difficult process to complete just once a year, imagine the consternation of management if the process is done again every three months! To reduce the pain of this process, one should consider shifting away from the use of electronic spreadsheets for budgeting calculations, instead using commercially sold budgeting packages that allow for direct updating of budget information in the model over the Internet or the company intranet, while also allowing for easy changes to the budget model without the attendant calculation errors that are so common in an electronic spreadsheet. By making this change, budgeting iterations are much easier to complete.

Cost: **Installation time:** 🕰️ 🕰️

5–24 Simplify the Budget Model

A company that has used the same budgeting model for many years will find that it gradually becomes more complicated. This is because there are incremental changes each year—a new analysis page here, extra departments there, perhaps some assumptions as well. Though the changes seem minimal if looked at for just one year, the accumulation over many years makes the model very cumbersome, difficult to understand, and prone to error. For example, if formulas are added to the budget that require inputting the final balance sheet numbers from the previous year, it is possible that no one will remember this when the next budgeting cycle arrives in the following year, especially if the person who made the change in the previous year is no longer with the company, or if the change was not documented anywhere. As the number of these changes pile up over the years, it becomes increasingly difficult to complete the budget on time. The person managing the budget model becomes increasingly indispensable, for no one else knows how to use it.

To avoid these problems, it is necessary to regularly simplify the budget model. This does not mean that the simplification can be done once and then dropped. On the contrary, the standard budget procedure should begin with a review of the model from the previous year to ensure that all budget line items and calculations are thoroughly documented and understandable, and that they are still needed. There should also be a step that specifically requires the budget manager to review the need for extra line items and formulas, with an eye to eliminating as much as possible from the budget model every year. Though it may not be possible to completely streamline the budget model in one year, a continuing effort in this area will yield excellent results as long as the review is continual.

An added benefit of simplifying the budget model is that less budgetary "gaming" arises. For example, when a large number of expense categories are used, managers tend to resort to all kinds of expense juggling as the budget year progresses in order to ensure that actual expenses incurred exactly match the amounts budgeted. These games are a waste of corporate resources, since they take management time away from the corporate mission. By summarizing many revenue and expense line items into just a few budgetary line items, managers will have the leeway to run the business in response to ongoing developments in the marketplace, rather than in accordance with the dictates of the budget.

Though the main focus of this best practice is to reduce the complexity of the budget model, it is sometimes sufficient to ensure that the model is adequately documented. Some businesses really become more complex over time and therefore require more detailed budget models. This is particularly true of companies on a fast growth track, especially if they are growing by acquisition and must account for the operations of many new businesses. In these cases, the budget manager should review the model at the end of each budget cycle to see what has been added to the model this year, and verify that complete and thoroughly understandable descriptions have been included in the budget procedure that note the reasons for the changes, how they work, and the resulting impact on the entire budget model. This step may be all that is needed for some companies.

Cost: 💵   **Installation time:** ⏰

5–25 Use Online Budget Updating

One of the most difficult problems for a budget manager in a large company is bringing together the budget information arriving from a multitude of outlying company locations. For example, a location may send budget updates on paper or a compact disc, either of which requires the manual translation of this information into the budget model by the budget manager's staff. If there are many locations reporting budget information, this can result in a flood of work for several days. Also, the person reentering the budget information may make a typing error, thereby altering a budgeted amount from what a subsidiary intended, or may misconstrue the submitted data and list a budget number in the wrong account. In either case, the budget must be reviewed by the subsidiary and a request made to adjust the error, which takes still more time and effort.

An excellent best practice that entirely eliminates this problem is to give subsidiaries direct online access to the budget model. They can then enter it themselves, make any necessary changes, and review the results. By doing so, all errors are made, and must be corrected, by the subsidiaries, taking this chore away from the central accounting group.

There are two problems with this best practice. One is that all subsidiaries must acquire online access to the budget model. The second item is more critical: Anyone from any subsidiary can now have access to the entire budget model, with the ability to delete it, alter information for other parts of the company, or just observe the numbers budgeted for other divisions or departments, which can be confidential. To avoid this problem, it may be necessary to split the budget into different files, one for each subsidiary, and then give password access only to the portion of the budget assigned to each subsidiary. Another option is to keep the budget model in one piece, but to restrict access by passwords to

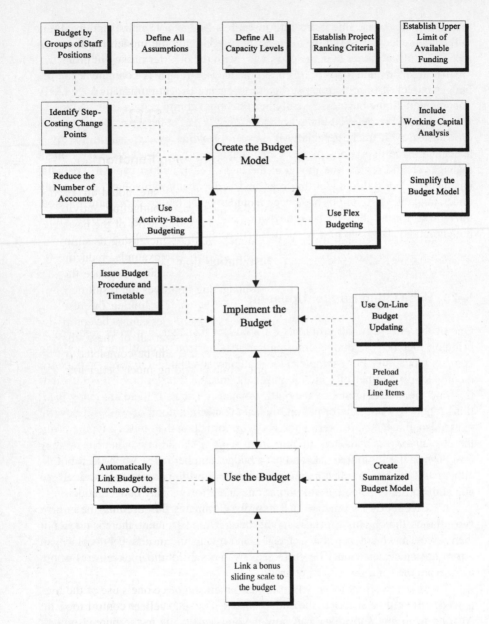

Exhibit 5.4 Impact of Best Practices on the Budgeting Function

just those account codes that apply to each subsidiary. The first option allows a company to use an electronic spreadsheet to contain the model, but the latter approach requires that it be stored in a database with better password protection than is typically available for an electronic spreadsheet. A company can pick either option based on its overall need for securing budget information.

Cost: Installation time:

Total Impact of Best Practices on the Budgeting Function

Most of the best practices discussed in this chapter are noted in Exhibit 5.4, where they are clustered around the three main budgeting activities— creating the budget model, implementing it, and using it. Most of the best practices impact the creation of the budget model, either by increasing its simplicity or by improving the information that goes into it. For example, reducing the number of accounts and budgeting by groups of staff positions reduce the size of the model, while using activity-based budgeting improves the resulting information. Finally, several methods are available for closely linking the resulting budget model to company operations, so that most activities cannot be completed without some interaction with budget information. What all of these changes amount to is a highly efficient budgeting process that can be completed in less time than the previous budgeting system, while providing much better information to the management team.

Summary

This chapter focused primarily on those best practices that improve a budget model's ease of use as well as the quality of the information it produces. These are the very issues most managers complain about, since many budget models take an eternity to produce and are not that accurate when released. Since the bulk of the changes in this area are easy and inexpensive to implement, there is no reason why an active and enterprising accounting manager cannot swiftly replace the old budgeting system with one that is easy to use and results in excellent budgeting information.

There was a lesser focus on best practices that enhance one's use of the budget once it has been produced. Since the budget is an excellent control tool, the best of these practices is one that ties the budget directly to the purchase order system, so that purchase orders can be automatically compared to the remaining available budget and rejected by the computer if there are no budgeted funds remaining. Another best practice links a bonus sliding scale to the budget, while another creates a summarized budget model for further financial modeling work by members of management. These are effective ways to maximize the budget once it has been produced.

Chapter 6

Cash Management Best Practices

This chapter covers the best practices that can be used to create a more efficient cash management function. Though this area falls into the finance function at many larger companies, it is typically under the authority of the controller in a smaller company, and so is covered in this book.

The best practices in this chapter are primarily concerned with creating an orderly flow of cash into and out of a company's coffers, leaving no cash in the system that is not being properly utilized to the fullest extent. This method frees up the largest possible amount for investment purposes. The vast majority of these best practices are complementary, working most effectively if they are all used at once.

This chapter begins with a discussion of the implementation problems associated with each best practice and then moves on to cover the advantages and disadvantages of using each one. The final section discusses how to use most of these best practices as a group to achieve a cash management system with a high degree of efficiency.

Implementation Issues for Cash Management Best Practices

All of the best practices covered in this chapter are noted in Exhibit 6.1, which shows the cost and duration of each item. In nearly all cases, cash management implementations are quite inexpensive and can be completed in a short time. The reason for these easy setups is that there is no custom programming involved, and no need to involve other departments. Without these two problem areas, it becomes an easy matter to install a whole range of best practices in short order. To make the situation even easier, a company's bank is usually eager to help install most of these items, because they involve creating close banking ties, which keeps a company from moving its banking business elsewhere. A bank can also charge fees for many of these services, which gives it an added incentive to help out. Thus, cash management is an area in which a controller can enjoy great success in improving operations.

Though all of the best practices noted in Exhibit 6.1 are covered in some detail later in this chapter, it is useful to see how the most important ones fit together into a coherent set of cash management practices. Accordingly, there is a flowchart in

Exhibit 6.1 Summary of Cash Management Best Practices

	Best Practice	Cost	Install Time
6–1	Access bank account information on the Internet	💵	⏰
6–2	Automatically apply cash	💵💵	⏰⏰
6–3	Avoid delays in check posting	💵	⏰
6–4	Collect receivables through lockboxes	💵💵	⏰⏰
6–5	Install remote deposit capture	💵	⏰
6–6	Consolidate bank accounts	💵	⏰⏰
6–7	Implement physical cash sweeping	💵	⏰⏰⏰
6–8	Implement notional pooling	💵	⏰⏰⏰
6–9	Implement controlled disbursements	💵	⏰
6–10	Negotiate faster deposited-check availability	💵	⏰
6–11	Open zero-balance accounts	💵	⏰
6–12	Shift money with electronic funds transfer	💵	⏰

Exhibit 6.2 that shows how lockboxes and cash sweeping can be used to accumulate cash from customers and forward it into a central bank account, from which cash is distributed only as needed to a payroll zero-balance account (for payments to employees) and a controlled disbursements account (for payments to suppliers). By using this approach, cash can be quickly sent to the main bank account and doled out only when company checks are cashed, which allows the cash management staff to transfer all remaining funds to an investment account where it can earn interest, rather than lying idle in any number of corporate checking accounts.

6–1 Access Bank Account Information on the Internet
                                                                ✔ Author's Choice

If the accounting staff needs to know the current balance outstanding on a loan, savings, or checking account, the most common way to find out is to call the company's bank representative. This is a slow and sometimes inaccurate approach, since the representative may not be available or will misread the information appearing on the screen.

An easier approach is to provide bank customers with direct access to their account information through a Web site. This access is free, requires no special

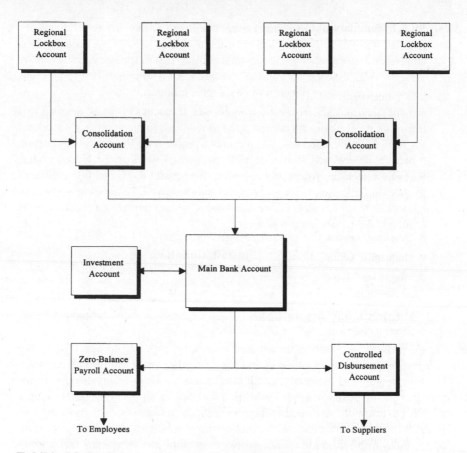

Exhibit 6.2 Bank Account Structure Using Best Practices

software besides an Internet browser. The more advanced sites allow users to download check images, initiate wire transfers, and move funds between accounts.

When conducting on-line bank reconciliations, it is best to do so on a daily basis. There are three reasons for using a daily reconciliation. First, it improves one's knowledge of the current cash position. Second, there is little reconciliation work remaining at month end, which contributes to a faster close. Finally, a daily review will uncover control problems more quickly, possibly leading to reduced fraud.

There are a few procedural issues to be aware of when conducting daily bank reconciliations:

- *High transaction volume.* If there are many daily transactions to cross-check, it is easy to miss one. If so, either reconcile in clusters by type of transaction (deposits first, checks second, etc.) or print the bank's daily transactions and manually cross off each one as it is reconciled.

- *Missed days.* It is easy to forget to reconcile every day. To avoid this problem, list it in the daily work log to be the first item handled each day, so it is completed before other issues arise and force it into the background. Also, always verify that the accounting records were reconciled for the previous day when conducting the current day's reconciliation.

- *Record electronic transactions on weekends.* If batches of check deposits and incoming ACH payments are recorded as received in the company's accounting records on the same day, this presents a problem for the person completing a daily bank reconciliation. An ACH payment will clear the bank at once, whereas a check payment may not clear for several days, making it difficult to check off all receipts for that day as being received. To avoid this problem, record electronic receipts on weekend dates, when there are no check receipts to muddy the reconciliation process.

Cost: **Installation time:** 🕐

6–2 Automatically Apply Cash   ✔*Author's Choice*

Even a well-run accounting department cannot be expected to apply incoming cash to outstanding receivables in less than one day, using traditional methods. The time required to manually match checks against open receivables, with the attendant problems of incorrect application and deduction management, is simply too great to allow for any notable improvements in process time. A good way out of this trap is to avoid it entirely by automating the bulk of all cash applications. When fully implemented, an automatic cash application system (sometimes known as AutoCash) can apply more than 90 percent of all cash receipts. This also results in lower days sales outstanding and provides a clear audit trail that may be useful for a Sarbanes-Oxley controls review.

The usual beginning point for an automated cash application is the lockbox. The lockbox operator records the magnetic ink character recognition (MICR) number and total payment amount from each received check, rather than the full remittance detail, and consolidates this information into an electronic feed that is sent directly into the company's accounting system. When performed manually, the lockbox data-entry cost per check is usually in the range of 15 to 30 cents.

The company's computer system uses the customer's bank account number (which is located within the MICR number) to match the check payment to the correct customer. The system then uses cash application rules to determine which invoices are being paid. Examples of these rules are:

1. Only apply the check to an invoice if the check exactly matches the amount of a single invoice. This is the most simplistic rule, and will result in the majority of all checks being kicked out for manual application.

2. Apply the check to multiple invoices that exactly match the check amount. To avoid excessive computer processing time to calculate all possible invoice combinations, this algorithm is usually restricted to just those invoices coming due for payment within the next few days, or those that are already overdue.

3. In addition to either of the first two options, match against the total shown on the most recent account statement sent to each customer.

4. In addition to any of the first three options, include an allowance for such deductions as freight or advertising allowances, which can be set by amount or percentage of invoice by individual customer.

Automatic cash application does not work with certain customers who continually take outsized deductions or refuse to pay freight charges or sales taxes. In these cases, it is best to flag the customers' payments for immediate manual application. By doing so, the cash misapplication rate can be greatly reduced, though the overall cash application rate will also decline.

The AutoCash system must also determine if there is a possibility of a duplicate match, where the payment could match any one of several invoices or invoice combinations. Duplicate matches are usually kicked out for manual application.

The overall cash application rate will gradually improve over time, as the user matches more MICR codes to customers, determines how to handle different types of deductions, and incorporates the payment patterns of customers into its system.

AutoCash applications are available on several ERP systems, including SAP and Oracle, and can also be found as an online application through 9ci, Inc.

Cost: 💵💵   **Installation time:** ⏰⏰

6–3 Avoid Delays in Check Posting

When there is a sudden influx of checks, the accounting staff may require an extra day to post them all against the accounts receivable database. This delay can also occur when the payments being made are slightly different from the invoices that they are paying, which requires some delay while the differences are reconciled. Though these problems can create a real bottleneck in the accounting department, they also result in a lengthening of the time interval before the checks are deposited at the bank, which in turn results in lost investment income.

To avoid this problem, the accounting staff can photocopy checks as they arrive, so that postings can be done from the copies, rather than the original checks. This allows the deposit to be made at once, rather than later. The main problem is the danger that a check will not be copied or that the copy will be lost, which results in a missed posting to the accounts receivable database. This problem leads to downstream collections and research problems involving backtracking to find the missing checks, thought it can be avoided through proper reconciliation procedures that match the total number of copied checks to the total number of actual checks, as well as the total amount posted to the total amount on the copied checks.

Cost: 💵   **Installation time:** ⏰

6–4 Collect Receivables through Lockboxes   ✔*Author's Choice*

There are a number of problems associated with receiving all customer payments at a company location. For example, checks can be lost or delayed in the mailroom, given to the wrong accounting person for further processing, or delayed in transit from the company to the bank. It is also necessary for the mailroom staff to log in all received checks, which are later compared to the deposit slip sent out by the accounting staff to ensure that all received checks have been deposited—this is a nonvalue-added step, though it is necessary to provide some control over received checks. All these steps are needed if checks are received and processed directly by a company.

The answer is to have the bank receive the checks instead. To do so, a company's bank sets up a lockbox, which is essentially a separate mailbox to which deposits are sent by customers. The bank opens all mail arriving at the lockbox, deposits all checks at once, copies them, and forwards the copies and anything else contained in customer remittances to the company. This approach has the advantage of accelerating the flow of cash into a company's bank account, since the lockbox system typically reduces the mail float customers enjoy by at least a day, while also eliminating all of the transaction-processing time that a company would also need during its internal cash-processing steps. The system can be enhanced further by creating lockboxes at a number of locations throughout the country, with locations very close to a company's largest customers. Customers will then send their funds to the nearest lockbox, which further reduces the mail float and increases the speed with which funds arrive in a company's coffers. If there are multiple lockboxes, a company should periodically compare the locations of its lockboxes to those of its customers, to ensure that the constantly changing mix of customers does not call for an alteration in the locations of some lockboxes to bring the overall mail float-time down to the lowest possible level. In short, there are some exceptional advantages to using lockboxes.

There are two problems with lockboxes. First, a bank will charge both a fixed and variable-rate fee for the use of a lockbox. There is a small, fixed monthly fee for the lockbox, plus a charge of a few cents for every processed check. For a company with a very small number of incoming checks, these costs may make it uneconomical to maintain a lockbox. Second, the work required to convince customers to change the company's pay-to address can be considerable. Every customer must be contacted, usually by mail, to inform them of the new lockbox address to which they must now send their payments. If they do not comply (a common occurrence), someone must make a reminder call. If there are many customers, this can be a major task to complete and may not be worthwhile if the sales to each customer are extremely small—the cost of contacting them may exceed the profit from annual sales to them. Thus, a company with a small number of customers or many low-volume customers may not find it cost-effective to use a lockbox.

An additional issue is the number of lockboxes to be used. A company cannot maintain an infinite number of them, since each one has a fixed cost that can add up. Instead, a common approach is to periodically hire a consultant, sometimes provided by a bank, who analyzes the locations and average sales to all customers, calculates the average mail float for each one, and offsets this information with the cost of putting lockboxes in specific locations. The result is a cost-benefit calculation that trades off excessive mail float against the cost of additional lockboxes to arrive at the most profitable mix of lockbox locations.

A final issue is that some customers will ignore all lockbox addresses and continue to send their checks directly to a company. When this happens, the controller can either process the checks as usual, using all the traditional control points, or simply have the mailroom staff put all the checks into an envelope and mail them to the lockbox. The latter approach is frequently the best because it allows a company to completely avoid all cash deposit procedures. The only case where the traditional cash-processing approach may still have to be followed is when a company is in extreme need of cash and can deposit the funds more quickly by walking them to the nearest bank branch to deposit immediately. Otherwise, all checks should be routed through the lockbox.

Consequently, one or more lockboxes can be a highly effective way to avoid the cumbersome check deposit procedure, while also accelerating the speed of incoming cash flows. In only a minority of situations will a lockbox not be a cost-effective alternative.

Cost: 💸💸   **Installation time:** ⏰⏰

6–5 Install Remote Deposit Capture   ✔ *Author's Choice*

If a company does not use a lockbox to accelerate its cash flow from check receipts, then it must physically transfer all checks from the accounting department to the local bank. If the person normally assigned to handle this task is not available, or if the department is too short-staffed to spare a person, then the company misses an extra day before the checks are deposited. If the bank is located relatively far away, then depositing also wastes a fair amount of time by the person assigned to make the deposit.

A much better alternative is to install a remote deposit capture system on-site. This involves scanning all checks through a scanner that is linked to a computer, and then sending the scanned check images over the Internet to the bank. This avoids all of the time that would normally be spent walking the checks over to the bank, and so pays for the monthly scanner rental fee just with the saved staff time. The process also results in a slight reduction in check clearing time.

The mechanics of the check scanning process are as follows:

1. Sort checks by the bank account name into which they will be deposited.
2. Add up the check totals for each bank account.
3. Enter the first batch total in the scanning software.
4. Scan the checks related to that batch.
5. Verify that the scanned totals match the batch total. If not, adjust either the batch total or individual check amounts.
6. Approve the batch for transmission to the bank.
7. Print a deposit slip for internal documentation.
8. Retain the checks for 15 business days, and then shred them.

Remote deposit capture does not work for foreign checks, which must still be manually deposited at the bank.

Cost: 💵   **Installation time:** ⏰

6–6 Consolidate Bank Accounts   ✔*Author's Choice*

A time-consuming chore at the beginning of each month is to complete reconciliations between the bank statements for all the company's bank accounts and the book balances it maintains for each of those accounts. For example, a retail store operation may have a separate bank account for each of hundreds of locations, each of which must be reconciled. Also, if it is the controller's policy to wait for all bank accounts to be reconciled before issuing financial statements, this can be the primary bottleneck operation of the monthly close. Finally, having many bank accounts raises the possibility that cash will linger in all of those accounts, resulting in less total cash being available for investment purposes. To use the previous example, if there are 100 retail stores and each has a bank account in which is deposited $5,000 (a decidedly modest sum for a single location), then $500,000 has been rendered unavailable for investment. Thus, having a multitude of bank accounts leads to a variety of downstream problems, which can seriously impact the efficiency of some portions of the accounting department, while also reducing the amount of cash readily available for investment purposes.

The best solution is to merge as many of them together as possible. To use the previous example, rather than give a bank account to each store, it may be possible to issue a fixed number of checks to each location, all of which will be drawn upon the company's central bank account. This reduces the number of bank accounts from 100 to one. If anyone feels that there is a danger of someone fraudulently cashing a large check on the main bank account, this problem can be resolved by mandating a maximum amount for each check, above which the bank will not honor the check. By limiting the amount per check and the number of checks, this control effectively resolves any risk of a major fraud loss by consolidating all bank accounts. This is also an effective approach when acquiring another company, since its bank accounts can be merged into the existing account. In both cases, reducing the number of accounts also makes it much easier to track the cash balances in each account. Thus, account consolidation is an effective approach for improving accounting efficiency as well as the management of cash flows.

There are some problems to consider before consolidating bank accounts. First, there may be automatic withdrawals taken out of an account. If the account is closed down and merged into a different account, the automatic withdrawal will be terminated, resulting in an unhappy supplier who is no longer receiving any money. To avoid this problem, the transactions impacting each account must be reviewed to ensure that all automatic withdrawals are being shifted to the consolidated account. Also, there are legal reasons for keeping some accounts separate, such as a flexible spending account, into which employee deductions are deposited and from which a plan administrator withdraws funds. Finally, consolidating too many bank accounts may result in a very difficult bank reconciliation chore. Sometimes it is easier to keep a small number of separate accounts, just to make the reconciliation process somewhat easier to untangle and resolve. However, with the exception of these few cases, it is generally possible to reduce the number of bank accounts to a bare minimum, resulting in greater efficiency and more cash available for investment.

Cost: **Installation time:** 🕰 🕰

6–7 Implement Physical Cash Sweeping   *✔ Author's Choice*

When a company sets up a *zero-balance account*, its bank automatically moves cash from that account into a concentration account, usually within the same bank. The cash balance in the zero-balance account (as the name implies) is reduced to zero whenever a sweep occurs. If the account has a debit balance at the time of the sweep, then money is shifted from the concentration account back into the account having the debit balance. An example is shown in Exhibit 6.3.

In the example, two of three subsidiary accounts initially contain credit (positive) balances, and Account C contains a debit (negative) balance. In the first stage of the sweep transaction, the cash in the two accounts having credit

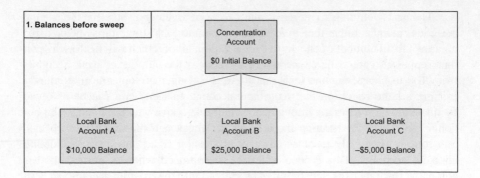

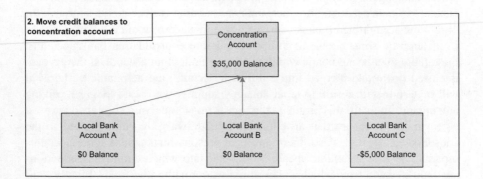

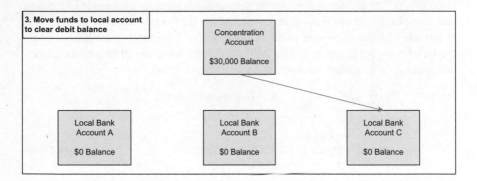

Exhibit 6.3 Zero-Balance Sweep Transaction

balances are swept into the concentration account. In the next stage of the sweep, sufficient funds are transferred from the concentration account to offset the debit balance in Account C. At the end of the sweep, then, there are no credit or debit balances in the zero-balance accounts.

It is also possible to use *constant balancing* to maintain a predetermined minimum balance in a subsidiary account, which involves sweeping only those cash levels above the minimum balance, and reverse sweeping cash into the subsidiary account if the balance drops below the minimum balance.

Daily sweeping may not be necessary outside of a company's designated core currencies. This is especially likely when noncore currency account balances are relatively low. If so, it may be more cost-effective to sweep them less frequently, or to implement *trigger balances*. A trigger balance is an account balance level above which excess funds are swept out of the account.

Some concentration banks can also monitor a company's account balances at third-party banks using SWIFT[1] messages, and create transfer requests to move excess cash to the concentration bank. The key point with account sweeping is to fully automate it—the effort involved in manually tracking account balances and shifting funds on a daily basis is not only expensive but also likely to cause errors.

In most sweeping transactions, the sweeps occur on an *intraday* basis, which means that balances are transferred to the concentration account before the end of the day. Consequently, some cash may be left behind in subsidiary accounts, rather than being centralized. This occurs when cash arrives in an account after execution of the daily sweep. The cash will remain in the subsidiary account overnight, and be included in the following day's sweep. If a bank can accomplish true *end-of-day* sweeps, then no cash will be left behind in local accounts. If a company is not dealing with such a bank, then a proactive approach to depositing checks before cut-off times is the best way to avoid unused cash.

There may be a need to track the amounts of cash swept from each zero-balance account into the concentration account; if so, the company records an inter-company loan from the subsidiary to the corporate parent in the amount of the cash transferred through the cash concentration process. Here are four reasons for doing so:

1. *Subsidiary-level financial reporting requirements.* A subsidiary may have an outstanding loan, for which a bank requires the periodic production of a balance sheet. Since account sweeping shifts cash away from a subsidiary's balance sheet, detailed sweep tracking is needed to put the cash back on the subsidiary's balance sheet for reporting purposes. This can be done by recording an intercompany loan from the subsidiary to the corporate parent in exchange for any swept cash, which can then be reversed to place the cash back on the subsidiary's balance sheet.

---

[1] Society for Worldwide Interbank Financial Telecommunication

2. *Interest income allocation.* A company may elect to allocate the interest earned at the concentration account level back to the subsidiaries whose accounts contributed cash to the concentration account. Some countries require that this interest allocation be done, to keep a company from locating the concentration account in a low-tax jurisdiction, where the tax on interest income is minimized. Thus, the amounts of cash swept into and out of a subsidiary account must be tracked in order to properly allocate the correct proportion of interest income to that account.

3. *Interest expense allocation.* Some tax jurisdictions may require the parent company to record interest expense on intercompany loans associated with the transfer of cash in a physical sweeping arrangement. If so, the company must track the intercompany loan balances outstanding per day, which is then used as the principal for the calculation of interest expense. The interest rate used for these calculations should be the market rate; any other rate can be construed by local tax authorities to be transfer pricing designed to shift income into low-tax regions.

4. *Central bank reporting.* Some central banks require that they be sent reports on transfers between resident and nonresident accounts. This may be handled by the company's bank, but can still increase the administrative burden associated with the sweep.

Some banks have the capability to track the amount of balance sweeps from each subsidiary account on an ongoing basis, which a company can use as its record of intercompany loans.

Cost: **Installation time:** 🕰 🕰 🕰

6–8 Implement Notional Pooling

Notional pooling is a mechanism for calculating interest on the combined credit and debit balances of accounts that a corporate parent chooses to cluster together, without actually transferring any funds. This approach allows each subsidiary company to take advantage of a single, centralized liquidity position, while still retaining daily cash management privileges. Also, since it avoids the use of cash transfers to a central pooling account, there is no need to create or monitor intercompany loans, nor are there any bank fees related to cash transfers (since there are no transfers). In addition, it largely eliminates the need to arrange overdraft lines with local banks. Further, interest earnings tend to be higher than if investments were made separately for the smaller individual accounts. Also, it offers a solution for partially owned subsidiaries whose other owners may balk at the prospect of physically transferring funds to an account controlled by another entity. And finally, the use of notional pooling is not a long-term commitment; on the contrary, it is relatively easy to back out of the arrangement.

Where global notional pooling is offered (usually where all participating accounts are held within a single bank), the pool offsets credit and debit balances on a multicurrency basis without the need to engage in any foreign exchange transactions. An additional benefit of global notional pooling lies in the area of intercompany cash flows; for example, if there are charges for administrative services, the transaction can be accomplished with no net movement of cash.

Once a company earns interest on the funds in a notional account, interest income is usually allocated back to each of the accounts composing the pool. For tax management reasons, it may be useful for the corporate parent to charge the subsidiaries participating in the pool for some cash-concentration administration expenses related to management of the pool. This scenario works best if the corporate subsidiaries are located in high-tax regions where reduced reportable income will result in reduced taxes.

The main downside of notional pooling is that it is not allowed in some countries, especially in portions of Africa, Asia, and Latin America (though it is very common in Europe). In these excluded areas, physical cash sweeping is the most common alternative. Also, the precise form of the notional pooling arrangement will vary according to local laws, so that some countries allow cross-border pooling while others do not.

In addition to the prohibition against notional pooling in some countries, it is difficult to find anything but a large multinational bank that offers cross-currency notional pooling. Instead, it is most common to have a separate notional cash pool for each currency area.

Cost: 💵   **Installation time:** ⏰ ⏰ ⏰

6–9 Implement Controlled Disbursements

The person who is in charge of managing corporate cash flows is always trying to find ways to retain cash for investment purposes, thereby earning interest for a company. There are unethical ways of doing so, such as not paying suppliers even when previously agreed-upon pay dates have been surpassed. However, these activities can destroy a company's reputation with its suppliers and even impact its credit rating.

A legitimate way to retain cash for an extra day or two is to use controlled disbursements. This best practice is based on the principle of mail float, which means that one can print and immediately mail a check to pay for an invoice on its due date and the supplier can receive and cash it, but the check will not clear for a day or two longer than was previously the case, resulting in extra time during which a company still has control over its funds. For example, a company in Denver can issue checks that are made payable to a bank in Aspen, Colorado, which, due to its isolated location, requires an extra day for checks to clear. When checks are presented to the Aspen location for payment, a daily batch of cash required to cover the payments is forwarded to the company's primary bank. The company can access this cash requirement information every day and forward just enough money to the controlled disbursement account to cover cash requirements for that day. These extra steps give a company the capability to keep virtually all of its excess cash in investments, extracting only the bare minimum each day to cover immediate cash requirements. Thus, controlled disbursements not only allow a company to retain its cash longer, but also to use the new off-site bank account as a zero-balance account. Both of these actions can significantly increase the amount of a company's operating funds on hand.

One problem with a controlled-disbursements account is that the amount of additional float made available through this method is gradually shrinking, as the Federal Reserve Bank gradually eliminates those pockets of inefficient-check clearing throughout the country. This may require a company to periodically change the location of the bank that it uses as its check-clearing point. Eventually, the longest additional float time to be gained by this method will probably be limited to a single day. Also, the concept is one of the most expensive bank services. Consequently, the cost must be carefully calculated and offset against projected benefits to ensure that it is a worthwhile implementation project.

Given the cost of controlled disbursements, this is a best practice that is best used by a company with a significant volume of cash flow, which ensures that the incremental benefits of retaining a large amount of cash for an extra day or two will adequately offset the cost of this service.

Cost: **Installation time:** 🕰️

6–10 Negotiate Faster Deposited-Check Availability

One of the standard tricks used by banks to create a larger store of funds that they can invest is to delay the availability of money from deposited checks. One can see delays of as long as five days for some checks, and much longer periods for checks drawn on international banks, even though the checks may have cleared much sooner. As a general rule, if checks are not clearing the bank within two days, then it is time to either negotiate with the bank to reduce the amount of float it is taking or to switch to another bank that is willing to make money available within a shorter time frame.

This option is not a realistic one for smaller businesses, since they have minimal leverage with their banks. Also, some companies that deal with many out-of-state customers will experience a much slower actual check-clearing time than those whose customers are located within the same state—this simply reflects the mechanics of the check-clearing process, and cannot be accelerated below a minimum level.

Cost: 💵   **Installation time:** 🕰️

6–11   Open Zero-Balance Accounts

Whenever a company cuts a check to a supplier, it must deposit enough cash in its checking account to cover payment on the check. If it does not do so, then the bank may not honor the check when it is presented for payment, or it may advance payment but charge a fee for doing so. In either case, the penalties are considerable for not having sufficient cash on hand to cover company obligations. Many companies run the risk of not having sufficient funds on hand because they want to earn interest on their money for as long as possible (most checking accounts do not pay interest, or very little). Accordingly, the typical organization assigns someone the task of monitoring the rate at which checks are being cashed, guesses when checks will be cashed, and uses all sorts of time-consuming averaging methods to make a reasonable guess as to how much money should be left in the account each day. Not only is this an expensive way to manage cash, but sometimes those guesses are wrong, resulting in bounced checks or additional bank fees.

The zero-balance account is a better way. As its name implies, the zero-balance account requires no balance. Instead, when checks are presented to the bank for payment, the bank automatically transfers money from another company account, in the exact amount required to cover the check. This approach allows a company to store all funds in just one account, where it is easier to track and invest. There is also no problem with forgetting to manually transfer funds into the zero-balance account because all transactions are handled automatically. There is no risk of not having cash available to pay for a check, unless there are no funds in the account from which money is automatically being drawn. A common use of the zero-balance account is for payroll checks. A variation on this type of account is the controlled disbursement account (see the "Implement Controlled Disbursements" section earlier in this chapter), which is most commonly used for accounts payable checks. By using either or both of these types of accounts, a company can consolidate its funds into a central holding account, where it is both more visible and easily transferred out to various investment vehicles.

One problem with a zero-balance account is that the bank will charge a small monthly fee for maintaining the account, but this fee is easily offset by the interest earned on money that would otherwise have been sitting in the account. In addition, some very small companies with limited banking needs do not bother with a zero-balance account because they do not like the notion of having extra complexity in their banking procedures. These small organizations prefer to handle all banking transactions through a single bank account, which is certainly an acceptable approach when there is a limited volume of cash flow in and out of a company. With the exception of these two cases, however, most companies will find that having a zero-balance account is an excellent way to centralize their funds in a single location.

Cost: **Installation time:**

6–12   Shift Money with Electronic Funds Transfer

The cash management staff is sometimes called upon to make money transfers that are either very large or complex or are on a rush basis. An example is a large payment that must go to a supplier at once, possibly to avert a loss of credit standing. This may require a hand-carried local delivery or an overnight express delivery to the supplier. In any of these cases, the cash management staff will take an inordinate proportion of its time to process the movement of funds. There must be an easier way.

There is, and it is the wire transfer. This transaction is handled through a company's bank, which can shift money out of the company's bank account in minutes and route it to the supplier's account, even if it is located at another bank. There is little paperwork and no hand-carrying of checks. To function properly, a company needs the recipient's bank account number and bank routing number. The person sending the funds (who must be authorized to do so, with this authorization on file at the bank) then faxes the transfer information to the bank and waits for the transfer to take place. To make the process even more efficient, one can have fax forms already prepared for the most common wire transfer destinations, with all of the bank account information already filled in. A more advanced setup used by larger companies is to have all the wire transfer information stored in the computer system, so that wire transfer information can be sent electronically to the bank. Yet another version is to send wire transfers by accessing the bank's database on-line and performing all the work oneself. With all of these options for sending money to suppliers, there is bound to be an approach that meets the particular needs and resources of any company.

When a company sends funds internationally via a wire transfer, the recipient will likely be charged a stiff foreign exchange conversion fee by the receiving bank. The receiving bank can get away with a high fee (sometimes as much as 10 percent for smaller funds transfers) because it is the designated recipient, and so has a monopoly on the conversion of the funds into the local currency; the recipient cannot shop for a better exchange rate with other banks. To avoid these fees, the paying company can offer the recipient to pay in the recipient's currency in exchange for a lower price. The payer can then shop among several foreign exchange providers for the best exchange rate. At a minimum, a company should have its international customers quote in both the company's home currency and the supplier's local currency, so that the company can see if it can achieve a better exchange rate through its foreign currency provider.

Both the issuing and receiving banks in a wire transfer transaction charge high transaction fees. In particular, the payment recipient is charged a *lifting fee*, which its bank imposes for handling the transaction. This fee is deducted from the amount of the funds being transferred, which means that the amount ultimately received is always somewhat less than the amount expected, which interferes with account reconciliation.

If a company engages in a large number of wire transfer transactions, bank fees can add up to a significant expense. To avoid it, consider sending payments through the Automated Clearing House (ACH), an electronic network for the processing of both credit and debit transactions within the United States and Canada. ACH payments include direct deposit payroll, Social Security payments, tax refunds, and the direct payment of a variety of business-to-business and consumer bills. Within the ACH system, the *originator* is the entity that originates transactions and the *receiver* is the entity that has authorized an originator to initiate a debit or credit entry to a transaction account. These transactions pass through sending and receiving banks that are authorized to use the ACH system. The transaction costs associated with ACH payments are low, typically about 10 percent of the fees charged for wire transfers. In addition, it is easy to set up recurring payments through the ACH system, and settlements are fast. Consequently, the ACH system is the electronic payment method of choice within the geographic region where it can be used.

There is no comprehensive equivalent of the ACH system that is available worldwide. Instead, similar electronic payment systems have been created in a number of countries, which are intended for payment transactions within those countries. A few large international banks have created links between these systems, which simulate a global ACH system. Under their systems, a company enters payment information, which the banks then reformat into the standard format of the country where the payment will be made. As such integrated systems become more common, there will likely be a decline in wire transfers in favor of global ACH payments. These payments will be especially popular among recipients, who are not charged the lifting fees that are common for wire transfers.

Cost: 💰   **Installation time:** ⏰

Total Impact of Best Practices on the Cash Management Function

An accounting department is well advised to implement nearly all of the best practices advocated in this chapter, for most of them work well together to centralize funds for easier investment, while accelerating the flow of incoming cash and slowing its outflow. The layout of the recommended best practices is shown in the flowchart in Exhibit 6.4. That flowchart shows that most cash management best practices are concentrated in just two areas—the inflow of cash from customers and its outflow to suppliers. To make these best practices work most efficiently, it is best to implement them fully in either of these two main areas in order to achieve the most efficient flow of cash. For example, the subcategory of cash inflows should be completely implemented, which means installing the remote deposit capture, lockbox, and cash-sweeping best practices, prior to moving on to the other subcategory of cash outflows. If one were to take a more scattershot

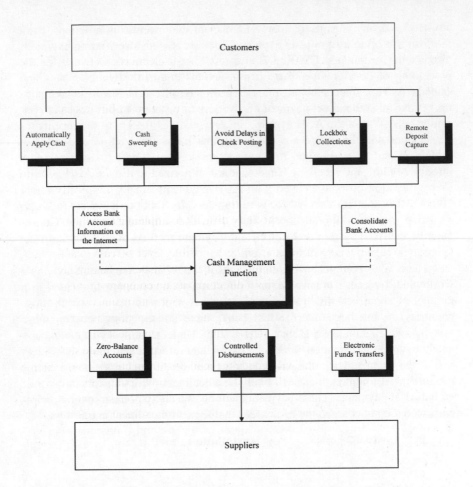

Exhibit 6.4 Impact of Best Practices on the Cash Management Function

approach to implementing these best practices, the efficiency of the overall process would be severely degraded. For example, implementing the lockboxes without cash sweeping would run the risk of having received funds sit idle in various bank accounts around the country, since the cash-sweeping practice, which automatically moves the funds into a central account, has not yet been implemented.

If it is not possible, for whatever reason, to implement a cluster of these best practices, then it is best to first implement either those with the greatest cost-benefit or else the one resulting in the greatest increase in operational efficiency. Under this scenario, the best practices with the greatest cost-benefit impact would be either controlled disbursements or lockboxes, since both approaches result in the retention of cash for a longer period, which gives a company more days to invest it. Alternatively, if efficiency is the main implementation criterion, then a controller should strongly consider a combination of cash sweeping and reducing the number of bank accounts—both practices result in much less work for the accounting staff in tracking where cash is located in a company's bank accounts. However, rather than focusing on a few best practices, it is best to implement a complete cash management system; the resulting impact on cash flows and profitability is worth the effort.

Summary

This chapter is unusual in that none of the best practices presented are mutually exclusive, nor are any of them especially difficult to implement, and most can be created at low cost. As a result, this is a prime area for an accounting manager to explore in order to achieve the highest possible level of cash management efficiency. Best of all, efficiency in this area directly equates to having more cash available for investments, which has a direct impact on company profits—one of the few functions covered in this book in which corporate management can see an immediate and measurable impact as a result of implementing best practices.

Given the high visibility of implementing cash management best practices, it is important to install as many of them as possible. In particular, there should be a set of lockboxes in place that will reduce the mail float from customers, as well as cash-sweeping processes that accumulate funds from the lockbox accounts and move them to the central bank account. There should also be zero-balance accounts to handle cashed payroll checks, and a controlled-disbursement account for paying suppliers. If this array of bank accounts is in place and is properly managed, there should be a noticeable increase in the average amount of funds on hand that can be profitably invested.

Chapter 7

Collections Best Practices

One of the worst jobs in any company is collecting on overdue accounts receivable. The person who must do the collecting never knows if an invoice has gone unpaid due to the company's fault or the customer's. There may be a very valid problem caused by the company that is making the customer wait on payment of the invoice, such as a damaged product shipment, a billing for the incorrect amount, or pricing that does not match the customer's purchase order amount. In these cases, the collections person apologizes to the customer for the company's sins and then tries to correct the internal problems responsible for the collection trouble. In other cases, the collections problem may be caused by the customer, who either cannot pay or who is deliberately stretching the payment period past the agreed-upon date. In such situations, the collections person must diplomatically bring pressure to bear on the customer, which is a difficult skill. No matter what the reason for an invoice being overdue, the collections person must ascertain the correct reason for the problem and fix it.

This chapter provides many best practices that allow a collections staff to reduce the error rate of invoices being sent to customers, while also providing new tools to force customers to pay by the due dates listed on company invoices. In addition, there are several best practices here that can enhance the operational efficiency of the collections staff. In short, this chapter makes the collections task easier, while reducing the amount of overdue accounts receivable at the same time.

Implementation Issues for Collections Best Practices

There are a surprisingly large number of best practices that can be applied to collections. Some are located in other functions, such as sales and credit, that have a direct impact on the collections function, while others are more directly associated with the activities of the collections department. Most of these best practices are relatively inexpensive and easy to implement, as noted in Exhibit 7.1. The exhibit notes the estimated cost and install time of implementation for each best practice. In most cases, it is a relatively simple matter to complete an implementation, with the exception of those items that require custom computer programming or that involve the participation of another department. In these two cases, either the risk of a lengthy programming project or the refusal of another department to

Exhibit 7.1 Summary of Collections Best Practices

	Best Practice	Cost	Install Time
Collection Management			
7–1	Accept check payments by fax	💵	⏰⏰
7–2	Clearly define account ownership	💵	⏰
7–3	Optimize the collections staff	💵	⏰
7–4	Designate a skip tracing specialist	💵💵	⏰
7–5	Educate the sales staff about revenue recognition	💵	⏰⏰
7–6	Utilize collection call stratification	💵	⏰
7–7	Base deduction management on transaction volume	💵	⏰
7–8	Require customer billing of marketing deductions	💵	⏰⏰
7–9	Conduct customer conference calls with sales staff	💵	⏰
7–10	Grant percentage discounts for early payment	💵💵	⏰
7–11	Conduct immediate review of unapplied cash	💵	⏰
7–12	Outsource collections	💵💵💵	⏰
7–13	Prepare a customer bankruptcy action plan	💵	⏰
7–14	Sell your bankruptcy creditor claim	💵	⏰
7–15	Simplify pricing structure	💵💵	⏰⏰⏰
7–16	Write off small balances with no approval	💵	⏰
7–17	Create an accurate bad debt forecast	💵	⏰
Collection Systems			
7–18	Use automated ACH debits	💵	⏰
7–19	Compile customer assets database	💵💵	⏰⏰
7–20	Maintain access to customer orders database	💵	⏰
7–21	Subscribe to special event notifications	💵	⏰
7–22	Set up automatic fax of overdue invoices	💵💵💵	⏰⏰⏰
7–23	Issue dunning letters automatically	💵💵	⏰⏰
7–24	Automate email delivery of overdue invoice information	💵💵💵	⏰⏰⏰
7–25	Use a collection call database	💵💵	⏰⏰⏰

Exhibit 7.1 *(Continued)*

	Best Practice	Cost	Install Time
Collection Systems			
7–26	Access up-to-date collection agency information	💵	⏰⏰
7–27	Implement customer order exception tracking system	💵💵	⏰⏰
7–28	Install a dispute tracking system	💵💵💵	⏰⏰⏰
7–29	Report on ongoing customer complaints	💵	⏰⏰
7–30	Link to comprehensive collections software package	💵💵💵	⏰⏰
7–31	Use real-time cash application techniques	💵	⏰

cooperate can jeopardize a successful implementation. An example of the first problem is automatically faxing overdue invoices to customers, while a good example of the second problem is persuading the sales department to adopt a simplified pricing structure. However, with the exception of these two problem areas, one will find that improving the collections function with the best practices contained in this chapter is a relatively easy endeavor.

7–1 Accept Check Payments by Fax

A serious collection dilemma for the collections person is having a dilatory customer say the check is being mailed—which then takes an unpardonable amount of time to arrive, indicating that the check was not mailed right away. If the collections person asks that a check be sent by overnight delivery service, then either the customer balks at the extra cost or the company must pay the fee.

An alternative delivery method is check-by-fax. Under this approach, the customer faxes the completed and signed check to the collections person, who promptly enters information from the check into check-printing software that is readily available from a number of companies. The company then prints the checks using approved check security paper, which is readily available from an office supply store. The check is created using standard printer ink, not magnetic ink character recognition (MICR) ink. The check will not have a signature line. Instead, it will contain a block of text where the signature line was, stating something similar to the following:

> **SIGNATURE NOT REQUIRED**
>
> Payment has been authorized by the depositor.
> Payee to hold you harmless for payment of this document.
> This document shall be deposited only to credit of payee.
> Absence of endorsement is guaranteed by payee's bank.

The company then deposits the check with its bank. The bank may need to process the check manually, since it does not use MICR ink, but it should accept the check. The net result of this process is that the company has eliminated the mail float from the collection process.

Because the company must obtain the customer's authorization, it is useful to retain a copy of the faxed check. A variation is to send the customer a check authorization form, which the customer fills out and returns by fax, along with a voided check. The information used in this process can also be collected over the phone, but that approach is not recommended, since it is prone to error and also results in no documentary evidence from the customer.

Cost: **Installation time:** 🕰️ 🕰️

7–2 Clearly Define Account Ownership

The sales staff is frequently unwilling to make collection calls on behalf of the accounting staff, because this takes away from their time in making new sales. However, the best contact with the customer is the salesperson, who has probably met with the customer multiple times and has built up a firm relationship, thereby making the salesperson the most effective collections person a company has.

To improve the collections process, a company should clearly define who "owns" each customer account and assign collection responsibility to the salesperson who has been given account ownership. "Ownership" means that the salesperson's name or sales region number should be included in the accounting database for each customer name. This does not mean that the bulk of the sales staff's job is now collections, but rather that the accounting department's collections staff can now call on specific individuals in the sales department when they feel that they will not otherwise collect payment on an invoice. To enhance the cooperation of the sales staff in the enforcement of collections, the compensation of the sales department manager should be tied to the proportion of cash collected from customers, which will entice this person to force the cooperation of his or her staff with the accounting department.

This concept should also be extended to the collections staff. There are usually specific customer issues associated with the nonpayment of an invoice, which must be repetitively researched if a collection problem is circulated throughout the collection staff. A better approach is to assign customer accounts to specific collections personnel. By doing so, they gain an understanding of each customer's particular issues, as well as have a chance to build relationships with their accounts payable counterparts at the customers' place of business, which frequently results in faster resolution of issues and therefore quicker payment by customers.

Cost: **Installation time:**

7–3 Optimize the Collections Staff   ✔ *Author's Choice*

The effectiveness of the collections department depends on the ability of its staff to collect the highest possible percentage of funds from overdue customers. However, consider the tasks they are assigned—reviewing the aging report for target customers, looking up contact information, pulling account files, contacting customers, tracking promise dates, sending out letters, and so on. Of these tasks, only one results in collections—the actual customer contact. All of the other activities reduce the effectiveness of the collections staff because they are administrative in nature.

If those employees who are best at collections must handle all associated activities, then they will have far less time to make collection calls, so that the department manager must either hire and train additional employees to be collectors or accept a low level of favorable collection results.

The solution is to hire administrative staff to assist the collectors with all activities not directly associated with customer contacts. This means that someone else should determine which accounts should be contacted, look up contact information, pull account files, track promise dates, and send out follow-up letters—in short, every collections activity previously noted, except for the actual customer contact. Further, do not require collections personnel to attend unnecessary meetings or do anything that detracts from their core mission of collecting money from customers. If this seems like an expensive alternative, then consider how much more money the collections staff could obtain from customers if they had a laser focus on customer contacts, and nothing else.

The department manager must come to a key realization when taking this approach, which is that a top-quality collections person is a prized asset whose time must be carefully directed toward realizing the highest possible collection rate. Collectors are, in effect, the bottleneck in the collections department, so their time must be carefully managed.

Once the time of the collections staff has been fully optimized, the department manager can consider going a step further and assigning the best collections staff to the most difficult customers. This highly skilled group is the most likely to achieve the best possible collection percentage. However, this approach does not work so well if a bonus system is in place for rewarding high collection rates, because the best collections people are now being assigned the most intractable customers. This concept also gets away from the concept of giving all of the collections staff a level playing field for comparison to each other, since their portfolio sizes and clients are no longer comparable. Consequently, taking this extra step calls for considerable prior discussion of its downside impact on the staff.

Cost: **Installation time:**

7–4 Designate a Skip Tracing Specialist

The collections staff is trained in the art of collecting money from a company's customers, but it is not necessarily trained in how to track down those customers who do not wish to be found. If the staff cannot contact someone, it tends to stop all collection efforts or shift the account over to a collection agency, rather than invest any additional time in trying to track down the customer.

Skip tracing is the art of locating a debtor who does not want to be found. It requires knowledge of various databases that are not normally used by a collections person, natural inquisitiveness, and dogged determination. In other words, only a particular kind of person performs well in skip tracing, and that person is not necessarily a collections person. Instead, consider hiring an experienced skip tracer, and providing some of that person's compensation based on a share of any funds recovered.

An alternative is to outsource this function to a professional skip tracer. However, do not expect to pay a few dollars for a thorough skip trace. Though the Internet is replete with advertisements for skip traces costing $100 or less, such searches are only for perfunctory perusals of a few common databases. For a detailed search, expect to pay a skip tracer on an hourly basis, and set a maximum number of hours for each trace. If the company is searching for a judgment debtor, then many states allow the company to add collection fees to the principal amount of the judgment, which may make this a more palatable alternative.

Before conducting a skip trace, be sure to make a rational, hard-headed decision regarding whether this is worth the time. A really thorough skip trace can require many hours, so is it worth the effort if the amount owed by the debtor is not large? With this issue in mind, most skip tracers will initially conduct only a brief search of easily accessible databases before proceeding further. Part of this initial search should include bankruptcy records, since a recent bankruptcy will likely force the skip tracer to cancel any additional activities.

Here are some location techniques that skip tracers use:

1. *Send an empty envelope to their latest known address, with "Do Not Forward—Address Correction Requested" stamped on it.* The Post Office will return it in about a week with the target's forwarding address.

2. *Use People Search on www.411.com.* This online database is a simple way to locate anyone by their name who resides in the United States. The skip tracer can also enter their phone number or email address in the same site, and it will sometimes return an address. The results are spotty, but this is worth a few minutes of staff time.

3. *Use caller ID on incoming calls.* Sometimes enough inquiries will result in the target calling the skip tracer, just to see what the person wants. If so, have caller ID, so the skip tracer can identify them and store their phone number. Then use the Reverse Phone search on *www.411.com* to determine their address.

4. *Conduct a search on a search engine.* Though a name search on Google may return thousands of Web links, putting the name in quotes and adding a few key words about the target will rapidly reduce the number of relevant links.

5. *Conduct a search through a paid database service.* These online sites provide access to records of inmates, births and deaths, marriages, divorces, reverse phone records, and Department of Motor Vehicle records. Expect to pay anywhere from $7.50 for a simple record search to $50 for a thorough analysis.

6. *Contact friends, co-workers, relatives, and neighbors.* Though time consuming, this can be an extremely effective approach. The target usually slips and lets someone know their new address, so persistence pays. An especially effective approach is to contact the former landlord, who may have the target's credit application on file. If so, this may contain all kinds of useful tracing information.

Whatever method used, the skip tracer should keep a formal log of results that includes the target's key personal information, as well as the results of every type of search already listed. This consolidates records in one place and ensures that the skip tracer does not duplicate any steps.

Cost: Installation time:

7–5 Educate the Sales Staff About Revenue Recognition

The sales staff is the primary engine of corporate profitability, and so is inclined to offer a broad array of deal sweeteners or custom terms to customers in order to ensure that a sale is finalized. Examples of special deals include free training, free maintenance, reduced pricing on the next product upgrade, and delayed payments. These alterations can present a major problem for the accounting department, since special deals can result in multielement sales transactions that trigger complex revenue recognition rules. While it is common to have the accounting department review the terms of proposed sale agreements prior to their approval, those deals have likely already been discussed with customers, and so are difficult to change. Also, having the accounting staff constantly alter deal terms introduces delay into the closing process.

A better approach is to conduct ongoing training sessions for the sales staff about revenue recognition rules. Training should be offered frequently, since turnover in the sales department can be high. Also, it is useful to construct training sessions using examples of both good and bad contracts, so that the sales staff can easily see which contract terms are most likely to cause problems. Such training should be accompanied by a rules guidebook that includes examples of acceptable deal structures, or by posting the same information on a company Web site. Training and supporting materials should be updated at once if related accounting rules change.

This approach gives the sales staff an excellent view of the general revenue recognition rules under which the company operates, so they are more likely to structure deal terms that will be immediately acceptable to the accounting department. The result is simplified and shorter reviews by the accounting staff, with contract rejections or alterations becoming extremely unlikely. This has the added benefit of shortening the time required for contract review, which leads to more deals being closed more quickly.

Cost: **Installation time:** 🕗 🕗

7–6 Utilize Collection Call Stratification

The typical list of overdue invoices is so long that the existing collections staff cannot possibly contact all customers about all invoices on a sufficiently frequent basis. This problem results in many invoices not being collected for an inordinately long time. Additional problems requiring time-consuming research may include an incorrect product price, missing shipping documentation, or a claim that the quantity billed is incorrect. Consequently, collection problems linger longer than they should, resulting in slow collections and substandard cash flow.

A good approach for improving the speed of cash collection is to utilize collection call stratification. The concept behind this approach is to split up, or stratify, all of the overdue receivables and concentrate the bulk of the collections staff's time on the very largest invoices. By doing so, a company can realize improved cash flow by collecting the largest dollar amounts sooner. The downside is that smaller invoices will receive less attention and therefore take longer to collect, but this is a reasonable shortcoming if the overall cash flow from using stratified collections is improved. To implement it, one should perform a Pareto analysis of a typical accounts receivable listing and determine the cutoff point above which 20 percent of all invoices will constitute 80 percent of the total revenue. For example, a cutoff point of $1,000 means that any invoice of more than $1,000 is in the group of invoices that represents the bulk of a company's revenue. When it is necessary to contact customers for collections work, a much higher number of customer contacts can be assigned for the invoices over $1,000. For example, a collections staff can be required to contact customers about all high-dollar invoices once every three days, whereas low-dollar contacts can be limited to once every two weeks. By allocating the time of the collections staff in this manner, it is possible to improve cash flow.

The stratification approach can also be expanded to include other members of a company. If there is an extremely large invoice that must be collected at once, the collections staff can be authorized to request the services of other departments, such as the sales staff, in making the collection. This approach needs to be limited to large-dollar invoices, since the sales staff does not want to be making collection calls all day. However, using the stratification approach, it is reasonable to request their assistance in collecting just the largest invoices.

Cost: 💵   **Installation time:** ⏰

7–7 Base Deduction Management on Transaction Volume

The collections staff may be experiencing a flood of payment deductions or just a trickle. If there is a considerable volume of deductions, then the accounting manager will have a difficult time allocating deduction resolution work among the staff, which will resist the extra workload that is added to their other chores. Conversely, if there are just a few deductions, the common response is to let them pile up until a sufficient volume exists to keep someone busy for a longer block of time—which results in deductions lingering on the accounts receivable aging report.

The best approach for managing these deductions varies based on the incoming volume. For instance, if the collections staff is inundated with deductions, it makes more sense to assign deduction resolution work to people who specialize in a particular type of deduction, such as problems with shipment damage, pricing complaints, or product returns. This means that if a customer takes multiple types of deductions on one invoice, it may receive calls from a different clerk for each of the deductions. This may not seem efficient from the customer's perspective, but works well for the company.

A different approach is used when there is a low volume of deductions. In this scenario, it makes more sense to leverage the collection staff's personal knowledge of each customer to resolve items on a case-by-case basis. Further, there is not enough deduction volume to make it cost-effective to employ a clerk full time on deductions in general or on a single type of deduction.

A hybrid approach is to assign a specialist deduction clerk to a single type of deduction for which the company is experiencing high volume, but not for other types of deductions with lower volume levels.

Cost: 💵   **Installation time:** ⏰

7–8 Require Customer Billing of Marketing Deductions

Customer payment deductions can be caused by a variety of problems and issues, such as damaged goods, incorrect pricing, and marketing promotions. It is extremely difficult for the accounting staff to sort through the various deduction causes and disposition them. Of particular concern are deductions for marketing promotions, since the accounting staff probably has no access to the promotions, and does not know which ones are valid.

One way to completely avoid marketing deductions is to require customers to invoice the company for them, rather than taking them as deductions. By doing so, the accounts payable staff merely forwards them to the marketing department for approval, and the company pays the customer; the accounts receivable staff no longer sees these deductions at all, which can reduce the overall volume of deductions considerably.

The accounting staff should assist the marketing manager in writing a procedure for customers, stating the process flow to be followed for the reimbursement of marketing promotions. Many customers have gotten into the habit of taking these promotions as deductions, so a considerable amount of customer retraining may be required.

A variation on this approach can be used when the marketing department creates "co-op" advertising allowances for customers. If these allowances are stored in the accounting system, then all deductions can be automatically charged against a customer's co-op allowance total. While this approach does eliminate deductions, it does so indiscriminately, with some nonmarketing deductions inevitably disappearing into the co-op allowance bucket.

Cost: Installation time: 🕰 🕰

7–9 Conduct Customer Conference Calls with Sales Staff

The credit and collections staff historically has a combative relationship with the sales department, since the sales staff sometimes pushes for high-risk sales that the credit and collections group does not want to collect. However, these two groups possess a great deal of knowledge about customers, and both parties can learn from each other. A good way to do so is to schedule a monthly conference call for both departments to discuss customers.

The agenda should include topics of interest to both departments, so one group will not think it is handing over information and receiving nothing in exchange. For example, the credit and collections staff can discuss collection problems with specific customers, while the sales staff can address large upcoming sales for which they'd like to receive advance credit approval. To be even more fair, a manager from each department can take turns coordinating the discussion in successive conference calls.

To keep the discussion focused, an agenda should cover such ongoing topics as collection problems, credit requests, transaction errors, capital purchases needed to improve operations, and the status of outstanding problems from the previous conference call.

It may also be useful to bring in representatives from the customer support department, who can possibly offer additional insights about customer issues.

Cost: 🔲   **Installation time:** ⏰

7–10 Grant Percentage Discounts for Early Payment

Some companies have large customers that pay late all the time. These customers are important to the company, and the customers abuse the one-sidedness of the relationship by stretching out their payments. In these cases, a company has little leverage, for it will lose a significant volume of sales if it cuts off the errant customers or cuts back on their credit limits.

In these cases, a company may have no choice other than to grant an early payment discount to customers in order to bring in cash sooner. This approach is especially effective if a company is in immediate need of cash. Also, accounts receivable that are outstanding for a long time period will require a number of collection actions, whereas one that is paid immediately will not require any; thus, the use of an early payment discount reduces the cost of collections.

The discount is an easy one to implement. A company usually prints the discount on its invoices so that customers will see it the next time an invoice is mailed to them. However, most customers already have payment terms included in their payment databases and a sudden change in terms may not be noticed. Accordingly, it may be necessary to call the customers' accounts payable staffs to notify them of the change. An alternative approach is to offer the discount only to a few key customers representing a high volume of sales or who are constant late-payers. By reducing the number of customers who take discounts, a company can make more selective use of this tool. Another variation is to only offer the early payment discount if a customer pays the full invoice amount. With this rule in place, customers will be less likely to subtract deductions from the invoice amount, since they will be losing a valuable early payment discount. The rule still allows customers to dispute payments after making a payment, but at least the company now has received full payment, and so has better control over the dispute.

There are three problems with using an early payment discount. One is the cost. To entice a customer into an early payment, the discount rate must be fairly high. A common discount rate is 2 percent, which translates into a significant expense if used by all customers. Another problem is that it is somewhat more difficult to apply cash against accounts receivable if a discount is taken. Depending on the facility of the accounting software, an accounting clerk may have to go to the extreme of manually calculating the discount amount taken and charging off the difference to a special discounts account. Finally, a discount can be abused. If a customer is already stretching its payments, it may take the discount rate without shrinking its payment interval to the prescribed number of days. This can lead to endless arguments over whether the discount should have been taken, which the customer will win if it makes up a large enough percentage of a company's sales.

Granting early payment discounts can significantly reduce the amount of a company's overdue accounts receivable, but this is at the high cost of the discount, which can be abused by some customers. Accordingly, this best practice should be used with care to improve the payment performance of selected customers.

Cost: **Installation time:**

7–11 Conduct Immediate Review
of Unapplied Cash   ✔ *Author's Choice*

It is a common occurrence for a collections person to call a customer about an overdue invoice, only to be told that the check was already sent. Upon further investigation, the collections staff finds that, for a variety of reasons, the errant check has been sitting in an accounting clerk's "in" box for several weeks, waiting to be applied to an invoice in the accounts receivable aging. Common reasons for not performing this cash application include not having enough time, not understanding what the check is intended to pay, or because there are unexplained line items on a payment, such as credits, that require further investigation before the check can be applied.

None of the reasons for not applying cash are valid, given the consequences of wasting the time of the collections staff. Only two solutions need to be installed to ensure that cash is applied at once. First, cash application is always the highest priority of whomever is responsible for it, thereby avoiding all arguments regarding other items taking priority, or not having enough time to complete the task. Second, *all* cash must be applied, even if it is only to an "unapplied cash" category in the accounts receivable register for those items that cannot be traced immediately to an open invoice. In these cases, simply having the total of unapplied cash for a customer clearly shown in the aged accounts receivable listing is a clear sign that the customer is correct—it has paid for an invoice and now the collections person knows how to apply the cash that was already received. Applying cash to accounts receivable as soon as it is received is critical to ensuring that the collections staff has complete information about customer payments before calling a customer.

Ensuring that cash is applied on time is a key internal auditing task. Without periodic review by a designated auditor, the person in charge of cash applications may become lazy and delay some application work. To avoid this problem, audits must be regularly scheduled and should verify not only that all cash is applied in a timely manner, but that the amount of cash received each day matches the amount applied. If these controls are rigidly followed, it becomes an easy matter to enforce this most fundamental of best practices.

Cost: 💵   **Installation time:** ⏰

7–12 Outsource Collections

Some companies have a very difficult time creating an effective collections department. Perhaps the management of the function is poor, or the staff is not well trained, or it does not have sufficient sway over other departments, such as sales, to garner support in changing underlying systems in a way that will reduce the amount of accounts receivable to collect. Whatever the reason or combination of reasons may be, there are times when the function simply does not work. A variation on this situation is when a collections staff is so overwhelmed with work that it cannot pay a sufficient amount of attention to the most difficult collection items. This is a much more common problem. In either case, the solution may be to go outside the company for help.

One solution is to outsource the entire function or some portion of it. When doing so, a company sends its accounts receivable aging report to a collections agency, which contacts all customers with overdue invoices that have reached a prespecified age—perhaps 60 days old, or whatever the agreement with the supplier may specify. The supplier is then responsible for bringing in the funds. In exchange, the collections agency either requires a percentage of each collected invoice (typically one-third) as payment for its services or it charges an hourly rate for its efforts. It is almost always less expensive to pay an hourly fee for collection services, rather than a percentage of the amounts collected, though going with an hourly approach gives the supplier less incentive to collect payments. One way to reduce the cost of a collections agency is to have a ten-day free demand period in the contract. This means that a payment made by a debtor within ten days of placing the account with the agency will not require an agency collection fee. To counteract the reduced level of incentive, it is useful to continually measure the collection effectiveness of the supplier, and switch to a new supplier if only a low percentage of invoices is being collected. This can be an effective approach for quickly bringing a trained group of collection professionals to bear on an existing collections problem.

Before deciding on the outsourcing route, one must consider a variety of important issues that make this a solution for only a minority of situations. One problem is cost. It is always cheaper to keep the collections function in-house because the fees charged by any supplier must include a profit, which automatically makes its services more expensive. This is a particularly important problem if the payment method is a percentage of the invoices collected, since the percentage can be considerable. Another problem is that this approach does not allow one to use most of the other best practices that are discussed in this chapter—by moving the entire function elsewhere, there is no longer any reason to improve the department's efficiency. Only a few best practices, those that involve other departments, such as the sales and credit departments, are still available for implementation. Finally, and most importantly, outsourcing the collections function puts the emphasis of the department squarely on collecting money, rather than on the equally important issue of correcting the underlying problems that are causing customers to not pay their bills on time. A collections supplier has absolutely no incentive to inform a company of why customers are not paying, because by doing so it is giving a company information that will reduce the number of overdue invoices and reduce the amount of its business. For example, if a customer does not pay its bills because a company repeatedly misprices the products it is selling, the collections agency will not inform the company of its error because then the invoices will be fixed and there will be fewer invoices to collect. All of these issues are major ones, requiring considerable deliberation before a company decides to outsource its collections function. Typically, this best practice should only be used in situations where a company wants to outsource the collection of a few of its most difficult collection problems. In most other cases, it is infinitely less expensive to go in search of a qualified manager who can bring the collections department up to a peak level of efficiency.

Cost: **Installation time:**

7–13 Prepare a Customer Bankruptcy Action Plan

When a customer files for bankruptcy protection, a company may find itself losing access to valuable assets if it does not act in a rapid and coordinated manner across several departments. Accordingly, the controller should create a customer bankruptcy action plan, and activate it immediately upon notice of a customer's bankruptcy filing. Here are six key steps to include in the plan:

- *Stop shipments in process or transit.* Contact the warehouse manager to see if any shipments are in transit, and have them recalled, if possible. Similarly, contact the production scheduling staff and cancel any of the customer's production orders.
- *Demand product reclamation.* Make a demand in writing within ten days of the customer's receipt of goods that the company has shipped to it, asking for the immediate return of those specific goods. Although the bankruptcy court might not allow the return, it might allow the company better treatment of its claim, such as payment in front of general creditors.
- *Stop payables in process.* Contact the accounts payable manager and halt any payments that may be in process to the customer. The company can use these payables to offset an unpaid debt owed by the customer to the company.
- *Review customer contracts.* Contact the corporate legal department for a copy of any current contracts between the company and the customer to see if the company is under any delivery obligations to the customer, and what the

company's rights are in terminating the contract. This is a particular problem if there is a master purchase order (MPO) between the company and the customer, since the company must continue to honor the MPO until it expires.

- *Obtain critical vendor status.* If the company has a key supplier relationship with the customer, the customer can request that the bankruptcy court authorize it to immediately pay the company's claim, or some portion of it, in exchange for the company continuing to sell to the customer on credit.

- *Copy the notice to corporate counsel.* Be sure to send the bankruptcy notice to corporate counsel, who may wish to take additional actions if the company is owed a substantial amount by the customer.

In addition to these steps, the accounting staff should review the customer's list of debts owed to the company and file a proof of claim with the bankruptcy court if the document is missing any debts. The proof of claim form should include the name of the company, the amount claimed, the documents proving the claim, and whether the claim is secured. If the claim is secured, then it is assigned a priority ahead of unsecured claims, so be sure to indicate this in the claim. However, filing a proof of claim occurs some months after the initial bankruptcy notice, and so does not require the immediate action demanded by the steps just described.

    Cost: **Installation time:**

7–14 Sell Your Bankruptcy Creditor Claim

Despite a company's best efforts at credit screening, customers will occasionally end up in bankruptcy court. Though one may have a reasonable claim with an expectation of eventually being paid, it still may take well over a year for the customer to pay all claims, usually at pennies on the dollar. Further, payments are likely to be in the customer's stock, rather than cash, and the stock will probably be restricted. Also, someone on the company's accounting or legal staffs must take the time to monitor the case as it drags through bankruptcy court. Finally, the company's bank will not allow any receivables from a bankrupt customer in the calculation of its borrowing base, which restricts the amount of money that the company can borrow.

A reasonable alternative is to see the claim to a third party for cash. The third party then pursues the claim, with the hope of eventually earning a good return on its investment. The usual approach is for a potential purchaser to estimate the proportion of the claim likely to be paid, and then discount this amount based on the likely duration of the bankruptcy process before the claim is paid. If the creditor offers to sell its claims for an amount equal to or less than the discounted value calculated by the purchaser, then the deal will likely be completed. Claims purchasers also acquire multiple creditor claims in order to have greater control over approval of the bankrupt company's workout plan, potentially increasing the potential payout to the claims purchaser.

To ensure the highest possible value when selling a creditor claim, the accounting staff should complete five steps:

- *Maximize the claim.* If the customer is disputing any part of the claim, then contact the customer to resolve the issue immediately. Also, if the customer has understated its debt to the company on its Schedule F, then file a proof of claim with the bankruptcy court. Disputed claims are worth much less than undisputed ones.
- *Sell early.* Pricing on creditor claims tend to drop over time, as more information becomes available about the financial condition of the customer. Conversely, pricing is higher just after the customer issues its Schedule F, detailing all creditor claims, since this is the first time when claims purchasers have access to this information, and may bid up prices.
- *Shop the claim.* It is generally best to delay acceptance of the first offer received, because claims purchasers first try a general low-ball offer to many creditors, hoping to scoop up low prices from inexperienced sellers. Instead, contact other claims purchasers to see if better offers are available. If the claim has a security interest senior to that of general unsecured creditors, then it is worth a great deal more than an unsecured claim.
- *Demand immediate payment.* If a claims purchaser wants to delay payment, it may not have sufficient capital to issue the payment. Instead, sell to a purchaser who offers immediate cash.
- *Negotiate the claim refund provision.* The claims purchaser will insist on a claims refund provision, whereby the company must pay back the purchaser (with interest) if the court disallows or reduces the company's claim. It is difficult to avoid this clause, but the company's attorney should negotiate down the interest rate, additional fees, and the definition of a disallowance or claim reduction.

It is generally a good idea to sell a creditor claim, but proper attention to the points noted here will both reduce a company's risk of being taken advantage of by a claims purchaser and also maximize the size of the payment.

Cost: 💵   **Installation time:** ⏰

7–15 Simplify Pricing Structure

A common problem for the collections staff is when it tries to collect on an invoice containing a pricing error. This problem most commonly arises when the order entry staff has a complicated set of rules to follow when deriving pricing. For example, rather than using a single price for each product, there may be a different price for various volume levels a customer orders—perhaps $1 per unit if 1,000 units are ordered and $2 if only 500 units are ordered. The situation can become even more complicated if there are special deals in place, such as an extra 10 percent discount if an order is placed within a special time period, such as the last week of the month. When all of these variations are included in the pricing structure (and some companies have even more complicated systems), it is a wonder that the order entry staff ever manages to issue a correct product price! A special circumstance under which pricing becomes nearly impossible to calculate is when the order entry department of an acquired company is merged with that of the buying company, leaving the order entry people with the pricing systems of the purchased company, as well as that of their own. The inevitable result is that customers will frequently disagree with the pricing on the invoices they receive and will not pay for them without a long period of dissension regarding the correct price. Alternatively, they will pay the price they think is the correct one, resulting in arguments over the remainder. In either case, the collections staff must become involved.

The solution is a simplification of the pricing structure. The easiest pricing structure to target is one that allows only one price to any customer for each product, with no special discounts of any kind. By using this system, not only does the collections staff have a much easier time, but so does the order entry staff—there is no need for them to make complicated calculations to arrive at a product price. However, there are two main implementation barriers to this approach: the sales staff and customers. The sales staff may be accustomed to a blizzard of promotional discounts to move product and may also have a long tradition of using volume discounts as a tool for shipping greater volume. Similarly, customers may be used to the same situation, especially those that benefit from the current tangle of pricing deals. To work through these barriers, it is critical for the controller to clearly communicate to senior management the reasons why a complicated pricing structure causes problems for the collections and order entry staffs. The end result is usually a political tug-of-war between the sales manager and controller; whoever wins is the one with the most political muscle in the organization.

Thus, simplifying the pricing structure is one of the most obvious ways to reduce the difficulty of collections, but it can be very difficult to implement because of resistance from the sales staff. One must build a clear case in favor of pricing simplification and present it well before the concept can become a reality.

Cost: 💵💵   **Installation time:** ⏰⏰⏰

7–16 Write Off Small Balances with No Approval

The typical procedure for writing off a bad debt is for a collections person to complete a bad debt approval form, including an explanation of why an account receivable is not collectible, which the controller must then review and sign. The form is filed away, possibly for future review by auditors. This can be a time-consuming process, but a necessary one if the amount of the bad debt is large. However, some bad debts are so small that the cost of completing the associated paperwork exceeds the bad debt. In short, the control point costs more than the savings for small write-offs.

The obvious solution is to eliminate approvals for small amounts that are overdue. One should determine the appropriate amount for the upper limit of items that can be written off; an easy way to make this determination is to calculate the cost of the collections staff's time, as well as that of incidental costs, such as phone calls. Any account receivable that is equal to or less than this cost should be written off. The timing of the write-off, once again, depends on the particular circumstances of each company. Some may feel that it is best to wait until the end of the year before writing off an invoice, while others promptly clear them out of the accounts receivable aging as soon as they are 90 days old. Whatever the exact criteria may be, it is important for management to stay out of the process once the underlying guidelines have been set. By staying away, management is telling the collections staff that it trusts employees to make these decisions on their own, while also giving managers more time to deal with other issues. If managers feel that they must check on the write-offs, they can let an internal audit team review the situation from time to time.

By avoiding the approval process for writing off small accounts receivable, the collections staff avoids unnecessary paperwork while managers eliminate a waste of their time.

Cost: **Installation time:** 🕧

7–17 Create an Accurate Bad Debt Forecast

Creating an accurate bad debt forecast can be similar to reading tea leaves or consulting a crystal ball—it is very difficult to make actual results come anywhere near the forecast. The usual approaches are to either create a forecast based on specific expected losses or to assign a loss probability based on the age of various receivables. Neither approach works especially well.

An alternative with a greater level of accuracy involves assigning a risk class to each customer, and then assigning a loss probability to open receivables based on the risk class. Risk classifications can be calculated with elaborate in-house risk scoring systems, but there are many commercially-available alternatives available, such as FICO (Fair, Isaac and Company) scores for individuals or the Dun & Bradstreet Paydex and Financial Stress scores for businesses.

Here are the steps needed to create a bad debt forecast based on risk scoring:

1. Periodically obtain new risk scores for all current customers, excluding those with minimal sales.

2. Load the scores for each customer into an open field in the customer master file.

3. Print a custom report that sorts current customers in declining order by risk score.

4. Divide the sorted list into fourths (low risk through high risk), and determine the bad debt percentage for the previous year for each category.

5. Use the format in the following example to derive the bad debt percentage:

Risk Category	Current Receivable Balance	Historical Bad Debt Percentage	Estimated Bad Debt by Risk Category
Low risk	$ 9,500,000	0.8%	$ 76,000
Medium low	7,250,000	1.6%	116,000
Medium high	3,875,000	3.9%	151,125
High risk	750,000	7.1%	53,250
Totals	$21,375,000	1.9%	$396,375

Cost: Installation time: 🕐

7–18 Use Automated ACH Debits

In some industries, the invoices sent to customers are exactly the same every month. This is common in service industries, where there are standard contracts providing the same services for the same price and for long periods of time. Examples of such cases are parking lots or health clubs, both of which put their customers on long-term contracts to pay fixed monthly amounts. In these cases, a company issues invoices for the same amount every month to all of its customers. The customers then pay the same amount every month and the accounts receivable staff enters the same amounts into the accounting software as having been received.

When the same amount is due every month, a company can use automatic ACH debits from the bank accounts of customers. This approach eliminates the need to run any invoices, since the customers do not need them to make a payment. There are also no collection problems, since payments are automatic. Thus, this approach can completely eliminate the invoicing and collection steps from the accounting department.

Before implementing automatic deductions, one must first review the obstacles that stand in the way of a successful project. One issue is that some invoices will still be needed if a company elects to "grandfather" its existing customers, so that they do not have to pay through bank deductions. Another problem is that invoices are also required for the first month or two of business with a new customer, because it usually takes some time before the automatic deduction is set up and operating smoothly. A regular invoice may also be necessary for a new customer because the first month of service may be for only part of the month (e.g., if the customer starts at the middle of the month, rather than at the beginning), which is easier to bill through an invoice than a deduction. Another issue is if the customer's bank account is canceled. Though these appear to be a significant number of issues, they are still a small minority of the total number of transactions processed. Generally speaking, if a company has a large base of customers for whom there are consistent and identical billings, a very effective best practice is to convert those customers to automatic bank deductions.

Cost: 💵   Installation time: ⏰

7–19 Compile Customer Assets Database

If a collections person finds that a customer will not pay, the usual recourse is to reduce or eliminate the customer's credit limit and to use threats—dunning letters and phone calls. These instruments are frequently not sufficient to force a customer to pay. However, what a collections person does not always realize is that there may be some other customer assets on the premises that the company can refuse to ship back to the customer until payment is made. When these assets are grouped into a database of customer assets, the collections staff has a much better chance of collecting on accounts receivable.

A customer assets database lists several items the customer owns, but which are located on the company premises. One common customer asset is consigned inventory. This is stock the customer has sent to the company either for resale or for inclusion in a finished product the company is making for the customer. Another customer asset is an engineering drawing or related set of product specifications. Yet another is a mold, which the customer has paid for and which a company uses in the plastics industry to create a product for the customer. All of these are valuable customer assets, which a company can hold hostage until all accounts receivable are paid.

The best way to keep this customer assets information in one place is to store it in the inventory database, because it is already set up in most accounting systems and includes location codes, so that it is easy to determine where each asset is located. Most important in using this database, a collections person can designate a customer in the accounting system as one to which nothing can be shipped (with a shipping hold flag of some kind), which effectively keeps the shipping department from sending the asset to the customer—it cannot print out shipping documentation or remove the asset from the inventory database. This is an extremely effective way to keep customer assets in-house, rather than inadvertently sent back to a customer that refuses to pay its bills.

The only problem with this best practice is making sure that customer assets are recorded in the assets database when they initially arrive at the company. Otherwise, there is no record of their existence, making it impossible to use these assets as leverage for the collections staff. The best approach is to force all receipts through the receiving department, whose responsibility is to record all receipts in the inventory database. The internal auditing staff can review the receiving log to verify that this action has been completed. The only customer asset that may not be recorded in this manner is a set of engineering drawings, which enters the company site through the engineering department, rather than the receiving dock. The only way to record this information is by fostering close cooperation with the engineering manager, who must realize the need for tracking all customer assets. These steps will result in tight control over customer assets and a better chance of collecting overdue accounts receivable by the collections staff.

Cost: 💵💵   **Installation time:** ⏰⏰

7–20 Maintain Customer Orders Database

The previous section noted the need for compiling a listing of customer assets that can be used to apply leverage to customers to collect on overdue accounts. The same approach applies to customer orders. If a customer has a large open order with a company, it is likely that the customer will be quite responsive to pressure to pay for open invoices when those orders are put on hold. Consequently, an excellent best practice to implement is to give the collections staff current knowledge of all open orders.

Implementation of this practice is an easy one for most companies; just give password access to the existing customer orders database to the collections staff. This access can be read-only, so there is no danger of a staff person inadvertently changing key information in a customer order. An additional issue is that someone must be responsible for flagging customers as "do not ship" in the customer orders database. This is a necessary step since orders will inadvertently pass through the system if there is not a solid block in the computer on shipments to a delinquent customer. However, many companies are uncomfortable with allowing the collections staff to have free access to altering the shipment status of customers, since they may use it so much that customers become irritated. Consequently, it may be better to allow this access only to a supervisor, such as an assistant controller, who can review a proposed order-hold request with the sales staff to see what the impact will be on customer relations before actually imposing it.

In summary, giving the collections staff access to the open orders database for customers results in better leverage over delinquent customers by threatening to freeze existing orders unless payment is made. The use of this database should be tempered by a consideration for long-term relations with customers; it should only be used if there is a clear collections problem that cannot be resolved in some other way.

Cost: 💵   **Installation time:** ⏰

7–21 Subscribe to Special Event Notifications

The collections department can be completely blindsided by a sudden drop in the credit rating of a customer, possibly resulting in bankruptcy and the loss of all accounts receivable to that customer. Though a company can track payment histories over time, talk to other suppliers of a customer, or periodically purchase credit records from a credit analysis group, all of these options require a continual planned effort. Many collections departments do not have the time to complete these extra tasks, even though the cost of being blindsided can be very high. They just take the chance that customers will continue to be financially stable.

Rather than undergo the embarrassment of losing an account receivable through the sudden decline of a customer, it is better to arrange for automatic notification of any significant changes to the credit standing of a customer. To do this, a company can contract with a major credit rating agency, such as Dun & Bradstreet. This organization can fax or e-mail a notification of any changes to the status of a customer, such as a change in the speed of its payment, adverse legal judgments, or strikes, which may signal a decline in the customer's ability to pay its bills. With this information in hand, a credit manager can take immediate steps to shrink a customer's credit limit and put extra emphasis on collection efforts for all outstanding accounts receivable, thereby avoiding problems later on, when a customer may sink into bankruptcy. The credit manager can be especially effective in taking action if several triggering events have occurred over a short period of time, indicating a steep decline in a customer's financial condition.

The only problem with advance notification of a customer's credit standing is that the credit agency will charge a fee for its work. However, the price of the notification, usually in the range of $25 to $40, is minor compared to the potential loss of existing accounts receivable. The only case where a company would not want to have advance notification set up is for customers that rarely make orders and usually of a small size when they do; in this case, a small credit limit is adequate protection against any major bad debt losses.

Cost: 💰   **Installation time:** ⏰

7–22 Set Up Automatic Fax of Overdue Invoices

The most common request that a collections person receives from a customer is to send a copy of an invoice that the customer cannot find. To do so, the collections person must either access the accounting computer system to print out a copy of the invoice or go to the customer's file to find it. Then the collections person must create a cover letter and fax it and the invoice to the customer. In addition, the fax may not go through, in which case the collections person must repeat this process. This process is typically the longest of all collections tasks—a collection call may only take a few minutes, but faxing an invoice can take several times that amount.

Few companies have found a way around the faxing problem. Those that have done so automatically extract an invoice record from the accounting database and fax it to the customer—all at the touch of a button. To do so, a company must link the invoice file in the accounting database to another file containing the name and fax number of the recipient, combine these two files to create a cover letter and invoice, and route the two records to a fax server for automatic transmission, one that will keep transmitting until the fax goes through, and then notify the sender of successful or failed transmissions. The advantages of this approach are obvious: immediate turnaround time, no need for the collections person to move to complete a fax, and automatic notification if there is a problem in completing a fax. For a company with a large collections staff, this represents a monumental improvement in efficiency.

The trouble with setting up an automatic invoice-faxing system is that one must put together several functions that are not normally combined. This almost certainly calls for customized programming and may have a risk that the system will periodically fail, due to the complex interlinking of different systems. To give a picture of the complexity of this approach, the front end of the system must include an input screen for the collections person that allows entry of the customer's contact name and fax number, as well as any accompanying text that should go on the cover letter to accompany the faxed invoice. On the same screen, one should be able to enter an invoice number so that the software automatically searches the invoice file and selects the correct invoice. There may be an additional step at this point, where the system presents a text image of the invoice so the collections person can verify that the correct invoice is about to be transmitted. Next, both the invoice text and the information that goes on the cover letter must be converted to a digital image that can be transmitted by fax. After that, the images are transmitted to a server that is a standalone fax transmission device. The server will repeatedly fax out the images to the recipient for a fixed number of attempts. If the transmission is not successful, the fax server will notify the sender via an e-mail message (which requires a preexisting email system); conversely, it should also send a message indicating a successful transmission.

Obviously, it is a difficult task to combine the accounting database with a fax server and an email system and expect it all to work properly at all times. Common problems are that information will not be successfully transmitted between the various components of the system, resulting in no fax transmission, or that the e-mail notification system does not work, resulting in no messages to the collections staff, who have no idea if their faxes are being sent or not. Consequently, most companies with small collections staff do not deem it worth the effort to attempt such an installation. Only the largest corporations, with correspondingly large collections staffs, use this best practice.

Cost: 💵💵💵   **Installation time:** ⏰⏰⏰

7–23 Issue Dunning Letters Automatically

Some companies have so many small accounts to collect that they cannot possibly take the time to call all of them to resolve payment disputes. This is an especially common problem for very small accounts receivable, where the cost of a contact call may exceed the amount of revenue outstanding. In other cases, there is some difficulty in contacting customers by phone, usually because all collection calls are automatically routed to the voice mail of the accounts payable departments. In these cases, a different form of communication is needed.

The best way to contact either unresponsive customers or accounts with very small overdue balances is the dunning letter. This is a letter that lists the overdue amount, the invoice number, and date, and requests payment. There are normally several degrees of severity in the tone of the dunning letter; the initial one has a respectful tone, assuming that there has been some mistake resulting in nonpayment. There is a gradual increase in severity. The final letter is the most threatening and usually requires immediate payment within a specific number of days or else the account will be turned over to a collection agency, the customer will be converted to cash-on-delivery for all future sales, or some similar dire warning. As it is impossible to craft a separate dunning letter for every customer situation (given the cost of doing so), a collections department must create a standard set of dunning letters that can be used for all customers. Though an informal way of communicating, a form letter still gets the point across to the customer. There is also a standard time interval between the issuance of each in a series of dunning letters—perhaps two weeks past the initial invoice due date before the first letter is sent, with additional letters being sent every two weeks thereafter. This use of a series of dunning letters, issued at standard intervals, is an effective and low-cost way to reach customers with whom it is not cost effective or otherwise possible to communicate.

There are various degrees of automation that can be applied to the use of dunning letters. The easiest approach is to have a standard preprinted letter, easily copied and mailed to a customer. The next level of automation is to store standard letters in a computer network, where all collections personnel can access them and make small modifications to match the customers to whom they are being sent. Though simple, both of these approaches suffer from the same complaint—there is no way to automatically issue dunning letters at set intervals. Instead, one must rely on the collections staff to remember to send out the letters. A more automated approach that takes into account the time interval since the last letter is merging the dunning letters into the accounting software. To do so, some custom programming is required. The programming must automatically access a text file as soon as an invoice reaches a certain number of days past due and issue a dunning letter. A different text file must be accessed as the number of days past due increases, since more strident letters must be sent as the invoices become older. The letters can then be printed and mailed out each day in a batch. Though this last method provides the tightest control over the standard issuance of the correct kinds of dunning letters, it is more complicated to set up, so it is generally best to calculate the programming cost of making such a significant enhancement before proceeding.

The automatic issuance of dunning letters is a cost-effective method for establishing a continual communication with customers regarding overdue invoices. It is particularly suitable to those situations where it is impossible to create personal relationships with customers through more expensive collection calls.

Cost: 💵💵   Installation time: ⏰⏰

7–24 Automate Email Delivery of Overdue Invoice Information

The process of engaging in a dispute with a customer over an overdue invoice payment usually requires a number of steps, where the two parties eventually establish the reason for nonpayment and then exchange information supporting their sides of the dispute.

A company can clear away most of its side of this paperwork if it is willing to create a system that automatically assembles a standard set of documents and emails them to the primary customer contact. This approach can save a great deal of time by the collections staff, which would otherwise need to accumulate it manually, and does so on a fixed schedule, so that the information is issued as soon as a receivable payment is overdue.

Creating such a system requires a considerable amount of work. It must extract a copy of the invoice from the accounting system, the customer's original order from the order entry system, the proof of delivery from the warehouse management system, and possibly even a copy of the master pricing contract from the purchasing system—and then assemble it into a PDF-formatted package for email transmission. Given the considerable cost of this system, a company must have a large collections group that will save a large proportion of its time by having this level of automation installed. A lower-cost alternative is to incrementally add information from more company systems over time, gaining feedback from the collections staff to see what other information should be added that will assist in the collection effort.

Cost: 💵💵💵   Installation time: ⏰⏰⏰

7–25 Use a Collection Call Database   ✔*Author's Choice*

A poorly organized collections group is one that does not know which customers to call, what customers said during previous calls, and how frequently contacts should be made in the future. The result of this level of disorganization is overdue payments being ignored for long periods, other customers being contacted so frequently that they become annoyed, and continually duplicated efforts. To a large extent, these problems can be overcome by using a collection call database.

A typical collection call database is a simple one recorded on paper, or a complex one that is integrated into a company's accounting software package. In either case, the basic concept is the same—keep a record of all contacts with the customer, as well as when to contact the customer next and what other actions to take. The first part of the database, the key contact listing, should contain the following information:

- Customer name
- Key contact name
- Secondary contact name
- Internal salesperson's name with account responsibility
- Phone numbers of all contacts
- Fax numbers of all contacts

The contact log comprises the second part of the database and should contain:

- Date of contact
- Name of person contacted
- Topics discussed
- Action items

The information noted is easily kept in a notebook if there is a single collections person, but may require a more complex, centralized database if there are many collections personnel. In the latter case, a supervisor may need to monitor collections activities for all employees, and he or she can do this more easily if the data is stored in a single location. However, a notebook-based database can be set up in a few hours with minimal effort, whereas a computerized database, especially one that is closely linked to the accounting records for each account receivable, may be a major undertaking. The reason for the added effort (and expense) is that it may be necessary to custom-program extra text fields into the accounting software so that notations can be kept alongside the record for each invoice; this is a surprisingly difficult endeavor, given the number of changes that must be made to the underlying database. The most difficult situation of all is if a company uses a software package that is regularly updated by a software supplier. Any changes made to the software (such as adding text fields) will be destroyed as soon as the next upgrade is installed, since the upgrade will wipe out all changes made in the interim.

A good midway approach for avoiding these difficulties with a computerized database is to use a separate tracking system not linked to the accounting software. Such software packages are commonly used by the sales department to track contacts with customers and can be easily modified to work for a collections department. They can be modified for use by multiple employees, resulting in a central database of contact information easily perused by a collections manager.

The only problem with this approach is that there is no linkage between the customer contact information contained in the accounting software (e.g., names and addresses) and the same information in the tracking software. This contact information must be reloaded manually from the accounting software into the tracking software. Likewise, any change to the contact information in the tracking software must be manually updated in the accounting system. Despite its limitations, maintaining a separate tracking system in the computer is an inexpensive way to maintain a centralized contact database.

Cost: 💵💵   **Installation time:** 🕐🕐🕐

7–26 Access Up-to-Date Collection Agency Information

Most companies have an in-house collection system in place, which they use to track the status of collection efforts on overdue invoices. This approach works fine until the in-house collections staff forwards receivables to third-party collection agencies for more aggressive collection efforts. At this point, the company has no way to update its receivable information, short of calling each agency and manually updating information about each invoice. Though this solution may be sufficient for companies with a small volume of outsourced collection work, a more automated solution is needed for higher-volume entities. Here are some solutions that improve the flow of collections information back to the company:

- *Allow collection agencies online access to the corporate collections database.* Though this approach does result in the use of a single corporate database, as well as no need for additional staff data entry, it also presents several problems. First, collection agencies may obtain access to the company's entire receivables database, including information about other receivables and collection agencies. Also, the company must provide training to the collection agency, and also runs the risk that any data entered will be inaccurate. Further, because of the company's training investment, it will be more likely to use only a few collection agencies, rather than trying out new ones.

- *Obtain online access to collection agency databases.* This approach creates more labor for the company, which must extract data from collection agency systems and manually update its own database with this information. This approach also requires a learning curve, which will force the company to use a very small number of collection agencies in order to learn fewer systems.

- *Manage your own hosting service.* A company doing a sufficient amount of business with collection agencies can use a variation of the last bullet point, and create its own Web-based hosting service. By doing so, it makes selected collection data available on the Internet to its collection agencies, and provides them with data entry screens that they use to update collection status—which is then ported back into the company's collections database.

The last approach is the ideal one, but only for larger companies. The relevant solution will be the one most cost-effective to a company, given the volume of its collection activity and the nature of its in-house collection systems and technical support.

Cost: 💸   **Installation time:** 🕐 🕐

7–27 Implement Customer Order Exception Tracking System

Many of the problems that result in collections work begin much earlier, from the time an order is entered into the system to the time it is produced, shipped, and invoiced. This interval is not one that the collections staff has any direct control over (unless the collections manager happens to run the entire company!), which means that problems upstream from the collections department will nonetheless have a direct and continuing impact on the quantity and type of problems that the collections staff must handle.

A good best practice for rooting out problems before they become collection issues is to set up a reporting system to track exceptions for customer orders as they move through all of a company's various processes. By keeping close tabs on these reports, the manager of the collection function can tell when there will probably be collection difficulties. By determining problems with specific customer orders in advance, the collections manager can work with the managers of other departments (mostly by suggestion) to correct problems before orders are shipped. A crucial factor in the success of this best practice is the interpersonal skill of the collections manager, who must bring customer order exceptions to the attention of other managers in such a way that they will not reactive negatively, but rather work with the presented information to make prompt corrections to their systems.

Another use of the reports is to recognize which orders are likely to result in collection problems and to use this information to make collection calls earlier than normal, so that any customer problems can be discovered, addressed, and resolved before the associated accounts receivable become inordinately old. By using the exception reports to manage accounts receivable more closely, it is possible to maintain a high accounts receivable turnover ratio, which frees up working capital for other purposes.

The number of reports used to track customer order exceptions will vary dramatically, depending on the types of systems already in place, the services or products offered to customers, and the type of industry. This range of options makes a complete list of all exception reports impossible to present, but the following list is a representative sample of the types of information that a collections manager should consider using as the foundation of a comprehensive order exception tracking system:

- Customer orders with nonstandard prices
- Customer orders for which the delivery date has exceeded the requested date

- Customer orders for which the quantity on hand is less than the amount ordered
- Customer orders for which the scheduled production is later than the requested delivery date
- Customer orders for which partial deliveries have been sent
- Customer orders requiring special-order parts
- Customer orders requiring a special form of transportation
- Customer orders requiring a special form of packaging

All of these exception reports focus on nonstandard customer orders, or orders for which there is some kind of shortfall. They are a very effective tool for honing in on those orders for which there will probably be customer complaints, which may result in collection problems.

The ability of a collections manager to create all these reports will depend on the type of computer database used to collect data about customer orders. Also, there should be a good report-writing tool or a willing programming staff to assist in the creation of these reports. If these factors are in place, a collections department can benefit greatly from an advance knowledge of which customer orders are likely to result in collection problems.

Cost: Installation time: ⏰ ⏰

7–28 Install a Dispute Tracking System

Customers usually deduct payment amounts from invoices they owe because of problems caused by the originating company. Examples of these problems are product returns caused by faulty products or incorrect order processing, product damage due to incorrect shipment packaging, incorrect sales deals issued by sales personnel, and promotional or advertising deductions for deals that were not clearly specified by the marketing staff. Unfortunately, none of the staff in these areas in which the problems originated are likely to hear about the resulting collection problems, because the collection task is placed in the hands of a clerk, in either the accounting or treasury departments, who is thoroughly overworked, and who certainly has neither the tools nor the authority to drive corrective changes back through the organization.

The solution is to give this person the tools to do so, which can then be accessed by a high-enough level of manager to ensure that corrective actions are taken. A properly functioning deduction investigation system requires workflow software in which one can route information about the problem to the appropriate party. The software must be able to shift the action routing to different parties if action is not taken by predetermined dates, thereby ensuring that action is taken to correct deduction-related problems. A key part of the dispute tracking system is the reason code assigned to each dispute. The list of available reason codes should be carefully defined, standardized, and kept to a relatively short list. Although this issue may appear simple enough, it is extremely difficult to aggregate dispute information if the same types of disputes are identified using different reason codes. If a workflow management system routes disputes to different people based on assigned reason codes, then it is quite possible for disputes to be routed to the wrong person. The system must also allow one to review the linked electronic images of related documentation associated with the specific problem, which calls for a document digitizing system. Further, the system must periodically summarize the various issues causing deductions to be taken, and route this information to the senior management team, where they can spot emerging problems and ensure that they are resolved. Finally, an implementing company must have a central database for its various functional areas, such as is provided by an enterprise resource planning (ERP) system, so that all parties can have ready access to the various stores of information throughout the company that relate to the issue at hand. Clearly, these requirements are expensive, but they give one the opportunity to continually monitor the reasons for deductions and fix the underlying problems causing them. This capability is invaluable not only from the perspective of improving customer relations, but also because it reduces the ongoing cost of dealing with payment deductions.

A crucial result of a dispute tracking system is the identification of repeat offenders. These are the companies that always find a reason (or no reason at all) to dispute payments, thereby delaying their payments to the company. With a dispute tracking system in place, management can determine the average aggregate amount of disputed items outstanding with each repeat offender, estimate the in-house cost of dealing with these disputes, and then decide if it is still profitable to continue doing business with these customers or if it would be better to prune them out of the accepted customer list.

Cost: 💵💵💵   **Installation time:** ⏰⏰⏰

7–29 Report on Ongoing Customer Complaints

Some customers deliberately issue a series of complaints about an order, with the sole intention of extracting concessions from the company in the form of payment deductions, late payments, and product upgrades. Such a customer initially appears to be profitable, based on the standard profit on the products ordered. However, when the cost of employee time, deductions, and delayed payments are netted against the initial profit, transactions with these customers frequently end up being a loss.

The collections staff is probably well aware of these customers, since they must deal with them constantly. However, management does not deal with customers on a daily basis, and so needs a reporting system that can reliably pinpoint who is causing problems on an ongoing basis. They can then use this information to determine when the company should stop doing business with selected customers.

The reporting system should compile a customer complaints score based on the number of problems accumulated by the customer, in the form of such factors as deductions taken, calls recorded in the customer service database, and average days to pay. The report should accumulate this information over the recent past, such as the last three months or six months, and present customer scores in declining order, so the worst customers are listed at the top of the report.

If this reporting structure is too difficult to assemble, then at least manually summarize the various types of problems for the small subset of customers causing the most trouble and present it on a trend line. The use of a trend line is important, since it will highlight those customers who are continually causing problems, rather than those who have had legitimate issues with a single order.

Cost: **Installation time:** 🕰 🕰

7–30 Link to Comprehensive Collections Software Package

Many of the other system-related best practices noted in this chapter are based on the assumption that a company wants to incrementally create separate applications that are directly linked to an existing accounting computer system. If so, a fair amount of programming work will be required to arrive at a complete in-house solution. This can be both expensive and time consuming. For those who prefer to install a complete solution on a more rapid time schedule, it is also possible to purchase a software package that incorporates many of the system-related best practices for collections.

An example of this breed of software is Sungard's GetPAID. This product is linked to a company's legacy accounting systems (specifically, the open accounts receivable and customer files) by customized interfaces, so there is either a continual or batched flow of information into it. A key feature it offers is the assignment of each customer to a specific collections person, so that each person can call up a subset of the overdue invoices for which he or she is responsible. Within this subset, the software will also categorize accounts in different sort sequences, such as placing those at the top that have missed their promised payment dates. Also, the software will present on a single screen all of the contact information related to each customer, including the promises made by customers, open issues, and contact information. The system will also allow the user to enter information for a fax, and then route it directly to the recipient, without requiring the collections person to ever leave his or her chair. It can also be linked to an auto-dialer, so that the collections staff spends less time attempting to establish connections with overdue customers. To further increase the efficiency of the collections staff, it will even determine the time zone in which each customer is located and prioritize the recommended list of calls, so that only those customers in time zones that are currently in the midst of standard business hours will be called.

The GetPAID system does not just store collections data—it can also export it to other systems, where it can be altered for other uses or reformatted for management reporting purposes (though the package contains its own reporting features, as well). Some of the standard reports include a time-series report on performance of individual collection personnel, as well as the same information for each customer. It can also create reports that are tailored by recipient—for example, all of the collection problems for a specific salesperson's customers can be lumped into one report and sent to that salesperson for remedial action. The software can also export data files into Excel or Access. Finally, the system allows customers to log in so they can upload payment dates into the system and resolve disputes online.

Several collection software packages of this type are Web-based, so there is no local software installation at all. Instead, users can log into a Web site. This approach eliminates all local IT support and also makes it easier to roll out the package to new locations.

There are several cost issues to consider when installing this type of software—not only of the software itself, but also for staff training time, installation by consultants, and ongoing maintenance costs. Offsetting these problems is a much shorter time period before a company will have an advanced collections software system fully operational. The record time period for a GetPAID installation is just five days, though a more typical installation speed is 60 days. For those companies with a serious collections problem and that need help right away, a comprehensive collections software package may be the answer.

Cost: 💵💵💵   Installation time: ⏰⏰

7–31 Use Real-Time Cash Application Techniques

There are few things more annoying for the collections staff than to waste time contacting a customer about an "overdue" payment, only to find that they have not only already paid, but the company has already cashed the check! Here are three ways to ensure that incoming cash receipts are properly applied to accounts receivable as fast as possible, so the collections staff will not experience this problem:

- *Review the unapplied cash account every day*. When the cash application staff does not know how to apply a check, it usually drops it into an unapplied cash account, with the intent of researching it further when there is time. However, it may be a long time before the staff gets around to the research work. To keep this delay from occurring, assign an experienced senior clerk to the job of clearing out the unapplied cash account every day, and have a manager inquire about the status of all items in the account on a regular basis. Also, do not evaluate the performance of the cash application staff based on how fast they can apply cash—this just drives them to dump more difficult items into the unapplied cash account.

- *Review the bank account every day.* Many customers now use ACH payments instead of checks, so review the bank account first thing each morning to see what has arrived. Don't wait for the bank statement to arrive at month-end to conduct this review, since customer payments may have been languishing in the account for up to a month.

- *Review lockbox online.* If the bank handling your lockbox posts check images online, then treat it just like a daily bank account review—don't wait a couple of extra days for customer payment information to arrive by mail.

Cost: **Installation time:** 🕰

Total Impact of Best Practices on the Collections Function

This section covers a group of collections best practices that, when used together, will result in a very efficient collections department. The group does not include all of the best practices covered in this chapter, for a small number are mutually exclusive. In particular, outsourcing the collections function does not allow one to implement many of the other best practices. Accordingly, it is assumed that collections work is kept in-house, so a number of other improvements can be implemented.

The recommended best practices are laid out in Exhibit 7.2 in order of the typical transaction flow that results in a completed collection activity. There are many best practices to make the collections task more efficient: lockbox collections, immediate cash application, unapproved write-offs of small balances, early payment discounts, stratified collections, and automatic faxing of overdue invoices and dunning letters, as well as special-event notifications. One can supplement these activities with three databases (e.g., customer assets, customer orders, and collection calls) to assist in making more effective collection calls. Nearly all of these changes can be completed in a relatively short time, with only a few requiring significant investments. Consequently, the activities shown in Exhibit 7.2 can all be implemented in most companies, resulting in a profound difference in the level of efficiency of the collections department.

Summary

The job of collecting accounts receivable is a hard and thankless one. The person who performs well in this position is the one who finds out why a customer pays late and then works with other departments to ensure that the customer has

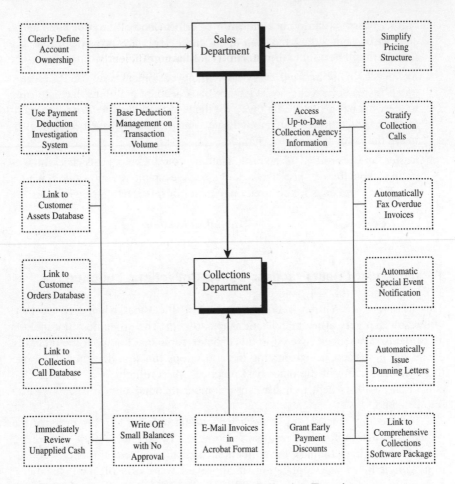

Exhibit 7.2 Impact of Best Practices on the Collection Function

fewer reasons for doing so in the future. This approach is embodied by many of the best practices presented in this chapter, such as simplifying the pricing structure and examining customer orders to see if there are any shipment problems. It is also important for a good collections person to keep accounts receivable from becoming overdue in the first place. Some of the best practices in this chapter address this issue, such as granting early payment discount terms and immediately applying all cash as soon as it is received. Another part of the collections job is to perform collection calls as efficiently as possible; this task is addressed by other best practices, such as using automated faxes of overdue invoices and dunning letters, as well as a collection call database. Finally, the collections staff must use all possible pressure points to collect from customers, which it can do with the use of collection call stratification and a database of customer assets. When all of these tools are properly utilized, a collections staff not only can perform its job more efficiently, but can reduce significantly the amount of overdue accounts receivable at the same time.

For more information about collections best practices, please refer to Bragg, *Billing and Collections Best Practices* (John Wiley & Sons, 2005).

Chapter 8

Credit Best Practices

In a surprising number of companies, there is no credit function at all. Instead, the standard practice is to invoice all and sundry and hope that they pay approximately on time. Only when a company accumulates a few large bad debt losses does management finally take action and institute credit analysis for its customers. However, the initial foray into credit analysis tends to be understaffed and poorly funded, with only cursory customer analysis; bad losses are only avoided by good luck, rather than through detailed analysis. It is only after management approves the formation of a well-run and fully funded credit department that the imposition of a comprehensive set of operating policies and procedures will achieve a reduction in bad debt losses.

This chapter provides many best practices that a credit department can use to tighten or ease its credit policy to meet varying circumstances, as well as provide access to more useful customer credit information, and tools for extending credit with the minimum of risk to the company. When integrated into a solid set of policies and procedures, the credit department can become surprisingly effective.

Implementation Issues for Credit Best Practices

Exhibit 8.1 shows that nearly all of the credit best practices involve a minimal amount of funding and very little time to implement. The key issue with credit best practices implementation, therefore, is not based on having sufficient resources available. Instead, the key factor is the willingness of the management team to impose a sufficient level of credit controls to reduce bad debt losses. In many companies whose orientation is strictly customer-focused, this can be a hard decision to reach. Instead, there is a tendency toward minimal credit practices, which results in less imposition on customers, but also higher levels of bad debt losses.

8–1 Create a Credit Policy

One of the chief causes of confusion not only within the credit department but also between the credit and sales departments is the lack of consistency in

Exhibit 8.1 Summary of Credit Best Practices

	Best Practice	Cost	Install Time
Credit Issues			
8–1	Create a credit policy	💵	⏰⏰
8–2	Modify the credit policy based on product margins	💵	⏰
8–3	Modify the credit policy based on changing economic conditions	💵	⏰
8–4	Modify the credit policy based on potential product obsolescence	💵	⏰
8–5	Centralize credit risk analysis	💵💵	⏰⏰
8–6	Preapprove customer credit	💵	⏰⏰
8–7	Subscribe to a credit report database	💵💵	⏰
8–8	Create an internal credit scoring system	💵💵💵	⏰⏰⏰
8–9	Modify credit application terms to favor the company	💵	⏰
8–10	Create a credit application guidebook	💵	⏰
8–11	Create standardized credit level determination system	💵	⏰
8–12	Require a new credit application if customers have not ordered in some time	💵	⏰
8–13	Review the credit levels of all customers who stop taking cash discounts	💵	⏰
8–14	Call new customers and explain credit terms	💵	⏰⏰
8–15	Issue a payment procedure to customers	💵	⏰⏰
8–16	Join an industry credit group	💵	⏰⏰
8–17	Refer a potential customer to a distributor	💵	⏰
8–18	Require intercorporate guarantees	💵	⏰
8–19	Obtain check verification and guarantee coverage	💵💵	⏰
8–20	Obtain credit insurance	💵💵	⏰
8–21	Obtain an export credit guarantee	💵💵	⏰
8–22	Shorten the terms of sale	💵	⏰
8–23	Insist on lien rights	💵	⏰

dealing with customer credit issues. This includes who is responsible for credit tasks, what logical structure is used to evaluate and assign credit, what terms of sale are used, and what milestones are established for the collections process. Without consistent application of these items, customers never know what credit levels they are likely to be assigned, collections activities tend to jolt from one step to the next in no predetermined order, and no one knows who is responsible for what activities.

Establishment of a reasonably detailed credit policy goes a long way toward resolving these issues. A well-written credit policy should clearly state the mission and goals of the credit department, exactly which positions are responsible for the most critical credit and collections tasks, what formula shall be used for assigning credit levels, and what steps shall be followed in the collections process (though a true collections maestro might balk at the thought of using a boringly consistent methodology!). Further comments are as follows:

- *Mission.* The mission statement should outline the general concept of how the credit department does business—does it provide a loose credit policy to maximize sales, or work toward high-quality receivables (implying reduced sales), or manage credit at some point in between? A loose credit policy might result in this mission: "The credit department shall offer credit to all customers except those where the risk of loss is probable."

- *Goals.* This can be quite specific, describing the exact performance measurements against which the credit staff will be judged. For example, "The department goals are to operate with no more than one collections person per 1,000 customers, while attaining a bad debt percentage no higher than 2 percent of sales, and annual days sales outstanding of no higher than 42 days."

- *Responsibilities.* This is perhaps the most critical part of the policy, based on the number of quarrels it can avert. It should firmly state who has final authority over the granting of credit and the assignment of credit hold status. This is normally the credit manager, but the policy can also state the order volume level at which someone else, such as the CFO or treasurer, can be called on to render final judgment.

- *Credit level assignment.* This section may be of extreme interest to the sales staff, the size of whose sales (and commissions) are based on it. The policy should at least state the sources of information to be used in the calculation of a credit limit, such as credit reports or financial statements, and can also include the minimum credit level automatically extended to all customers, as well as the criteria used to grant larger limits.

- *Collections methodology.* The policy can itemize what collection steps shall be followed, such as initial calls, customer visits, emails, notification of the sales staff, credit holds, and forwarding to a collections agency. This section can be written in too much detail, itemizing exactly what steps are to be taken after a certain number of days. This can constrain an active collections staff from taking unique steps to achieve a collection, so a certain degree of vagueness is acceptable here.

- *Terms of sale.* If there are few product lines in a single industry, it is useful to clearly state a standard payment term, such as a 1 percent discount if paid in 10 days; otherwise full payment is expected in 30 days. An override policy can be included, noting a sign-off by the controller. By doing so, the sales staff will be less inclined to attempt to gain better terms on behalf of customers. However, where there are multiple industries served with different customary credit terms, it may be too complicated to include this verbiage in the credit policy.

Cost: Installation time: 🕐🕐

8–2 Modify the Credit Policy Based on Product Margins ✔*Author's Choice*

Company management can cause significant losses if it attempts to loosen the corporate credit policy without a good knowledge of the margins it earns on its products. For example, if it only earns a 10 percent profit on a product that sells for $10 and extends credit for one unit on that product to a customer who defaults, it has just incurred a loss of $9 that will require the sale of nine more units to offset the loss. However, if the same product had a profit of 50 percent, it would require the sale of only one more unit to offset the loss on a bad debt. Thus, loosening or tightening the credit policy can have a dramatic impact on profits when product margins are low.

The obvious solution is to review product margins with management on a regular basis, whenever management wants to alter the credit policy, or when new products are about to be released. The concept can be taken a step further by altering the credit policy for each product family, so the credit limit is more closely aligned with product profit levels. This approach allows one to fine-tune credit policy to maximize profits. At its most advanced level, one can consider the credit policy in advance for products that are still in the design stage. If a company is using target costing to more precisely define product costs during the design stage, this can be an effective approach for linking credit policy with the product rollout to achieve maximum profitability upon product release.

Cost: Installation time: 🕐

8–3 Modify the Credit Policy Based on Changing Economic Conditions

When economic conditions within an industry worsen, a company whose credit policy has not changed from a more expansive period will likely find itself granting more credit than it should, resulting in more bad debts. Similarly, a restrictive credit policy during a boom period will result in lost sales that go to competitors. This latter approach is particularly galling over the long term, since customers may permanently convert to a competitor and not come back, resulting in lost market share.

The solution is to schedule a periodic review of the credit policy with senior management to see when it should be changed to match economic conditions. A scheduled quarterly review is generally sufficient for this purpose. To prepare for the meeting, one should assemble a list of leading indicators for the industry, tracked on a trend line, that show where the business cycle is most likely to be heading. This information is most relevant for the company's industry, rather than the economy as a whole, since the conditions within some industries can vary substantially from the general economy. If a company has international operations, then the credit policy can be tailored to suit the business cycles of specific countries.

Cost: **Installation time:** 🕰️

8–4 Modify the Credit Policy Based on Potential Product Obsolescence

If a company manufactures or resells products with a short shelf life, or that are subject to rapid technological obsolescence or fashion trends, completed products sitting in the warehouse may be subject to obsolescence in the very short term. If so, a tight credit policy can result in limited product sales that leave excess quantities on hand. In such cases, the company is faced with the choice of scrapping the remaining inventory or selling it off at fire sale prices.

The alternative is to loosen the credit policy on those selected inventory items most likely to become obsolete in the near term. The logic is that, even if inventory is sold to customers with a questionable ability to pay for the goods, this at least presents higher odds of obtaining payment than if the company trucks the goods to the nearest dumpster.

To make this best practice work, the credit department must be kept regularly informed of the obsolescence status of inventory items, preferably on a daily or weekly basis. The easiest way to do this is to have the sales, marketing, and logistics staffs regularly flag potentially obsolete items in the inventory database and give the credit department online access to this information. When customers send in orders, the credit staff can call up this information in the computer system, verify the obsolescence status of the items ordered, and modify the credit policy as needed. If the company also has a credit scoring system, it should consider linking this data feed from the inventory database into the scoring model, so the model automatically issues different credit recommendations based on the items being ordered.

Cost: **Installation time:** 🕰️

8–5 Centralize Credit Risk Analysis

Credit risk analysis is frequently managed at the business unit level. A credit manager decides on the appropriate level of risk that the business unit wants to accept by investing in receivables from a specific customer, and manages the customer's orders to that level. However, what if there are a number of similar business units within a company, and the same customer is doing business with several of them? This means that the company's exposure in aggregate is considerably higher than the maximum level allowed by the credit managers in each business unit. If the customer were to go bankrupt, the entire company might suddenly find itself facing a much larger loss than anyone had previously suspected.

There are two ways to handle this problem. One approach is to centralize credit risk analysis, so that a single credit group can see the aggregated total credit level for each customer. This approach works best if the same accounting system is used throughout a company, which makes it easier to aggregate information relevant to the credit decision. However, it will face resistance from the local business unit managers who prefer to run their own credit operations. A less intrusive alternative is to have a corporate-level analyst periodically aggregate receivable balances and credit limits by customer for all business units, and then flag those customers doing a significant amount of business with the company as a whole. The corporate controller can bring potential credit problems to the attention of the business unit controllers, and come to a mutual agreement regarding credit reductions.

Cost: 💵💵   Installation time: ⏰⏰

8–6 Preapprove Customer Credit

The collections staff suffers severely from credit that is granted after the sales force makes a sale to a customer. The typical situation is that a salesperson finds a new customer and makes an inordinately large sale to it; the salesperson then badgers the credit department to grant a large credit limit to the customer since there is a large commission on the line. The credit staff yields to this pressure and allows more credit than the supplier's credit history warrants, resulting in a difficult collection job for the collections staff. The answer to this quandary lies in fixing the credit-granting process well before the collections staff even knows the new customer exists.

The solution is to work closely with the sales staff to create a "hit list" of new customer prospects before any sales effort is made to contact them. The credit staff then reviews existing credit information about these customers, which is easily gleaned from credit reporting agencies, and calculates the credit levels that it is comfortable granting. These credit levels are given to the sales staff, which now knows the upper limits of what it is allowed to sell to each customer. This approach greatly reduces the pressure that salespeople are wont to bring on the credit staff for higher credit limits. A major byproduct of this process is that the collections staff no longer has to deal with inordinately high accounts receivable with customers who have no way of paying on time.

The only problem with this approach is that a great deal of intradepartmental discipline is needed. The sales manager, in particular, must be able to carefully plan in advance for upcoming sales campaigns and control the sales staff in following sales targets. In addition, this person must see the importance of setting up credit levels in advance and be able to work closely with the credit department in granting appropriate credit levels. If this type of person is not running the sales department, it will be difficult to enforce this best practice.

One way to gain the cooperation of the sales manager is to run a cost-benefit analysis that compares the cost of credit prescreening to the resulting reduction in marketing costs. If the accounting manager can show that a company failing the prescreen can then be excluded from all marketing mailing lists, the marketing budget will benefit from reductions in expensive mailings and follow-up contacts. The sales manager may find that this represents a significant cost reduction, and will then support the prescreening concept. To achieve these cost reductions, this approach requires that prescreen failures be retained in a separate file, which is then subtracted from the marketing database.

Thus, planning carefully to grant appropriate levels of credit to customers before the sales force contacts them is an excellent way to reduce the number of customers the collections staff must contact.

Cost: 🖅   **Installation time:** ⏰ ⏰

8–7 Subscribe to a Credit Report Database

When a customer calls to place an order on credit, the credit department is operating from a clean slate. It has no idea whether the information the customer enters into a credit application is correct. Although a painstaking amount of labor can eventually verify this information, a large time penalty is required to do so. Meanwhile, customers must wait for the application to be completed, which may take days, sending frustrated customers elsewhere.

One solution is to download credit reports on customers over the Internet. These reports list company locations, names, officer information, credit histories, legal problems, banking relations, financial information, and other data of great use to the credit department. The largest purveyors of these reports are Dun & Bradstreet (www.dnb.com) and Equifax (www.equifax.com). There are also a number of reporting services that specialize in credit reports by industry: the equipment leasing, food, home furnishings, manufacturing, and plastics industries are served in this manner.

It is easiest to buy a subscription to these reports, which considerably reduces the price per report. Lower-cost reports include only basic customer information, such as corporate names, locations, ownership, and corporate history, whereas the more expensive reports include a variety of financial and payment information. Equifax reports present information more graphically, but the two report providers issue essentially the same information.

If a small business has just a few owners, it is entirely possible that the finances of the business and the owners are intertwined, either because the owners rely on their businesses for the bulk of their personal income or because they are willing to use personal resources to shore up a failing company. Thus, if the finances of an owner begin to decline, this is a strong leading indicator that the finances of the business will begin to decline soon thereafter. Accordingly, the periodic review of owners' personal credit reports can be an exceedingly useful tool in evaluating the credit of smaller businesses. The periodic review of the credit reports of both small businesses *and* their owners at the same time provides the best possible early warning system for credit problems.

The cost of these reports can build up rapidly if many customers require a review, so the credit manager should use some discretion in determining what credit level requires the use of a credit report.

Cost:    **Installation time:** 🕰

8–8 Create an Internal Credit Scoring System

When a company becomes large enough to have a large customer base, a key concern is the development of a reliable credit scoring model to determine which customers should be granted or denied credit. Though adequate credit scoring systems are available from third parties, larger firms can potentially save millions of dollars by creating credit solutions that are fine-tuned to their specific needs, especially because internal data about customers provide a much more powerful predictor of customer risk than a model based on just the information provided by an external credit report agency. Ultimately, an internal credit scoring system allows a company to avoid the maximum number of bad debts, while lowering the rejection rate on accounts that will not become bad debts. It can also lead to the adjustment of existing credit limits to reflect each customer's underlying credit quality. There are four basic types of credit scoring systems:

- *Rules-based.* Creates a score based on a set of rules constructed from the company's past experience. However, the weights assigned to the various scoring factors are highly judgmental and may not improve scoring results.

- *Neural network–based.* Uses artificial intelligence algorithms to find relationships between account characteristics and the probability of default. However, this is "black box" software, so its results are hard to evaluate.

- *Statistics-based.* Uses statistical analysis to estimate the probability of customer default or delinquency. However, it requires a statistics expert to implement.
- *Genetic algorithm–based.* Uses a trial and error approach to select the best prediction model. However, this is a very new approach and is not yet well understood within the credit analysis field.

A company should not attempt to create its own credit scoring system from scratch, since commercial off-the-shelf packages are available. The implementation of these systems can be lengthy, but the quality of the underlying software will exceed anything that a company's own programming staff can develop.

Such models make sense if a company feels that the information it has accumulated about customers or specific sectors of the economy is so valuable that it can lead to credit scores having much higher levels of accuracy. The information that can be incorporated into such a scoring system could include a multiyear history of customer payments, customer service records of contacts with customers, customer financial statements, and customer trade references.

Once the model has been constructed, a significant amount of testing should be done to see how well it operates. One testing method is to compare the internal credit rating to the ratings produced by outside credit reporting agencies. Any major inconsistencies between the internal and external ratings should be investigated. A large variance does not mean that the company's scoring system is necessarily wrong, but someone should verify what specific information is causing the discrepancy, and whether that information improves the accuracy of the score.

Creating an in-house system is extremely time consuming, requiring labor for data preparation, the selection of variables, searches for data correlations, and model fitting. The expense of creating this system is considerable, and so it is only an option for large, well-funded companies who need improved scoring on large numbers of customers.

Cost: 💵💵💵   **Installation time:** ⏰⏰⏰

8–9 Modify Credit Application Terms
to Favor the Company   ✔*Author's Choice*

Too many companies create credit applications that are boilerplate models they copied from the Internet or purchased through an office supply store. The terms of these agreements may include loopholes that customers can exploit to avoid or delay payments.

The credit application is perhaps the only document that a credit department will persuade a customer to sign (if they want a line of credit), thereby turning it into a legal document; therefore, modify it to enhance the company's ability to collect overdue receivables. Consider including the following clauses:

- *ACH debit clause*. Include a clause stating that the customer agrees to have the company debit its bank account for open accounts receivable as of a specific number of days following billing, and leave space for the customer to enter bank account information.

- *Arbitration clause*. The steps followed in the arbitration process are similar to those used in normal legal proceedings, but they follow a more compressed timeline, with judgment being rendered by an arbitrator. The clause should specify which issues will be subject to arbitration, and the steps both parties will follow during the process. Keeping the arbitration clause as specific as possible will keep the two parties from wrangling over how the arbitration is to be conducted, thereby shortening the period before the company achieves final resolution of the contested issue.

- *Credit venue provision*. If a customer defaults on a payment, the company will want to litigate the case as close to home as possible in order to avoid travel costs. This can be achieved by inserting a clause that any recourse to the courts will be settled in the company's state of residence.

- *Duty to inspect*. A customer may claim well after the date of receipt that a delivery was damaged and use this as the basis for nonpayment. To sidestep this issue, insert a clause requiring the customer to inspect received goods and issue a complaint to the company within a specific period of time, after which the customer waives any further claims.

- *Security interest provision*. This clause gives the company a security interest in any goods shipped to the customer. If used, the company needs a procedure for perfecting any security interests received. This is time sensitive, because the first security interest publicly filed has priority over later claims.

- *Personal guarantee*. Company owners frequently have more assets than their companies, so obtaining a personal guarantee is certainly worth a try.

- *Reimbursement for collection fees*. The collection department may resort to the use of a collection agency or attorney to collect a past-due account. By having the customer agree in advance to reimburse the company for these added expenses, it may be possible to use the threat of this clause to accelerate customer payment.

- *Reimbursement for NSF fees*. If a customer pays with a check that does not clear because there are not sufficient funds (NSF) in the account, the company will be charged a fee by the bank. The customer should agree to reimburse the company for this charge. Better yet, include a standard fee in the credit application that is even higher than the bank's fee, so the company is also compensated for its transaction-handling costs.

- *Charge for duplicate invoices*. If customers continually ask for a duplicate of an invoice that was already sent, this is a likely sign of a payment delaying tactic. If there is a clause in the agreement that specifies a modest fee for supplying additional copies, the collections staff can trigger it if it suspects a customer is abusing the service.

- *Signature is binding.* A customer could claim that the person signing the credit application is not an officer of the company, and that the agreement is therefore not binding. To avoid this, include a clause stating that the person executing the agreement acknowledges that he/she has the authority to enter into the terms and conditions of the credit application.

If any provision is listed on the back of the credit application or on any page other than the signature page, include an extra signature or initials line on that page of the application, thereby giving legal proof that the customer has acknowledged and agreed to the provision.

A customer who objects to any of these clauses can always cross them out and put his or her initials next to the alteration. It is then up to the credit manager to proceed with the application in light of these changes or to reject the application.

If the security interest or personal guarantee provisions are signed, the credit application becomes a valuable legal document, so make sure that a procedure is in place to appropriately store the application.

Cost:    Installation time: 🕰

8–10   Create a Credit Application Guidebook

A company's credit application may contain quite a few fields to be completed, and there may be a history of having incomplete or incorrect information in some of those fields. If so, consider asking the company's sales staff to sit with the customer and help the person fill out the form. This approach is particularly useful when the sales staff has a guidebook from the accounting department in which the application is fully described. In particular, the accounting staff should point out those questions that are more likely to be responded to incorrectly and should point out the types of answers that the credit staff is looking for. The guide can even include a sample completed version. Another possibility is to anticipate various questions that a customer may have in completing the application and note a complete answer in the guide. It is also useful to include a flowchart of the credit application process, as well as a timeline by which credit decisions are usually made.

If the guide is excessively long or packed with text, then the sales staff and customers are less likely to use it. A better approach is to create a graphically intensive layout that imparts the most important information over the shortest number of pages.

Cost: 💵   Installation time: 🕰

8–11   Create Standardized Credit Level Determination System

A common complaint of the collections staff is that there does not appear to be any reasoning behind the credit levels granted to customers, resulting in inordinately high credit levels for some customers that cannot begin to repay their debt. This results in considerable effort for the collections staff to bring in cash from these customers, as well as pleas to the credit department to lower credit to levels that have some reasonable chance of being repaid. This condition is caused by the approach of many credit departments to granting credit, which is that they grant the highest possible credit level to meet the latest order received from a customer. This approach is advocated heavily by the salesperson who stands to receive a substantial commission if the sale is approved. Consequently, granting credit based on the size of a customer's order rather than its ability to pay leads to considerable additional collections work.

A solution is to create a procedure for granting credit that uses a single set of rules that are not to be violated, no matter how much pressure the sales staff applies to expand credit levels. The exact procedure will vary by credit department and the experience of the credit manager. As an example, a credit person can obtain a credit report for a prospective customer and use this as a source of baseline information for deriving a credit level. A credit report is an excellent basis upon which to create a standard credit level, for the information contained in it is collected in a similar manner for all companies, resulting in a standardized and highly comparable basis of information. Such a credit report should include a listing of the high, low, and median credit levels granted to a customer by other companies, giving a credit manager the range of credit that other companies have determined is appropriate. However, just using the range of credit levels is not normally sufficient, since one must also consider the number of extra days beyond terms that a customer takes to pay its customers. This information is a good indicator of creditworthiness and is also contained in a credit report. A good example of how the "payment" information can be included in the calculation of a credit level is to take the median credit level other companies granted as a starting point and then subtract 5 percent of this amount for every day that a customer pays its suppliers later than standard payment terms. For example, if the median credit level is $10,000, and a customer pays an average of ten days late, 50 percent of the median credit level is taken away, resulting in a credit level for the customer of $5,000. The exact system a company uses will be highly dependent on its willingness to incur credit losses and expend extra effort on collections. A company willing to obtain more marginal sales will adopt the highest credit level shown in the credit report and not discount the impact of late payments at all, whereas a risk-averse company may be inclined to use the lowest reported credit level and further discount it heavily for the impact of any late payments by the potential customer.

The range of standard procedures for granting credit levels is infinite. The main point is to have one consistent basis for creating reasonable customer credit levels, which gives the collections staff far less work to collect on sales that exceed the ability of a customer to pay.

Cost: Installation time: 🕐

8–12 Require a New Credit Application if Customers Have Not Ordered in Some Time

If a customer has not placed an order recently, perhaps for a year or more, its financial situation may have changed considerably, rendering its previously assigned credit level no longer valid. This is a particular problem when the customer may be shopping through an industry to see who will accept an order, and is forced back to the company when no other suppliers are willing to deal with it anymore. If the company's credit department simply dusts off the old credit review and allows the same credit limit, there could be a bad debt lurking in the immediate future.

One solution is to require customers to complete a new credit application after a preset interval has passed, such as two years. This represents a significant additional workload for the credit staff, so require this additional review only if the old credit level was a sufficiently high one to represent a noticeable potential bad debt loss. Though the computer system can be designed to flag these customers for a credit review when new orders arrive, an alternative is to simply purge from the accounting database all customers with whom there has been no business in the past two years. Then, when an order arrives and the accounting system shows no customer record, the credit staff knows it needs to get involved.

Cost: 💵   Installation time: 🕐

8–13 Review the Credit Levels of All Customers Who Stop Taking Cash Discounts

When a customer stops taking cash discounts, it may mean only that a new payables person is not aware of the discount and just needs a reminder from the company in order to start doing so once again. However, a more likely scenario is that the customer's financial condition has declined to the point where it no longer has the cash to make an early payment.

Not taking early payment discounts is an excellent early warning of a decline in a customer's financial condition. If the cash application staff notices this change, they should notify the credit manager at once, who can reevaluate the customer's credit limit.

The real problem with this best practice is noticing when cash discounts stop. Unless a customer's payments are so large that their absence is clearly noticeable, there is not usually an automated way to note their absence. Instead, it may be necessary for a manager to regularly compare a list of customers who usually take discounts to the accounts receivable aging. Though this manual approach can be time-consuming, it can save the company from incurring a bad debt loss. This review should be conducted by a credit or collections person, on the grounds that they have the largest vested interest in spotting this problem as early as possible.

Cost: **Installation time:** 🕭

8–14 Call New Customers and Explain Credit Terms   ✔*Author's Choice*

When a new customer receives its first invoice from a company, the standard sequence of events for the accounts payable staff is to enter the "pay to" information in the computer system, accept the corporate default payment days (such as 30), and press the ENTER key. By doing so, the customer has completely ignored the company's payment terms, not to mention any early payment discounts that may have been added (and possibly negotiated at some length with the customer). This is a particular problem early in a company's relationship with a new customer, since the credit department is keeping an especially watchful eye on the payment situation. If payments arrive late, the business partners are off to a bad start.

The solution is to contact the customer at the beginning of the relationship and explain the payment terms. By taking the time to make this contact, the customer is now aware that the company takes payment terms seriously, and expects them to be observed. This contact can take the form of a phone call, personal meeting, or letter. A phone call or personal meeting is the best alternative, since it gives the customer a chance to bring up any special payment issues that could interfere with timely invoice payment.

The key point is to make sure this contact is made with the correct person, or else the time invested in this best practice will serve no purpose. The best contact is the accounts payable manager. As an alternative, try the payables clerk to whom invoices will be sent; this is a less optimal choice, since account responsibilities may be shuffled among the clerks on a regular basis.

Cost: 💵   **Installation time:** 🕭 🕭

8–15 Issue a Payment Procedure to Customers

When a company sends an invoice to a customer, the customer assumes that the usual payment arrangements apply—the industry standard number of days to pay, ship back defective goods without notice, and call the company salesperson if there are any questions. If the company's systems are not set up to handle transactions in this manner, this can cause trouble.

A better approach is to develop a short payment procedure for new customers. It should certainly list the company's payment terms, but then go further to list company contact information as well as the exact process for returning goods and how to claim a credit. The procedure can even extend to the use of an application form for payments via Automated Clearing House (ACH). This approach can greatly reduce the number of problems that the collections staff normally deals with.

Getting the procedure into the hands of all customers can take some work. It can go out with the next batch of invoices, or be delivered by the sales staff, or be issued as a separate mailing. If any of the information on the procedure changes, the distribution must occur again, which can be a chore if there are many customers.

Cost: Installation time:

8–16 Join an Industry Credit Group

Credit reports are an extremely useful way to obtain information about customer locations, business names, and general credit condition. However, they do not yield the most up-to-date information about a customer's immediate financial condition. It is entirely possible that a customer will enter a serious financial decline a number of months before any hint of its condition appears on a credit report. In the meantime, the company may have issued a substantial amount of credit to the customer, leaving the credit manager in a tenuous position.

An excellent solution is to join an industry credit group. These groups exchange information about specific customers, such as recent problems with not-sufficient-funds (NSF) checks, bankruptcies, accounts being sent to collections, and other financial difficulties, so the credit department can take quick action to tighten credit where necessary. This is also an excellent opportunity for networking, so credit personnel across the industry can more easily exchange information.

The National Association of Credit Management (NACM), which can be reached at *www.nacm.org,* maintains a listing of national credit management groups, including those in Exhibit 8.2. The NACM lists meeting intervals and contact information for each group's administrator.

Cost: Installation time:

8–17 Refer a Potential Customer to a Distributor

After reviewing a customer's credit application, the credit department may conclude that it has no interest in providing any type of credit to a prospective customer. If the customer is not willing to provide either cash in advance or some form of security, there may be no further avenue for the company to make a sale.

Exhibit 8.2 NACM List of National Credit Management Groups

National Agricultural Credit Conference	National Musical Instrument
National Christian Suppliers	National Paper Packaging Credit Group
National Coated Paper and Film Manufacturing	National Professional Apparel Manufacturers
National Electronics and Communications	National Seed Distributors
National Fundraising Manufacturers	National Steel Mill
National Garage Door and Operating Devices	National Suppliers to Window Manufacturers Credit Group
National Home Centers Credit Group	National Tool and Accessories Manufacturers
National Housewares / Consumer Products	National Truck, Trailer and Equipment Credit Group
National Lawn and Garden Suppliers	
National Leisure Living Manufacturers	National Vinyl Fence Credit Group
National Metal Building and Components	National Water Products Manufacturers
National Metal Producers	National Waterway Carriers / Suppliers

Even if the company itself cannot grant credit, it is possible that a distributor will have a looser credit policy. If the company has a distribution network, refer the customer to a distributor. This approach can indirectly result in a sale for the company, though of a lesser size than it would have experienced with a direct sale (due to the distributor commission or markup). Nonetheless, if the credit department considers a customer to have significant credit risk, this may be a viable alternative.

Cost: Installation time: 🕰

8–18 Require Intercorporate Guarantees

A credit manager is sometimes confronted with a situation where a customer does not have a good credit record and its managers are hired staff who have no intention of adding their personal guarantees to an order. Is there a way to still grant credit?

It is possible that the company is a subsidiary of another corporate entity. If so, request that the parent company issue a guarantee making the parent liable for the subsidiary's debt. If the company chooses to exercise this guarantee, it is customary to warn the customer that the company intends to contact the guaranteeing entity, not only as a courtesy, but also because this makes the customer more likely to pay.

This approach calls for the examination of the parent's credit in place of the subsidiary, so an additional credit review must be conducted. Also, this type of guarantee may be unenforceable if there is no obvious consideration given to the guaranteeing entity in exchange for its guarantee. If this may be a problem, clearly specify the form of consideration given within the guarantee document. Further, review the guaranteeing company's board minutes, articles of incorporation, or bylaws to see if it is authorized to grant a guarantee—if not, the guarantee is unenforceable.

If the guarantee is granted, be sure to store it in a locked file for safekeeping, and make note of the guarantee in the customer file.

Cost:    Installation time: 🕐

8–19 Obtain Check Verification and Guarantee Coverage

Retail organizations accept large quantities of checks from their customers, and many of those checks will not clear the bank, causing a loss for the company. They can resolve this issue by no longer accepting checks, but that solution can reduce sales.

An alternative is to use a check verification service. Verification means that the company submits each check it receives from customers through a check scanner, which extracts account information from each check and transmits it to an outside *National Negative Database,* which compares it to a listing of bad check writers. If the customer has a history of writing bad checks, then the system declines the check. The fee for this service is a few cents per check submitted, plus a monthly fixed fee.

An expansion of the check verification service is the check guarantee program. It is essentially a credit insurance service where the provider guarantees payment on each check submitted to it. The guarantee process is the same as the verification process just described, except that the check guarantee provider will issue a specific approval; the company is now guaranteed payment on that specific check. The company is also responsible for obtaining some additional information from the customer, such as a driver's license number and phone number. Upon acceptance, the check is converted into an electronic check, and payment will be sent directly to the company's designated bank account. If a customer complains about having a check rejected, the employee handling the transaction can hand over the business card of the check verification service and suggest that the customer contact the service directly.

If the check guarantee provider ends up paying the company for a disproportionate number of bad checks, the provider may cancel the guarantee program with the company. The check guarantee fee is based on a per-check fixed charge, plus a percentage of the amount of the check.

The total cost to the company is roughly the same as or somewhat lower than the fees charged under a credit card program. Generally, the verification service is sufficient; the extra percentage fee required for a guarantee program is frequently higher than the losses on bad checks that a company would otherwise have experienced.

When looking for the best check verification and guarantee coverage, select the one with the largest possible National Negative Database, since this will provide the best coverage of potential bad check writers.

Cost: 💸💸   **Installation time:** ⏰

8–20 Obtain Credit Insurance

Letters of credit take time to set up, are difficult to monitor, and must be followed to the letter in order to be paid. This process makes smaller companies less than willing to enter into international sales. Also, companies of any size may be unwilling to grant large lines of credit or even smaller ones if customers have some risk of nonpayment. In both instances, a prudent credit manager may recommend dropping a potential sale.

An increasingly common solution to this dilemma is the use of credit insurance. This is essentially a guarantee against customer nonpayment. It is faster to set up than a line of credit, can be used for both domestic and international receivables, and allows a company to increase its credit lines to customers. Also, for those companies willing to take on some credit risk themselves, they can extend a larger credit line than the credit insurance company may allow, thereby giving themselves the opportunity to earn additional revenue. Further, a company using credit insurance can reduce the size of its bad debt reserve, as well as offer a higher-quality accounts receivable base as collateral for a line of credit. Credit insurance is available for domestic credit, export credit, and coverage of custom products prior to delivery, in case customers cancel orders.

If a credit insurance policy stipulates a maximum credit limit per customer, the insurance company must make the decision to increase the credit limit, or the company can take on the uninsured risk of granting extra credit. If the policy contains no maximum limit at all, the insurance company has control over the credit limit granted to each customer. If a customer is considered by the insurance agency to be high risk, it will likely grant no insurance at all. Also, goods being exported to countries with a high perceived level of political risk will not be granted credit insurance.

The cost of credit insurance can exceed 0.5 percent of the invoiced amount, with higher costs for riskier customers and substantially lower rates for customers considered to be in excellent financial condition. The company does not have to absorb this cost; where possible, consider rebilling it to the customer, who may be willing to pay it in order to obtain a larger line of credit than would otherwise be the case.

When entering into a credit insurance policy, be sure to focus on its exclusionary language. For example, credit insurance does not necessarily include disputes, such as when goods arrive late or damaged. It is useful to itemize the various exclusions and then review how many receivable disputes would have fallen into those exclusions in the past year, to see if a proposed credit insurance policy is truly cost-effective.

Cost: 💵💵   Installation time: ⏰

8–21 Obtain an Export Credit Guarantee

Sometimes, a company cannot obtain credit insurance or a letter of credit for a potential sale to a foreign customer, resulting in the painful decision to either extend credit in a risky situation or to walk away from a potential sale.

The Export-Import Bank of the United States (www.exim.gov) offers an export credit guarantee to anyone shipping domestic goods to a foreign customer, which can provide an excellent boost to sales. Also, because the U.S. government now guarantees a company's foreign receivables, the company will have a much better chance to obtain debt that is collateralized by its receivables. Furthermore, the Bank's multibuyer policy guarantees payment on *all* qualifying international sales on open account terms. Other policies are available for short- and medium-term sales to individual buyers. The Bank's minimum policy premium of $500 is much lower than that of most private insurers, which makes this a good option for smaller businesses.

It is also possible to obtain preshipment coverage, so a company will not have to worry about an order cancellation for a custom order requiring a long time period to prepare for shipment. Further, the Bank may grant credit guarantees even for sales into high-risk countries that a private insurer will avoid.

To obtain a guarantee, the exporting company must submit an application containing information about the customer, such as a credit report (containing a Dun & Bradstreet Paydex score of at least 50, indicating average payments no more than 30 days slow) and trade references; larger shipments also require the customer's financial statements (audited for several years, if the proposed guarantee exceeds $1 million). Also, the customer must have been in the same general line of business for at least three years. Finally, for large transactions, operating and net profit, current ratio, and total liabilities/net worth standards must be met. If accepted, the exporting company must pay the full amount of the coverage premium in advance. Premiums will vary by the amount of coverage, evaluation of the customer, and the country in which the customer is based. The guarantee is only for a portion of the net contract value on domestic goods (usually 95 percent), so the company must still incur some of the risk of nonpayment. Also, this guarantee is not available for military sales or to countries that have not been approved by the government.

One issue with using the Bank is that it establishes fees on a fixed schedule that only changes infrequently, so that its prices can vary considerably from those of private insurers. This can result in significant overpricing from time to time.

Cost: Installation time: 🕰

8–22   Shorten the Terms of Sale

There may be cases where a customer wants to place a large number of small orders with a company, cumulatively resulting in a large credit line before the company's typical terms period has expired. For example, it may plan to place 10 orders for $3,000 each within the company's standard 30-day terms period, resulting in a required credit line of $30,000. However, the customer's financial condition may not warrant this level of credit risk by the company.

A solution is to shorten the terms of sale. In the above scenario, reducing payment terms to 15 days would mean that the customer should be able to purchase the same quantity of goods from the company on a credit line of just $15,000.

This approach works only if a customer is placing many small orders rather than one large one, the orders are evenly spaced out, and the customer's own cash receipts cycle allows it to pay on such short terms. Thus, this best practice applies to only a minority of situations.

Cost: 💵   Installation time: 🕰

8–23   Insist on Lien Rights

If a company is supplying labor or equipment under the terms of a construction contract, it is likely that the contract contains a lien waiver. Under this provision, the company cannot file a lien on the customer in the event of customer nonpayment. This is an especially common provision that a customer will insist on in exchange for paying the company. This is not a large problem if the customer is large and well-funded, but it can be a major problem if the customer is small and undercapitalized.

When initially signing a construction contract with a customer, review it for a lien waiver and either strike it or modify it to only waive the lien to the extent of progress payments already made to the company. Further, the waiver should only apply if the customer does not file for bankruptcy within 90 days after the funds clear. In the event of a bankruptcy, the company will likely be sued for the return of any funds paid to it within 90 days before the filing, so it is important to retain lien rights in order to protect the receivable. If the customer attempts to impose the waiver at a later date, then the company should have the same objective in dealing with it.

Cost: 💵   Installation time: 🕰

Summary

If a company implements most of the credit best practices noted in this chapter, the result will be an extremely active credit group that is constantly examining the corporate credit policy, as well as the credit standing of its customers as defined by a variety of key criteria. The credit process will be proactive, with the credit group contacting customers directly to explain credit terms and payment procedures, while also joining industry credit groups to learn more about their customer base. Although these are all excellent activities that should be encouraged, this group will require additional funding, which must be offset against the savings they generate from reduced bad-debt losses.

Chapter 9

Commissions Best Practices

The application of best practices to commissions hardly seems to be worth a separate chapter; however, there are a surprisingly large number of actions that can streamline the calculation of commissions and their payment to sales personnel.

This chapter contains 12 best practices, and the main factor to keep in mind is that they are designed to improve the operations of the accounting department only. Though none of them will worsen the systems in the sales department, the other area that is directly impacted, they may have an opposite impact on the morale of that department. For example, one best practice is to replace convoluted commission structures with a simplified model. Though this will obviously lead to easier commission calculations by the accounting staff, it may also have the negative impact of reducing the sales incentive for those salespeople who are no longer receiving such a good compensation package. Accordingly, before installing any of the following best practices, it is a good idea to first gain the approval of the sales manager to any changes that will directly or indirectly impact the sales department.

Implementation Issues for Commissions Best Practices

This section illustrates the relative degree of implementation cost and duration for commission best practices, as displayed in Exhibit 9.1. The level of implementation difficulty in this area is quite polarized because of one major issue—some of the recommended changes require the complete cooperation of the sales manager, who will probably actively resist at least a few of them. Accordingly, the duration of implementation for these best practices is rated as difficult and long, though they are actually quite simple if the agreement of the sales manager can somehow be obtained in advance.

Those best practices that can be completed by the accounting staff without any outside approval are rated as both inexpensive and short installations. An example of such a best practice is paying commissions through the traditional payroll system. The only exceptions to the easy internal accounting changes are two items that may require some expensive programming assistance. Thus, the range of implementation difficulty is extraordinarily wide in this functional area.

Exhibit 9.1 Summary of Commissions Best Practices

	Best Practice	*Cost*	*Install Time*
Commission Calculations			
9–1	Automatically calculate commissions in the computer system	💵💵💵	⏰⏰
9–2	Calculate final commissions from actual data	💵	⏰⏰⏰
9–3	Construct a standard commission terms table	💵	⏰
9–4	Periodically issue a summary of commission rates	💵	⏰
9–5	Simplify the commission structure	💵	⏰⏰⏰
Commission Payments			
9–6	Include commission payments in payroll payments	💵	⏰
9–7	Lengthen the interval between commission payments	💵	⏰⏰⏰
9–8	Only pay commissions from cash received	💵	⏰⏰⏰
9–9	Periodically audit commissions paid	💵💵	⏰
Commission Systems			
9–10	Install incentive compensation management software	💵💵💵	⏰⏰⏰
9–11	Post commission payments on the company intranet	💵💵	⏰⏰
9–12	Show potential commissions on cash register	💵💵	⏰⏰

9–1 Automatically Calculate Commissions in the Computer System

For many commission clerks, the days when commissions are calculated are not pleasant. Every invoice from the previous month must be assembled and reviewed, with notations on each one regarding which salesperson is paid a commission, the extent of any split commissions, and their amounts. Further, given the volume of invoices and the complexity of calculations, there is almost certainly an error every month, so the sales staff will be sure to pay a visit as soon as the commission checks are released in order to complain about their payments. This results in additional changes to the payments, making them very difficult to audit, in case the controller or the internal audit manager wants to verify that commissions are being calculated correctly. The manual nature of the work makes it both tedious and highly prone to error.

The answer is to automate as much of it as possible by having the computer system do the calculating. This way, the commission clerk only has to scan through the list of invoices assigned to each salesperson and verify that each has the correct salesperson's name listed on it and the correct commission rate charged to it. To make this system work, there must be a provision in the accounting software to record salesperson names and commission rates against invoices, a very common feature on even the most inexpensive systems—though if it does not exist, an expensive piece of programming work must be completed before this best practice can be implemented. Then the accounting staff must alter its invoicing procedure so that it enters a salesperson's name, initials, or identifying number in the invoicing record for every new invoice. It is very helpful if the data-entry screen is altered to *require* this field to be entered, in order to avoid any missing commissions. Once this procedure is altered, it is an easy matter to run a commissions report at the end of the reporting period and then pay commission checks from it. This is a simple and effective way to eliminate the manual labor and errors associated with the calculation of commissions.

The main problem is that it does not work if the commission system is a complex one. For example, the typical computer system only allows for a single commission rate and salesperson to be assigned to each invoice. However, many companies have highly varied and detailed commission systems, where the commission rates vary based on a variety of factors and many invoices have split commissions assigned to several sales staff. In these cases, only custom programming or a return to manual commission calculations will be possible, unless someone can convince the sales manager to adopt a simplified commission structure. This is rarely possible since the sales manager is the one who probably created the complicated system and has no intention of seeing it dismantled.

Cost: 💵💵💵   **Installation time:** ⏰⏰

9–2 Calculate Final Commissions from Actual Data

A common arrangement for departing salespeople is that they are paid immediately for the commissions they have not yet received, but which they should receive in the next commission payment. Unfortunately, the amount of this commission payment is frequently a guess, since some sales have not yet been completed and orders have not even been received for other potential sales on which a salesperson may have been working for many months. Accordingly, there is usually a complicated formula in the typical salesperson's hiring agreement that pays out a full commission on completed sales, a partial one on orders just received, and perhaps even a small allowance on expected sales for which final orders have not yet been received. The work required to complete this formula is highly labor-intensive and frequently inaccurate, especially if an allowance is paid for sales which may not yet have occurred (and which may never occur).

A better approach is to restructure the initial sales agreement to state that commissions will be paid at the regular times after employee termination until all sales have been recorded. The duration of these payments may be several months, which means that the salesperson must wait some time to receive full compensation, but the accounting staff benefits from not having to waste time on a separate, and highly laborious, termination calculation. Instead, they take no notice of whether a salesperson is still working for the company and just calculate and pay out commissions in accordance with regular procedures.

There are three problems with this approach. First, if the commission calculation is made automatically in the computer system, sales will probably be assigned to a new salesperson as soon as the old one has left, requiring some manual tracking of exactly who is entitled to payment on which sale during the transition period. The second problem is that if a salesperson is fired, most state laws require immediate compensation within a day or so of termination. Though the initial sales agreement can be modified to cover this contingency, one should first check to see if the applicable state law will override the sales agreement. Finally, this type of payout usually requires a change to the initial employee contract with each salesperson; the existing sales staff may have a problem with this new arrangement since they will not receive payment so quickly if they leave the company. A company can take the chance of irritating the existing sales staff by unilaterally changing the agreements, but may want to try the more politically correct approach of grandfathering the existing staff and only apply the new agreement to new sales employees. In short, delaying the final commission payment runs the risk of mixing up payments between old and new salespeople, may be contrary to state laws, and may only be applicable to new employees. Despite these issues, it is still a good idea to implement this best practice, even though it may be several years before it applies to all of the sales staff.

Cost: 💵   Installation time: ⏰ ⏰ ⏰

9–3 Construct a Standard Commission
Terms Table   ✔ *Author's Choice*

As salespeople may make the majority of their incomes from commissions, they have a great deal of interest in the exact rates paid on various kinds of sales. This can lead to many visits to the commissions clerk to complain about perceived problems with the rates paid on various invoices. Not only can this be a stressful visit on the part of the commissions clerk, who will be on the receiving end of some very forceful arguments, but it is also a waste of time, since that person has other work to do besides listening to the arguments of the sales staff.

A reasonable approach that greatly reduces sales staff complaints is a commission terms table. It should specify the exact commission arrangement with each salesperson so there is absolutely no way to misconstrue the reimbursement arrangement. Once this is set up, it can be distributed to the sales staff, who can refer to it instead of the commissions clerk. There will be the inevitable rash of complaints for the first few days after the table is issued since the sales staff will want clarification on a few key points, possibly requiring a reissuance of the table. However, once the table has been reviewed a few times, the number of complaints should rapidly dwindle. The only problem is that listing the commission deals of all the sales staff side-by-side on a single document will lead to a great deal of analysis and arguing by those sales personnel who think they are not receiving as good a commission arrangement. To avoid this problem, separate the table into pieces so each salesperson sees only that piece of it that applies to the individual. By following this approach, the number of inquiries and commission adjustments that the accounting staff must deal with will rapidly decline.

Cost: 🏷️   **Installation time:** ⏰

9–4 Periodically Issue a Summary of Commission Rates

Even companies with a simplified and easily understandable commission structure will sometimes have difficulty communicating this information to the sales staff. The problem is that the information is not readily available for sales personnel to see, and so they are always breeding rumors about commission alterations impacting their income. This causes a continuing morale problem, frequently resulting in needless inquiries to the accounting department.

The simple solution is to periodically issue a summary of commission rates. If management is comfortable with revealing the entire commission structure for all personnel, it can issue a commission table to the entire sales force. If not, it can issue a salesperson-specific commission listing. The table should be issued no less frequently than annually. A good way to present the commission information is to include it in the annual review, allowing each salesperson time to review it and ask questions about it. Also, the commissions table should be reissued and discussed with the sales force *every time* there is a change in the table, which keeps the accounting staff from having to explain the changes after the fact when the sales staff calls to inquire about the alterations. In short, up-front communications with the sales staff is a good way to keep the accounting department from having to answer inquiries about commission information.

Cost: 💵   **Installation time:** ⏰

9–5 Simplify the Commission Structure   ✔*Author's Choice*

The bane of the accounting department is an overly complex commission structure. When there are a multitude of commission rates, shared rates, special bonuses, and retroactive booster clauses, the commission calculation chore is mind-numbing and highly subject to error, which causes further analysis to fix. An example of such a system, based on an actual corporation, is for a company-wide standard commission rate, but with special increased commission rates for certain counties considered especially difficult regions in which to sell, except for sales to certain customers, which are the responsibility of the in-house sales staff, who receive a different commission rate. In addition, the commission rate is retroactively increased if later quarterly sales targets are met, and are retroactively increased a *second* time if the full-year sales goal is reached, with an extra bonus payment if the full-year goal is exceeded by a set percentage. Needless to say, this company went through an endless cycle of commission payment adjustments, some of which were disputed for months afterwards. Also, this company had great difficulty retaining a commissions clerk in the accounting department.

The obvious resolution is a simplification of the overall commission structure. For example, the previous example can be reduced to a single across-the-board commission rate, with quarterly and annual bonuses if milestone targets are reached. Though an obvious solution and one that can greatly reduce the work of the accounting staff, it is only implemented with the greatest difficulty because the sales manager must approve the new system, and rarely does so. The reason is that the sales manager probably created the convoluted commissions system in the first place and feels that it is a good one for motivating the sales staff. In this situation, the matter may have to go to a higher authority for approval, though this irritates the sales manager. A better and more politically correct variation is to persuade the sales manager to adopt a midway solution that leaves both parties partially satisfied and still able to work with each other on additional projects. In the long run, as new people move into the sales manager position, there may still be opportunities to more completely simplify the commission structure.

Cost: 💵   Installation time: 🕐 🕐 🕐

9–6 Include Commission Payments in Payroll Payments

If a company has a significant number of sales personnel, the chore of issuing commission payments to them can be a significant one. The taxes must be compiled for each check and deducted from the gross pay, the checks must be cut or a wire transfer made, and, for those employees who are out of town, there may be other special arrangements to get the money to them. Depending on the number of checks, this can interfere with the smooth functioning of the accounting department.

A simple but effective way to avoid this problem is to roll commission payments into the regular payroll processing system. By doing so, the payroll calculation chore is completely eliminated, once the gross commission amounts are approved and sent to the payroll staff for processing. The system will calculate taxes automatically, issue checks or direct deposits, or mail to employees, depending on the distribution method the regular payroll system uses. This completely eliminates a major chore.

There are two problems with this best practice. First, the commission payment date may not coincide with the payroll processing date, which necessitates a change in the commission payment date. For example, if the commission is always paid on the fifteenth day of the month, but the payroll is on a biweekly schedule, the actual pay date will certainly not fall on the fifteenth day of every month. To fix this issue, the commission payment date in the example could be set to the first payroll date following the fifteenth of the month. Second, by combining a salesperson's regular paycheck with the commission payment, the combined total will put the employee into a higher pay bracket, resulting in more taxes being deducted (never a popular outcome). This issue can be resolved either by setting employee deduction rates lower or by separating the payments into two separate checks in the payroll system in order to drop the payee into a lower apparent tax bracket. As long as these issues are taken into account, merging commissions into the payroll system is a very effective way for the accounting staff to avoid cutting separate manual commission checks.

Cost: 🖅   **Installation time:** ⏰

9–7 Lengthen the Interval between Commission Payments

Some commissions are paid as frequently as once a week, though monthly payments are the norm in most industries. If there are many employees receiving commission payments, this level of frequency results in a multitude of commission calculations and check payments over the course of a year.

It may be possible in some instances to lengthen the interval between commission payments, reducing the amount of commission calculation and paycheck preparation work for the accounting department. This best practice is only useful in a minority of situations, however, because the commissions of many sales personnel constitute a large proportion of their pay and they cannot afford to wait a long time to receive it. However, there are some instances where salespeople receive only a very small proportion of their pay in the form of commissions. In this situation, it makes little sense to calculate a commission for a very small amount of money and is better to only do it at a longer interval, perhaps quarterly or annually. Though it can be used only in a few cases, this best practice is worth considering.

Cost:    Installation time: ⏰ ⏰ ⏰

9–8 Pay Commissions Only from Cash Received

A major problem for the collections staff is salespeople who indiscriminately sell any amount of product or service to customers, regardless of the ability of those customers to pay. When this happens, the salesperson is focusing only on the commission that will result from the sale and not on the excessive work required of the collections staff to bring in the payment from the supplier, not to mention the much higher bad debt allowance needed to offset uncollectible accounts.

The solution is to change the commission system so that salespeople are paid a commission only on the cash received from customers. This change will instantly turn the entire sales force into a secondary collection agency, since they will be very interested in bringing in cash on time. They will also be more concerned about the creditworthiness of their customers, since they will spend less time selling to customers that have little realistic chance of paying.

There are a few problems that make this a tough best practice to adopt. First, as it requires salespeople to wait longer before they are paid a commission, they are markedly unwilling to change to this new system. Second, the amount they are paid will be somewhat smaller than what they are used to receiving, since inevitably there will be a few accounts receivable that will never be collected. Third, because of the first two issues, some of the sales staff will feel slighted and will probably leave the company to find another organization with a more favorable commission arrangement. Accordingly, the sales manager may not support a change to this kind of commission structure.

A problem directly related to the accounting systems (and not the intransigence of the sales department!) is that since commissions are now paid based on cash received, there must be a cash report to show the amounts of cash received from each customer in a given time period, in order to calculate commissions from this information. Alternatively, if commissions are based on cash received from specific invoices, the report must reflect this information. Most accounting systems already contain this report; if not, it must be programmed into the system.

Cost: 🫰   Installation time: ⏰ ⏰ ⏰

9–9 Periodically Audit Commissions Paid

Given the complexity of some commission structures, it comes as no surprise that the sales staff is not always paid the correct commission amount. This is particularly true of transition periods, where payment rates change or new salespeople take over different sales territories. When this happens, there is confusion regarding the correct commission rates to pay on certain invoices or whom to pay for each one. The usual result is that there are some overpayments that go uncorrected; the sales staff will closely peruse commission payments to make sure that *under*payments do not occur, so this is rarely a problem. In addition, there is a chance that overpayments are made on a regular basis, since any continuing overpayment is unlikely to be reported by the salesperson on the receiving end of this largesse.

The best way to review commissions for this problem is to schedule a periodic internal audit of the commission calculations. This review can take the form of a detailed analysis of a sampling of commission payments or a much simpler overall review of the percentage of commissions paid out, with a more detailed review if the percentage looks excessively high. Any problems discovered through this process can result in some retraining of the commissions clerk, an adjustment in the commission rates paid, or a reduction in the future payments to the sales staff until any overpayments have been fully deducted from their pay. This approach requires some time on the part of the internal audit staff, but does not need to be conducted very frequently and so is not an expensive proposition. An occasional review is usually sufficient to find and correct any problems with commission overpayments.

Cost:    **Installation time:**

9–10 Install Incentive Compensation Management Software

Commission tracking for a large number of salespeople is an exceedingly complex chore, especially when there are multiple sales plans with a variety of splits, bonuses, overrides, caps, hurdles, guaranteed payments, and commission rates. This task typically requires a massive amount of accounting staff time spent manipulating electronic spreadsheets, and is highly error-prone. Most of the other best practices in this chapter are designed to *simplify* the commission calculation structure in order to reduce the amount of accounting effort. However, an automated alternative is available that allows the sales manager to retain a high degree of commission plan complexity while minimizing the manual calculation labor of the accounting staff.

The solution is to install incentive compensation management software, such as that offered by Synygy and Callidus Software. It is a separate package from the accounting software, and requires a custom data feed from the accounting database, using the incoming data to build complex data-tracking models that churn out exactly what each salesperson is to be paid, along with a commission statement. The best packages also allow for the what-if modeling of different commission plan scenarios, as well as the construction of customized commission plans that are precisely tailored to a company's needs, and can also deliver commission results to salespeople over the Internet. The trouble with this best practice is its cost. The software is expensive and requires consulting labor to develop a data link between the main accounting database and the new software; thus, it is only a cost-effective solution for those organizations with at least 100 salespeople.

Cost: 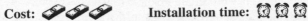   Installation time: 🕐🕐🕐

9–11 Post Commission Payments on the Company Intranet

A sales staff whose pay structure is heavily skewed in favor of commission payments, rather than salaries, will probably hound the accounting staff at month-end to see what their commission payments will be. This comes at the time of the month when the accounting staff is trying to close the accounting books, and so increases their workload at the worst possible time of the month. However, by creating a linkage between the accounting database and a company's intranet site, it is now possible to shift this information directly to a Web page where the sales staff can view it at any time, and without involving the valuable time of the accounting staff.

There are two ways to post the commission information. One is to wait until all commission-related calculations have been completed at month-end, and then either manually dump the data into an HTML (HyperText Markup Language) format for posting to a Web page or else run a batch program that does so automatically. Either approach will give the sales staff a complete set of information about their commissions. However, this approach still requires some manual effort at month-end (even if only for a few minutes while a batch program runs).

An alternative approach is to create a direct interface between the accounting database and the Web page, so that commissions are updated constantly, including grand totals for each commission payment period. By using this approach, the accounting staff has virtually no work to do in conveying information to the sales staff. In addition, sales personnel can check their commissions at any time of the month, and call the accounting staff with their concerns right away—this is a great improvement, since problems can be spotted and fixed at once, rather than waiting until the crucial month-end closing period to correct them.

No matter which method is used for posting commission information, a password system will be needed, since this is highly personal payroll-related information. There should be a reminder program built into the system, so that the sales staff is forced to alter their passwords on a regular basis, thereby reducing the risk of outside access to this information.

Cost: 💵💵   Installation time: 🕐🕐

9–12 Show Potential Commissions on Cash Register

The sales manager can have difficulty in motivating the sales staff to sell those products with the highest margins. This is a particularly galling issue when there are so many products on hand it is almost impossible to educate the staff about margins on each one. Consequently, the sales staff sells whatever customers ask for, rather than attempting to steer them in the direction of more profitable products, resulting in less-than-optimal corporate profitability.

A rarely used best practice is to itemize the commission rates salespeople earn on individual products right on the cash register. When combined with a listing of the commissions on a range of related products, the sales staff can quickly scan the data, identify those that will make the most money, and steer customers toward them. Since the products with the highest commissions will presumably have the highest margins, this practice should result in higher company margins. The tool can also be used to emphasize sales on products the company is discontinuing and wishes to clear out of stock. Thus, by providing detailed information to the sales staff that is also tied to sales incentives, a company can increase its margins while also better managing its mix of on-hand products.

One problem is that this approach is usable only in a retail environment where salespeople ring up sales on the spot. It would not be functional at all, for example, if a salesperson conducts multiple sales calls on the road, though the concept can be modified by loading commission rates by product into a laptop computer, which the salesperson can consult during sales calls. Another issue is that the commission database will be a very complicated one, especially if commissions on products are changed frequently, necessitating a listing of commissions by both product and date. This can be a major programming job, requiring significant computer resources. Finally, the cash registers must include video display terminals of a sufficient size to show multiple products and their commissions—if such terminals do not exist, all retail locations using the system must be equipped with them, a significant extra expense. If these problems can be overcome, however, the posting of product commissions on cash registers can lead to a major improvement in corporate profitability.

Cost: **Installation time:**

Total Impact of Best Practices on the Commissions Function

This section describes the overall impact of best practices on the commissions function. The best practices noted in this chapter have an impact on four major accounting activities, as noted graphically in Exhibit 9.2. They impact the motivation of sales personnel, the calculation of commissions, and their payment and subsequent reporting. The vast majority of these best practices are centered on the calculation of commissions, since this step requires the most work from the accounting department. All of the best practices associated with commission calculations can be implemented together—none are mutually exclusive. Though the permission of the sales manager is required for several of these items, the end result—standardized commissions that are regularly audited, automatically calculated, and paid only from actual cash receipts—reduces the work of the

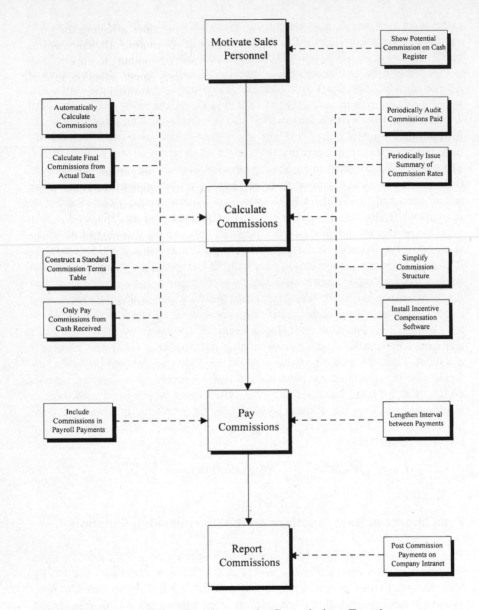

Exhibit 9.2 Impact of Best Practices on the Commissions Function

accounting staff to a remarkable degree. Those best practices affecting the payment of commissions have a much smaller impact on accounting efficiency, while the one item affecting the motivation of the sales staff does nothing to improve the accounting department. Accordingly, the bulk of management attention in this area should go to improving the efficiency of calculating commissions.

Summary

This chapter concentrated primarily on ways to reduce the time, effort, and number of errors in the calculation of commissions, with a reduced emphasis on better ways to pay commissions once they have been calculated. They are mostly easy best practices to implement. However, as noted several times in this chapter, several of them will directly affect the sales staff and so require the approval of the sales manager before they can be implemented. Since some of these changes will not be popular with the salespeople, do not be surprised if that approval is not forthcoming. If so, an occasional review of unapproved best practices may eventually find a more malleable sales manager in place, with a different result. Thus, if at first you don't succeed, try, try again.

Chapter 10

Costing Best Practices

This chapter is concerned with those best practices impacting the cost of products and the valuation of inventory. They are grouped into three main areas: information accuracy, cost reports, and costing systems. The first category, information accuracy, covers several best practices that review the accuracy of key information driving the costing of inventory: bills of material, labor routings, and units of measure. The second category, cost reports, is covered by the largest number of best practices. These are concerned with modifying or even eliminating the current cost-reporting systems in favor of a tighter focus on direct costs, materials, costs trends, and obsolete inventory. The final category, costing systems, addresses the two costing systems that should at least supplement, if not replace, traditional costing systems: activity-based costing and target costing. When the complete set of best practices advocated in this chapter has been implemented, a company will find that it has a much better grasp of its key product costs and how to control them.

Implementation Issues for Costing Best Practices

This section covers the general level of implementation cost and duration for each of the best practices discussed later in this chapter. Each best practice is noted in Exhibit 10.1, along with a rating of the cost and duration of implementation for each one. Generally speaking, these are easy best practices to install because most of them can be completed with no other approval than the controller's, and they have a short implementation duration and are quite inexpensive to install and operate. The main exceptions are target costing and activity-based costing, which require a major commitment of time and staff and the approval of other department managers, depending on their levels of involvement in the implementations. However, despite the level of installation difficulty for these two best practices, they both have the most significant positive impact of all the improvements noted in this chapter and thus are well worth the effort.

There are also several cost-reporting changes advocated in this chapter. Though the reports are not hard to alter or replace, it can be quite another matter to convince the report recipients that they are now receiving better information, especially if they are old-line managers who have received the same cost reports for decades. Consequently, the time required to insert a new cost report into a

Exhibit 10.1 Summary of Costing Best Practices

	Best Practice	*Cost*	*Install Time*
10–1	Audit bills of material		
10–2	Audit labor routings		
10–3	Eliminate high-leverage overhead allocation bases		
10–4	Assign overhead personnel to specific subplants		
10–5	Use perfect standards for material variance reporting		
10–6	Eliminate labor variance reporting		
10–7	Follow a schedule of inventory obsolescence reviews		
10–8	Eliminate the tracking of work-in-process inventory		
10–9	Implement activity-based costing		
10–10	Implement throughput accounting		
10–11	Implement target costing		
10–12	Track excess capacity		
10–13	Limit access to unit of measure changes		
10–14	Report on landed cost instead of supplier price		
10–15	Report on total customer price		
10–16	Review cost trends		
10–17	Review material scrap levels		
10–18	Revise traditional cost accounting reports		

company's standard reporting package can take much longer than one would normally expect.

10–1 Audit Bills of Material   ✔*Author's Choice*

When the accounting department issues financial statements, one of the largest expenses listed on it is the material cost (at least in a manufacturing environment). Unless they conduct a monthly physical inventory count, the accounting staff must rely on the word of the logistics department in assuming that the month-end inventory listed on the books is the correct amount. If it is not, the financial statements can be off by a significant amount. The core document used by the logistics department that drives the accuracy of the inventory is the bill of material. This is a listing of the components that go into a product. If it is incorrect, the parts assumed to be in a product will be incorrect, which means that product costs will be wrong, too. This problem has the greatest impact in a backflushing environment, where the bills of material determine how many materials are used to produce a product. Thus, the accuracy of the bills of material has a major impact on the accuracy of the financial statements.

The solution is to follow an ongoing program of auditing bills of material. By doing so, errors are flushed out of the bills, resulting in better inventory quantity data, which in turn results in more accurate financial statements. The best way to implement bill audits is to tie them to the production schedule, so that any products scheduled to be manufactured in the near future are reviewed the most frequently. This focuses attention on those bills with the highest usage, though it is still necessary to review the bills of less frequently used products from time to time. The review can be conducted by the engineering staff, the production scheduler, the warehouse staff, and the production staff. The reason for using so many people is that they all have input into the process. The engineering staff has the best overall knowledge of the product, while the production scheduler is the most aware of production shortages caused by problems with the bills, and the warehouse staff sees components returned to the warehouse that were listed in the bills but not actually used; the production staff must assemble products and knows from practical experience which bills are inaccurate. Thus, a variety of people (preferably all of them) can influence the bill of material review process.

Measuring a bill of material includes several steps. One is to ensure that the correct part quantities are listed. Another is to verify that parts should be included in the product at all. Yet another is that the correct subassemblies roll up into the final product. If any of these items are incorrect, a bill of material should be listed as incorrect in total. For a large bill with many components, this means that it will almost certainly be listed as incorrect when it is first reviewed, with rapid improvement as corrections are made. The target that a company should shoot for when reviewing bills of material is a minimum accuracy level of 98 percent. At this level, any errors will have a minimal impact on accuracy, cost of the inventory, and cost of goods sold.

If a controller can effectively work with the engineering, production, and logistics staffs to create a reliable bill of material review system, the result is a much more accurate costing system.

Cost: 🖅   **Installation time:** 🕰

10–2 Audit Labor Routings

The labor a company charges to each of its products is derived from a labor routing, which is an engineering estimate of the labor hours required to produce a product. Unfortunately, an inaccuracy in the labor-routing information has a major impact on a company's profitability for two reasons. One is that the labor hours assigned to a product will be incorrect, resulting in an incorrect product cost. By itself, this is not usually a major problem, because the labor cost is not a large component of the total product cost. However, the second reason is the real problem—since the labor rate is frequently used as the primary basis upon which overhead is allocated to products, a shift in the labor rate can result in a massive change in the allocated overhead cost, which may be much larger than the underlying labor cost. Thus, an inaccurate labor routing can have a major impact on the reported cost of a product.

The best practice that addresses this problem is auditing labor routings. By doing so, one can gradually review all labor records and verify their accuracy, thereby avoiding any miscosting of products. To do so, one must enlist the help of the engineering manager, who assigns a staff person to review this information on a regular basis and make changes as needed. The accounting department can assist in the effort by comparing the labor routings of similar products to see if there are any discrepancies and bring them to the attention of the engineering department for resolution. Also, it can review computer records (if they exist) to see when labor routings have been changed and verify the alterations with the engineering staff. Finally, the accounting staff can work with the production planning department to see if the assumed production-run quantities noted in the labor routings match actual production quantities. This last item is a critical one, for the assumed per-unit labor quantity will go down as the run length increases, due to the improved learning curve that comes with longer production runs, as well as the larger number of production units over which the labor setup time can be spread. Some unscrupulous businesspeople will assume very short production runs in order to increase the assumed labor rates in their labor routings, resulting in the capitalization of much higher labor and overhead costs in the inventory records. Thus, a continual review and comparison of labor-routing records by the accounting staff is a necessary component of this auditing process.

Cost: 🖊️   **Installation time:** ⏰

10–3 Eliminate High-Leverage Overhead Allocation Bases

There is nothing more damaging to a company than to make a management decision based on inaccurate information. Though the accounting department is devoted to presenting the best possible information to senior management at all times, there is one area in which it continues to provide inaccurate data: overhead costs. This is an increasingly large proportion of the costs of many companies, and it is critical to allocate it to various activities and products properly. To be blunt, most accountants do a very poor job of allocating these costs, resulting in cost reports that show inordinately high or low overhead costs being assigned to various items. When a manager acts upon this information, the decision may be a wrong one because the overhead cost component of the information was wrong. The reason why overhead costing information is incorrect in so many instances is a faulty allocation base. For example, the most common allocation base is to assign overhead costs to a product based on the amount of labor cost used to build it. The trouble is that labor is an increasingly small component of total labor costs, resulting in large overhead amounts being allocated based on tiny labor costs. The ratio of overhead to labor costs can reach absurd levels, such as $10 for every $1 of labor. When there are large differences between the proportion of overhead to the allocation base, even a slight change in the allocation base will result in a large swing in the overhead costs. Thus, minute month-to-month differences in the allocation base can falsely alter product costs by significant amounts.

The best practice that resolves this problem is to find new allocation bases that are not so highly leveraged. By doing so, there is less chance of having unusual cost swings based on small alterations in the allocation base. A good rule of thumb is to keep the ratio of allocation base to overhead cost no higher than one to one and preferably much less. This way, small changes in the allocation base will result in similarly small changes in the overhead cost. If the allocation base is not monetary, use an allocation base that is so large that any large changes are unlikely. For example, if square footage is used as the allocation base, the chance that the amount of square footage will suddenly change by an inordinate amount is quite small. In either case, the goal of reducing wide swings in overhead costs has been achieved.

This is a simple best practice to implement, usually requiring a modest investment in investigation time in order to find new allocation bases to replace the existing ones, as well as a few days of work to set up the allocation formulas. Since there is little or no programming required, and the approval of other departments is unnecessary, there is no reason why this implementation cannot succeed in short order.

This best practice addresses the problem of keeping overhead costs from changing significantly. Another best practice reviews the problem from a different angle, which is tightly linking overhead costs to specific activities, resulting in a more informed allocation of costs to those activities driving the costs. For more information, see the "Implement Activity-Based Costing" section later in this chapter.

Cost: 💵   **Installation time:** 🕐

10–4 Assign Overhead Personnel to Specific Subplants

One of the largest headaches for the cost accounting staff is determining what overhead costs are assigned to which products. Not only are these assignments subject to considerable personal interpretation, but also they can strongly impact the way management views the profitability of various products. For example, if the assignment is made to a product of overhead costs that are not related to its manufacture, storage, or use in any way, its costs will appear artificially high, and management may even stop manufacturing it on the false grounds that it is not profitable.

A possible solution is to divide the production area into subplants, each one assigned the task of manufacturing a subset of all company products. One can then assign most of the overhead personnel, such as buyers, shop supervisors, and materials handlers to specific subplants. By doing so, the cost accounting staff can much more easily allocate overhead costs to specific products. This approach meshes nicely with the activity-based costing concept previously discussed, since costs are more closely identified with specific products.

The trouble is the considerable effort required to reshuffle the production layout into subplants. Further, if subplants are too small, it may not be possible to assign staff full-time to just one subplant, forcing them to service several subplants at once, and reducing the efficiency of costing allocations.

Cost: Installation time: 🕐 🕐

10–5 Use Perfect Standards for Material Variance Reporting

The typical bill of materials contains a standard amount of scrap that is expected to occur as part of the manufacturing process. Once a reporting period is completed, the cost accountant summarizes the standard amount of expected scrap listed in the bills of material, and constructs variances by comparing the standard scrap to actual scrap. The problem with this approach is that the company adopts a mind-set that the standard scrap levels are acceptable, and so never undertakes any scrap reduction activities that will shrink the amount of "standard" scrap.

To avoid this mindset trap, assume a zero level of baseline scrap for variance reporting purposes. Also, rather than reporting a materials variance, instead report on the total amount of wasted materials (since there is no longer a baseline from which to calculate a variance). By making these changes, management can now see the total amount of scrap and presumably take action to reduce it to levels well below their former levels.

The cost accountant's variance reporting is now replaced with a detailed examination of the dollar value of various types of scrap, which helps management direct its efforts into the reduction of those sources of waste having the greatest dollar value. Thus, the cost accountant is constantly reshuffling the waste data to ascertain where the next waste reduction campaign can be most profitably initiated, which will likely include the use of root cause analysis. This change in reporting represents a significant alteration from the former reporting functions of the cost accountant, and may require retraining in problem analysis techniques.

Cost: Installation time: 🕐 🕐

10–6 Eliminate Labor Variance Reporting ✔ *Author's Choice*

The cost components of work-in-process and inventory goods will inevitably include some labor. However, the proportion of labor in the total cost mix has dropped markedly over the years, with material and overhead costs now predominating. Nonetheless, the costing reports the accounting staff has traditionally generated are mostly concerned with labor. Examples of these reports are those detailing overtime, comparing actual to standard labor rates or usage, and labor efficiency. By comparison, the reports concerned with the materials expense typically cover only scrap rates and purchase price variances, while many companies have no reporting for overhead costs at all. Hence, most accounting departments are misallocating their time in reporting on the smallest component of product costs.

The solution is to stop reporting on labor variances. The accounting staff will have more time to spend on reports concerning costs that make up a larger proportion of product costs. The problem with this best practice is the remarkable uproar it frequently incites, especially on the part of traditional production managers who were raised on the concept of tight labor cost controls. Thus, the best way to implement this item is to carefully educate the production staff on the following points:

- *Direct labor is really a fixed cost.* In many manufacturing situations, the direct labor staff cannot be sent home the moment there is no work left to do. Instead, a company must think about retaining them since they are trained and more efficient than other people who might be brought in off the street. Accordingly, it makes a great deal of sense to guarantee regular working hours to the direct labor staff. By doing so, it becomes apparent that direct labor is not a variable cost at all and requires much less detailed investigation and reporting work for the accounting staff.

- *Other reports are more valuable.* If the accounting department only has enough resources to issue a fixed number of reports, there is a good argument for eliminating the least useful ones (labor reporting) in favor of ones involving more costs, such as materials and overhead. One can reinforce this argument by formulating trial report layouts for new reports that will replace the labor reports.

- *Target costing is the real area of concern.* Many studies have shown that costs are not that variable once a product design is released to the factory floor. Instead, the primary area in which costs can truly be impacted is during the product design (see the "Implement Target Costing" section later in this chapter).

If production management can be convinced that these three points are accurate, it becomes much easier to eliminate labor variance reporting, either completely or in part.

The only situation in which this best practice should not be implemented is one where labor costs still make up the majority of product costs and where those costs are variable. If labor costs are highly fixed in nature, there is not much point in continuing to issue reports showing that the costs have not changed from period to period.

Cost: 💵   **Installation time:** ⏰

10–7   Follow a Schedule of Inventory
Obsolescence Reviews   ✔*Author's Choice*

A great many companies find that the proportion of their inventory that is obsolete is much higher than expected. This is a major problem at the end of the fiscal year, when this type of inventory is supposed to be investigated and written off, usually in conjunction with the auditor's review or the physical inventory (or both). If this write-off has not occurred in previous years, the cumulative amount can be quite startling. This may result in the departure of the controller, on the grounds that he or she should have known about the problem.

The solution is adopting and sticking to a schedule of regular obsolete-inventory reviews. This is an unpopular task with many employees because they must pore over usage reports and wander through the warehouse to see what inventory is not needed and then follow up on disposal problems. However, these people do not realize the major benefits of having a periodic obsolete-inventory review. One is that it clears space out of the warehouse, which may even allow for a reduction in the space this department needs. Also, spotting obsolete inventory as early as possible allows a company to realize the best salvage value for it, which will inevitably decline over time (unless a company is dealing in antiques!). Further, a close review of the reason why an inventory item is in stock and obsolete may lead to discoveries concerning how parts are ordered and used; changing these practices may lead to a reduction in obsolete inventory in the future. Thus, there are a number of excellent reasons for maintaining an ongoing obsolete-inventory review system.

The composition of the obsolete-inventory review committee is very important. There should be an accountant who can summarize the costs of obsolescence, while an engineering representative is in the best position to determine if a part can be used elsewhere. Also, someone from the purchasing department can tell if there is any resale value. Consequently, a cross-departmental committee is needed to properly review obsolete inventory.

The main contribution of the accounting department to this review is a periodic report itemizing those parts most likely to be obsolete. This information can take the following forms:

• *Last usage date.* Many computer systems record the last date on which a specific part number was removed from the warehouse for production or sale. If so, use a report writer to extract and sort this information, resulting in a report that lists all inventory, starting with those products with the oldest "last used" date.

- *No "where used" in the system.* If a computer system includes a bill of materials, there is a strong likelihood that it also generates a "where used" report, which lists all of the bills of material for which an inventory item is used. If there is no "where used" listed on the report, it is likely that a part is no longer needed. This report is most effective if bills of material are removed from the computer system as soon as products are withdrawn from the market; this more clearly reveals those inventory items that are no longer needed. This approach can also be used to determine which inventory *is going to be* obsolete, based on the anticipated withdrawal of *existing* products from the market.

- *Comparison to previous-year physical inventory tags.* Many companies still conduct a physical inventory at the end of their fiscal years. When this is done, a tag is usually taped to each inventory item. Later, a member of the accounting staff can walk through the warehouse and mark down all inventory items with an inventory tag still attached to them. This is a simple visual approach for finding old inventory.

- *Acknowledged obsolete inventory still in the system.* Even the best inventory review committee will sometimes let obsolete inventory fall through the cracks and remain in both the warehouse and the inventory database. The accounting staff should keep track of all acknowledged obsolete inventory and continue to notify management of those items that have not yet been removed.

Any or all of these reports can be used to gain a knowledge of likely candidates for obsolete-inventory status. This information is the mandatory first step in the process of keeping the inventory up-to-date. Consequently, the accounting staff plays a major role in this process.

Cost: 💵   **Installation time:** 🕰️

10–8 Eliminate the Tracking of Work-in-Process Inventory

One of the most complex and error-ridden tasks for the cost accountant is the tracking and accumulation of costs for work-in-process (WIP) inventory. Because inventory can pass through many workstations, picking up machining and labor costs as it progresses through the production facility, there can be a multitude of transactions to accumulate and charge to inventory. Also, because inventory-tracking systems are typically at their worst in the production area (as opposed to the controlled environment in the warehouse), it is common to see inventory records disappear. Materials themselves can also disappear, since scrap can occur throughout the production process. The end result is a labor-intensive accounting mess that frequently yields inaccurate costing results.

The solution requires the conversion of the production process to cellular manufacturing and the elimination of WIP queues in the production area. Once this has been accomplished, WIP levels will have been driven so low that there is no point in tracking WIP at all. Instead, the cost accounting staff will continue to record items as being in raw materials inventory until they are assembled into final products, after which they are transferred directly into the finished goods inventory.

The problem is certainly not with the elimination of WIP inventory—the cost accounting staff will adopt this practice with enthusiasm. The issue is the massive alteration in production practices leading to the minimization of WIP inventory.

Cost: 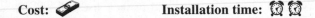   Installation time:

10–9 Implement Activity-Based Costing

The vast majority of companies only accumulate and report on costs by department and product. The first method is tied to responsibility accounting, whereby the costs of the specific department are tied to the performance bonus of its manager. The second method assumes that the cost of overhead—mostly made up of those departmental costs noted in the first method—is assigned to products based on the amount of labor they accumulate. The problem with this approach is that the two methods should be combined so that *all* company costs, to the greatest extent possible, are tied to the actual cost required to produce a product. Without this information, a company is doomed to make incorrect decisions related to the correct pricing of products, or even if they should be continued or discontinued. The same problem applies to determining the cost or profit associated with each customer. Again, a company can work incorrectly to increase its business with a high-maintenance customer that results in much lower overall profits, while abandoning other customers that are really much more profitable. Poor costing methodologies are at the bottom of many bad corporate decisions.

The solution to this problem is a system called activity-based costing. Under this approach, a company summarizes all of its costs into a number of cost pools, then allocates the expenses in those pools to a variety of activities, using a large number of allocation measures. It becomes much easier to accurately assign the costs of these activities to various products and customers, based on their usage of the activities. Though this may seem like nothing more than an elaborate allocation of overhead, it is actually a carefully constructed methodology for determining the true cost of a company's products and services. Along with target costing, it is the most significant advance in costing methodologies in the last few decades, eminently worth the effort of putting in place.

However, installing an activity-based costing system is not that easy. The cost pools must be constructed, allocation measures determined, and new systems created to store, calculate, and report all of this information. In addition, the cooperation of other departments is necessary to ensure that new allocation measures are properly and consistently calculated. Finally, management must be apprised of the content of the new reports that will come out of this system and how they can be used. Given the considerable cost, time, and training required to ensure that this system becomes fully operational and accepted by management, it is no surprise that many such installations have not been completed, and even completed ones do not enjoy the full support of upper management. Thus, it is not so strange that activity-based costing is the best cost-accounting tool available and yet does not enjoy universal popularity or usage.

From the perspective of the accounting department, installing this system is a difficult chore. Depending on the size of the company, one or more staff people should be allocated to the project full-time for many months. In addition, the existing accounting software almost certainly does not track activity-based costs; a secondary software package must be purchased that takes information from the general ledger, as well as allocation bases from a variety of locations, summarizes data into cost pools, allocates it to activities, and charges costs to products. Also, given the newness of this approach and the lack of instruction about it at the college level, the services of a consultant may be worth the added cost. Further, a considerable amount of management time must go into planning and controlling the work effort, so that it is completed on time without exceeding the budgeted expenditure level.

Cost: 💸💸   **Installation time:** ⏰⏰⏰

10–10 Implement Throughput Accounting ✔*Author's Choice*

The preceding best practice recommended the use of activity-based costing (ABC) as a central costing technique. However, ABC suffers from a key assumption that can result in incorrect decision making in the short term—it assumes that all costs are variable. Over the long term, this assumption is correct, since even the largest assets, such as a building, can be eliminated. However, these costs are fixed in the short term, and so should not be allocated for short-term order acceptance or manufacturing prioritization purposes. Thus, ABC can result in the allocation of an excessive amount of "fixed" costs to a product, resulting in decisions not to accept customer orders that could have yielded short-term profits.

An alternative system to use for these short-term decisions is throughput accounting. Under this approach, only the cost of direct materials is considered to be variable, with all other costs assumed to be fixed in the short term. This assumption results in significantly larger product gross margins than would be the case if ABC were used, so that lower price points will now be considered to yield acceptable gross margins. Throughput accounting is especially valid for manufacturing facilities that use large amounts of machinery, since these assets are substantially less variable in the short term than would be the cost of manufacturing labor.

This technique is especially useful for monitoring the usage of work centers that are bottleneck operations, especially in regard to how the flow of orders through bottleneck operations impact total profits generated by the manufacturing system.

Cost: **Installation time:** 🕰 🕰

10–11 Implement Target Costing

A cost accounting staff can create the best costing reports in the world, constantly update this information, and hound the production, engineering, and purchasing staffs incessantly to improve the situation, and find little change in product costs. The reason is that most product costs are locked in when the product is *designed*. For example, a poor microwave oven design will lead to production inefficiencies because the product was not designed for ease of manufacturability. Similarly, if the oven was not designed to be sufficiently sturdy, there will be a number of customer returns, resulting in added engineering and manufacturing costs to fix the problem. Further, the oven may contain nonstandard parts that are both difficult and expensive to obtain and that may not allow for the use of existing parts used with other products. Thus, cost accounting is focusing on the wrong target—product costs during *production*, instead of product costs during the *design* stage.

The best practice that addresses this issue is called target costing. Under this concept, the existing market is reviewed and a target price is determined at which a certain set of product specifications will probably sell quite well. A design team is then assigned the task of creating a product with those specifications and a maximum cost. The maximum cost figure allows a company to sell for the previously determined price while still making an acceptable profit. If it is impossible to produce the product for the maximum assigned cost, the project is abandoned. This approach is in contrast to the more traditional method of designing a product, determining how much it costs when the project is finished, and then adding on a profit percentage to arrive at a selling price.

The obvious advantage of target costing is that a company has total control over product costs before any product reaches the production floor. It is easy to determine which products should be produced and which ones abandoned, thereby keeping losing or marginally profitable products out of a company's product mix. From the accounting department's perspective, its costing work shifts away from tracking production costs and into tracking costs during the design phase. This means that a cost accountant should be reassigned from the first activity to the latter so there is a daily review of the range of costs into which target costs are likely to fall. By shifting the direction of the accounting department's costing analysis, one can report on the activities which truly have the greatest impact on product costs.

Cost:    Installation time: 🕭 🕭

10–12 Track Excess Capacity

The typical company has excessive production capacity in multiple production operations, which are constrained by just a few bottleneck operations. Company management may not realize the extent to which some of its asset investment is underutilized, which can seriously impact the company's return on investment.

A solution is to track excess production capacity by work center or individual machine or person. By doing so, management can ascertain if some assets or employee positions can be eliminated or even outsourced. However, there are some issues with this best practice. First, the excess capacity reporting must take into account the maximum levels of usage that occasionally occur. For example, a machine may work at only 15 percent capacity on average, but have periodic bursts of activity reaching near 100 percent of capacity when certain types of products having unique machining requirements are scheduled for production. In these cases, the excess capacity level should be graphed on a timeline, so that management can see the level and duration of these capacity utilization spikes. If the spikes are of short duration, management may conclude that it can still eliminate some assets and simply outsource the excess levels of work.

A second problem with excess capacity reporting is that management will have a tendency to use it to eliminate *all* excess assets, resulting in a "balanced plant" where there is exactly enough capacity throughout the facility. The trouble with this approach is that shifting manufacturing requirements and unexpected work center downtime create a considerable degree of demand fluctuation that requires some excess capacity to overcome. Thus, some level of excess capacity is still needed in the production system in order to achieve an optimal production flow.

Cost: 💵   Installation time: 🕭

10–13 Limit Access to Unit of Measure Changes

The unit of measure field, an innocuous field in the computer system, can have a major impact on the accuracy of product costs. When the quantity in a bill of material or inventory record is created, it has a unit of measure listed next to it. For example, one inch of tape on a bill of materials will have a quantity of one and a unit of measure of "IN," or "inch." However, if the unit of measure is changed to "RL," or "roll" without a corresponding reduction in the amount of tape listed in the quantity field, the amount of tape picked for production will increase from one inch to an entire roll. The same problem applies to the inventory, where a change to the unit of measure field without a corresponding change in the quantity field will result in a potentially massive change in the amount of inventory on the books. This seemingly minor issue can result in a major change in the cost of goods sold.

The solution is to limit access to the unit of measure field in the computer system, preferably to one person or position. By doing so, all changes must be reviewed by one person, who will presumably be trained well enough to realize the relationship between units of measure and quantities. If access by multiple people cannot be avoided, then a less-reliable variation is to require approval by a manager before making a change. However, as someone can make a change without approval, this system is too easy to bypass. A third variation is to carefully review changes in the unit of measure fields after the fact, perhaps with an occasional internal audit, but this approach only finds problems after they have already been made; the best solution is always to keep the problem from occurring in the first place.

An excellent alternative is to set up the computer system so that multiple units of measure are allowed. To use the previous example, the roll of tape can be listed as both one roll or 1,760 inches in the same inventory or bill of material record; this approach eliminates anyone's need to change the unit of measure field, since all possible variations are already described. Unfortunately, not all accounting and manufacturing software packages contain this feature; it is not normally available unless a company is willing to invest in some complicated and expensive programming.

Cost: 💵   Installation time: ⏰

10–14 Report on Landed Cost Instead of Supplier Price   ✔ *Author's Choice*

When the purchasing department focuses exclusively on reducing the purchase price charged by suppliers, it is not seeing the entire expense associated with bringing a product to the company. There is also the transportation cost associated with the purchase, as well as the lot sizes in which items are shipped (and associated storage requirements), damage incurred while in transit, the potential for foreign exchange losses, and shipping insurance. For example, the purchasing department may use an overseas supplier in an attempt to reduce the per-unit cost of an item. However, by doing so, it must order in much larger lot sizes and several weeks earlier than was previously necessary. It must also pay for shipping insurance, as well as the services of an international shipping broker. The net result is no change in the total cost of the product once it arrives at the company's receiving dock.

The solution for the accounting department is to focus the company's attention on the landed cost of purchased items rather than the supplier price. By doing so, the purchasing department gains a better understanding of the total cost of bringing items to the company, and avoids incorrect purchasing decisions that might otherwise increase company expenses.

The downside is the extra work required by the accounting department. Rather than simply recording the amount listed on the supplier invoice as the total product cost, the accounting staff must accumulate expenses from several other sources, such as foreign exchange costs from the finance department, shipping insurance and loss claims from the materials management department, and order lot sizes from the purchasing department. Given the extra accounting effort required, one should concentrate recurring landed cost reporting efforts on only the largest-dollar item purchases, with spot checks of other items.

Cost: **Installation time:** 🕑 🕑

10–15 Report on Total Customer Price

The sales department uses the company's standard price list to determine how much it is charging customers—but is that really the entire price that the customer pays? The price may actually include a number of other items, such as insurance, sales taxes, customs fees, and freight. When a customer compares these total costs that it must absorb to buy the company's products, it is entirely possible that the total cost is higher than if the customer bought from other competitors. They may be located closer, so that freight costs are lower, or they may be willing to absorb insurance costs, and so forth. The result may be that a customer unexpectedly switches to a competitor, even though the company's posted price for the same product appears to be lower.

The cost accounting staff can estimate such costs to see what the total cost is for key customers, not only if they buy from the company but also if they buy from a selection of key competitors instead. Being aware of these differences in the total price to the customer allows the sales staff to make informed decisions regarding whether to change the company's pricing structure or issue special deals. For example, if a customer is located near a key competitor, and therefore will pay less freight to buy from that competitor, then the company can offer to absorb the freight cost on deliveries. As another example, if an international customer is shipping with partial ship containers, the company can offer to adjust payment terms, so the customer can consolidate purchases into less-expensive full container lots.

Reporting on the total customer price obviously includes a great deal of assumptions about customer costs and the prices of competitors. However, if it points out a significant pricing disparity, the sales staff should know about the problem immediately and should be prepared to counter it.

Cost: **Installation time:** 🕑 🕑

10–16 Review Cost Trends

The typical cost accounting report shows the current cost of each product, perhaps in relation to a standard cost that was put in place when the product was first created. Though this report does give management a snapshot of how existing costs relate to standards, there is no way to see if the cost was gradually increased or decreased from the preset standard cost, if the actual cost was ever close to the standard cost, or if there have been sudden changes in costs which are probably related either to step-costs in the overhead category (such as adding a new facility) or to material cost changes. Given the lack of information, management has no way of knowing if the current costing situation reflects a deterioration in costs or an improvement.

The solution is to switch to reporting based on cost trends. An example is shown in Exhibit 10.2. As noted in the exhibit, the report starts with a base cost established with actual cost data when the product was first released to production. Then the series of columns in the middle of the report show the historical total cost of each product, based on any time period that is most appropriate (quarterly costs are shown in the exhibit). Then the projected target cost that the company is striving for is noted to the far right of the report, with a final column noting the percentage difference in cost between the most recent cost and the target cost, along with the date by which the company is expecting to achieve the target cost. This format allows management to easily determine where costing problems are developing, or if there are potential problems with reaching a targeted cost by the due date. This approach gives management a much more potent tool to use in tracking product costs.

Exhibit 10.2 Sample Cost Trend Analysis

Product Description	Base Cost	Actual Cost 3/31/10	Actual Cost 6/30/10	Actual Cost 9/30/10	Target Cost	Variance from Target	Target Date
Pail	$ 4.00	$ 4.12	$ 4.15	$ 4.29	$ 3.98	8%	03/31/08
Bucket	3.92	3.92	3.90	3.88	3.75	3%	03/31/08
Trowel	1.57	1.65	1.72	1.67	1.57	6%	03/31/08
Spade	8.07	9.48	10.93	10.93	8.07	35%	06/30/08
Shovel	8.08	9.49	10.94	10.94	8.08	35%	06/30/08
Hose	15.01	14.98	14.95	14.90	14.90	0%	06/30/08
Sprinkler	23.19	28.01	28.77	27.75	23.00	21%	06/30/08

Supplemental information can enhance the information shown on the cost trend chart. For example, it can include a column showing either unit or dollar volume for each item, allowing management to quickly determine where it should invest the bulk of its time in fixing problems—on those products that have a large dollar impact on total revenues, as opposed to those that may have large cost variances but that have only a negligible profitability impact. It may also be useful to include the price and margin in the table, though this can be difficult to determine if pricing varies significantly by customer, perhaps due to variations in the volumes sold to each one. Another reporting possibility is to issue a subsidiary-level report that breaks down product costs into multiple components, so management can determine which costs are deviating from expected values. If this option is used, there should be matching target costs for each component, so management can compare actual to expected costs in all categories and see where there are problems. Finally, if there are many variations on a standard product design, the report may become too lengthy and unwieldy to be easily readable. For example, this can happen when the same product is issued in ten different colors, resulting in a report with ten line items—one for each product variation. In this instance, it is useful to cluster each product group into a single line item resulting in a much shorter and more readable report. All or some of these reporting variations can give management a better idea of the cost trends to which their products are subject.

Cost: **Installation time:** 🕰

10–17 Review Material Scrap Levels

There are a number of ways to tell if a production process is not operating as efficiently as it could. For example, labor hours are higher than expected, material usage exceeds the standard, or delivery times are chronically late. However, the accounting department does not do well in reporting on late deliveries, since this does not involve the database of financial information that the accounting staff normally accesses. Also, the direct labor pool tends to be relatively fixed in the short term, and so is surprisingly difficult to reduce. Thus, accounting reports showing excessive labor may not result in an immediate impact on this area. However, reporting on material scrap rates is well worth the effort. The reason is that a high scrap rate is the primary indicator of a host of potential problems in the production process. For example, scrap can be caused by poor operator training, bad machine maintenance, an excessive level of work-in-process inventory, and design flaws. By using material scrap as the prime indicator of problems in the production process, management can locate the reasons for it, target those problems, and eliminate them.

The problem for the accounting department is how to issue a valid material scrap rate report. If the report is inaccurate, management will not believe the numbers and will not use the information to improve the production process. It is vital to derive the most accurate information possible from the evidence at hand. There are a variety of scrap reporting methods available, noted in the following bullet points:

- *Weigh the scrap.* The simplest method for determining the amount of scrap is to put it in a pile and weigh it. This is a practical approach if a company can recycle the bulk of its scrap and therefore keeps it in recycling bins. One can then weigh the bins and multiply the weight by the average cost of the scrap to determine a total scrap cost.

- *Summarize receipts from scrap purchasers.* An even easier approach is to let the scrap purchaser weigh the scrap bin and use this information to derive the total cost of the scrap.

- *Compare standard to actual material usage.* The approach that results in the most detailed information about exactly which material has been scrapped is a comparison of standard material quantities to actual usage. This requires accurate bills of material, production records, and inventory counts; without them, a comparison of these records will not result in an accurate determination of scrap costs.

- *Create a floor reporting system.* This is the approach used the most by those companies with poor production records. If they cannot use the preceding option due to the existence of inaccurate bills of material, production records, or inventory records, they must require the production staff to manually track the scrap they are generating. This approach tends to underreport scrap, since production personnel do not like to report on the inefficiencies of their own department. Also, the scrap reporting by the manufacturing personnel can be voluminous and may require extra staff to summarize and analyze. Thus, this approach is prone to inaccuracy and high reporting costs.

Of the previous scrap reporting methods, some are not accurate enough to provide more than a rough guess at the exact items that were scrapped; these include weighing the scrap or perusing the receipts from scrap purchasers. The other two reporting systems reveal the most useful information because they detail the exact items that were scrapped. Of the two, comparing actual to standard usage is the easiest to implement, since it requires no additional reporting by manufacturing personnel; however, the standards must be accurate, or the basis of comparison will not function properly. If the standards (e.g., bills of material, production records, and inventory records) are not accurate, one is faced with the problem of either correcting the underlying information or implementing the final reporting option, which is creating a shop floor reporting system for tracking actual material scrap rates. The exact reporting method used will depend on the level of reporting detail needed, as well as the accuracy of a company's production database.

Cost: **Installation time:**

10–18 Revise Traditional Cost Accounting Reports

Though many of the other best practices advocated in this chapter involve doing away with or replacing the existing set of cost accounting reports, there are instances in which they can be modified sufficiently to still be of great use. This section deals with a number of small changes that can greatly enhance these reports. Though it would be best to install all of these upgrades, even using just one or two of them would bring about an incremental improvement in costing information. The changes are as follows:

- *Assemble products into reporting groups.* Too often, a cost report presents a list of hundreds of products, sorted by product number. Though there may be plenty of valid information in such a report, there is no easy way for a busy executive to determine where it is. Instead, it should be grouped into relevant categories, such as clustering all product variations into a single summary number or clustering product sales by customer. These clusters should always contain subtotals so managers can take in the total cost impact of each group at a glance.

- *Give rapid feedback.* There is no point in compiling a perfect cost analysis if it is done months after a product is produced. Instead, a good cost report should be issued as soon as possible after a product is completed, allowing management to make changes to improve costs the next time the product is made. The best case of all is when a cost report is issued to management while a product is still being made (and preferably near the beginning of a production run) so immediate alterations will result in a rapid cost reduction.

- *Only report on exceptions.* Some companies have such enormously long cost reports that there is no way to glance through them and spot the problem situations. To resolve this issue, reports should be issued that only show exceptions. For example, a report may only show those products with negative cost variances of at least 10 percent. By doing so, a voluminous report can be reduced to a short memo revealing those items requiring immediate attention.

- *Report on costs by customer.* All too many cost reports only focus on product costs, not the total costs of dealing with each customer. By widening the focus of a traditional cost report to include this extra information, one can reveal some startling information, especially if a customer that was previously thought to be highly profitable is eating up an outsized proportion of a company's resources in such areas as purchasing, warehousing, and order entry.

- *Use direct costing.* Many costing reports only show product margins after overhead is included in the total costing mix. However, if the overhead allocation is not valid, management has no way of knowing what margins really are and usually ends up ignoring the cost reports entirely. An easy way to avoid this problem is to insert an extra pair of columns in the cost report, in which are inserted the dollar margin after direct costs (i.e., price minus labor and materials) and the direct cost margin percentage. Though this variation leaves no room for any overhead cost at all, it does result in a good analysis of direct costs.

These best practices focus on assembling information into a format that is easy to read, relevant, does not require the reader to wade through vast amounts of data, and presents information as rapidly as possible. By installing them, one can make the existing cost reports much more relevant to the decisions that management must make every day.

Cost: 💵💵💵   **Installation time:** ⏰⏰

Total Impact of Best Practices on the Costing Function

This section describes the impact of all the best practices described in this chapter on the costing function. They address three main areas within the costing function, as noted in Exhibit 10.3. Auditing various sources of costing information will improve its accuracy. Eliminating old costing reports and replacing them with ones that focus on scrap levels, obsolescence, cost trends, and direct costs will have a major impact on the quality of information presented to the rest of the organization. Finally, implementing activity-based costing and target costing systems will drastically improve the types of cost information that management can use to make costing-related decisions.

Of all these best practices, it is difficult to pick out one or two that must be implemented before all others, due to their impact, becauset these best practices are highly interrelated. For example, an activity-based costing system provides valuable new information, but no one will see it if the new data is shoehorned into the same old cost accounting reports. Similarly, new costing reports are vital but will still contain inaccurate information unless the underlying data is improved through regular audits. Thus, it is necessary to install these best practices as a group in order to obtain the maximum impact of quality information presented in a new and informative format.

If all of these best practices are installed, the primary impact on the organization will be much better costing information than what was previously available. However, the reports will not have an impact on the organization unless they are acted upon. This calls for a very active controller, who must peruse the new information, devise action plans based on it, and aggressively market both the reports and his or her conclusions to management on a continuing basis. Without this proactive approach, senior managers will receive the new reports and not realize that they are holding a powerful new tool in their hands. Thus, the

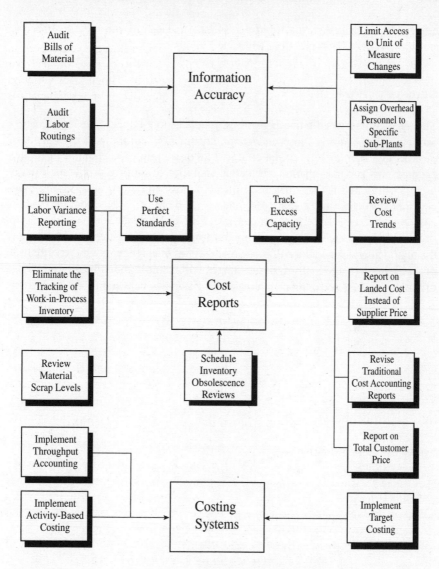

Exhibit 10.3 Impact of Best Practices on the Costing Function

controller is the key to the rapid acceptance and use of the new costing data resulting from the best practices advocated in this chapter.

Summary

This chapter described a number of best practices that impact inventory costing. Some involve auditing those underlying documents with the greatest impact on profitability, such as bills of material and labor routings. Others alter or replace existing cost reports, resulting in better visibility of costing problems. Finally, target costing and activity-based costing systems can be installed, giving much control over costs (in the first case) and vastly more accurate information about costs (in the latter case). These are generally easy implementations, with the exception of the two new costing systems, but implementing the reports will require the approval and acceptance of those members of management who read them. If properly implemented, all of these changes will result in much better knowledge of costs, which, if acted upon, can make the difference between profits and losses.

Chapter 11

Filing Best Practices

This chapter covers the best practices that can be used to create a more efficient filing system for an accounting department. Though this may seem like such an easy topic that it does not warrant its own chapter, there are actually many steps that a progressive accounting staff can take to greatly enhance the efficiency of its filing work.

This chapter does not focus on doing a better job of filing documents. On the contrary, filing is a totally nonvalue-added activity, so the focus here is on finding ways to completely avoid filing. This can be done through a variety of approaches, including an increased use of electronic documents, standard procedures for destroying old documents, and keeping paper from being used in the first place. All of these document prevention techniques are designed to keep paper from ever reaching the filing staff, thereby allowing a company to reduce the clerical work associated with filing, while also reducing the amount of space needed to store documents. These major benefits deserve a separate chapter, no matter how minor the subject matter may at first appear to be.

Implementation Issues for Filing Best Practices

This section discusses the relative ease or difficulty of implementation of the best practices to be covered later in this chapter. Each best practice is noted in Exhibit 11.1. For each best practice, there are columns noting the cost and duration of implementation. These are relative measures and will vary considerably depending on the circumstances in each company. In general, the overall level of implementation is considered to be easiest if they are entirely within the control of the accounting department, such as for adopting a document-destruction policy. However, if they involve the cooperation of another department, or if they require special computer programming to implement, which is the case for many of the best practices related to storing data on a computer, then the implementation is assumed to be much more difficult to complete.

The two most expensive best practices are document imaging and extending the time period before computer records are purged from primary computer storage. The reason for this assessment is data storage—document imaging requires extremely large amounts of storage, usually involving a compact disc jukebox with storage levels in the very high gigabyte range, as does increasing primary

Exhibit 11.1 Summary of Filing Best Practices

	Best Practice	Cost	Install Time
Mailroom Improvements			
11–1	Improve the mailroom interface	💵	⏰
Computer-Related Filing Issues			
11–2	Reduce keystroke errors	💵	⏰⏰
11–3	Use multiple OCR engines for data capture	💵💵💵	⏰⏰⏰
11–4	Add digital signatures to electronic documents	💵	⏰
11–5	Archive computer files	💵💵	⏰
11–6	Implement document imaging	💵💵💵	⏰⏰⏰
11–7	Eliminate stored paper documents if already in computer	💵	⏰⏰
11–8	Extend time period before computer records are purged	💵💵💵	⏰⏰
11–9	Extend use of existing computer database	💵💵💵	⏰⏰⏰
11–10	Improve computer system reliability	💵💵	⏰⏰
11–11	Track documents with RFID	💵💵	⏰⏰
Other Filing Issues			
11–12	Adopt a document-destruction policy	💵	⏰
11–13	Eliminate attaching back-up materials to checks for signing	💵	⏰
11–14	Eliminate reports	💵	⏰⏰
11–15	Move records off-site	💵💵	⏰⏰
11–16	Reduce number of form copies to file	💵	⏰⏰

storage to extend the time period over which records are kept in the computer system. In both cases, one should carefully research costs with the assistance of the computer department before taking any additional implementation steps.

The remainder of this chapter covers the best practices for the filing function as presented in Exhibit 11.1.

11–1 Improve the Mailroom Interface

The proportion of all incoming mail going to the accounting department is usually well over half the total. Given this volume, the accounting manager has considerable interest in ensuring that the mail is properly routed to the accounting department. A wide variety of efficiencies can apply here, including the outright elimination of incoming mail, electronic forms, and the digitization and electronic distribution of received mail. At a more basic level of incremental efficiency, you can even copy Affiliated Computer Services (ACS), which speeds mail opening and reduces torn letters by opening mail with a belt sander (!). Here are some possibilities to consider:

- *Reroute the mail.* This means sending checks to a lockbox. Rather than run the risk of having the mailroom mishandle a check, just have customers send them straight to a lockbox.

- *Use electronic forms.* If you want customers to complete and send in forms, such as credit applications or W-9 forms, consider putting an electronic form on your Web site that allows them to send information straight into your computer system and bypass the mailroom.

- *Mailroom opens all mail.* Don't just let the mailroom forward envelopes to employees without first opening them (unless they are marked "confidential"), since some customers like to send payments to the salesperson assigned to them—and that person might not open his mail for some time, thereby impeding cash flow.

- *Digitize all incoming mail.* The mailroom can scan every incoming piece of mail and e-mail it to employees, which eliminates routing time and stores a permanent record of the mail in the e-mail system.

    Cost: 💵   **Installation time:** ⏰

11–2 Reduce Keystroke Errors

One of the primary ongoing tasks of any accounting manager is to avoid data-entry errors, since they cause errors in the reporting of financial results and can be extremely time consuming to locate and correct. Some traditional techniques include dual data entry with matching by the computer to spot discrepancies, as well as bar coding. More recently, Internet-based forms require customers to enter their own orders, while RFID promises to yield additional improvements in data-entry error rates.

One of the key problems that managers tend to overlook is the massive disparity in the error rates for the keying of alphanumeric data versus numeric data. There are many studies on this topic whose results vary by such factors as the size of the keyboard used (bigger is better) and the skill of the typist. However, the relationship between the two error rates is clear enough—entering alphanumeric data through a keyboard is 100 times more likely to result in an error than numeric data entered through a keypad, assuming the skills of a normal

60-words-per-minute typist. The error disparity drops to 25 times for an expert typist, but the difference is still enormous.

How does this impact the accountant? Clearly, it makes a great deal of sense to replace as much alphanumeric data as possible with numeric data. For example, warehouse bin locations could be converted to numeric codes instead of the more common Aisle A, Rack 3, Bin R style. Similarly, product codes should be purely numeric. Also, don't try to create different versions of an invoice, such as invoice number 1234A. Further, avoid using transaction identifiers, such as a purchase order that is coded as PO-45678. By focusing on using just numeric codes, an accounting department can drastically reduce its keypunching error rates.

Cost: 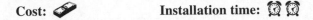   **Installation time:** 🕐 🕐

11–3 Use Multiple OCR Engines for Data Capture

A common efficiency technique is for accounting departments to digitize paper documents with a scanner, allowing the documents to be accessible through the corporate computer system. However, it is more difficult to go beyond storage of the scanned image and also extract the data stored on the scanned images.

Most scanning systems come with built-in optical character recognition (OCR) software that extracts data from digital images. Unfortunately, some documents contain handwritten text or are damaged, resulting in incorrect OCR interpretation, sometimes with laughably inaccurate results. An alternative approach that spots these errors is a technological advancement on the old technique of having two data-entry operators enter the same information, and checking each other's work for mistakes. In this case, two different OCR systems can be used to interpret the same image, with differences between the two interpretations being flagged for operator intervention.

In high-volume environments where manual intervention is not possible, some multiple-OCR systems will instead assign an accuracy value to an interpreted character, with the system storing the interpreted value having a higher score. Thus, the OCR engines can vote for which interpretation is correct. This does not mean that the resulting interpretation will actually be correct, but at least that the one with the highest probability of accuracy was retained.

Please note that multiple OCR engines are only one aspect of high-accuracy data interpretation. Other issues include the quality of the scanner, smudges and background color on documents, and scan resolution levels.

Cost: 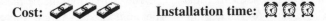   **Installation time:** 🕐 🕐 🕐

11–4 Add Digital Signatures to Electronic Documents

One of the primary difficulties with converting paper-based forms to electronic ones is that many documents require a signature to be affixed to them. This results in an electronic form being printed out, signed, and then either scanned back into a digital format or else used from that point forward as a paper document. As a result, the multitude of benefits associated with digital documents—minimal storage costs, infinite replication, ease of search, and so on—are lost. This problem has been corrected through the passage of a federal law in June 2000 legalizing the use of digital signatures.

It is still unclear how the courts will rule on the multitude of variations that can arise in relation to the type of digital signature used. At this time, it is quite possible that a character-based name on a message will be sufficient, though encrypted digital signatures that are much more difficult to duplicate will likely become the norm.

As more companies take advantage of this new law, we will see efficiency improvements in all of the following areas:

- *Customer orders.* A customer order typically requires a signature by a corporate manager, which is then hand-carried, mailed, or faxed to the receiving company. Digital signatures can cut much of the delivery time out of this process by sending orders by email straight to the recipient, which will greatly speed up the order fulfillment process. In addition, it reduces the risk that an order will be lost (as is frequently the case when orders are faxed).

- *Human resources.* The human resources department is awash in documents that require signatures—W-4 forms, I-9 forms, 401(k) forms, benefit forms, and so on. By switching to digital signatures, a company could not only avoid much of the physical paper flow that is currently needed, but also reduce much of the face-to-face time between human resources staff and other employees that is now needed to complete paperwork. This could be replaced by a vastly greater degree of automation that would convert the human resources staff from paper processors to managers of the process.

- *Legal documents.* Many business agreements require the transfer of documents back and forth between the concerned parties, usually by expensive overnight delivery service, to ensure that signatures are appropriately affixed before the documents are finalized. This extra time period can be avoided by the use of e-mail documents.

- *Purchasing.* The purchasing staff can issue purchase orders to suppliers by email, with full digital authorization, rather than having to laboriously print out a purchase order, find an authorized signer for it, and fax or mail it to a supplier. This improved process will greatly increase the speed and efficiency of the purchasing department.

The exact type of digital signatures used will become more apparent as the cost-effectiveness and security of various solutions become more apparent in the marketplace. At the moment, the market leaders include Entrust Technologies and Verisign.

Cost: 💸 **Installation time:** ⏰

11–5 Archive Computer Files

Some companies have elected to use computer records as a direct replacement
for their paper documents (see the group of best practices shown later in Exhibit
11.4). When this happens, they have certainly eliminated the majority (if not all)
of their filing work, but they have also put themselves at risk of losing electronic
documents if they are not archiving computer records. In a typical organization,
all records are purged from the computer system after one or two years, usually
because maintaining a larger on-line database will require an inordinate amount
of expensive storage space. However, purging these records runs counter to the
document-destruction policies noted later in the section, "Adopt a Document-
Destruction Policy," in which nearly all documents must be retained for longer
than one or two years. Consequently, storing all documents on a computer system
is not legally possible if the system is to be systematically purged of all records
from time to time.

The answer to the purging problem is to archive data before they are
purged. This means that the database must be transferred to some reliable storage medium, such as back-up tape or compact disc. By doing so, one can retrieve
the back-up storage medium at some later date and review it for data, extracting
any electronic document needed. Though this may seem like a simple matter of
inserting an extra back-up tape into the daily computer back-up procedure and
then putting the extra tape in permanent storage, there are some extra issues to
consider. One is that back-up tapes are not especially reliable over many years.
The data on them will degrade. A better storage medium is a compact disc (CD-
ROM), though using it requires a company to purchase a special storage device
that will write onto the CD-ROM. The other main problem is that the archived
data may be in a format that will be unreadable a few years from now—after all,
how many companies today have equipment that can read data stored on one
of the old storage mediums from 20 years ago, such as paper tape or computer
cards? The answer to this problem is a difficult one. It is possible to transfer all
key electronic document images to microfilm or microfiche, or to store all data
in the most "bombproof" of current data storage formats, American Standard
Code for Information Interchange (ASCII). However, technological trends may
shift away from using ASCII in the future, so storing in this format still has risks.
Another option is to go back to all archived data and convert them to whatever
the current data language may be whenever a company changes its systems, an
expensive endeavor. As there is no clear answer to these storage problems, a
company may need to store data in multiple file formats and carefully review the
integrity of the data from time to time to ensure that the files are still readable.

Carefully archiving all key computer files prior to purging them from the
primary computer system is a fundamental best practice necessary for a fully
digitized filing system to function properly.

Cost: 💵💵   **Installation time:** ⏰

11–6 Implement Document Imaging

Many companies find themselves in the situation of constantly searching for files. Perhaps several departments need them at once and the files are constantly shifted back and forth, resulting in no one able to consistently locate them. Also, some employees are better than others at returning files when they are finished with them, while other companies just have a hard time obtaining a qualified group of staff people who can reliably file documents in the right place. Whatever the case may be, it is a common problem and one that can seriously impact operations.

One answer to this quandary is to convert all paper documents into digital ones and store them in the central computer system so that, potentially, all employees can access them from all locations—and do so at the same time. Digital documents have the advantage of never being lost (with one caveat, noted later in this section), never being destroyed (as long as there are proper back-up routines taking place), and being available to anyone with the correct kind of access. These are formidable advantages and have caused many larger corporations to adopt this approach as the best way to avoid the majority of their filing problems.

To implement a document-imaging system, one must first obtain a document scanner with a sufficiently high throughput speed and resolution to allow scanning a multitude of documents, as well as scanning with a sufficient degree of clarity to obtain a quality digital image. This scanner must be linked to a high-capacity storage device, usually one using multiple compact discs that is called a "CD jukebox" and a file server containing the index file that tracks the location of all digital documents stored in the jukebox. A number of terminals are also necessary to link to this system, so that users may access digitized documents from as many company locations as necessary. A graphical view of this layout is shown in Exhibit 11.2.

There are some problems with digital document storage that make it useful in only selected cases. One is cost—the entire system, especially the storage device, can easily bring the total cost into the six-digit range, with high-end systems for large corporations exceeding a million dollars. Also, there is a considerable workload required to set up the system, for a large portion of a company's existing documents must be scanned into the system, as do new documents that are generated every day. There is also an issue with legality, for it may be necessary to continue to retain some paper documents, given the murky nature of the law regarding the acceptability of digitized documents in a legal action. In addition, if a document is not properly indexed when it is first scanned into the system (i.e., given an access code that allows a user to more easily find it), it is possible that there will be great difficulty in later locating it in the computer; in effect, the document is lost in the storage device. Thus, there are a number of issues to be aware of before installing such a system. Generally speaking, the cost consideration alone will keep smaller companies from implementing this solution, unless

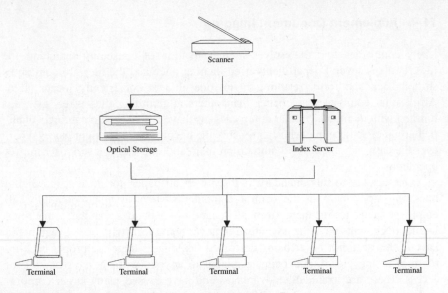

Exhibit 11.2 Overview of the Document-Imaging Process

they are in industries that require enormous amounts of paperwork, such as the legal or medical professions.

Cost: 💵💵💵   **Installation time:** ⏰⏰⏰

11–7 Eliminate Stored Paper Documents If Already in Computer

Most companies store the bulk of their data in their computer systems and then periodically print out records and file them away—even though all of the data still exist in the computer system. Though an argument can be made that employees are accustomed to handling paper documents more readily than digital ones, and that computer systems are too unreliable to constitute the sole repository of information, these are objections that can be overridden with the proper degree of training and system changes. In Exhibit 11.4, shown later in the "Total Impact of Best Practices on the Filing Function" section, there are a number of other best practices listed that will make a computer system essentially *bombproof* and therefore make it available for use during normal business hours with very few exceptions. Those best practices, which are described elsewhere in this chapter, are as follows:

- Archive computer files
- Avoid purging computer records
- Extend use of the computer database

- Improve computer system reliability
- Use document imaging

Once all or most of these best practices have been put in place, it is time to implement the one described in this section—to eliminate any paper documents already stored in the computer system. This is a step that must be completed with extreme care, for the computer system must be thoroughly proven to be fully operational and virtually incapable of failure before the paper files are removed from the corporate premises. The logical sequence of steps to follow for this implementation is to wait for a sufficient period of time to pass to verify that the computer system is thoroughly bombproof; then to shift all paper documents to an off-site location, so that they can still be called back in case of an emergency, and then, after a longer interval, to completely eliminate those documents except the ones required for legal purposes. This is a long implementation process that may require several years to complete, but it is essential that the elimination of paper documents does not interfere with the daily conduct of company business, which can fail or be severely impacted if the conversion to digital documents does not go as planned.

Cost: Installation time: 🕑 🕑

11–8 Extend Time Period before Computer Records Are Purged

An accounting department that relies on the data stored in its computer system to handle day-to-day transactions has a problem when those records are purged. The purging process usually occurs during the month-end or year-end closing process, typically destroying all transaction records that are more than one year old. When this happens, the accounting staff goes from having immediate access to all records via their computer terminals to having to retrieve paper documents, frequently from an off-site storage location. Clearly, this is a major reduction in the speed and efficiency of the department as it relates to the retrieval of data.

The reason why records are purged is that they take up a considerable amount of space in the hard drive storage of the computer system. By purging old records from time to time, it is possible to reduce storage requirements, which makes it unnecessary to purchase additional storage devices. The best practice advocated here is actually a set of variations on retaining some or all storage space, as noted:

- *Delay purging old records.* The most comprehensive way to avoid additional filing work is to extend the period before which records will be deleted. For example, an automatic purge after one year can be shifted to a purge after two years. However, this policy will greatly expand a computer system's storage requirements, a serious consideration, especially when the purge period extends so far back in time that there is a diminishing return on the usefulness of the data in comparison to the cost of the extra computer storage. Though this is the most common version of the best practice currently in use, it should not extend storage too far back in time, given the high cost of doing so.

- *Only purge selected files.* Rather than purge all records, it may be possible to only purge those files containing specific types of records. For example, management may not feel that it is necessary to retain accounts payable records for more than one year, whereas it may want to retain sales records for a considerably longer period. Accordingly, the best approach in this case is to delete specific files regularly, while retaining others for longer periods. This is an effective way to retain data in the system while spending less money on computer storage. It is most effective when those files containing the largest numbers of records (and thus the ones that take up the most storage space) are deleted first, such as daily inventory transaction files.

- *Only purge obsolete records.* An approach that is even more selective than purging specific files is to purge only specific records. For example, management may decide to eliminate the records of all customers with which the company has not done business for at least two years, while retaining the records of all current customers for five years. It is usually a simple matter to extract data from the database that clearly shows which customers can be deleted, along with all associated information. This method is more labor-intensive than doing a blanket purge with a single keystroke, but it retains the information that is most likely to be called into use.

- *Use slower access storage media.* Large corporations that can afford the expense may transfer older computer files to slower and less expensive tape back-up systems still linked to the primary computer storage system. By using this approach, they can allow fairly rapid access to data, even if the data are several years old, by any employee with access to the computer system. However, since the slower storage devices are still much more expensive than simply purging data and leaving paper documents in a warehouse, this is typically an option that is only explored by companies with large computer system budgets.

Any of these alternatives will give the accounting staff better access to old records, which allows them to avoid the onerous task of manually picking through old files for needed records. When selecting one alternative over another, it is necessary to determine the need for various kinds of records and to retain only those for which there is a reasonable expectation that some data retrieval will be needed.

Cost: 💵💵💵   **Installation time:** ⏰⏰

11–9 Extend Use of Existing Computer Database

Whenever the person responsible for filing makes the recommendation to have everyone access data directly through the computer system, rather than through documents, the response is usually that not everyone has access to the system. That is, some employees cannot access the correct files they need, they do not know how to access the information, or they do not have access to the computer network in order to do so. In most cases, this is not an idle complaint; these people really will not be able to function unless significant changes are made to the computer system.

This best practice is a mandatory one if online access to data is to take the place of paper documents. It involves several steps that are needed to open up access to the computer system. This is not an item that can be completed in a haphazard manner, for it is too complicated to complete without using a rigid, step-by-step approach, which is as follows:

1. *Determine who uses information.* Before opening up computer access to employees, it is necessary to determine who needs the access. For example, it makes no sense to provide computer terminals to everyone in a company, only to discover that half of them do not have the slightest need for information. Accordingly, one should interview all employees to see what they need and determine where in the computer system that information can be found.

2. *Calculate changes in access volumes.* If the new system will result in a massive increase in user access to the system, this should be calculated well in advance, so the central computer system can be upgraded to handle the extra workload. Additional software licenses may also have to be purchased to cover the extra users.

3. *Construct new interface screens.* Some of the data that are needed, as discovered in the first step, may not reside in one place in the computer system and may require the construction of new screens in the computer that bring all of the necessary data together for easier use. This can be a laborious step with a large programming budget. It is also next to impossible to complete if a company uses a packaged software system that is regularly updated by the supplier, since each update will probably wipe out any custom programming.

4. *Determine type of access.* Once all of the data have been clustered into the appropriate groups for employee use, it is very important to determine who gets to change the information. If some employees will not be allowed to, they must be given read-only access rights in the computer system; these rights may vary by screen, and should be set up well in advance so this task does not interfere with later implementation steps.

5. *Add terminals.* There may be a need for extra terminals so that all employees have easy access to the system. This may require stringing additional cable

or the addition of broadband links to other locations for off-site access. It is also important to ensure that there are enough printers provided to meet the needs of the additional users.

6. *Train employees.* The last step before going live with the new system is to train employees in how to use the computer system. This training should be custom-tailored to the exact needs of each group that will be accessing different information in the system, and the employees should train on the terminals, so they know exactly what to do. They should also be given one-page summaries showing them how to access the information they need.

These steps can take quite a long time to complete and will require a significant budget, so it is important to verify in advance that there is a reasonable payback to the company from implementing it—either through reduced filing costs or by improving the efficiency of the corporation as a whole.

Cost: 💵💵💵   **Installation time:** ⏰⏰⏰

11–10 Improve Computer System Reliability

Many of the recommendations in this chapter are based on the assumption that paper-based documents can be eliminated by calling up their electronic counterparts in a company's computer system. However, many controllers find that this assumption will not work, and it meets with great resistance throughout a company because the computer system has a bad reputation for not being functional at all times. If the system is down and there are no paper documents that are immediately available to serve as back-up information, a company can literally stop functioning at once.

There are a number of steps that a company can take to improve the reliability of its computer systems. As many as possible of the following actions should be taken to improve system reliability. Though even one of them is helpful, the entire group will go a long way toward creating a bombproof system that employees will have confidence in. The best practices for improving system reliability are as follows:

- *Battery back-ups.* A computer system will experience power failures from time to time, as well as power spikes or brownouts. All of these problems result in computer system crashes, which corrupt data and keep the system down for long periods of time. This problem is an especially vexing one in a manufacturing environment, where power spikes may occur when large machinery is turned on in the same power grid as a company's computer system. The solution to this problem is a simple one—just install a battery back-up, also known as an uninterruptible power supply (UPS) on all file servers or larger computers, as well as every personal computer, terminal, router, and hub—in short, everything attached to a computer network that requires electricity. By doing so, a computer system can be completely protected from all power fluctuations. Also, batteries will become worn out and fail over time, so it is critical to have a battery replacement schedule in place designed to replace batteries shortly before their scheduled failure dates.

• *Disk mirroring.* Some companies that cannot afford to have any system downtime at all will use two primary computers to record all transactions, rather than the more traditional single computer. Under this system, all transactions are recorded by two computers that are linked together and that mirror each other's functions. If one of these computers develops a problem, the other one takes over all processing and continues operating on its own so that users have no idea that there is a problem. The damaged computer can be repaired while the other unit continues to operate. Though this is a more expensive approach, it guarantees a very high level of system reliability.

• *Emergency planning and testing.* No matter how many precautions a company takes, it is likely that there will be system crashes from time to time. Rather than passively hope that these incidents do not occur, it is better to develop a formal plan for how to deal with them before they happen. By writing down the precise recovery steps to be followed, one can save a significant amount of time in fixing systems. This plan can also be used for practice; by scheduling periodic training sessions for recovering from system crashes, one can determine the weak points in the emergency plan, and fix them before a real emergency occurs. By using this approach, a company can keep system downtime to a minimum.

• *Redo cabling.* Some employees have difficulty staying online with their central computer systems. This is caused by poorly constructed network cabling, which may in turn be caused by excessive cable lengths without repeaters, cables running near power sources (such as machinery), or the wrong types of cabling. In some cases, the best way to eliminate this problem is to completely redo the cabling. This may require the installation of top-quality, high-capacity fiber optic cabling, as well as new hubs. Also, if there are links to distant locations, it may be necessary to convert from a dial-up modem access, which runs on standard copper cabling, to a high-capacity T1 phone line, which is much more reliable, although also much more expensive to operate. By making these changes, a number of system reliability problems can be eliminated.

• *Scheduled downtime.* One of the most common employee complaints regarding system downtime is that maintenance occurs during regular business hours, rather than at other times. When maintenance, such as system back-ups, testing, or software upgrades, is going on, other users cannot access the system, which keeps them from performing their jobs. To avoid this problem, it is very important to cluster standard maintenance work together in a batch and run it automatically during low-usage periods, such as late at night. Similarly, any other system work that may bring the computer system down must be carefully scheduled to match low-transaction periods during the workweek, such as just before or after the regular working hours, or during the lunch period. The best way to ensure that these times are properly scheduled is to create a work schedule for the computer department that identifies the periods when the system must be brought down, so employees can be adequately prepared in advance for these periods, and so additional planning can be done to ensure that the downtime periods are kept to an absolute minimum.

- *System testing.* There is a saying that all systems have bugs in them—you just may not have found them yet. This is a major problem if a company implements a new system without proper testing. A rigid testing program will ensure that new systems have the appropriate back-up systems, will operate as promised, can handle large transaction volumes, and will handle unusual transactions. If a new system successfully passes all of these tests, then it can be put into service. If not, it must be fixed and tested again. Only by rigidly adhering to tough testing standards can a company provide reliable computer systems to its employees.

While all of the preceding system reliability improvements are being implemented, it is extremely important to publicize the progress of the work. If the improvements are undertaken quietly, employees may still be influenced by a long tradition of system problems and their opinions will not be changed for a long time. Instead, to more quickly bring employees to the point of accepting the computer system as their primary source of documents, it is necessary to publicize current system improvement projects, upcoming ones, and before-and-after measurements that clearly show the improvement in system reliability. Advertising system changes to employees is one of the best ways to get them to support a move to eliminate paper-based backup systems.

Cost: 💵💵   **Installation time:** ⏰⏰

11–11 Track Documents with RFID

Radio frequency identification (RFID) was invented in 1999 at a think tank located at the Massachusetts Institute of Technology. It involves the attachment of a tiny transceiver to an object, allowing it to be tracked by a network of receivers. The most obvious use for RFID is inventory tracking at the pallet or case level within a business location, since this allows for a tightly confined tracking area, moderate RFID cost, and tracking of what is frequently a company's largest-dollar asset. The long-term intent of RFID backers is to create a large-scale RFID tracking network capable of tracking inventory across large areas, so that companies have a precise picture of where their inventory is located anywhere in the supply chain, on a real-time basis.

It is also possible to use RFID in the accounting department. One possibility is the tracking of documents. Though many accounting departments already have document scanning systems in place that would appear to render RFID unnecessary, consider again—what about truly sensitive documents, such as signed legal documents, internal audit work papers, insurance folders, archived documents, and the like? In many cases, employees remove these documents from their customary locations and leave them all over the accounting department, making it more difficult to locate when they are needed on short notice. Perhaps adding RFID tags to these types of documents and adding receivers in the accounting area would be a reasonable way to ensure that they can always be found.

Cost: 💵💵   **Installation time:** ⏰⏰

11–12 Adopt a Document-Destruction Policy   ✔*Author's Choice*

Many companies keep on storing more documents year after year because they have no idea of when they are supposed to get rid of them. By default, they typically remain in a heap in the back corner of the most distant warehouse, eating up space that can be put to better uses. For companies that have been in operation for many years, this can become a considerable burden due to the many years paper has been allowed to accumulate, especially if management has a habit of purchasing expensive filing cabinets in which to store old records, rather than less expensive cardboard storage boxes.

One solution is to work with a company's lawyers and certified public accountants (CPAs) to construct a document-destruction policy similar to the comprehensive one shown in Exhibit 11.3. The policy should take into account

Exhibit 11.3 Detailed Document-Destruction Policy

Type of Record	Retention
Accident reports/claims (settled)	7 years
Accounts payable ledgers/schedules	7 years
Accounts receivable ledgers/schedules	7 years
Advertisement for a job opening	1 year
Age records	3 years
Applications for advertised job openings	1 year
Bank reconciliations	1 year
Capital stock records	Permanent
Chart of accounts	Permanent
Checks (canceled)	7 years

(continues)

Exhibit 11.3 *(Continued)*

Type of Record	Retention
Citizenship or authorization to work (I-9)	3 years from hire or 1 year after separation (whichever is longer)
Contracts and leases (expired)	7 years
Contracts and leases in effect	Permanent
Deeds, mortgages, bills of sale	Permanent
Demotion records	1 year
Discrimination or enforcement charges	3 years
Earnings per week	3 years
Employer information report	Keep most recent report
Employment contracts	3 years
Financial statements	Permanent
General ledgers (year-end)	Permanent
Hazardous materials exposure/monitoring	30 years
Hiring records	1 year from date record made or personnel action taken, whichever is later
Insurance policies (expired)	3 years
Insurance records, claims, reports	Permanent
Insurance/pension/retirement plans	1 year after termination
Internal audit reports	3 years
Inventory records	7 years
Invoices to customers	7 years
Invoices from suppliers	7 years
Layoff selection	1 year
Material safety data sheets	30 years
Minute books, including bylaws and charter	Permanent
Notes receivable ledgers and schedules	7 years
Occupational injuries	5 years
Payroll records—pay data	3 years
Payroll records—Employment data	3 years from termination
Physical inventory tags	3 years
Physical/medical examinations	Duration of employment, plus 30 years
Plant cost ledgers	7 years
Polygraph tests	3 years from date of test

Exhibit 11.3 *(Continued)*

Type of Record	Retention
Promotion records/notices	1 year from promotion
Property appraisals	Permanent
Property records	Permanent
Purchase orders	7 years
Receiving sheets	1 year
Sales and purchase records	3 years
Sales records	7 years
Stock and bond certificates (canceled)	7 years
Subsidiary ledgers	7 years
Tax returns	Permanent
Termination records	1 year
Time cards	3 years
Time worked records	2 years
Transfer records	1 year
Wage-rate tables	3 years

the document-retention requirements of all federal, state, and local regulatory agencies, always adopting the longest required retention period. Once this policy has been completed, the existing pile of paperwork can be sorted through with an eye to eliminating all items for which there is no legal reason to keep them. When conducting this elimination process, however, it is important to keep all documents for which there is no termination date whatsoever, such as corporate minute books, titles to automobiles, or project files for special machinery built for customers.

Once a document-destruction policy has been created to eliminate unnecessary paperwork, a common result is for a company to realize a significant savings in storage space as well as filing cabinets, both of which may be sold off or used for other more profitable purposes.

Cost: 🖅   **Installation time:** 🕑

11–13 Eliminate Attaching Back-Up Materials to Checks for Signing

A common cause for extra filing work is that many check-signers require back-up documentation to accompany all checks presented to them for signing. They want the extra information so they can tell exactly why a payment is being made.

The extra paperwork typically includes the complete packet of accounts payable documents: the supplier's invoice, the company's purchase order, and receiving documentation. To fulfill the wishes of the check-signers, the filing staff must extract the accounts payable items from files, attach them to checks, wait for the checks to be signed, and then detach them from the checks and file them away again. All of this movement of paper also raises the risk that documents will be misfiled during the process of taking them out of files and then putting them back in. When this happens, an inordinate amount of time may be required to locate and refile the missing documents. These activities can take up a considerable proportion of the filing staff's time.

The solution is to stop attaching accounts payable backup information to checks about to be signed. Though this seems like a simple and obvious step, it can be a difficult one to convince the check-signers to agree with. By eliminating the back-up materials, the check-signers have no way of knowing what the company is paying for. The best way to deal with this complaint is to set up control points earlier in the accounts payable process, so that the check-signers are so comfortable with the level of control that goes into creating a check, they no longer care about what they are signing. Typically, the best control point is the purchase order. If no checks are cut without a purchase order in hand approved by the correct manager, there is no need for the additional control point of having one last review of the back-up documents by the check-signer. It can take some time for a good purchase order control system to be implemented; it is especially important that all exceptions be rooted out of the accounts payable system so that all payments are authorized by a purchase order. The check-signers may want proof of the efficacy of the new system before they relinquish the back-up documentation, so the controller should work with the internal audit staff to schedule a review of the purchase order control system and make any changes that the auditors recommend, in order to ensure that the new control system works properly. If these changes can be made, there is no longer any need for back-up documentation for the check-signers, and a significant proportion of filing time can therefore be eliminated.

Cost: **Installation time:**

11–14 Eliminate Reports   ✔ *Author's Choice*

Most companies are awash in reports. Typically, someone asks the accounting department to generate a report, which it does—and continues to do for the foreseeable future because no one has told it to stop doing so. The majority of these reports are really only needed once—perhaps to check on the profitability of a specific product line, or the cost of a service, or the usage of some equipment. Even though their usage is limited, the accounting department continues to churn them out and distribute them because the recipients are not aware of the cost of creating them. A further problem is the distribution of the reports. It is common for someone who does not realize the expense of distributing a report to have it sent to everyone in the company who might use it and to many who most certainly do not. Over time, the accumulation of, in many cases, hundreds of reports, and the enormous distribution lists creates a startlingly large filing burden. Not only are these reports stored in case someone needs them, but they are distributed, and it is the job of the filing staff to do both things.

The solution to the reports problem is to reduce the number of reports as well as the number of recipients, but the method of implementing this best practice is worth some careful consideration. One approach is to simply stop distributing reports and to see who complains. However, this is not a very astute political move by the controller, since an abrupt halt to reporting can irritate the heads of any departments who receive the information. Instead, it is better to use the following steps:

1. *Issue a list of outstanding reports and distributions.* Sometimes it is sufficient to bring to the attention of other departments the extent of the report list that is being used. If issued along with a list of report recipients, as well as a plea from the controller to review the lists and cross out any reports and recipients that are no longer needed, it is usually possible to put a considerable dent in the accounting department's reporting and filing chore.

2. *Notify recipients of the cost of reports.* If a simple notification of the number of reports does not result in any significant change, it may be necessary to notify management of the total cost of creating and issuing those reports. If the cost is considerable, the management team may authorize the elimination of several additional reports.

3. *Combine reports.* Once the report list has been pruned with the previous steps, it is time to interview the report recipients and see what information on each report is actually being used. It may then be possible to combine the data on several reports, resulting in fewer reports that are really needed. For many companies, these first three steps will bring about a sufficient reduction in the number of reports without having to proceed to the final two steps.

4. *Charge recipients for reports.* If there are still a number of reports left to produce, it may be necessary to charge back the recipients for the cost of both creating and distributing the reports (with an extra charge for each additional person who is sent each report). Incurring an expense for information almost invariably will cause department managers to take a serious look at cutting back on their use of reports, which bodes well for the filing staff.

5. *Post reports on the computer network.* This last option can be substituted for the previous step of charging for report usage. This one allows the filing staff to avoid all distribution work by posting electronic reports on the computer network, where users can access it for themselves. This approach may not work for some reports that do not convert readily to a readable format for all

computer terminals, nor is it available to those report recipients who do not have a computer or access to one. Still, given the recent surge in the use of corporate intranets, this may be the preferred approach of the future for report distribution.

These steps, taken in the order presented, are usually sufficient to bring about a drastic reduction in the number of reports being used and issued, which has a correspondingly large and favorable impact on the quantity of filing work that can be eliminated.

Cost: 💵   **Installation time:** ⏰⏰

11–15 Move Records Off-Site

A controller can have an exceedingly inefficient accounting operation for no other reason than the presence of an immense amount of records in the accounting area, which makes it difficult to find a sufficient amount of operating space and renders it difficult to find the most current information. Frequently, these records are kept near the accounting staff on the erroneous grounds that there will be times when they are needed and that it will be an exceptional hassle to recover them if they are stored elsewhere. This is a particularly difficult problem if the accounting staff has been in place for many years and is accustomed to having records kept close at hand.

The solution is to review the dates of the records and move the oldest items to a secondary location. The cut-off date for which records will be moved is usually for anything that is not in the current year of operations. There may be a few cases where additional records should be kept, such as records from the previous year that the auditors might request during their annual audit. However, in general, these records can be moved out with minimal impact on current operations.

The main objectors to this approach will be those staff members who have grown accustomed to keeping files close at hand, but this objection will usually recede over time, especially if a good index clearly identifies which storage box contains which records, so that retrieving paperwork is an easy affair. The resulting benefits from the change will be a considerable increase in working space and less need for expensive office space and fewer expensive filing cabinets. The best improvement of all is that it contributes to overall efficiency, for the amount of paperwork remaining will be so greatly reduced that it will be simple to determine where the really crucial files are located, which reduces search time. Moving records off-site is an excellent method for reducing occupancy costs and clutter in the accounting area.

Cost: 💵💵   **Installation time:** ⏰⏰

11-16 Reduce Number of Form Copies to File

Over time, it is a common occurrence for a company to continually add to the number of copies of printed documents. For example, an invoice that starts with two copies—one for the customer and one for the company—may later have another copy added so that invoices can be filed in numerical order, and perhaps another copy so that the customer service department (or some other department) can have an extra copy. These additional documents are usually added without much thought to the consequences for the filing staff, which must put away all the extra copies. Also, additional document copies result in more expensive documents (since there is more paper involved), as well as a more heavy-duty printer that can punch through such a thick sheaf of documents (which can also bunch up quite easily, causing a printer jam). Thus, a large number of document copies results in a multitude of problems, not the least of which is a considerable increase in the workload of the filing staff.

The solution is to reduce the number of copies. However, this is not a simple matter of ordering new documents with fewer parts. Both costs and politics can become an issue when implementing what appears to be, on the surface, a very simple matter. The main cost is that there may be many documents still in stock with extra copies. If so, it makes little sense to throw them all out. Instead, use them up, throwing away the extra copies that are generated, and then order new documents when the old ones are gone. The main problem is politics. If there is an extra copy being generated, it is a good bet that someone in the company asked for the extra copy and that person will not be happy when the copy is eliminated. If the person who wants the extra copy is a highly placed manager, it is unlikely that the change will go unnoticed or tolerated. Instead, if persuasion does not work, it is probable that implementation will be impossible until that person leaves the company or moves to a position having less influence over the decision. Also, before eliminating a document copy, it is mandatory that the exact use of the copy be clarified with all users to ensure that there is not a problem if it is no longer printed.

Despite the number of possible problems, this is a best practice that can usually be implemented at least in part and will result in immediate gains for the filing staff in exchange for a moderate amount of implementation effort.

Cost: 💵   **Installation time:** ⏰⏰

Total Impact of Best Practices on the Filing Function

This section groups together all of the best practices described in this chapter and shows how they can be applied in a typical corporate environment. As opposed to the best practices in most other chapters of this book, all of the filing best practices can be installed together, for they are not mutually exclusive.

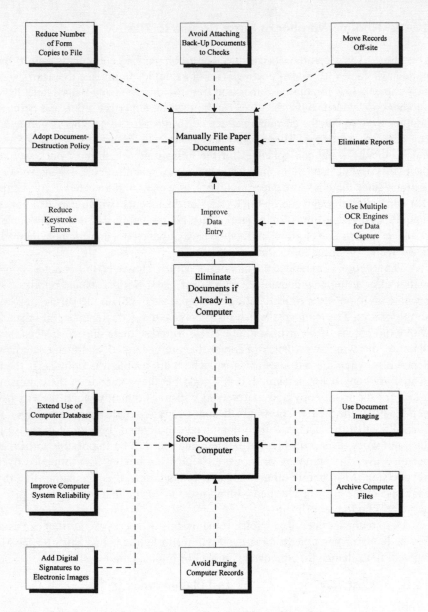

Exhibit 11.4 Impact of Best Practices on the Filing Function

They tend to cluster into two categories: those concerned with the reduction of manual filing labor and those intended to completely avoid filing by using a company's computer system as the primary data storage point. Though the computer system is obviously the more advanced and efficient method of storage, it takes a long time to convert a company entirely to that storage medium (if only because of employee resistance), so it is recommended that all of the best practices, including those for manual filing, be implemented.

As noted in Exhibit 11.4, there are six best practices associated with the manual filing function. Some involve cleaning up the work area by either moving old documents off-site or by using a document-destruction policy to entirely eliminate them. Other best practices eliminate documents before they ever have a chance to be filed, by such means as stopping the use of reports and reducing the number of form copies. The other main category of best practices assumes that there will be less need for filing work if documents are stored in a company's computer system. If so, the main focus is on increasing computer access to the largest possible number of employees, while also increasing the reliability of the computer system and storing a considerable amount of information on it. By implementing the largest possible combination of these activities, one can bring about a reduction in a company's filing workload, and may even be able to eliminate the majority of the work.

Summary

This chapter covered two main categories of best practices for filing. One focused on ways to reduce the amount of filing work needed, on the assumption that some filing of paper documents must always be done. The second cluster of best practices covered how to use a computer system as the logical storage location for information, rather than a filing cabinet. This second alternative is the preferred approach, since it gives everyone with computer access the ability to call up a document without any risk of damaging or losing the information on the digitized document. However, there are a number of steps that a company must take to ensure that information is properly stored on its computer system and that the system is sufficiently operational during working hours to act as a proper substitute for a manual filing system. Thus, the best practices described in this chapter cover the two main filing alternatives—the filing cabinet and the computer system.

Chapter 12

Finance Best Practices

This book is primarily about improving the accounting function, not the finance function. However, this area is commonly integrated into the accounting department in smaller organizations, where the cost of a treasury staff cannot be justified. Thus, this area becomes part of the accounting function, and so a limited set of best practices are included here.

Only in one case is an expensive and time-consuming best practice listed—the use of a treasury workstation. It is really only cost-effective for a larger company, but is included here because it does such a good job of integrating and improving on a number of rote treasury functions. It is highly recommended for those organizations that can afford it, but its substantial cost should be carefully reviewed before a decision is made.

This chapter begins with a short review of the level of implementation difficulty for each finance best practice, and then moves on to individual discussions of each one. There is no final section that describes how these items can be used in concert, since these functions operate just as well if implemented individually—there is little efficiency to be gained through overlapping finance best practices.

Implementation Issues for Finance Best Practices

This section notes in Exhibit 12.1 the level of implementation difficulty that one can expect when installing the finance-related best practices in this chapter. Exhibit 12.1 describes the cost and duration of implementation for each best practice.

The duration of implementation for these Internet-based applications is listed as "medium" in the exhibit, though a company can make them operational in a relatively short time. The reason for the longer expected implementation duration is that one may find that a specific Web site does not precisely match one's expectations, which may result in some shopping among related sites to find a better match. Alternatively, some missing functionality may have to be shifted in-house, which also requires more time to implement.

12–1 Use an Investment Strategy for
Short-Term Investments   ✔ *Author's Choice*

At the most minimal level of investment strategy, one can do nothing and leave idle balances in the corporate bank accounts. This is essentially an *earnings*

Exhibit 12.1 Summary of Finance Best Practices

	Best Practice	Cost	Install Time
Financing and Investment Activities			
12–1	Use an investment strategy for short-term investments	💵	🕐🕐
12–2	Securitize receivables	💵💵	🕐🕐
12–3	Purchase debt directly from the government	💵	🕐
12–4	Sell securities under the Regulation A exemption	💵💵💵	🕐🕐
12–5	Sell securities under the Regulation D exemption	💵💵💵	🕐🕐
12–6	Set up supply chain financing	💵	🕐🕐
12–7	Take a business unit public	💵💵💵	🕐🕐🕐
Option Management			
12–8	Automate option tracking	💵💵💵	🕐🕐
Pension Management			
12–9	Automate 401(k) plan enrollment	💵	🕐🕐
12–10	Grant employees immediate 401(k) eligibility	💵	🕐🕐
Risk Management			
12–11	Consolidate insurance policies	💵	🕐🕐🕐
12–12	Obtain key man life insurance for the CFO	💵💵	🕐
12–13	Obtain advance rating assessments	💵💵	🕐🕐
12–14	Rent a captive insurance company	💵💵💵	🕐🕐🕐
12–15	Use netting to reduce foreign exchange settlements	💵💵	🕐🕐🕐
12–16	Install a treasury workstation	💵💵💵	🕐🕐🕐
12–17	Connect to the SWIFT network	💵💵	🕐🕐
12–18	Optimize the organization of treasury operations	💵💵💵	🕐🕐🕐
12–19	Hedge foreign exchange with forward exchange contracts	💵💵	🕐🕐
12–20	Hedge foreign exchange with currency futures	💵💵	🕐🕐
12–21	Lock in interest rates with an interest rate swap	💵💵	🕐🕐

credit strategy, since the bank uses the earnings from these idle balances to offset its service fees. If a company has minimal cash balances, then this is not an entirely bad strategy. The earnings credit can be the equivalent of a modest rate of return, and if there is not enough cash to plan for more substantive investments, leaving the cash alone is a reasonable alternative.

A *matching strategy* simply matches the maturity date of an investment to the cash flow availability dates listed on the cash forecast. For example, ABC Company's cash forecast indicates that $80,000 will be available for investment immediately, but must be used in two months for a capital project. One can invest the funds in a two-month instrument, such that its maturity date is just prior to when the funds will be needed. This is a very simple investment strategy that is more concerned with short-term liquidity than return on investment, and is most commonly used by firms having minimal excess cash.

A *laddering strategy* involves creating a set of investments that have a series of consecutive maturity dates. For example, ABC Company's cash forecast indicates that $150,000 of excess cash will be available for the foreseeable future, and its investment policy forbids any investments having a duration of greater than three months. One could invest the entire amount in a three-month instrument, since this takes advantage of the presumably somewhat higher interest rates that are available on longer-term investments. However, there is always a risk that some portion of the cash will be needed sooner. In order to keep the investment more liquid while still taking advantage of the higher interest rates available through longer-term investments, an alternative is to break the available cash into thirds and invest $50,000 in a one-month instrument, another $50,000 in a two-month instrument, and the final $50,000 in a three-month instrument. As each investment matures, the money can be reinvested into a three-month instrument. By doing so, ABC always has $50,000 of the invested amount coming due within one month or less. This improves liquidity, while still taking advantage of longer-term interest rates.

A *tranched cashflow strategy* requires one to determine what cash is available for short, medium, and long-term investment, and to then adopt different investment criteria for each of these investment tranches. The exact investment criteria will vary based on a company's individual needs, but here is a sample of how the tranches might be arranged:

1. The short-term tranche is treated as cash that may be needed for operational requirements on a moment's notice. This means that cash flows into and out of this tranche can be strongly positive or negative. Thus, return on investment is not a key criterion—instead, the focus is on very high levels of liquidity. The return should be the lowest of the three tranches, but should also be relatively steady.

2. The medium-term tranche includes cash that may be required for use within the next 3 to 12 months, and usually only for highly predictable events, such as periodic tax or dividend payments, or capital expenditures that can be

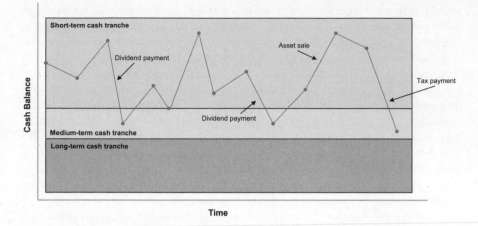

Exhibit 12.2 Investments by Cashflow Tranches

planned well in advance. Given the much higher level of predictability in this tranche, one can accept longer-term maturities with moderate levels of volatility that have somewhat higher returns on investment.

3. The long-term tranche includes cash for which there is no planned operational use, and that can be safely invested for at least one year. The priority for this tranche shifts more in favor of a higher return on investment, with an attendant potential for higher levels of volatility and perhaps short-term capital loss, with a reduction in the level of liquidity.

Portrayed graphically, the tranches would appear as noted in Exhibit 12.2. The corporate cash balance should rarely decline into the long-term tranche, with occasional forays into the medium-term tranche, while the cash level will vary considerably within the short-term tranche.

Exhibit 12.3 Returns from Tranched Cashflow Strategy

	Baseline Return	+	Additional Basis Points	Percent of Portfolio	Return Enhancement
Short-term tranche	1-month Treasuries	+	0	50%	0 bps
Medium-term tranche	1-month Treasuries	+	15	40%	+6 bps
Long-term tranche	1-month Treasuries	+	60	10%	+6 bps
			Total Incremental Return		+12 bps

An example of the numerical result of a tranched cashflow strategy is shown in Exhibit 12.3, which assumes a baseline return to be the return on one-month Treasuries, with a target of increased basis points (BPS) above that standard for the medium-term and long-term tranches.

To engage in the tranched cashflow strategy, one should regularly review the cash forecast, and adjust the amounts of cash needed in each of the three tranches. Inattention to these adjustments could result in an unanticipated cash requirement when the cash in the company's long-term tranche is tied up in excessively long-term, illiquid investments.

Cost: 💵   **Installation time:** ⏰⏰

12–2 Securitize Receivables

A large company can consider securitizing its accounts receivable, thereby achieving one of the lowest interest rates available for debt. To do so, it creates a special-purpose entity (SPE) and transfers a selection of its receivables into the SPE. The SPE then sells the receivables to a bank conduit, which, in turn, pools the receivables that it has bought from multiple companies, and uses the cash flows from the receivables to back the issuance of commercial paper to investors, who, in turn, are repaid with the cash flows from the receivables.

Receivables securitization is clearly a complex process to initially create; the primary benefit of doing so is that a company's receivables are isolated from the company's other risks, so that the SPE has a higher credit rating than the company, with an attendant decline in borrowing costs. To achieve the AAA credit rating typically needed for receivables securitization, a credit rating agency will review the performance record of receivables previously included in the pool, debtor concentrations in the pool, and the company's credit and collection policies.

A lesser reason for using receivables securitization is that a company is not required to record it as debt on its balance sheet. However, this sometimes leads to an outcry from the investing community that a company is hiding liabilities, so companies sometimes voluntarily record the transaction as debt on their balance sheets.

A key factor in preserving the stellar credit rating of the SPE is to maintain an adequate degree of separation between the company and the SPE. To do so, the transfer of receivables is supposed to be a nonrecourse sale, so that the company's creditors cannot claim the assets of the SPE if the company goes bankrupt. This means that there should be no mechanism by which the company can regain control of any receivables shifted to the SPE.

Receivables securitization is only available to large companies having a broad customer base whose receivables experience minimal defaults. Further, there must be adequate tracking systems in place to monitor the creditworthiness of those debtors whose receivables are included in the SPE, delinquency statistics, and customer concentrations, as well as frequent reporting on receivable collections.

Cost:    Installation time: 🕰 🕰

12–3   Purchase Debt Directly from the Government

A company that has excess cash is typically constrained by its lending policies to investments in a limited number of high-grade debt instruments that carry minimal risk and can be easily liquidated. In many cases, the only allowable investments are Treasury notes, bills, and bonds of the United States government. However, companies have been forced to pay commissions to brokers and resellers in order to obtain these types of investments.

But there is no transaction fee for purchasing government debt directly from the United States Treasury through its *www.publicdebt.treas.gov* Web site. One can use the site to create a TreasuryDirect account for making electronic purchases of debt. Though the intent of the site is to sell debt that is held to maturity, one can request a debt sale through the Federal Reserve Bank of Chicago via the Treasury's Sell Direct system; the government will then sell one's debt investments on the open market in exchange for a small fee per security sold. The usual investment will be in Treasury bills, since they have the shortest term to maturity and can therefore liquidate prior to any need for a commissionable sale to a broker or reseller. More information about this service is available by downloading the TreasuryDirect Investor Kit from the aforementioned Web site.

Cost: 💵   Installation time: 🕰

12–4   Sell Securities under the Regulation A Exemption

Regulation A is described in the SEC's Rules 251 through 263 and provides an exemption from the securities registration requirements of the Securities Act of 1933, on the grounds that a smaller securities issuance does not warrant registration. Regulation A allows exemption from registration if the offering is no larger than $5 million in aggregate per year. Of this amount, no more than $1.5 million can be attributed to the secondary offering of securities currently held by existing shareholders; the secondary offering cannot include resales by company affiliates if the company has not generated net income from continuing operations in at least one of the past two fiscal years. The exemption is restricted to American and Canadian companies, and it is not available to investment and development-stage companies (such as *blank-check* companies). Anyone using this exemption must also create an offering circular, similar to the one that would be required for a registered offering.

There are a number of critical advantages to the exemption provided under Regulation A. First, there is no limit on the number of investors, nor must they pass any kind of qualification test (as would be the case under Regulation D, as described next in "Sell Securities under the Regulation D Exemption"). Further, there are no restrictions on the resale of any securities sold under the Regulation. Finally, the key difference between a Regulation A offering and a registered offering is the absence of any periodic reporting requirements. This is a major reduction in costs to the company, and is the most attractive aspect of the exemption.

In addition, and unlike a registered offering, the Regulation allows a company to "test the waters" with investors in advance of the offering, in order to determine the level of investor interest. To take advantage of this feature, the company must submit the materials used for this initial testing of the waters to the SEC on or before their first date of use. The materials must state that no money is being solicited or will be accepted, that no sales will be made until the company issues an offering circular, that any indication of interest by an investor does not constitute a purchase commitment, and also identify the company's CEO, as well as briefly describe the business. The company can only "test the waters" until it has filed an offering circular with the SEC, and can only commence securities sales once at least 20 days have passed since the last document delivery or broadcast.

When a company is ready to notify the SEC of securities sales under this Regulation, it does so using Form 1-A. Once the Form is filed, the company can conduct a general solicitation, which can include advertising the offering, as long as the solicitation states that sales cannot be completed until the SEC qualifies the company's preliminary offering circular. This preliminary document does not have to include the final security price, though it should contain an estimate of the range of the maximum offering price and the maximum number of shares or debt securities to be offered. Advertising can only state where the offering circular can be obtained, the name of the company, the price and type of security being offered, and the company's general type of business.

Although a company is permitted to advertise its offering as soon as the Form 1-A is filed, it must follow a specific procedure to conduct actual security sales. Once the Form 1-A has been qualified by the SEC, the company must furnish an offering circular to each prospective purchaser at least 48 hours prior to mailing a confirmation of sale. If a broker/dealer is involved with the sale, this entity must provide a copy of the offering circular either with or prior to the confirmation of sale.

If the information in an offering circular becomes false or misleading due to changed circumstances or there have been material developments during the course of an offering, the company must revise the offering circular.

Once securities sales are underway, the company must file Form 2-A with the SEC every six months following the qualification of the offering statement, describing ongoing sales from the offering and use of proceeds. In addition, it must file a final Form 2-A within 30 calendar days following the later of the termination of the offering or the application of proceeds from the offering.

The Regulation has provisions that can disqualify a company from using it. It is not available if a company has had a variety of disclosure problems with the SEC in the past five years, or if the company currently has a registration statement being reviewed by the SEC, or if any affiliates or the company's underwriter have been convicted within the past ten years of a crime related to a security transaction.

Cost: 💵💵💵   Installation time: ⏰⏰

12–5 Sell Securities under the Regulation D Exemption

A company can avoid the lengthy and expensive securities registration process by using the Regulation D exemption. Securities can only be sold under the Regulation D exemption to an *accredited investor*. An accredited investor is one whom the issuing company reasonably believes falls within any of five categories at the time of the securities sale:

1. A bank, broker-dealer, insurance company, investment company, or employee benefit plan
2. A director, executive officer, or general partner of the issuing company
3. A person whose individual net worth (or joint net worth with a spouse) exceeds $1 million
4. A person having individual income exceeding $200,000 or joint income with a spouse exceeding $300,000 in each of the last two years, with a reasonable expectation for reaching the same income level in the current year
5. Any trust with total assets exceeding $5 million

There are several additional types of accredited investors, and some restrictions on the accredited investor types just noted; please review Rule 501 of Regulation D for more details. Nonetheless, the previous definitions describe the primary types of accredited investors.

The information that must be sent to accredited investors as part of the financing is minimized if the issuing company is already meeting its financial reporting requirements under the Exchange Act. Additional reporting requirements are applicable if this is not the case. Please consult Rule 502 of Regulation D for further details.

The issuing company is not allowed any form of general solicitation for the sale of securities under Regulation D. This prohibits the use of advertisements and articles via any medium of publication. It also prohibits the sale of securities through seminars to which attendees were invited through any form of general solicitation. In order to avoid having a general solicitation, a company must pre-screen any investor to whom an inquiry is sent, usually by using an underwriter or promoter who already has a list of qualified potential investors.

A Regulation D offering may span a number of months; if so, there may be some question about which securities sales fall within its boundaries. The consideration of a sale transaction as being integrated into a specific Regulation D offering is a judgmental one. The following factors would lead to the presumption of integration:

- The sales are part of a single financing plan.
- The sales involve the issuance of the same class of securities.
- The sales are being made at approximately the same time;
- The same type of consideration is involved.
- Securities sales are made for the same general purpose.

Securities sold under a Regulation D offering cannot be resold without registration. For this reason, the issuing company is required under Rule 502 of the Regulation to "exercise reasonable care to assure that the purchasers of the securities are not underwriters . . ." To do so, the company must take the following three steps:

1. Inquire of purchasers if they are acquiring the securities for themselves or for other parties.
2. Disclose to each purchaser that the securities have not been registered and therefore cannot be resold until they are registered.
3. Add a legend to each securities certificate, stating that the securities have not been registered, and stating the restrictions on their sale or transfer.

Cost: 💵💵💵   **Installation time:** ⏰⏰

12–6 Set Up Supply Chain Financing

A company may try to improve its working capital situation by negotiating for longer payment terms with its suppliers. Of course, this simply shifts the working capital burden to the suppliers who are effectively providing funds to the company. If a supplier offers an early payment discount, then the company may make an early payment, but now the supplier is losing a substantial amount on the discount. Another problem is that suppliers tend to call the payables staff more frequently about payment dates when payment terms are longer.

An alternative is supply chain financing. Under this solution, a company sends its approved payables list to its bank, specifying the dates on which invoice payments are to be made. The bank makes these payments on behalf of the company. However, in addition to this basic payables function, the bank also contacts the company's suppliers with an offer of early payment, in exchange for a financing charge for the period until maturity. If a supplier agrees with this arrangement and signs a receivables sale contract, then the bank delivers payment from its own funds to the supplier, less its fee. Once the company's payment dates are reached, the bank removes the funds from the company's account, transferring some of the cash to those customers electing to be paid on the prearrangement settlement date, and transferring the remaining funds to its own account to pay for those invoices that it paid early to suppliers at a discount.

This arrangement works very well for suppliers because they may be in need of early settlement. In addition, they receive a much higher percentage of invoice face value than would be the case if they opted for a factoring arrangement with a third party, where 80 percent of the invoice is typically the maximum amount that will be advanced. Also, the amount of the discount offered by the bank may be quite small (much less than if the supplier were offering an early payment discount), if the company is a large and well-funded entity having excellent credit. Finally, the arrangement is usually nonrecourse for the supplier, since the arrangement with the bank is structured as a receivables assignment.

The arrangement also works well for the bank, which has excellent visibility into the company's bank balances and cash flow history, and so knows when it can offer such financing at minimal risk to itself. Also, it obtains fees from the company in exchange for disbursing funds on behalf of the company.

This is also a good deal for the company, whose suppliers now have ready access to funds. Further, since the bank is contacting suppliers with payment dates, they will no longer make inquiries of the company regarding when they will be paid.

Supply chain financing is less useful when payment terms are relatively short, since there is not much benefit for suppliers in being paid just a few days early. However, it is an excellent tool when standard payment terms are quite long.

Cost: 💵   **Installation time:** ⏰ ⏰

12–7 Take a Business Unit Public

A company with multiple business units can have numerous problems related to them: Investors are unclear about the operating results of each unit, there may be significant differences in the perceived market value of some units, other units do not fall into the core business area, and unit managers have no incentive to improve their stock performance when their units have only a minor impact on overall corporate results. All of these issues can be addressed to some degree by taking a business unit public.

One approach for going public is the equity carve-out. Under this approach, a company creates a separate legal entity for a subsidiary, with a separate board of directors, and sells shares in it to the public through an initial public offering. This approach is usually taken when the unit has a high perceived value by the equity markets that will result in a high share price, and therefore considerable cash received by the corporate parent. Usually, the parent company retains some measure of ownership over the business unit.

Another option is the spinoff, which is a simple distribution of shares in the business unit to existing shareholders as a stock dividend. This approach is usually taken when the corporate parent wishes to completely sever its ownership of a business unit, frequently because it does not fit into the overall area of corporate focus.

Finally, the corporate parent can issue a tracking stock in a business unit. This requires no new legal entity, and therefore no separate board of directors. Shares are usually issued as a stock split from the shares of the corporate parent, with shareholders receiving a claim on the future earnings of the designated business unit; the parent continues to control the unit. This approach is usually taken when the parent feels the value of the unit will increase on the equity market, resulting in gains for shareholders.

No matter which of these approaches is taken, there are a number of benefits. First, investors receive operating and financial information about a specific business unit, which gives them more information upon which to make investment decisions. Second, the value of shares is more tightly linked to the performance of specific business areas, which is also of use to investors. Third, business units can bring in equity capital for their own use, which may improve the amount of cash available to them than would be the case if they were competing for corporate funding with other business units. Fourth, subsidiaries can use their own stock to engage in merger and acquisition activities. Finally, creating stock for a business unit is a powerful incentive for its business managers if they are given stock options linked to those shares, since the managers have a major impact on the future value of the business unit.

Cost: 💵💵💵   **Installation time:** ⏰⏰⏰

12–8 Automate Option Tracking

When a large number of employees have company options, either the finance or human resources department will be the target of ongoing questions about the vesting, valuation, and tax implications of these options. Because the tax laws are so complex in this area, employees keep returning with follow-up clarification questions, as well as to run what-if scenarios on what they should do under various circumstances. Given a large number of employees with many option grants, this can turn into a major drain on company resources. In addition, a company runs the risk of giving bad advice to its employees, which may have legal repercussions if employees using this advice lose money through the exercise of options.

A solution for larger companies is to purchase an options tracking package, which they can use alternatively as an in-house solution or as a featured service on the external site of an application service provider. An example of such software is Express Options, which is sold by Transcentive, Inc. The system stores all options information in a single database, allowing one to handle multiple grant types, determine vesting schedules, track option exercises and cancellations, and provide employees with tax-related information. It also calculates option valuations, exports data to the company stock transfer agent, and provides a variety of reports for regulatory purposes. By using Transcentive's add-on product, Express Desktop, employees can access such information about their options as portfolio valuations based on different stock pricing assumptions, what-if modeling, transaction histories, and frequently asked questions. They can also place orders to exercise their options through the system.

For this type of service, one can expect to pay a minimum of $15,000 annually, with the price exceeding one-third of a million dollars per year for larger installations. Given its cost, this best practice is most applicable to corporations with at least several hundred option holders.

Cost: 💵💵💵   **Installation time:** ⏰ ⏰

12–9 Automate 401(k) Plan Enrollment

In smaller organizations, the accounting department is tasked with the management of 401(k) plan additions, changes, and deletions. This is not an efficient process, for someone must arrange for a meeting with each employee who has now been working for the minimum amount of time, as specified in the plan documentation, explain the plan's features to them, wait for them to take the plan materials home for review, and, finally, enter the returned documents into the system of the 401(k) provider. This is a lengthy and time-consuming process.

An alternative is to automatically enroll employees in the 401(k) plan. This is also known as a *negative election*, since an employee must make a decision *not* to be enrolled in the plan, rather than the reverse. This approach has the considerable advantage of reducing the paperwork needed to enter a person into the 401(k) plan, since it is done as part of the hiring process, along with all other paperwork needed to set up a new employee.

There are only minor downsides to this best practice. With more employees in the plan, there will be somewhat higher fees charged by the 401(k) service provider (which are typically charged on a per-person basis). Also, there will still be some paperwork associated with those employees who *do* make a negative election. Finally, since the group of employees who tend to be added to the 401(k) plan through this method are at the lower end of the income stratum, it is more likely that they will want to take out loans against their invested funds, each of which calls for more paperwork.

Cost: 💵   **Installation time:** ⏰ ⏰

12–10 Grant Employees Immediate 401(k) Eligibility

The most common way to enroll employees into a company's 401(k) pension plan is to make them wait either 90 days or a year from the date of hire. This calls for the maintenance of a list of dates for newly hired employees that must be watched to ascertain when someone becomes available for this benefit. Then they must be contacted and scheduled for a short lecture about how the plan works and how to invest in it. Then they complete paperwork to enroll, which is forwarded to the payroll department so that deductions can be made from their paychecks for advancement to the 401(k) plan administrator. All of the steps can more easily be compressed into the hiring process, as was just noted in the "Automate 401(k) Plan Enrollment" section in this chapter. However, the issue can be taken one step further not only by completing all of the paperwork at the time of hire, but also by actually allowing *immediate* participation in the plan at the time of hire. This represents less a matter of improved efficiency than of giving new employees a fine new benefit, for they can begin investing funds at once, which may lead to a reduced level of employee turnover.

The main problem is that new employees can impact a company's ability to pass pension plan nondiscrimination tests, especially if the new hires are at low pay scales. If these new employees do not invest a reasonable proportion of their salaries in the 401(k) plan, this can force highly compensated employees to limit their plan contributions to less than the maximum amounts. Nonetheless, if there is a perception that immediate eligibility for the plan will improve the employee turnover rate, then this should be considered the overriding issue.

Cost: Installation time: 🕐 🕐

12–11 Consolidate Insurance Policies

Insurance policies are frequently added to a company's insurance portfolio in a piecemeal manner. Someone on the management team decides that some additional coverage is needed to mitigate a perceived risk, and so an additional policy is added—sometimes beginning at a different time of the year from the other policies already in existence, and perhaps with different insurance companies. This can be an expensive approach, for each insurer must factor in potential loss costs plus operating expenses and profit—on each policy it issues.

A better alternative is to aggregate the policies with a single insurer. By doing so, insurers can see that their administrative cost will be the same, despite the much higher volume of insurance, and so they can reduce their insurance prices. Also, there is little risk that claims will arise on every single policy held, so the overall risk to the insurer declines—which in turn can reduce prices yet again.

This option is best used by large companies with large-dollar insurance policies, since insurers will want their business badly enough to be willing to reduce prices based on the factors just noted.

Cost: Installation time: 🕐 🕐 🕐

12–12 Obtain Key Man Life Insurance for the CFO

It is common for companies to take out key man life insurance policies on their chief executive officers or the holders of key product knowledge—but what about the CFO?

First, let's look at the reasons for key-man insurance. It is intended to at least cover the cost of recruiting and training a replacement, and can also be used to fulfill any contractual pay or benefit obligations to the person's surviving spouse. The most justifiable use of this insurance is when the partners in a partnership need the resources to buy out the shares of any partner who dies.

These traditional reasons do not warrant the purchase of key-man insurance for the CFO. Companies should have a sufficiently deep management team to be able to promote a CFO from within, or at least adequately backfill the position until an outsider is hired.

However, there is a scenario when such insurance might make sense. If the current CFO is deeply involved in financing arrangements and there is a serious risk that the financing could be lost in the event of the CFO's demise, then the insurance proceeds could compensate for the lost funds. If this scenario is the reason for having key-man life insurance, then the amount of the insurance should approximate the amount of funding at risk of being lost.

Cost: Installation time:

12–13 Obtain Advance Rating Assessments

A company with publicly held debt can never be sure about the change in its rating by a major rating service after it has taken some significant action, such as an acquisition or a major capital investment. If the rating agency decides after the fact that the company's action has downgraded the credit level on its debt, then the reduced ranking may trigger a number of adverse financial items—such as a drop in the market price of the debt in order to increase its effective interest rate, or difficulty in obtaining additional debt at a reasonable price.

This problem can be overcome by using Standard & Poor's Rating Evaluation Service. This service allows a company to obtain a confidential review of its credit rating by a Standard & Poor's analyst who will issue a prospective credit rating based on the proposed action. This is a particularly valuable service when a company has a range of action items to choose from and is willing to change its strategic direction based on which action results in the best credit rating. Since the ratings derived by Standard & Poor's are based on prospective actions that may never be implemented, the ratings will be kept confidential until such time as the company makes its plans public. Examples of possible activities that could require a prospective credit analysis are asset sales or divestitures, stock buy-backs, mergers or acquisitions, financial restructurings, recapitalizations, expansions into new lines of business, and modifications to the corporate legal structure.

The primary difficulty with this best practice is the considerable fee required to have these analyses performed. The fee charged will increase for each additional strategic option a company wishes to have analyzed, so having a broad range of possible actions reviewed will be expensive.

Cost: 💵💵   Installation time: ⏰⏰

12–14 Rent a Captive Insurance Company

Companies are having increasing difficulty obtaining reasonably priced insurance of all types, if they can obtain insurance at all. Captive insurance companies have been used to provide access to insurance. They are run by a single company, an association of companies, or by an entire industry in order to solve particular insurance problems. Though the use of captive insurance companies has been a longstanding option for obtaining at least some of the necessary insurance, this option has required extensive legal analysis, incorporation costs, and significant initial capitalization fees that have limited their use. Also, sharing a captive with other companies has, until now, meant that a company must share in the risks incurred by other companies, which can present an uncomfortably high risk profile.

Over the past few years, changes in the legal requirements for captive insurance companies have brought about the creation of the rent-a-captive. Under this legal structure, a captive insurance company has already been created by a third party that rents it out for use by multiple companies. The structure is usually in the format of "protected cells," whereby each company using one can shield its contributed capital and surplus from other renters that are also using the captive. Not only does this format prevent a company from dealing with the initial start-up costs of a captive insurance company, but it also allows it to retain any underwriting profit and investment income from contributed funds. The company can even recover a low-claim bonus at the end of the rent-a-captive contract, though it can also be liable for additional claims payments that exceed its initial or subsequent contributions into the captive. This format is especially useful for those companies faced with moderate risks that have reduced their frequency of claim incurrence. Conversely, it is less useful for companies seeking catastrophic coverage or that have high volumes of small-claim activity.

The creators of rent-a-captive insurance companies usually charge a percentage fee of premiums paid into the captives in exchange for their use, while some also take a share of the investment profit. This option is cost-effective for those companies paying at least half a million dollars in insurance expenses per year. One should also pay for up-front legal advice on both the applicability of this approach and the tax deductibility of contributions made into a rent-a-captive.

Cost: 💵💵💵   Installation time: ⏰⏰⏰

12–15 Use Netting to Reduce Foreign Exchange Settlements

A company that regularly conducts business in multiple countries must spend a considerable amount of time settling foreign exchange transactions. It may buy and sell the same currencies many times over as it processes individual payables and receivables. There are three ways to reduce the volume of these transactions, depending on the number of parties involved:

1. *Unilateral netting.* A company can aggregate the cash flows amongst its various subsidiaries to determine if any foreign exchange payments between the subsidiaries can be netted, with only the (presumably) smaller residual balances being physically shifted. This reduces the volume of foreign exchange cash flows, and therefore the associated foreign exchange risk.

2. *Bilateral spreadsheet netting.* If two companies located in different countries transact a great deal of business with each other, then they can track the payables owed to each other, net out the balances at the end of each month, and one party pays the other the net remaining balance.

3. *Multilateral centralized netting.* When there are multiple parties wishing to net transactions, it becomes much too complex to manage with a spreadsheet. Instead, the common approach is to net transactions through a centralized exchange, such as Arizona-based EuroNetting (*www.euronetting .com*). Under a centralized netting system, each participant enters its payables into a centralized database through an Internet browser or some other file upload system, after which the netting service converts each participant's net cash flows to an equivalent amount in each participant's base currency, and then uses actual traded exchange rates to determine the final net position of each participant. The exchange operator then pays or receives each participant's net position and uses the proceeds to offset the required foreign exchange trades.

Each type of netting arrangement can involve a broad array of payment types, covering such areas as products, services, royalties, dividends, interest, loans, and hedging contracts.

When bilateral or multilateral netting is used, the parties usually sign a master agreement that itemizes the types of netting to be performed, as well as which contracts or purchase orders are to be included in the arrangement.

Although netting can be a highly effective way to reduce foreign exchange transaction costs, some governments do not recognize the enforceability of netting arrangements, because they can undermine the payment rights of third-party creditors. Consequently, consult a qualified attorney prior to entering into a netting arrangement.

Cost: 💵💵   **Installation time:** ⏰⏰⏰

12–16 Install a Treasury Workstation

The multitude of treasury-based transactions can take up a large part of the finance staff's workday and is highly subject to error. These tasks involve management of a company's cash position, investment and debt portfolio, and risk analysis. The normal approach to these tasks is to track, summarize, and analyze them on an electronic spreadsheet, with manual input derived from all of the company's banks and investment firms on a daily basis. In addition, any changes resulting from this analysis, such as the centralization or investment of cash, must be manually shifted to the general ledger. Given the highly manual nature of these tasks, this frequently results in errors that must be corrected through the bank reconciliation process. A treasury workstation can greatly reduce many of these work steps.

A treasury workstation is a combination of hardware and software that will manage cash, investments, debt issuance and tracking, as well as provide some risk analysis functions. It is an expensive item to purchase, typically ranging from $30,000 for a bare-bones installation to $300,000 for a fully configured one. The difference between these prices is the amount of functionality and bank interfaces added to the treasury workstation—if a buyer wants every possible feature and must share data with a large number of financial suppliers, then the cost will be much closer to the top of the range. Given these costs, this best practice is not cost-effective for companies with sales volumes under $50 million. Also, because of the large number of interfaces needed to connect the workstation to other entities, the installation time can range from one to nine months.

Why spend so much money and installation time on a treasury workstation? Because it automates so much of the rote finance tasks. For example, if an employee enters an investment into the system, it will create a transaction for the settlement, one for the maturity, and another for the interest. It will then alter the cash forecast with this information, as well as create a wire transfer to send the money to an investing entity. Here are some of the other functions that it can perform:

- *Bank reconciliation.* It can do the bulk of a bank reconciliation, leaving just a few nonreconciling items to be resolved by an employee.
- *Cash forecasting.* It can determine all company cash inflows and outflows from multiple sources in order to derive a cash forecast.
- *Cash movement.* It can originate electronic funds transfers.
- *Debt tracking.* It can follow short-term debt with a link to a dealer-based commercial paper program.
- *Financial exposure.* It can identify and quantify financial exposure.
- *Foreign exchange.* It can determine a company's cash positions in any currency.
- *Investment tracking.* It can track and summarize a company's investment positions in money markets, mutual funds, short-term and fixed-income investments, equities, and options.

- *Risk analysis.* It allows an employee to use it as a giant calculator, performing what-if analyses with yield-curve manipulation and scenario analysis.

Based on this lengthy list, it is evident that a large company can derive a sufficient benefit from a treasury workstation to offset its substantial cost.

Cost: 💵💵💵   Installation time: ⏰⏰⏰

12–17 Connect to the SWIFT Network

The Society for Worldwide Interbank Financial Telecommunication (SWIFT) operates a worldwide network that banks use to exchange standardized electronic messages that are known as SWIFT MT codes. The SWIFT network is highly secure, and is designed strictly to transport messages between participants—it does not provide a clearing or settlement service. By accessing the SWIFT network, a company can streamline a number of treasury transactions, which makes the entire system more cost-effective to operate.

Companies are now able to access the SWIFT network by any one of four methods:

- *Standardized Corporate Environment (SCORE).* Under this approach, a company can communicate with all member banks in a closed user group. Companies allowed to use this method must be listed on selected stock exchanges in specific countries, which include most of Western Europe, North America, and some countries in Eastern Europe, Latin America, and Asia. SWIFT invoices companies directly for their message traffic. This is the most efficient method, because users have direct access to nearly all banks.

- *Member-Administered Closed User Group (MA-CUG).* A company can join a separate MA-CUG for each bank with which it wishes to communicate. Each MA-CUG is administered by a bank, rather than SWIFT. The bank running each CUG will invoice member companies for their message traffic. This approach may call for membership in multiple MA-CUGs, which is less convenient than the SCORE method. However, it is available to all types and sizes of companies.

- *Alliance Lite.* SWIFT has made this method available to smaller companies having low transaction volumes. It allows them to use either a manual browser-based payment entry system or to integrate directly into their treasury management systems.

- *SWIFT bureaus.* Third-party providers have set up their own access to the SWIFT network, and allow companies access through their systems for a per-transaction fee. This approach avoids the need for any in-house systems maintenance, but connectivity to any in-house treasury management systems is likely to be limited.

In none of these access methodologies is a company allowed to deal directly with another corporation; it can only send messages through bank intermediaries.

Access to the SWIFT network is important for larger companies, because they can link their treasury management systems directly into the SWIFT network. By doing so, they avoid having to establish individual interfaces with the reporting systems of all the banks with which they do business, and instead can rely on a single standard messaging format to initiate transactions with and acquire information from bank accounts all over the world.

Each SWIFT MT code used to send messages within the SWIFT network contains a standard set of information fields. Thus, a different SWIFT MT code is used for each type of transaction. For example, a company can issue an MT 101 to move funds, an MT 104 to debit a debtor's account, an MT 300 for a foreign exchange confirmation, an MT 320 for a loan confirmation, and an MT 940 to request bank account information. Given the high degree of standardization, these messages can be automatically generated by a company's treasury management system and transmitted through SWIFT, while all incoming messages can also be dealt with by the treasury management system in a highly automated manner.

In summary, there are multiple ways for a company to gain access to the SWIFT system, which it can then integrate into its treasury management system.

Cost: 💵💵   **Installation time:** ⏰⏰

12–18 Optimize the Organization of Treasury Operations

A large multinational company typically became large at least in part through acquisitions, which leaves it with a complex set of banking relationships and accounts, as well as a highly dispersed treasury management group that resides in a multitude of locations. This results in the inefficient use of cash, which in turn reduces interest income and does not allow a company to pay down the optimal amount of debt.

These problems can be mitigated by implementing regional treasury management centers, usually one per continent. By doing so, the treasurer can concentrate those treasury staff with the highest levels of expertise in the same locations, while also achieving a much higher level of control over the underlying cash pooling and foreign exchange transactions, not to mention better clerical tracking of any resulting intercompany loans. By concentrating activities into this smaller number of regional treasury centers, the treasurer can also more easily obtain online access to the overall status of cash flows for the entire company.

The price of this increased level of efficiency is a considerable amount of resistance by individual companies within the corporate conglomerate, since local controllers and chief financial officers will be reluctant to hand over the administration of their cash flows to a regional center that is outside of their control. Also, such a high level of cash management calls for centralized information flows that can only be provided by a companywide enterprise resource planning (ERP) system, which is an extremely expensive system to purchase and install. Consequently, the multinational optimization of treasury activities is so expensive that it is a reasonable option only for the largest companies.

Cost: 💵💵💵   **Installation time:** ⏰⏰⏰

12–19 Hedge Foreign Exchange with Forward Exchange Contracts

Under a forward exchange contract, which is the most commonly used foreign exchange (FX) hedge, a company agrees to purchase a fixed amount of a foreign currency on a specific date, and at a predetermined rate. This allows it to lock in the rate of exchange up front for settlement at a specified date in the future. The counterparty is typically a bank, which requires a deposit to secure the contract, with a final payment due in time to be cleared by the settlement date. If the company has a credit facility with the bank acting as its counterparty, then the bank can allocate a portion of that line to any outstanding forward exchange contracts and release the allocation once the contracts have been settled. The forward exchange contract is considered to be an over-the-counter transaction because there is no centralized trading location and customized transactions are created directly between parties.

EXAMPLE

Toledo Toolmakers has a 100,000 euro receivable at a spot rate of 1.39079. Toledo can enter into a forward FX contract with a bank for 100,000 euros at a forward rate of 1.3900, so that Toledo receives a fixed amount of $139,000 on the maturity date of the receivable. When Toledo receives the 100,000 euro payment, it transfers the funds to the bank acting as counterparty on the forward FX contract, and receives $139,000 from the bank. Thus, Toledo has achieved its original receivable amount of $139,000, even if the spot rate has declined during the interval.

The price of a currency on the maturity date (its forward price) comprises the spot price, plus a transaction fee, plus or minus points that represent the interest rate differential between the two currencies. The combination of the spot rate and the forward points is known as the *all-in forward rate*. The interest rate differential is calculated in accordance with these two rules:

1. The currency of the country having a higher interest rate trades at a discount
2. The currency of the country having a lower interest rate trades at a premium.

For example, if the domestic interest rate is higher than that of the foreign currency, then forward points are deducted from the spot rate, which makes the foreign currency less expensive in the forward market. The result of this pricing is that the forward price should make the buyer indifferent to taking delivery immediately or at some future date. Thus, if the spot price of euros per dollar were 0.7194 and there was a discount of 40 points for forwards having a one-year maturity, then the all-in forward rate would be 0.7154.

The calculation of the discount or premium points follows this formula:

$$\text{Premium/discount} = \text{Exchange rate} \times \text{interest rate differential}$$
$$\times \frac{\text{Days of contract duration}}{360}$$

EXAMPLE

The six-month U.S. dollar money market rate is 2.50 percent and the six-month euro money market rate is 3.75 percent. The USD/EUR exchange rate is 0.7194. The number of days in the forward exchange contract is 181. Because the euro interest rate exceeds the dollar interest rate, the dollar is at a premium to the euro. Thus, the USD/EUR forward exchange rate exceeds the spot rate. The premium is calculated as:

0.7194 spot rate × .0125 interest differential × (181/365 days) = .0045 premium

The premium is therefore 45 points, which results in a USD/EUR forward exchange rate of 0.7194 + 0.0045, or 0.7239.

There are a few problems with forward exchange contracts. First, because they are special transactions between two parties, it can be difficult to sell them to a third party. Also, the transaction premium offered may not be competitive.

Another problem is that the arrangement relies on the customer paying the company on or before the date when the forward FX contract matures. To continue using Toledo Toolmakers in an example, its terms to a European Union customer may require payment in 60 days, so it enters into a forward contract to expire in 63 days, which factors in an allowance of three extra days for the customer to pay. If the customer does not pay within 63 days, then Toledo still has to deliver euros on that date to fulfill its side of the forward contract.

Cost: **Installation time:** 🕰️🕰️

12–20 Hedge Foreign Exchange with Currency Futures

A currency future is the same as a forward exchange contract, except that it trades on an exchange. Each contract has a standardized size, expiry date, and settlement rules. The primary currency futures center with substantial volume is the Chicago Mercantile Exchange (CME). The CME offers futures trading between the major currencies, as well as some of the emerging market currencies. However, the volume of contracts in the emerging market currencies is quite low.

These contracts are normally handled through a broker, who charges a commission. There is also a margin requirement, so that the buyer may be called on to submit additional funds over time if the underlying futures contract declines in value. Part of this margin is an initial deposit whose size is based on the contract size and the type of position being acquired. All futures contracts are marked to market daily, with the underlying margin accounts being credited or debited with the day's gains or losses. If the balance of the margin account drops too far, then the contract buyer must contribute more funds to the margin account. If the buyer does not update the margin account as required, then it is possible that the position will be closed out.

Since currency futures have standard sizes and expiry dates, it is quite likely that a futures hedging strategy will not exactly match the underlying currency activity. For example, if a company needs to hedge a projected receipt of 375,000 euros and the related futures contract only trades in units of 100,000 euros, then the company has the choice of selling either three or four contracts, totaling 300,000 and 400,000 euros, respectively. Further, if the projected currency receipt date varies from the standard futures contract expiry date, then the company will be subject to some foreign exchange risk for a few days. Thus, the standardized nature of currency futures contracts result in an imperfect hedge for users.

EXAMPLE

Toledo Toolmakers ships product to a German customer in February, and expects to receive a payment of 425,000 euros on June 12. Toledo's CFO elects to hedge the transaction by selling a futures contract on the CME. The standard contract size for the EUR/USD pairing is 100,000 euros, so Toledo sells four contracts to hedge its expected receipt of 425,000 euros. This contract always expires on Fridays; the nearest Friday following the expected receipt date of the euros is on June 15, so Toledo enters into contracts having that expiry date. Because the standardized futures contracts do not exactly fit Toledo's transaction, Toledo is electing not to hedge 25,000 euros of the expected receipt, and it will also retain the risk of exchange rate fluctuations between its currency receipt date of June 12 and its currency sale date of June 15.

Cost: **Installation time:**

12–21   Lock in Interest Rates with an Interest Rate Swap

The *interest rate swap* is an agreement between two parties (where one party is almost always a bank) to exchange interest payments in the same currency over a defined time period, which normally ranges from one to ten years. One of the parties is paying a fixed rate of interest, while the other is paying a variable rate. The variable interest rate is paid whenever a new coupon is set, which is typically once a quarter. Fixed interest is usually paid at the end of each year.

By engaging in a swap, a company can shift from fixed to variable payments, or vice versa. Thus, if a company uses a swap to shift from variable to fixed interest payments, it can better forecast its financing costs and avoid increased payments, but loses the chance of reduced interest payments if rates were to decline. If it takes the opposite position and swaps fixed rates for variable rates, then it is essentially betting that it will benefit from a future decline in interest rates. An interest rate swap is especially useful for a company with a weak credit rating, since such entities must pay a premium to obtain fixed-rate debt. They may find it less expensive to obtain variable-rate debt and then engage in an interest rate swap to secure what is essentially a fixed-rate payment schedule.

The parties to an interest rate swap deal directly with each other, rather than using a standard product that is traded over an exchange. They customarily use the standard master agreement that is maintained by the International Swaps and Derivatives Association (*www.isda.org*). The ISDA represents participants in the privately negotiated derivatives industry, and maintains standard contracts for derivatives transactions. The parties commonly modify a variety of features within the agreement to suit their needs.

EXAMPLE

ABC Company borrows $10 million. Under the terms of the agreement, ABC must make quarterly interest payments for the next three years that are based on the London Interbank Offered Rate (LIBOR), which is reset once a quarter under the terms of the borrowing agreement. Since the interest payments are variable, the company will experience reduced interest payments if LIBOR declines, but will pay more if LIBOR increases. ABC's management is more concerned about the risk of LIBOR increasing, so it eliminates this risk by entering into an interest rate swap in which it agrees to pay interest for three years on $10 million at a fixed rate, while its counterparty agrees to make floating interest rate payments for three years on $10 million to ABC. The first-year payment stream for the transaction is shown in the following table, where the counterparty makes quarterly payments to ABC, which vary based on changes in LIBOR. ABC makes a single fixed interest rate payment to the counterparty at the end of year one. The result of these transactions is that ABC experiences a net reduction in its interest expense of $20,000 in the first year of the swap agreement.

Payment Date	Loan Fixed Rate	Applicable LIBOR Quarterly Rate	Payments from the Counterparty to ABC Company	Payments from ABC Company to the Counterparty
March 31	–	4.20%	$105,000	
June 30	–	4.35%	108,750	
September 30	–	4.60%	115,000	
December 31	4.25%	4.65%	116,250	$425,000
Totals			**$445,000**	**$425,000**

The CFO should arrange for payments under an interest swap agreement to be as closely aligned as possible with the payment terms of the underlying debt agreement. Thus, it is not useful if a counterparty's payment to the company is scheduled to arrive several weeks after the company is scheduled to pay its bank under a loan agreement. Instead, the counterparty's payment should be scheduled to arrive just prior to the due date specified in the loan agreement, thereby better aligning the company's cash flows.

Cost: 💵💵   **Installation time:** ⏰⏰

Chapter 13

Financial Statements
Best Practices

This chapter covers the best practices that can be used to issue financial statements more rapidly. This creation process can be one of the most convoluted and time consuming of all activities, with a long time needed to complete a quality set of statements. When a long interval is regularly required to complete financial statements, it has two significant impacts: not allowing any time for the accounting staff to complete other activities, and an irate management team that never receives its information on time. These are serious problems that can be completely eliminated by the best practices noted in this chapter.

The primary purpose of the more than two dozen improvement suggestions in this chapter is to streamline the entire process of financial statement production. This is done in a variety of ways, such as completing some tasks before the end of the month, avoiding the bank reconciliation, and automating the month-end cutoff process. Most of these steps are simple ones and can be quickly and easily inserted into the existing process. A few, however, such as automating the period-end cutoff, require a significant amount of extra work and may carry some risk of providing imperfect financial information. Consequently, it is necessary to review each recommended best practice carefully and only use those that will most easily be inserted into the existing system without causing either a stoppage in financial statement production or a reduction in their quality.

This chapter begins with a brief analysis of the level of implementation difficulty for each of the best practices, proceeds to a detailed review of each one, and finishes with an overview of how most of them can be grouped together into a highly efficient financial statement production process.

Implementation Issues for Financial Statements Best Practices

This section notes the relative level of implementation difficulty for all of the best practices that are discussed later in this chapter. The primary source of information is contained in Exhibit 13.1, which shows the cost and duration of implementation for each best practice. For this group of improvements, the table makes it clear that, in most cases, changes are of little duration, easy to implement, and have little or no cost. The reason is that most alterations are confined to a small

Exhibit 13.1 Summary of Financial Statements Best Practices

	Best Practice	Cost	Install Time
Financial Reports			
13–1	Move operating data to other reports	💵	⏰
13–2	Post financial statements in an Excel PivotTable on the Internet	💵	⏰
13–3	Restrict the level of reporting	💵	⏰
13–4	Write financial statement footnotes in advance	💵	⏰
13–5	Create a disclosure committee	💵	⏰⏰
Work Automation			
13–6	Automate recurring journal entries	💵	⏰
13–7	Automate the cutoff	💵💵💵	⏰⏰⏰
Work Elimination			
13–8	Avoid the bank reconciliation	💵	⏰
13–9	Defer routine work	💵	⏰
13–10	Eliminate multiple approvals	💵	⏰⏰
13–11	Eliminate small accruals	💵	⏰
13–12	Reduce investigation levels	💵	⏰
Work Management			
13–13	Assign closing responsibilities	💵	⏰
13–14	Compress billing activities	💵	⏰⏰
13–15	Conduct transaction training	💵💵	⏰⏰
13–16	Continually review wait times	💵	⏰
13–17	Convert serial activities to parallel ones	💵	⏰⏰
13–18	Create a closing schedule	💵	⏰
13–19	Document the process	💵	⏰
13–20	Restrict the use of journal entries	💵	⏰
13–21	Train the staff in closing procedures	💵💵	⏰⏰
13–22	Use cycle counting to avoid month-end counts	💵💵	⏰⏰⏰
13–23	Use internal audits to locate transaction problems in advance	💵💵	⏰⏰

(continues)

Exhibit 13.1 *(Continued)*

	Best Practice	Cost	Install Time
Work Timing			
13–24	Compress public company closing activities	💵	⏰⏰
13–25	Use standard journal entry forms	💵	⏰
13–26	Complete allocation bases in advance	💵	⏰
13–27	Conduct daily review of the financial statements	💵	⏰

number of people within the accounting department, which makes it easier to alter the tasks of just that small group. Also, these are mostly procedural changes, ones that do not require expensive and problematic computer programming alterations. Further, there is little need for the participation of other departments. Thus, for all these reasons, the risk and investment associated with most of these best practices are low.

The two glaring exceptions are automating the period-end cutoff and using inventory cycle counting to avoid month-end inventory counts. In the first case, there is a need for programming; and in both cases, the complete cooperation of the warehouse staff is required. Given these two additional variables, these best practices become not only the most expensive and time-consuming ones to implement, but also the ones most likely to fail.

13–1 Move Operating Data to Other Reports   ✔*Author's Choice*

A major factor in the delay in completing financial statements is the inclusion of operating data in the statements. The reason is that this information, such as scrap rates or employee turnover, is not contained in the financial information that the accounting staff normally deals with, nor is it readily obtained by creating ratios or comparisons of the financial data. In short, this information can be hard to obtain. The situation is worsened by the lack of control of the accounting staff over who tracks the information, as well as its accuracy once it is obtained. For example, a subsidiary may forward information about its customer backlog that seems suspiciously high; the controller has the options of including the provided data in the financial statements or of holding off on the financial statement distribution while requesting and waiting for a review of the numbers by the subsidiary—which is under no obligation to do the review. Thus, including operating data in the financial statements not only can delay the issuance of the statements but also does nothing to ensure the accuracy of the operating information.

An easy way to avoid these problems is to separate all operating information from the financial statements so the statements can be issued in a timely manner, with the operating information sent out later in a separate document. By using this approach, there are fewer steps to complete when issuing financial statements, leaving fewer steps to delay the overall process. Also, if there are problems with the operating data, the controller can review the information at his or her leisure and verify that the information is correct before releasing it. Not only is this an easy best practice to implement, but it is also one that has no associated expense.

Cost: **Installation time:** 🕑

13–2 Post Financial Statements in an Excel PivotTable on the Internet

A number of companies have found that an effective way to increase investor knowledge of their activities is to post their financial statements on their Web sites. These tend to be a summary-level duplication of the most recent quarterly or annual results, as well as any accompanying financial notes. Though this is certainly a good way to communicate with investors, the concept can be taken a step further by loading the financial information into an Excel PivotTable, which is essentially a three-dimensional spreadsheet that reveals different layers of information to the user. By using a PivotTable, a reader of a financial statement can access the results for multiple years, or even different lines of business, within a summary-level financial statement. A good example of this layout can be found in the Investor Relations section of the Microsoft Web site. This is a relatively easy best practice to implement. The only downside is that investors must download the file, which creates the highly unlikely, yet possible, risk of importing a computer virus through the spreadsheet file.

Cost: 💵   **Installation time:** 🕑

13–3 Restrict the Level of Reporting

Over time, many older companies have gradually gotten into the habit of demanding (and receiving) immensely detailed financial statements from the accounting department. Besides the usual balance sheet and income statement, as well as departmental reports, there can be a plethora of additional schedules, such as sales by customer or region, inventory levels by type of inventory, and a complete activity-based costing analysis of every customer. Though some of these reports may be set up to run automatically as part of the regular package of financial statements (and thereby requiring no additional work), other reports may require the transfer of information to a different format, such as an electronic spreadsheet, for further analysis and regrouping into a customized report. In this case, the amount of time required to assemble and independently prepare the reports may exceed the time needed to create the primary financial statements. Thus, the more reports included in the financial statements, the more time it takes to issue the statements.

The solution is to make a list of all the reports included in the financial statements, ignore those that are automatically created by the accounting software, and focus on eliminating or delaying those that are created separately. It may be possible to strip these reports out of the basic financial reporting package, allowing the accounting staff to issue the basic underlying statements much more quickly. To achieve this goal, it may be necessary to explain to management that the reports will no longer be provided at all (which is normally not received well). Other variations are to issue the reports separately and at a later date, or to issue them less frequently, such as once a quarter or year. Usually, there is some combination of methods that will be agreeable to management, thereby allowing a controller to restrict the level of reporting in the financial statements to only the most basic information.

Management may take a better view of this reduction in the information provided if the controller or CFO makes it known that, while information will be delayed, other information will be provided more frequently in order to meet the operating needs of the company. For example, the accounting department could promise daily access to information about changes in revenues, discounts given to customers, and expenses, and weekly access to changes in headcount information. By providing this information so rapidly, it reduces the negative impact of restricting some information from the financial statements, while also providing a service by issuing key information even sooner than it had previously been issued.

Cost: Installation time: 🕰

13–4 Write Financial Statement Footnotes in Advance

Many footnotes accompany a well-documented set of financial statements. These typically include an executive summary, notes on the accounting methodologies, the amount of long-term debt (as well as the years in which it comes due), a commentary on insurance coverage, any customers with a high preponderance of a company's sales, and a historical comparison of the current results to prior years. Depending on the number of footnotes added to the financial statement package, this can be a considerable amount of work to update every period.

The solution is to separate them into two categories: boilerplate information that is rarely changed, and information that is closely linked to current financial results, requiring a great deal of updating. All footnotes in the first category should be clustered together to the greatest extent possible, reviewed prior to the end of the month, and even printed out and ready for inclusion with the remainder of the financial statements. By handling these items well in advance, there is less work to be done during the crucial period immediately following the end of a reporting period, when there is little time available for such work. Unfortunately, many footnotes *do* require updates based on current financial results and so cannot be completed in advance. In these cases, it is still possible to highlight those portions of each footnote that must be changed, either with different font sizes, underlining, or color changes in the computer, so that everything requiring examination can be spotted and checked easily. In addition, it is a good idea to create a checklist containing all of the data to be updated in each footnote. This checklist is an excellent way to avoid situations where footnotes are distributed that have not been updated to account for the most recent results.

Cost: 💵   Installation time: ⏰

13–5   Create a Disclosure Committee

Auditors have become increasingly sensitive to the completeness of financial statement disclosures, especially in the areas of potential commitments for which a company may be liable. The problem for company management is that the employees who may be creating these commitments (especially in the purchasing and legal departments) probably have no idea that their activities require disclosure. This is less of a problem in smaller, centralized companies where informal communication channels keep everyone apprised of ongoing activities, but can be a significant problem in larger firms where employees are widely distributed and communication systems are accordingly more difficult to maintain.

A solution is to assemble a disclosure committee, made up of representatives from every department whose employees are likely to create transactions requiring some form of disclosure. This group does not have to meet in person very frequently, but they should be encouraged to share information at regular intervals regarding their departments' activities. Further, every member of the group should be kept up to date by the accounting staff regarding changes in disclosure requirements, as well as the details of the disclosures currently being made. This approach not only improves the comprehensiveness of disclosures, but is also useful for correcting and updating existing disclosures.

Cost: 💵   Installation time: ⏰ ⏰

13–6   Automate Recurring Journal Entries

The average financial statement many require several dozen journal entries before it is completed. Some of these entries can be quite large, perhaps to redistribute payroll costs to a large number of departments or to allocate occupancy costs in a similar manner. If they are substantial, it is easy to incorrectly enter them occasionally, resulting in revenues and expenses being sent to the wrong accounts, making the financial statements very difficult to compare from month to month. If the journal entries have been highly inconsistent over time, it may even be necessary for the general ledger accountant to review all of them and create new journal entries to correct the original entries. All of this work takes time, of course—and time is in short supply during the financial statement closing process.

Many general ledger accounting software packages have a feature that allows one to avoid the continual reentry of journal entries every month by setting up recurring journal entries which the system will automatically generate every month, with no further manual interference. This type of entry is only for those situations where the exact amounts of the entries do not change from month to month (e.g., for the allocation of occupancy costs), so it will only apply to a portion of the total number of journal entries. Nonetheless, by setting up recurring entries in the computer, there are fewer journal entries to make.

The only problem with using recurring entries is that they will change at long intervals, necessitating a periodic update. To use the earlier example, occupancy costs may be reallocated based on changes in the square footage occupied by each department, so the closing schedule should include an annual review and updating of the amounts used in this entry. Another way to update recurring entries is to create a schedule of entry updates, so a controller knows the exact month or year in which a recurring entry is scheduled to change and can ignore it in the meantime. Either approach gives a sufficient amount of control over this type of journal entry, while still reducing the total amount of accounting time allocated to it.

Cost: **Installation time:** 🕪

13–7 Automate the Cutoff

The single most difficult issue at the time of each financial statement closing is the cutoff. This involves matching the invoices from suppliers with receipts to ensure that all expenses carry with them a corresponding benefit within the same period. The main problem in this area is the cost of goods sold, where large quantities of goods are received every day, usually comprising the bulk of all expenditures. If even a single high-value delivery is recorded in the wrong period, the cost of goods sold can be off significantly, either too high, because an expense is recorded without the corresponding receipt, or vice versa. To exacerbate the problem, the incorrect entry will reverse itself in the following accounting period, resulting in a continual fluctuation in the cost of goods sold, one period being too high and the next too low. This can be very embarrassing for a controller and is a grave matter for publicly held companies, which can be sued by shareholders for incorrectly reporting financial results. To avoid this problem, most controllers allocate an inordinate amount of staffpower to the comparison of accounts payable and inventory records.

To avoid the entire cutoff problem, it is absolutely mandatory that a company strictly adhere to a policy of turning away from the receiving dock any deliveries that do not have an accompanying purchase order number. By closely following this policy, it is possible to entirely automate the period-end cutoff. By immediately logging in all receipts against purchase orders in the computer system, it is possible to generate a computer report comparing all inventory receipts to the purchase orders entered into the computer system, as well as all received supplier invoices that match up against the purchase orders. This report yields a complete list of all receipts for which there are no supplier invoices, making it easier to accrue for all missing invoices. This carries with it the double benefits of not only avoiding the manual labor of determining a clean cutoff, but also eliminating the wait time that would otherwise be required before supplier invoices arrive.

Unfortunately, there are several problems with this excellent approach that limit a controller's ability to install it. First, it requires the cooperation of the computer services and warehousing departments—the first to program the changes needed to make it run in the computer system and the latter to agree to reject all items without purchase orders, as well as to enter all receipts in a computer at the receiving dock. Whenever additional departments are involved, the chances of completion drop, since there are more supervisors who can interfere with it. Also, due to the programming needs, this is an expensive implementation (unless there is already a packaged software solution on hand that contains the appropriate features). Further, the purchasing department must be persuaded to enter all purchase orders into the computer system in a timely manner. All of these issues, particularly the involvement of multiple departments, makes this a difficult and expensive best practice to implement, though it is also one of the most rewarding ones to have in place.

Cost: 💵💵💵   Installation time: ⏰⏰⏰

13–8 Avoid the Bank Reconciliation

The last item completed before issuing financial statements is usually the bank reconciliation. A company's bank takes a few days to compile bank statements for all of its customers following the end of the month, then a few more days pass while the statement travels through the mail. The typical company then receives it on about the fifth business day of the month, and someone in the accounting department must scramble to complete the bank reconciliation. Usually, there are bank fees noted on the statement that must be recorded on a company's books, as well as any unrecorded checks (always manual ones that were never entered into the computer system) to be recorded. Because of the delay built into receiving the statement and the time needed to complete the bank reconciliation, many companies cannot reduce the time needed to complete their financial statements to less than five or six days.

The solution is to not include the bank reconciliation in the month-end closing procedure. By doing so, there is no need to wait for the bank statement to arrive, nor is there any last-minute rush to complete the bank reconciliation.

However, there is a significant risk to consider, which is that there is an expense located on the bank statement that, if not recorded, will have a major impact on the level of reported profits in the financial statements. For example, a large manual check representing a major expense is listed on the bank statement as having been processed; this check will eliminate all monthly profits when recorded in the general ledger. This possibility is the main reason why many controllers insist on waiting for the bank reconciliation to be completed before they will consider issuing financial statements. Luckily, there are several steps one can take to reduce this risk. One is to accrue banking fees. These are usually about the same amount each month and so can be accrued and then reversed after the actual bank statement arrives. Second, one can call the bank and advance the date on which the bank statement is issued, say to the 25th day of the month, which allows the accounting staff to complete the bank reconciliation much sooner, though there is still a risk that the final few days of the month may contain an unrecorded expense that will not be found until the following month's bank statement. Also, the outside auditors will object to a bank statement that does not extend to the last day of the month, so the final statement of the year must be converted back to the traditional month-end variety. Third and best, the accounting staff can subscribe to its bank's on-line transaction review system (assuming it has one), which allows someone to review all checks received every day and to maintain a running bank reconciliation. By using this final approach, the bank reconciliation is always perfect and all expenses are spotted on the same day they are recorded by the bank. As a result, there is no need to worry about unexplained expenses appearing on the bank statement and the reconciliation can safely be shifted out of those few frenzied days when the financial statements are being produced. Though any of the three variations noted in this paragraph can be used, only the last one is a completely foolproof way to avoid missing something on a bank statement that should be recorded as a current expense.

Cost: Installation time: 🕰

13–9 Defer Routine Work

An accounting department is usually overwhelmed by its ongoing volume of work, without the extra crushing load of creating and distributing the periodic financial statements. Many of these tasks, such as payments to suppliers, invoicing to customers, daily or weekly reports to management, or the processing of cash, are vital ones, and cannot be delayed for long. As a result, the accounting staff is accustomed to working long overtime hours during the first week of each month, not to mention a blackout on vacation time during this period. Also, the following week is sometimes a frenzied one as well, since the accounting department must catch up on the necessary work it did not have a chance to complete in the previous week. In short, producing the financial statements is a hard lump for the accounting department to swallow.

The solution is to carefully review the tasks currently scheduled for completion during the first week of the month and see if there are ways to eliminate them or shift them into a later week. For example, management may be accustomed to receiving a daily report of sales and cash receipts; it may be possible to completely eliminate this report for a few days during the beginning of the month so that the workload is completely eliminated, rather than being shifted into the next week. Completely avoiding work is always the best option, but for some tasks, there is no alternative to shifting it forward a few days. Examples of this kind are paying suppliers or billing customers—this must be done, but a judicious delay of a few days will not do an excessive amount of harm to these basic processes. However, there may be a few cases, such as invoicing very large dollar amounts or paying suppliers in order to take a large early payment discount, where it pays to go ahead with the work in the current period, but only for key items; the remaining smaller items can still be deferred for a short time. This solution is an easy way to reduce the amount of overtime required to complete the financial statements.

Cost: Installation time:

13–10 Eliminate Multiple Approvals

A typical problem when financial statements are produced is to have employees wait for approvals before they are allowed to complete their tasks, or to pass along work to other employees, who cannot begin until the approvals are given. When there are many approvals to obtain, especially in areas where the approvals are holding up key work products, there can be a substantial impact on the speed of financial statement completion. Typical spots in the financial statement process that include approvals are journal entries, footnotes, the final version of the statements, and the final results from all of the major accounting modules: accounts payable, accounts receivable, payroll, and fixed assets. Given the number of approvals in some companies, it is a wonder that the financial statements are ever produced in less than a month.

There are several solutions that bypass the approvals problem. When reviewing them, one must consider the underlying reason for using approvals, which is to ensure that information is correctly processed. Without an approval, there must be a countervailing system in place to ensure that accurate information is still transmitted to the financial statements. Some solutions are as follows:

- *Designate a back-up approver.* If there is a continuing problem with finding the person who is allowed to issue approvals, then there should be a back-up approver available. This should still be a person who has a sufficient level of technical expertise, and so this solution is only a viable option for those companies with some extra employees on hand who are sufficiently qualified.
- *Increase training levels.* An excellent way to avoid approvals is to train the accounting staff in the closing procedures so that they all become experts in their jobs. After heavy and repeated training, it is quite common to find that

the staff is more technically proficient in their tasks than their bosses, with little need for any approval. Also, newcomers to the accounting department must receive similarly high levels of indoctrination.

- *Issue ranges within which approvals are not required.* The best way to handle the approval problem is not to require approvals at all. To do so, determine the comfort level of the controller in regard to how much an accountant is allowed to do without any supervisory review. For example, one can establish a limit of $2,500 for any journal entry, above which approvals are still required. This approach usually eliminates the bulk of the approvals, while still reserving the oversight privilege for those transactions large enough to truly warrant a review. This method usually requires a periodic review of all transactions to ensure that the preset ranges are being observed.

- *Reduce to one approver.* In cases where there is more than one approver, there is rarely a need for it. For example, if a journal entry for more than $5,000 must be approved by an assistant controller, but anything over $25,000 requires the approval of the controller, it is usually sufficient to give the assistant controller a much higher signoff authority, reserving only the most unusual situations for the involvement of the extra person. If a controller still insists on requiring a secondary review of all approvals, then either the controller is a certifiable micromanager (which may require counseling) or else the person issuing the first approval is not sufficiently qualified to give it (in which case he or she should have no approval authority at all).

- *Shift the approver to an available person.* A common occurrence is that a high-ranking person is the only one allowed to approve certain transactions. If that person frequently travels or is in meetings, then a process cannot be completed until the person becomes available to give an approval. Consequently, the best approach is to reassign the approval to a different person who is always on-site, usually an assistant controller or accounting manager.

All of these approaches are targeted at reducing the processing time required to track down a designated approver. Given a company's individual circumstances, especially involving the risks of not approving a processing step, the ultimate solution to this problem will be a mix of these options. The key issue to remember is that some situations do indeed require some kind of supervisory control, so there is always some approval requirement for at least a few key deliverables.

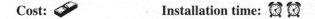

Cost: 💵   **Installation time:** ⏰ ⏰

13–11 Eliminate Small Accruals

In some companies, there is a focus on achieving perfectly accurate financial statements, no matter how many extra accruals are needed. Though there is a certain degree of professional satisfaction in issuing a set of absolutely accurate financial statements, this can use up a considerable amount of accounting resources, which could be better used elsewhere. For example, it may require 20 extra accruals, along with the attendant analysis, review, and approval effort, to yield financial statements that now have a profit altered by one or two percentage points. Realistically, such a slight change in the financial results will not have a noticeable impact on the decision making of the managers, stock analysts, or creditors who review the financial statements. So, despite an inordinate amount of extra effort, no one really cares about the slightly more accurate results.

The answer is to review all existing accruals and throw out all of the ones resulting in only very small accrual amounts. By doing so, less time is needed to produce the financial statements, opening up resources for other uses. However, when conducting the accrual review, it is important to check on a number of past journal entries to ensure that each accrual is always a small one—if there is even a slight chance of an accrual occasionally being a large one, it is best to keep it in place on the grounds that financial statement accuracy could be severely impacted by its absence at some point in the future. Thus, as long as an appropriate degree of caution is used when eliminating accruals from the financial statement closing procedure, it is reasonable to permanently eliminate the use of small accruals.

Cost: 💵   Installation time: 🕑

13–12 Reduce Investigation Levels

Before issuing the financial statements, they are subject to an intensive review by the controller, who compares each line item to the budgeted level and thoroughly investigates each item that varies significantly from the budget. This is an admirable and necessary practice, since it catches errors and also prepares the controller for any questions from the management team regarding those same variances. However, the practice can be taken too far. For example, it is almost impossible for any revenue or expense line item to match exactly the budgeted amount (unless it is related to a long-term contract that ensures totally predictable amounts), so a controller who investigates virtually all variances will be doomed to review every line item in the general ledger. This is an enormous task and also an unnecessary one, for the vast majority of variances are so small that there is no point in reviewing them—even if there is an error somewhere, the total impact is so insignificant that there will be no noticeable impact on corporate profitability.

A very simple best practice that eliminates most of this review work is to reduce investigation levels to the point where only the largest variances are checked for accuracy. This can take several forms. For example, a minimum dollar amount, such as $10,000, can be set for the amount of a variance that a controller will bother to investigate. Alternatively, it can be on a percentage basis, such as anything over a 30 percent variance. Also, there may be some accounts, such as payroll, that are better reviewed by checking headcount figures each month, thereby entirely eliminating them from the variance analysis. The best approach is usually a combination of all three techniques, which means that anything over a specific dollar variance is always reviewed, plus any large percentage variances that may fall under the preset dollar level, with the exception of certain accounts reviewed in other ways. This system can then be modified over time to allow for changes in the controller's comfort level with variance investigation, as well as to cover new accounts that may be added. By creating such a system of variance review levels, it is possible to greatly reduce the amount of review work that must be completed prior to issuing financial statements.

Cost: 💸   Installation time: ⏰

13–13 Assign Closing Responsibilities   ✔ *Author's Choice*

The typical financial statement preparation process can be a jumbled affair. It is not clear who is completing which task or when anything needs to be completed. This leads to disarray in the accounting department whenever the financial statements are to be produced.

The solution is to produce a document that clearly states exactly who is responsible for each task required to produce financial statements. As noted in Exhibit 13.2, it states the job position that must complete each task. In order to

Exhibit 13.2 Statement of Responsibilities for the Production of Financials

Task	Controller	Assistant Controller	General Ledger Accountant
Calculate depreciation		✓	
Calculate interest accrual		✓	
Compare to A/P detail			✓
Compare to A/R detail			✓
Compare to F/A detail			✓
Do recurring journal entries			✓
Prepare bank reconciliation		✓	
Prepare footnotes	✓		
Review cutoff		✓	

fully utilize this document, it is necessary to have a staff meeting prior to each closing period so the controller can go over the closing responsibilities. This reinforces the need for each person to complete each task exactly on time, so the accounting team can reliably issue financial statements every period. When combined with a detailed closing schedule, as described later in this chapter under the "Create a Closing Schedule" section, a controller has a complete set of documentation on hand for producing the financial statements.

Cost: 💵   **Installation time:** ⏰

13–14 Compress Billing Activities

When trying to achieve a fast close, many organizations find that the most intractable problem is how to get billings done sooner. Most other closing tasks can be shortened to a few minutes, but the problem with invoicing is that so much is shipped (or services billed) at month-end that the process becomes clogged and delays the closing. Here are five alternatives for improving the speed of the month-end invoicing process:

1. *Double up on invoicing labor.* Have twice as many people work on the month-end invoices. If this requires the use of less-trained staff, then have them do the easy invoices and reserve the complex invoices for the regular staff. This can be a problem if the accounting software has licenses for only a smaller number of concurrent users.
2. *See attached.* If fully extended billing information comes from a separate system and must be retyped into the billing software, then just put "see attached" on the invoice, along with the grand total, and then staple the detail to the invoice.
3. *Roll-forward error corrections.* If the underlying detail used to create an invoice contains an error, then try to roll it forward into the next month's invoice, or just issue a separate invoice in a few days, after the close is completed. The attitude should be that the first draft of an invoice will also be the last draft of that invoice.
4. *Cut and paste.* If the billing information from another system can be dumped into an Excel or flat file, then cut and paste it directly into the billing software to save typing time.
5. *Create custom reports.* Picky customers may want invoices in a certain format, which takes time to manually input. If these customers are likely to be long term, then invest in the report writing time to create special billing layouts just for them.

Of the five options shown above, the first three can be readily implemented, while the final two tend to be useful only in more limited circumstances.

Cost: 🪙   **Installation time:** 🕰 🕰

13–15 Conduct Transaction Training

Once the preliminary financial statements have been completed, the controller must carefully review all expense, revenue, and balance sheet items to see if there are unusual variances, investigate all of them, and make corrections that result in an accurate financial statement. Depending on the number of errors and the time it takes to research them, this error-checking phase can seriously extend the time required before financial statements are produced.

One way to reduce the number of these errors is to conduct detailed transaction training for all employees who have a role in entering transactions into the computer system (typically a sizeable group). The reason is that the controller's final review of the financial statements is only a method for removing errors after they have already been made; by eliminating these errors before they happen through proper training, the number of errors that the controller must later research will drop dramatically.

The training must be very specifically targeted at eliminating recurring errors. This is done through a feedback loop. All errors discovered in the financial statements should be noted in a log, along with the name and position of the person most likely to have caused the error. This information is reviewed each month, and a short training program is created, targeted both at the specific person who made the mistake and the type of error that occurred; if the error appears to be a common one for many employees to make, the training can be given to everyone who enters the same transaction. Also, the training programs may be used to update the initial training that all employees receive in transaction processing, thereby avoiding errors in the initial training program. Mandatory reinforcement training is also useful, both as a reminder for experienced staff and as a part of the core training for new recruits, thereby keeping the focus on error reduction over the long term.

The main problem with this approach is the cost of training. If there are many people entering transactions, the training required to cover all of them can be considerable. In these cases, it may be necessary to scale back to a small number of seminars per year, or else to issue bulletins describing problems, or to use on-line training through the computer system. All of these approaches are less expensive than comprehensive and frequent training, but are also less effective. At worst, there should be a follow-up program with the specific individuals who make errors, so the worst offenders can be targeted for immediate improvement. Also, some of the people who need training may work for other departments, so the controller may have to exercise some tact in asking other department heads for permission to repeatedly train their employees. However, these issues are minor ones, given the benefits of reduced transaction error rates.

Cost:    **Installation time:** 🕐 🕐

13–16 Continually Review Wait Times

A lengthy financial statement completion process has a number of spots built into it where there are long wait times. For example, the typical company waits five days before it receives a bank statement from the bank for each of its accounts necessary to complete a bank statement. Also, there is usually a wait of a few days while supplier invoices arrive, just to make sure that all expenses have been properly recorded. It is pauses like these that make it nearly impossible to issue financial statements in a rapid manner, no matter how quickly all other tasks are completed. For example, it may be possible to blaze through a bank reconciliation in an hour, but if one is still waiting five days to receive the bank statement, one is focusing on the speed of the wrong activity.

The solution is a continual review of wait times. This focuses attention on those activities a controller should really be attempting to reduce in size or eliminate. To review wait times, the best tool is a Gantt chart. This shows the typical start and stop dates for each closing activity. By closely examining the start dates for each activity and questioning why those dates cannot be accelerated, it brings attention to bear on any activities that are dependent on the prior completion of other activities. However, this is only a tool for pointing out where there are problems; it does not actually resolve them. To use the example from earlier in this section, a Gantt chart will only tell a controller that there is a substantial wait involved before all supplier invoices are received—the controller must still *do* something about it (that particular item is addressed in the "Automate the Cutoff" section earlier in this chapter).

There are no problems with using this best practice, for it is easily implemented, requiring only a brief review by the controller after each financial statement closing to determine if there have been any wait-time changes. It also needs no programming and does not involve other departments. In short, it is a simple best practice to install and provides valuable information for the targeting of further improvements.

Cost: 💵   **Installation time:** 🕐

13–17 Convert Serial Activities to Parallel Ones

A common problem, especially in smaller accounting departments, is that a considerable amount of wait time is built into the process because there are too many activities being conducted in a serial manner—that is, one process does not start until another is finished. A good example is in a small organization where just one person is in charge of completing several processing steps and does not have time to advance to additional tasks until the first one is complete. The same problem occurs in large organizations but usually not due to a lack of staffpower. Instead, the information that flows into one process must be supplied by another task, so the preceding step must be completely finished before the next one can be started. These issues create a great deal of difficulty in reducing the time needed to complete financial statements.

The solution is to convert serial activities into parallel ones. A parallel activity is one which can be completed without any need for data from a preceding process. An example of several parallel closing activities is shown in Exhibit 13.3, which depicts the accounts receivable, accounts payable, fixed assets,

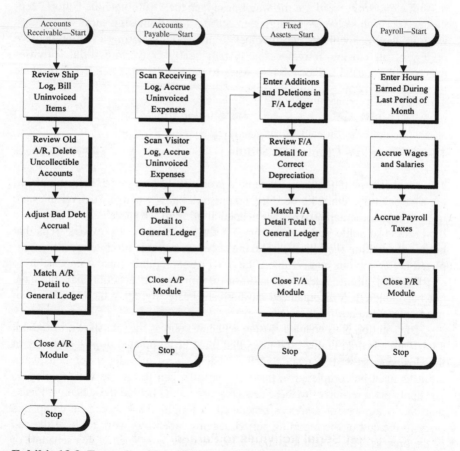

Exhibit 13.3 Example of Parallel Closing Activities

Reprinted with permission from Steven Bragg, *Just-in-Time Accounting* (New York: John Wiley & Sons, Inc., 1996), p. 334.

and payroll processes. Only in one case, where the final detail of the accounts payable process is needed as the starting point for the fixed assets process, is there any linkage between the separate processes. The trick to making this best practice work is to separate the individual processes that make up a financial statement closing so that they can be independently processed. An example of this is using a preliminary set of financial statements as the input into an allocation base from which occupancy costs are allocated to various departments. By using older information in the allocation base (see the "Complete Allocation Bases in Advance" section later in this chapter), there is no longer a linkage between the two processes, so they can now be processed as parallel activities. Similarly, the accounts payable function is not normally closed until several days have passed, while the company waits for a few supplier invoices to arrive. This serial processing issue is readily avoided by using computer systems and real-time entry of receipts at the warehouse (see the "Automate the Cutoff" section earlier in this chapter) to create an accrual for all missing supplier invoices without waiting for the actual invoices to arrive. Conducting a comprehensive review of all closing activities and systematically converting serial activities into parallel ones is one of the best ways to reduce the time needed to produce financial statements.

Cost: Installation time: 🕑 🕑

13–18 Create a Closing Schedule   ✔ *Author's Choice*

The worst enemy of a financial statement process is a disorganized closing. Without a sufficiently detailed procedure, no one will know when any deliverables are needed or if some deliverables are needed at all. Further, there is no sequence to the process so some steps are waiting for the completion of previous steps that no one is working on. For example, the accounts payable module must be completed before anyone can complete the fixed assets module since it is possible to overlook last-minute fixed asset additions if some of the accounts payable have not been entered. A disorganized closing can drastically delay the completion of financial statements.

The solution is to create a closing schedule such as the one shown in Exhibit 13.4. This schedule itemizes all tasks that must be completed during each day of the closing process. By creating such a schedule, it is immediately obvious when all tasks must be completed so that the controller can follow up with employees and apply extra resources to those tasks that are falling behind the schedule. Please note that a number of activities scheduled in Exhibit 13.4 should be completed *prior* to the end of the reporting period, leaving much less work to do at the end of the process. This schedule is most effective when combined with a schedule of responsibilities, such as the one noted earlier in Exhibit 13.2. The two schedules can even be combined so that the name or title of the responsible person is listed at the beginning of each activity in the closing schedule.

Exhibit 13.4 Sample Closing Schedule

- *Four days prior to period-end*
    1. Revise the closing schedule and distribute to staff.
    2. Verify that recurring journal entries are still correct for the current reporting period.
    3. Review financial statements with the most recent information and investigate any unusual variances.

- *Two days prior to period-end*
    1. Review the contract schedule and verify that all contractual agreements have been either paid out to suppliers or billed to customers.
    2. Complete all allocation bases.
    3. Review financial statements with the most recent information and investigate any unusual variances.

- *One day prior to period-end*
    1. Conduct an audit of the inventory to determine the accuracy level.
    2. Complete footnotes.
    3. Review financial statements with the most recent information and investigate any unusual variances.
    4. Go online with the bank and complete a preliminary bank reconciliation.

- *Day of period-end*
    1. Process the period-end closing program in the computer.
    2. Print all period-end reports.

- *First day after period-end*
    1. Compare all period-end reports to general ledger balances and reconcile differences.
    2. Accrue for unpaid payroll.
    3. Close the accounts receivable module.

- *Second day after period-end*
    1. Review cutoff information and accrue for any missing supplier invoices.
    2. Close the accounts payable module.
    3. Update the fixed assets schedule and calculate depreciation.
    4. Complete all remaining accruals.

- *Third day after period-end*
    1. Update detailed schedules for all balance sheet accounts.
    2. Complete all operating data for inclusion in the financial statements.
    3. Complete a preliminary set of financial statements.

Exhibit 13.4 *(Continued)*

- *Fourth day after period-end*
    1. Finalize the financial statements and issue.
    2. Calculate the borrowing base certificate and send it to the bank, along with a set of financial statements.

The only issue with creating a closing schedule is that it is a constantly changing document requiring regular updating and communication to the accounting staff. The reason for the regular updates is that the schedule will initially allow for a substantial number of days before statements are completed, but management will gradually shrink the number of days, requiring a constant reshuffling of tasks and responsibilities. The accounting staff will only follow changes to the schedule if the alterations are clearly communicated to them. In particular, the controller must listen to their objections regarding a reduction in the time to complete tasks so their requirements can be incorporated into the schedule. As long as these factors are considered, the closing schedule becomes the foundation document driving the timely completion of the financial statements.

Cost: **Installation time:**

13–19 Document the Process

Some organizations have created closing procedures and established responsibilities for those accounting people who are involved with the production of financial statements, which helps them to some degree in organizing the flow of work. However, they meet with great resistance when they take the next step and mandate reductions in the time needed to complete the statements. Employees grouse that there is not enough time to complete their work, that upstream work is not completed on time (which does not allow them to start *their* tasks on time), and that management does not know all the details required to complete their tasks. As a result, though the process appears to be more organized, there is no way to reduce the time and resources allocated to it.

The underlying reason why this problem arises is that the employees are right—the managers who are demanding shorter completion dates do not really know the process and cannot understand the plethora of additional necessary changes before the process will become truly streamlined. The only way to avoid this quagmire is to document the process thoroughly. This means that a team must interview all employees who are involved in the reporting process, write down detailed descriptions of what they do, and flowchart all activities. Only after these steps are completed can one see the bottlenecks in the process that must be eliminated. For example, an employee may be using a painfully slow allocation method for spreading occupancy costs, which can be easily altered by switching to a simpler method—but a controller will never know this without a complete documentation of exactly how the current allocation calculation is made. The documentation process can be a slow one, especially for a multidivision company including many employees and locations in the process. Nonetheless, it is the only way to gain a better understanding of the process, which leads to better decisions regarding how other best practices can be inserted to ensure better results.

It is possible to short-circuit some of the documentation process. One approach is to determine which people in the process are causing the obvious bottlenecks, since the work piles up at their desks. Their work should be documented and acted on first, while the efforts of others, whose work products are clearly coming in on time, can wait until any changes alter the process enough to make *them* the cause of the new bottlenecks. By using this variation on the documentation process, it is possible to more rapidly institute changes to the overall process.

Cost: 💵   **Installation time:** ⏰

13–20 Restrict the Use of Journal Entries

Journal entries can be the bane of the general ledger accountant who is desperately trying to issue accurate financial statements. The reason is that in the midst of cleaning up the general ledger in preparation for the issuance of financial statements, this person will sometimes find that a journal entry has miraculously appeared in the ledger, requiring a hurried investigation to determine who entered it, why it was made, and whether it was already duplicated by the general ledger accountant. After this added work, there is always the chance that even more entries will be made prior to the closing of the books for the reporting period. A particularly irritating problem is when a journal entry is made between the time when the financial statements are issued and the accounting period is closed in the computer system, since the change appears in the beginning balance for the next month, but does not show up in the financial statements! These problems are caused by allowing multiple people to create journal entries.

A much simpler approach is to restrict the task of making journal entries to a single person, the general ledger accountant. Even the controller should not be allowed to create journal entries. By using this approach, there is a single easily controlled point of entry into the general ledger, ensuring that the information entering the ledger has been verified in advance. The inevitable result will be fewer problems with the production of financial statements.

There are a few problems with this approach. Some accounting personnel will probably complain that they are entitled to make journal entries, while there may also be a problem if the general ledger accountant is not available at month-end to make entries; if so, there should be a back-up person on hand authorized to handle journal entries. Another issue for larger corporations is what to do if there are a number of general ledger accountants, all of whom must make entries at the same time, due to the volume of entries required. In this case, it is necessary to maintain a log, either manually or in the computer, in which every accountant must record all entries. By referring to other entries already in the log, any of the general ledger accountants can easily see what entries have already been made and can thereby avoid any duplicate entries. An alternatve approach is to assign responsibility for specific journal entries to certain general ledger accountants.

Cost: Installation time: 🕰

13–21 Train the Staff in Closing Procedures

One of the biggest problems with a new accounting staff, or one in which the responsibilities for producing financial statements have changed recently, is that they do not know what they are supposed to do. This results in a general level of confusion regarding responsibilities, as well as the slow completion of deliverables and their probable inaccuracy even when they *are* done. This is a nightmare situation for a controller, who must review everyone's work in great detail and check on everyone's progress to ensure that they will complete their assigned tasks on time. This scenario is almost guaranteed to result in the late production of financial statements, and probably ones with errors, as well.

A key factor that will reduce the level of confusion is proper training of the accounting staff. By doing so, error rates will decline, while the time needed to complete assigned tasks will drop dramatically. To achieve this end result, one must first have an adequate set of procedures from which to conduct training (see the "Document the Process" section earlier in this chapter). Once these procedures are written, use them to conduct personalized training of every person who is involved in the creation of financial statements. It is important to conduct training prior to the end of the reporting period so that the training can be done in a leisurely manner, giving everyone time to ruminate over the information and to have their questions answered thoroughly. If the training is conducted in the midst of the closing process, there will not be enough time for an adequate level of training. Also, once the initial training is complete, the controller must still monitor the progress of all the people on the accounting team and provide follow-up training as needed to ensure that they have fully absorbed what they have been taught and that any errors are corrected. Finally, the procedures used as a training tool must be given to the accounting staff for referral purposes, as well as being updated at once to reflect any ongoing changes to the closing procedure. Training is an extremely cost-effective method for ensuring that the accounting staff completes the financial statements in an efficient and effective manner.

Cost: 💵 💵   Installation time: 🕰 🕰

13–22 Use Cycle Counting to Avoid
Month-End Counts   ✔ *Author's Choice*

A common effort for companies with poor inventory recordkeeping systems is to count the inventory at the end of every reporting period. By doing so, the controller is assured of a reasonably accurate cost of goods sold figure, though at the cost of shutting down the business while the counting process goes on (since this may interfere with accurate inventory counts), which not only runs the risk of losing some business, but also requires paying some employees to conduct the decidedly *not* value-added inventory counting activity. Over the course of a year, this represents either a major loss of revenue, addition to expenses, or both.

The solution is to stop taking periodic inventory counts. By doing so, there is no stoppage of sales activities, nor is there any need to redirect activities to counting inventory. In addition, the accounting staff no longer has to spend valuable time during the end of the month to participate in the inventory count, which gives them more time to complete the financial statements more quickly. Unfortunately, this happy state of affairs brings with it some risks. The main one is that inventory may become quite inaccurate over time, resulting in cost-of-goods-sold numbers in the financial statements that will, over time, depart quite a long way from the actual situation. If this number is inaccurate, the borrowing base information a company presents to the bank will also probably be wrong, which may give the bank grounds for withholding additional borrowings. A final problem is that if the financial statements are incorrect, the controller may pay for this oversight by losing his or her job.

The best way to avoid all of these issues is to use cycle counting. This process involves a continual count of the entire inventory so that all items, especially the high-value or high-usage ones, have their quantities verified frequently. In addition, a trained cycle-counter is much more likely to obtain accurate inventory figures than the less knowledgeable group of counters typically employed for period-end counts. A good cycle-counter is trained to investigate *why* there are counting variances, resulting in changes to the underlying systems that originally caused the errors. By using this approach, it is very unlikely that the inventory will be very far off at any time, which gives a controller much greater confidence that the inventory figures at the end of the month are accurate, without the need for a periodic physical inventory count.

Cost: 💵💵   Installation time: ⏰⏰⏰

13–23 Use Internal Audits to Locate Transaction
Problems in Advance

The general ledger is, in a manner of speaking, the cesspool into which all corporate information flows—that is to say, all transaction errors will wend their way into this final repository of corporate information. Unfortunately, this is the only source of information from which the financial statements are created. Accordingly, poorly completed transactions upstream from the general ledger will eventually appear in the financial statements. This causes a great deal of extra work for the accounting staff, who must frantically research all of the problems that were caused upstream from the financial statements and issue journal entries to correct them—all in the few days during which the statements must be completed and issued. This problem occurs month after month unless something is done to find out where these problems are occurring and why.

The internal auditing staff can be brought in to discover where problems are occurring, why they are happening, who is causing the problems, and what can be done to fix them. By using the internal auditing staff, the controller can determine the exact nature of all the problems plaguing the financial statements. Though this best practice does not solve the problems, it at least identifies them, making it much easier for a controller to determine an appropriate response to each one. The long-term result of this approach is a gradual reduction in the number of errors in the financial statements, resulting in much less analysis time by the accounting staff to correct the preliminary version of the financial statements.

The main problem with this approach is caused by the internal audit department and its controlling audit committee. The department recommends to the audit committee (which is usually composed of members of the board of directors) a set of investigative projects for the upcoming year, which the committee typically approves without much discussion. The department creates this list based on the perceived payback from each potential audit, or because they are in potentially high-risk areas. If the controller cannot get the transaction review audit onto this annual project list (and repeatedly so, since this audit must be repeated time and again), there is no way that the best practice can ever be completed. It may take a considerable amount of influence with the internal audit manager or the audit committee to make sure that these audits are regularly conducted.

Cost: 💵💵   **Installation time:** ⏰⏰

13–24 Compress Public Company Closing Activities   ✔*Author's Choice*

A publicly held company must take one additional step in the issuance of its financial statements, which is to file those statements with the Securities and Exchange Commission (SEC). Unfortunately, the filing process requires the involvement of several outside parties, which makes it impossible to close the books in a single day. In fact, closing in a *month* can be considered a respectable accomplishment. Here are some ways to reduce the duration of the public company close:

- *Quarterly auditor review or audit.* The company's external auditors must conduct a review of the 10Q reports, plus a full audit of the 10K report. To reduce the time needed for this activity, insist on the retention of experienced audit staff on the company's audit or review, give the auditors maximum support by in-house staff, encourage the auditors to conduct preliminary testing well in advance of the audit, increase the strength of controls in order to avoid audit exceptions, and prepare detailed support for all disclosures included in the 10Q and 10K reports.

- *Quarterly legal review.* A company's legal counsel must review the 10Q and 10K reports to ensure that all legally mandated disclosures and supporting schedules have been included. This review also searches for incorrect or unsupportable statements made in the disclosures. Fortunately, the attorneys are looking for different issues than those being reviewed by the auditors, so it is quite possible to issue a review copy of the 10Q or 10K report to the attorneys before the auditors have completed their work. Any changes made by the attorneys can then be incorporated into the latest draft of the 10Q or 10K that the auditors are reviewing.

- *Officer certification.* Section 906 of the Sarbanes-Oxley Act stipulates that the CEO and CFO of a publicly held company must issue a written statement with every financial statement issued, certifying that the information contained within it fairly presents its financial condition and results of operations. If these officers issue such statements knowing that the financial statements do not present such information, then they can be fined up to $5 million and/or be imprisoned up to 20 years. Given the penalties involved, they obviously want some time to review the financials. This is not a significant problem because both officers can review the financial statements while the auditors are conducting their work. This gives them at least a week in which to read and comment on the financial statements before there is any possibility of filing the statements.

- *Audit committee approval.* The company's audit committee must also give its formal approval of the 10Q and 10K filings. The audit committee approval meeting is set several days in advance, to coordinate the schedules of the committee members. The group then discusses the report during a conference call, the controller notes all recommendations made during the meeting, and the accounting staff then creates an updated version of the report following the call. There are a few ways to achieve minor time reductions. One possibility is to issue a disclosure memo to the committee members well before they see the financial statements. A disclosure memo itemizes the accounting issues that the company is addressing in the current financial statements. If the committee members are aware of these issues in advance, they will be less likely to address them again during the committee meeting. Another possibility is to issue the financial statements to the committee members before the supporting footnotes and disclosures are released. The financial statements are usually complete several days earlier, so the committee can see them as soon as possible. Again, this leaves less material for discussion during the formal audit committee meeting.

- *EDGARizing.* The SEC accepts 10Q and 10K filings through its Electronic Data Gathering, Analysis, and Retrieval (EDGAR) system. Companies filing their reports with the SEC almost always forward them to a firm specializing in the conversion of their reports into HTML or XML (known as EDGARizing). The specialist converts the statements to the required format and then files them with the SEC on behalf of the company. Quarterly and annual filings usually arrive at an EDGARizing firm from multiple companies at about the same time, which can create a considerable backlog, and lengthens the time required to file. The best way around this problem is to file well before the SEC-mandated due dates, so that there are fewer competing filings. Another option is to retain the services of a smaller local EDGARizing firm, which will be more likely to put greater emphasis on completing a company's filings in a timely manner.

Cost: Installation time: 🕰 🕰

13–25 Use Standard Journal Entry Forms   ✔*Author's Choice*

The production of a typical set of financial statements requires the entry of a large number of journal entries. These must be made for a variety of reasons that even the best-run accounting department cannot avoid, such as cost allocations, accrued expenses for which a supplier invoice has not yet arrived, or the shifting of an expense to a different account than the one into which it was initially recorded. Recording each one of these entries can take a considerable amount of time, for a great deal of thought must go into which accounts are used, their account numbers, the amounts of money to be recorded in each account, and whether there will be a debit or credit entry. Consequently, the use of journal entries can take up a significant amount of the total time required to produce financial statements.

One way to reduce the time devoted to journal entries is to create a standard set of journal entry forms. These are used for the recording of standard journal entries where the amount of money to be recorded will vary, but the account numbers will stay the same most of the time. An example of such an entry is noted in Exhibit 13.5. This type of entry is a common one and probably applies to a majority of the journal entries every month. This type of journal entry standardization can be taken a step further by creating recurring journal entries, which are used for any entries having the exact same amount of money in the entry every time. For more information on this approach, see the "Automate Recurring Journal Entries" section earlier in this chapter.

Cost: Installation time: 🕰

Exhibit 13.5 Sample Journal Entry Form for the Allocation of Occupancy Costs

Account Description	Debit	Credit
Rent Expense		XXX
Utility Expense		XXX
Building Maintenance Expense		XXX
Accounting Department Occupancy Expense	XXX	
Engineering Department Occupancy Expense	XXX	
Logistics Department Occupancy Expense	XXX	
Marketing Department Occupancy Expense	XXX	
Production Department Occupancy Expense	XXX	
Sales Department Occupancy Expense	XXX	

13–26 Complete Allocation Bases in Advance

A number of expenses must be allocated among departments. These can include occupancy, telephone, insurance, and other costs. There is an allocation base for each allocation. For example, occupancy may be based on the square footage occupied by each department, while telephone costs are allocated based on the number of employees in a department. For each allocation base, someone in the accounting department must update all of the information based on the latest financial results, prior to creating a journal entry to allocate the costs to various departments. Because an allocation base usually includes the latest financial information before a final cost allocation is made, it tends to be one of the last action items the accounting department completes before it issues the financial statements. Because it falls so late in the process, it can have a direct impact on the total time required to issue financial statements.

The solution is a straightforward one—use information from the previous month as an allocation base. By doing so, there is no allocation base to update in the midst of the frantic release of financial statements. Instead, the update can be completed at everyone's leisure, since it does not have to be ready until the next month's financial statements are put together. In case there are any concerns regarding the relationship between the previous month's allocation base and the current month's expenses to be distributed, one can always release a study that shows the (almost invariably) minor changes in the allocation base from month to month. An alternative approach that may quash any fears of this sort is to use a three-month averaging allocation so that any unusual variations in the monthly allocation base can be spread out. The only remaining problem is the outside auditors, who may insist on an allocation base that uses information from the end of the year; if so, the allocation base can be updated for the final month of the fiscal year, but the system can revert to a previous-month system for all other months of the year. This is an easy way to shift some of the workload away from the busy days immediately following the end of an accounting period.

Cost: 💵   **Installation time:** ⏰

13–27 Conduct Daily Review of the Financial Statements

Sometimes the initial review of the period-end financial statements comes as quite a shock—the revenues or expenses may be wildly off from expectations. This results in a great deal of frantic research while the controller investigates possible causes, rapidly makes changes, and issues bland statements to the rest of the management team that the financial statements might be issued a bit late this month. If the financials are indeed substantially different from what management has been led to expect, the blame may even be pinned on the controller, who may lose his or her job as a result.

The best way to avoid this problem is to conduct a daily or weekly review of the financial statements. Yes, this means *prior* to the end of the month. By doing so, a controller can review revenues as soon as they are billed, and expenses as soon as they are incurred so that any obvious discrepancies can be resolved right away. In addition, if there is a real problem with the financial results, the controller will know about it immediately, rather than being taken by surprise at month-end, which carries the additional benefit of being able to warn the management team immediately, setting their expectations for the period-end financial results. Also, by finding and correcting problems well in advance, there are hardly any issues left to deal with by the end of the month, so the financial statements can be issued much more quickly. Thus, an ongoing review enhances the controller's knowledge of how the financial statements are likely to appear and gives advance warning of problems.

Many controllers would say that a daily review of the financial statements is an excessive use of their time, since a review on each business day of the month piles up into a formidable block of time. This is true, so the time must be used wisely. For example, if there are repeated accounting problems with just the revenue-recording part of the financial statements, it may be sufficient to review only the sales each day. Similarly, if transactions are only posted into the general ledger once a week, then the financial statements will only be updated once a week, reducing the number of times when it is necessary to review the statements. Also, if there are many minor problems throughout the financial statements, the daily review chore can be assigned to a financial analyst, with instructions to only notify the controller of major issues. By selecting a review interval that meets the needs of the specific situation, a controller can reduce the amount of labor assigned to this task.

Cost: 💵   **Installation time:** 🕰️

Total Impact of Best Practices on the Financial Statements Function

This section gives an overview of how and when the best practices described in this chapter should be implemented, and the total impact of these changes on the financial statement reporting function.

The "how" of implementing best practices in this area is answered by: "Do them in big blocks." The reason is that, in general, these best practices are very easy to implement and can be installed in clusters. Given their minimal impact on department operations, they rarely have much of an impact on employee morale, so there is no restriction on multiple implementation projects at the same time. A key issue is that a number of these implementations do not have a clear beginning and end. For example, training the staff in closing procedures, or reviewing wait times, will always require continuing review, because the state of the art will continually change, making it necessary to go back to these items constantly. Thus, the best approach is multiple best practice implementations, which are constantly reviewed.

The other key issue is implementation timing. For most of these best practices, it is best to conduct an implementation outside of the period when financial statements are prepared. This point is best illustrated by perusing Exhibit 13.6. This exhibit clusters all of the best practices into the time before the end of the reporting period, in the midst of it, or after it. The vast majority of the practices fall into the first category. This means that most financial statement best practices can be completed at leisure, when there is no rush to produce financial information. The main benefits of this timing issue are that implementations can be completed more smoothly; there is time to correct mistakes; and if there is an implementation problem, it can be deferred in favor of the procedure it is replacing. Therefore, timing of the changes tends to be a minor issue.

The overall impact of best practices on the financial statements function falls into two areas. One is that financial statements can be completed much more quickly, efficiently, and with fewer errors, all of which are greatly appreciated by upper management. The standard for world-class companies with multiple subsidiaries is to issue financial statements in four working days, while single-location companies have been known to issue them in as little as one day. These benchmarks are quite attainable if all of the best practices noted in this chapter are not only installed, but also constantly reviewed to ensure that they are being

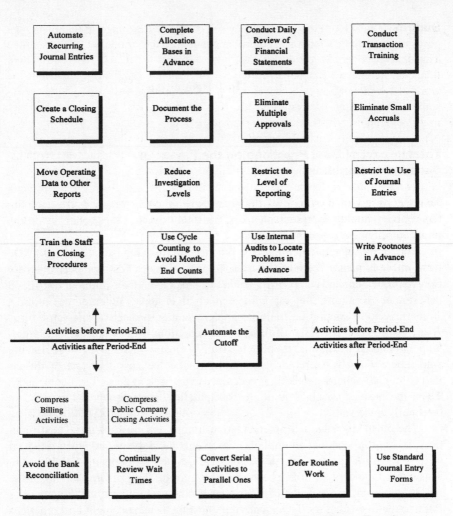

Exhibit 13.6 Impact of Best Practices on the Financial Statements Function

used in the most efficient manner. The other impact of best practices is that the workload for producing financial statements partially shifts into the week *prior to* the end of the reporting period from the week *following* it. The evidence of this shift is amply illustrated in Exhibit 13.6, where there are 16 listed activities that can be completed prior to the end of the reporting period. All accounting managers should integrate this shift in workloads into the schedules of their staffs, ensuring that there are no excessively high or low work periods resulting from the change in systems.

Summary

This chapter covered a variety of techniques for improving the speed with which financial statements can be distributed. These methods vary from shifting the work of the closing process to before the end of a reporting period to avoiding some of the closing work entirely. Most of the suggestions noted here will work in all companies, irrespective of the closing systems they already have in place. A few items require a careful appraisal of the current situation, however, such as avoiding the completion of the bank reconciliation and using an automated cutoff system—these require either special training or new computer systems and must be used with an eye to the risk of system or training failures and their impact on the accuracy of the financial statements. No matter which best practices are chosen from the list in this chapter, one overriding issue remains constant—this is a carefully choreographed dance of many people working together, requiring a good manager to control. For more information about financial statements best practices please refer to the author's *Fast Close*, 2nd ed. (John Wiley & Sons, 2009).

Chapter 14

General Best Practices

There are a number of best practices that do not fall into any of the categories listed in the other chapters of this book. They can be clustered into three primary areas: activities related to processes, personnel, and reporting, as shown later in Exhibit 14.9. These are all key areas that deserve special management attention to ensure that they operate properly. Examples of best practices related to processes include process centering and consolidating accounting functions, while examples of best practices for personnel include policies and procedures manuals and training programs. Finally, examples of best practices related to reporting include the use of on-line and balanced scorecard reporting. A review of this array of best practices allows one to enhance a number of key activities.

Implementation Issues for General Best Practices

This section covers the general level of implementation difficulty that will arise when installing the best practices discussed later in this chapter. This information is primarily contained in Exhibit 14.1, which shows the cost and duration of implementing each best practice.

The best practices noted in this chapter tend to require larger levels of management time than those noted in other chapters, as well as a longer project duration and higher cost. Examples of this are the consolidation of accounting functions and switching to on-line reporting, which require a great deal of planning and programming work, as well as (in the first case) the geographical transfer of employees.

Even if these difficult best practices are excluded, the remainder will at least require some advance planning, along with a week or more of work before they are fully operational. The biggest problem with most is that they are *systems*— they require their own procedures, training, and measurements to ensure that they work properly. Examples of systems best practices are the continual review of process cycles, training, and process centering. Due to the extra work required to create and maintain an entire system, one must be aware of the time and effort needed before some payback will be realized.

Finally, a few best practices are simple to initiate and complete, require minimal management attention, and need only a modest amount of follow-up work from time to time. These best practices include the creation of a contract terms database, issuing activity calendars, and outsourcing tax form preparation. However,

Exhibit 14.1 Summary of General Best Practices

	Best Practice	Cost	Install Time
Management			
14–1	Apply run charts to accounting processes	💵	⏰⏰
14–2	Apply check sheets to accounting processes	💵	⏰⏰
14–3	Apply value stream mapping to accounting processes	💵	⏰⏰
14–4	Apply the production cell layout to accounting	💵	⏰⏰⏰
14–5	Create a best practices support center	💵💵💵	⏰⏰
14–6	Consolidate all accounting functions	💵💵💵	⏰⏰⏰
14–7	Continually review key process cycles	💵	⏰⏰
14–8	Create a policies and procedures manual	💵💵	⏰⏰
14–9	Eliminate all transaction backlogs	💵💵	⏰⏰
14–10	Implement process centering	💵💵	⏰⏰
14–11	Issue activity calendars to all accounting positions	💵	⏰
14–12	Post the policies and procedures manual on the company intranet site	💵💵	⏰⏰
Reporting			
14–13	Switch to online reporting	💵💵💵	⏰⏰⏰
14–14	Track function measurements	💵	⏰⏰
14–15	Use Balanced Scorecard reporting	💵	⏰⏰
14–16	Discuss major accounting decisions with auditors	💵	⏰⏰
Systems			
14–17	Create a contract terms database	💵💵	⏰
14–18	Install a knowledge management system	💵💵💵	⏰⏰
14–19	Monitor fixed assets with wireless sensors	💵💵	⏰⏰
Taxation			
14–20	Create an online tax policy listing	💵💵	⏰⏰
14–21	Designate a tax liaison for each government jurisdiction	💵	⏰⏰

Exhibit 14.1 *(Continued)*

	Best Practice	Cost	Install Time
14–22	Assign tax staff to business units		
14–23	Outsource tax form preparation		
14–24	Submit electronic tax returns to the IRS		
14–25	Pay federal taxes online		
14–26	Subscribe to an online tax information service		

Training

14–27	Move intellectual property to an offshore holding company		
14–28	Create accounting training teams		
14–29	Create an ongoing training program for all accounting personnel		
14–30	Create computer-based training movies		
14–31	Implement cross-training for mission-critical activities		

restricting one's implementation of best practices to just these items would be a mistake, for the level of accounting efficiency will rise dramatically when the more difficult implementations are successfully completed.

The remainder of this chapter is grouped into sections, each of which covers one best practice. In each section, there is a discussion of the problems that a best practice can alleviate, how the best practice works, and any implementation problems that may arise.

14–1 Apply Run Charts to Accounting Processes

Run charts are used to display process performance over time, and are an effective way to visually spot trends and cycles in data. This is a high-level analysis, and it must be followed up with a detailed review of the data to locate and correct underlying causes. Run charts can also be used as a feedback loop to ensure that changes made to a process have resulted in improvements.

The typical run chart, shown in Exhibit 14.2, itemizes events on the y axis and the time period over which the events occurred on the x axis. As shown in the exhibit, it is also useful to include a line, running parallel to the x axis, showing the average for the events; anyone viewing the data can use the information to determine the extent by which events have departed from the average. The

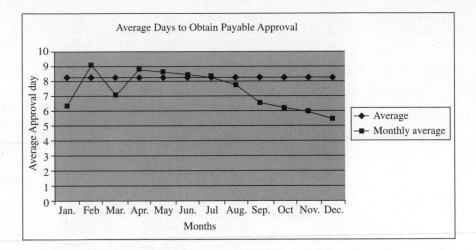

Exhibit 14.2 Run Chart for Payables Approval Period

example shows a run chart for the average number of days to obtain approval of supplier invoices, with a strong downward trend beginning in April, when the company begins the rollout of an electronic workflow management system for payable approvals.

When reviewing a run chart, be aware that there is some normal variation in the data, so always review the data over a sufficiently long period of time to determine the general min-max range within which the data normally fall. The main focus of attention should be on events that fall outside the normal range of data, and in particular, those events that do so in a repetitive manner. If the run chart contains a large number of data points and at least eight consecutive events appear on one side or the other of the average, then it is likely that a unique underlying cause has influenced the process.

For example, the invoice creation process typically requires a few hours from the point of service or product delivery, but there are valid reasons for occasional delays in this process, such as a salesperson needing to create a cover letter to accompany an invoice, or (at the other extreme) an automatic invoice delivery using electronic data interchange. But what if the creation process is delayed by the hiring of a new warehouse manager who is not fully conversant with the process of sending shipment information to the billing staff for conversion into an invoice? If so, the run chart in Exhibit 14.3 reveals that the delay in invoice creation suddenly jumps from an average of 3 business hours to 13 business hours (with an attendant delay of cash flow, which highlights the importance of this issue). The run chart makes a clear visual case for further investigation into the invoicing delay, which should ultimately result in the rapid reeducation of the new warehouse manager.

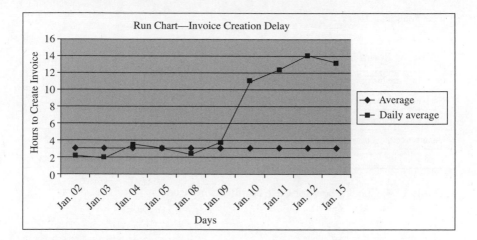

Exhibit 14.3 Run Chart for Invoice Creation Delay

Where else can the run chart be used in the accounting process? It works best for the analysis of high-volume transactions, so consider using it for process analysis in the billing, collections, inventory, payables, and payroll areas.

Cost: 🪙   **Installation time:** ⏰⏰

14–2 Apply Check Sheets to Accounting Processes

The check sheet is a structured form used for the collection and analysis of data. Its most common application is for the collection of data about the frequency or patterns of events. Data entry on the form is designed to be as simple as possible, with check marks or similar symbols. The check sheet is most frequently used in a production setting, but can be easily applied to the accounting function.

For example, what if the accounting manager is trying to increase the efficiency of the cash application process? The first step is to determine the frequency of various issues impacting the process, so that the accounting manager can focus her efforts on efficiency improvement. She discusses the project with the cash application staff and uses the staff's input to construct the check sheet shown in Exhibit 14.4. The cash application staff fills it in during a one-week period, resulting in the determination that unauthorized payment deductions are the most frequent problem encountered during cash application, followed by missing remittance detail information. This information could then be used to prioritize efficiency improvement activities.

Cost: 🪙   **Installation time:** ⏰⏰

Cash Application Issues

Reason	Day					
	Mon	Tue.	Wed.	Thu.	Fri.	Total
Customer double pay		II		I		3
No remittance advice enclosed	I	卌	II	I	IIII	13
Pays with multiple checks			I		I	2
Unauthorized deductions taken	卌	卌 II	IIII	卌 II	II	25
Total	6	14	7	9	7	43

Exhibit 14.4 Check Sheet for Cash Application Issues

14–3 Apply Value Stream Mapping to Accounting Processes

Value stream mapping (VSM) focuses on the identification of waste across an entire process. Once waste has been identified with this tool, one can focus on the elimination of the waste. A VSM chart identifies all of the actions required to complete a process, while also identifying key information about each action item. Key information will vary by the process under review, but can include total hours worked, overtime hours, cycle time to complete a transaction, error rates, and absenteeism.

The value stream chart shown in Exhibit 14.5 addresses the entire procurement cycle, from the initial placement of a requisition through processing of the resulting supplier invoice. Under each processing step, the VSM chart itemizes the amount of overtime, staffing, work shifts, process uptime, and transaction error rate. The chart then shows the total time required for each processing step, as well as the time required between steps, and also identifies the types of time spent between steps (e.g., outbound batching, transit time, and inbound queue time).

The chart reveals that most of the procurement cycle time is used between processing steps, especially in the transit time of orders from suppliers to the company. If total cycle time is an issue, then a reasonable conclusion would be to either source locally or expend more for faster delivery services. However, if the emphasis is on speedier in-house processing, then the chart shows that the purchase-order processing stage is the most time consuming; it is also probably a bottleneck operation, given the amount of overtime incurred. Likely conclusions would be to reduce the error rate in the purchasing area by working on a reduction of errors in the upstream requisitioning area (note how the two error rates are identical, since the purchasing staff is likely copying errors from requisitions directly onto the purchase orders), offloading purchasing work with procurement cards, or bolstering capacity by adding purchasing staff.

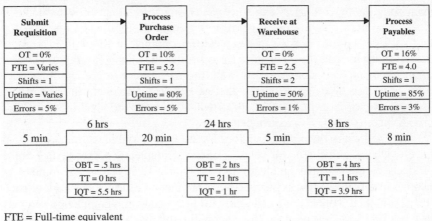

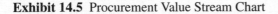

OBT = .5 hrs		OBT = 2 hrs		OBT = 4 hrs
TT = 0 hrs		TT = 21 hrs		TT = .1 hrs
IQT = 5.5 hrs		IQT = 1 hr		IQT = 3.9 hrs

FTE = Full-time equivalent
IQT = Inbound queue time
OBT = Outbound batch time
OT = Overtime
TT = Transit time

Exhibit 14.5 Procurement Value Stream Chart

Another option for shrinking the total cycle time is to have the receiving staff send receiving documents to the payables department more frequently than once every four hours. Cutting the outbound batch time in half would eliminate two hours from the total cycle time, though this would require two more trips to the payables department per day by the receiving staff.

Value stream mapping works best in highly focused, high-volume processes where it makes sense to spend time wringing a few seconds out of repetitive processes. Conversely, the analysis effort would be wasted in low-volume areas where the staff constantly switches between multiple tasks.

Cost: **Installation time:** 🕰️ 🕰️

14–4 Apply the Production Cell Layout to Accounting
✔Author's Choice

One of the reasons why a smaller accounting department tends to be so heavily cluttered with paperwork is that employees are called on to handle a multitude of tasks throughout the day—and be prepared to handle each one totally within the confines of their offices. This means that a single individual may need a multitude of computers, printers, filing cabinets, and/or binders for multiple activities—such as cash receipts processing, inventory valuation, and billing— all in one office. Switching between tasks throughout the day calls for putting away some documents, accessing others, changing accounting software modules, stocking printers with different types of forms or check stock, and other activities that increase the time needed to complete transactions. In addition, if management decides to centralize files in order to remove the clutter from each person's office, then employees now have to walk further in order to access information for their various tasks. So, it appears that we must either tolerate cluttered offices or more employee move time—both of which increase the level of transaction processing inefficiency. Is there a better way?

We can look to the production floor for a solution. Manufacturing operations have used production cells for years in order to completely process either entire products or major subassemblies—and all with a relatively small number of people, sometimes as few as one person. A production cell includes a set of carefully positioned workstations that allow for easy sequential completion of every task needed to create a product. If we apply this approach to the accounting area, the work layout will look substantially different. For example, one office can be set up to process nothing but invoices, with the necessary filing cabinets located within that office, a computer terminal always open to the billing software module, and invoice forms always loaded into the locally positioned printer. The same approach works for payroll, cash receipts processing, financial statement preparation, and so on.

There are some downsides to the use of production cells in accounting. For example, the smaller accounting departments to which this concept primarily applies may have as few as one employee who operates out of a single office. If so, setting up several production cells might require several offices. A possible solution is to reconfigure the work space of a single office so that different quadrants of the office are permanently configured to handle a single accounting transaction. There may also be control problems, such as permanently leaving check stock in a printer. In this case, the solution will be a trade-off between controls (removing check stock from locked storage) and convenience (taking the chance that someone will access the check stock).

Cost: Installation time: 🕰 🕰 🕰

14–5   Create a Best Practices Support Center

In a larger company having multiple accounting locations, a best practice may be installed with ease in one location, and stall badly in another. This problem can be due to a variety of environmental factors, differences in the comparative levels of expertise, implementation errors, or simply different levels of management support.

These issues can be mitigated by creating a best practices support center. The support center's staff can provide services to the rest of the organization at the strategic or tactical level. For example, it can review an accounting center's operations and provide a complete set of best practices recommendations with an implementation plan, or just help to change management aspects of a specific best practice. It can also prepackage best practices with supporting policies, procedures, controls, checklists, and training materials, which makes them much easier to install.

The support center can also engage in fine-tuning of existing best practices, going back to prior implementations to see what worked and what did not. It can work on entirely new best practices by prototyping them in a controlled environment or working on them with suppliers, and then rolling them out at test locations. If company managers want to use exactly the same best practices throughout the company (which makes them easier to implement and manage), then the support center's staff can derive the most optimized version of a best practice, put its "seal of approval" on it, and then manage the rollout of that specific version of the best practice.

If the support center is also assigned to conduct post-implementation reviews, then it can engage in audits that not only evaluate the success of a best practice but also measure it across multiple locations. This can lead to further evaluations to determine why a best practice works better in one location than another.

Essentially, the support center becomes a central repository of knowledge about best practices and how they can best be implemented, but can be expanded into a consulting and internal auditing practice.

Cost: Installation time:

14–6 Consolidate All Accounting Functions

A company with many locations will frequently have a separate accounting staff in each location. By doing so, the overall cost of accounting tends to be much higher than the industry average because there is a great deal of staff duplication. For example, each location requires its own controller, assistant controller, and accounting manager. Also, transaction volumes may not be great enough to fill the time of the accounting staff in each location, leading to underutilized personnel. Also, the quality of management may vary significantly between locations, resulting in differences in the level of efficiency, with locations experiencing the same transaction volume requiring significantly different volumes in the number of required accounting staff. Further, with accounting conducted in many locations, a well-run company must schedule a large number of internal audits in all of those locations to ensure that procedures are completed in accordance with corporate standards. Finally, extra labor is needed at corporate headquarters to consolidate all of the accounting records for financial reporting purposes. This formidable array of inefficiencies results in a significant increase in accounting expenses.

The solution to this tangled web of accounting problems is to consolidate all or most of the functions into the smallest possible number of locations. By doing so, fewer accounting managers are needed, while procedures can be standardized and enforced much more easily. Also, given the smaller number of locations, the work of consolidating financial results is simplified. The only case in which this solution does not work well is if a company has an extremely diversified set of subsidiaries. For example, the accounting operations of a railroad, an oil refinery, and a cement plant are so different that consolidating these functions would be extremely difficult. Conversely, the consolidation task becomes much easier for those companies doing business in a single industry and that have many locations that conduct the same kind of business using approximately the same procedures.

Here are the most common areas in which companies have had success in centralizing into shared services centers:

- Accounts receivable collections
- Cash application
- Cost accounting
- Employee expense report processing
- Intercompany accounts payable and receivable processing
- Inventory accounting
- Invoice processing
- Payroll processing

The level of centralization that can be achieved with shared services centers depends on the nature of the function being centralized. For example, a separate collections center may be required for each country, since this calls for considerable customer contact in the local language, as well as knowledge of the local laws regarding collections. Service centers can be more global if they involve services that are highly standardized and transactional in nature and that require minimal expertise.

However, this best practice requires a great deal of management skill and money. For example, combining the accounts payable functions of many locations requires the construction of a central processing facility, along with the transfer of staff to that location, retraining, the design of new systems, new audit procedures, and the orderly transfer of supplier invoices from many locations to a single one—and in the midst of this massive change, suppliers must still be paid on time so there is no disruption of deliveries to the company from suppliers. Given the size of this task, the major factors needed to ensure success are the appointment of an excellent manager to the consolidation process, the complete support of this project by top management, and sufficient funding to see it through to completion. In addition, given the amount of disruption involved, it would be wise to consolidate only one function at a time so that most activities are not interrupted at the same time. By taking these steps, the odds of successfully finishing a consolidation project are greatly enhanced.

Cost:    **Installation time:** 🕰 🕰 🕰

14–7 Continually Review Key Process Cycles

As a general rule, any system will begin to degrade as soon as it is created. For example, a new purchasing process cycle will begin almost immediately to encounter exceptions to the rules, as well as special situations that spawn a subset of extra procedures that do not appear anywhere in the procedures manual. Further, the process will not be maintained very well, resulting in lots of excess data in the system, such as the records of suppliers that have not been used in years, perpetually open purchase orders, even though the orders were filled long ago, and supplier invoices that have a permanent "hold" slapped on them so that they cannot be paid. The example is only for accounts payable, but the same problem applies to all processes. Thus, over time, all of an accounting department's processes will be in desperate need of a tune-up.

That tune-up is provided by a rarely used best practice in which a designated employee is in charge of constantly reviewing process cycles. In some companies, this person is called the "process owner," with responsibility for the flow of information through a specific process and for any changes to it. When someone is assigned to review process cycles, there should be a very detailed set of tasks to be reviewed. To use the previous example, the process owner should review the list of suppliers in the computer to see which can be deleted, check on open purchase orders to see what can be closed, review the list of suppliers with early payment discounts to verify that discounts are taken, check with the receiving staff to ensure that they receive only goods labeled with valid purchase order numbers, and review payment packets to verify that all payments were only for items authorized by the purchasing department. If the process is complex enough, one or more people may be assigned to it—otherwise, one person may be assigned multiple cycles and rotate through a review of them all so all primary cycles receive a tune-up several times a year.

One advantage of constantly reviewing process cycles is that few exception transactions will occur, resulting in far less research work to correct problems. Another factor is that employees involved in creating transactions will receive constant advice from the process owner regarding how they are supposed to be conducting their work, resulting in much better standardization of output. Further, the process owner constantly reviews why old transactions have not yet been completed, tracks down the reasons for the problems, and corrects them at the source. None of these changes are major, but when taken as a whole, they represent a considerable improvement in the way a company's key processes operate. This work is well worth the effort.

The main problem is that the process owner is a new position and adds to overhead. However, the number of mistakes this person finds and corrects will frequently pay back his or her salary. For example, finding and fixing a hole in the revenue cycle that lets shipments disappear from the system may keep a company from missing billings to customers. Similarly, keeping the accounts payable staff from making unapproved payments to suppliers will also save money. A second problem is that this position tends to step outside the boundaries of the accounting department, since the processes being reviewed are impacted by other departments, such as the shipping and receiving departments and the purchasing department. Because this may be looked on as interference by the accounting department, a process owner must be a very tactful person and strongly supported by upper management. If these issues can be overcome, the process owner becomes a major contributor to the smooth functioning of any company.

Cost: **Installation time:** 🕰 🕰

14–8   Create a Policies and Procedures Manual   ✔*Author's Choice*

As is noted several times in this chapter, an unorganized accounting department is inefficient, suffers from a high transaction error rate, and does not complete its work products on time. While other best practices noted in this chapter, such as general training, cross-training, and calendars of events, will contribute to a more structured environment, one of the very best ways to create a disciplined accounting group is to create and maintain a policies and procedures manual.

This manual should list the main policies under which the accounting department operates, such as those listed in Exhibit 14.6. These are the key issues that confront each functional area and are usually limited to just a few pages. Anything longer probably indicates an excessive degree of control or some confusion in the difference between a policy and a procedure.

A good example of a policy is one that sets a boundary for an activity. The first policy noted in Exhibit 14.6 states that an accounts payable clerk is allowed to process any supplier invoice within 5 percent of the amount listed on the original purchase order. By doing so, this policy clearly defines what the clerk is allowed to do. A procedure, by contrast, defines the precise activities that take place within the boundaries the policies create. An example of a procedure is shown in Exhibit 14.7, where there is a definitive listing of the exact steps one must follow in order to create and issue the annual budget. A procedure is usually sufficient to use as a guideline for an employee who needs to understand how a process works. When combined with a proper level of training, the policies and procedures manual is an effective way not only to increase control over the accounting department, but also to enhance its efficiency.

Though there are few excuses for not having such a manual, there are some pitfalls to consider when constructing it, as well as for maintaining and enforcing it. They are as follows:

- *Not enough detail.* A procedure that does not cover activity steps in a sufficient degree of detail is not of much use to someone who is using it for the first time; it is important to list specific forms used, computer screens accessed, and fields on those screens in which information is entered, as well as the other positions that either supply information for the procedure or to which it sends

Exhibit 14.6 Sample Policies Page

Accounts Payable:

- Any supplier invoice within 5 percent of the price indicated on the buyer's purchase order requires no additional authorization to pay.

Document Archival:

- Use the following format to determine when to dispose of old records:

Type of Record	Retention
Accounts payable ledgers/schedules	7 years
Advertisement for a job opening	1 year
Capital stock records	Permanent
Checks (canceled)	7 years
Deeds, mortgages, bills of sale	Permanent
Earnings per week	3 years
Financial statements	Permanent
General ledgers (year-end)	Permanent
Hiring records	1 year from date record made or personnel action taken, whichever is later
Insurance/pension/retirement plans	1 year after termination
Invoices to customers	7 years
Minute books, including bylaws and charter	Permanent
Payroll records—employment data	3 years from termination
Physical/medical examinations	Duration of employment, plus 30 years
Property records	Permanent
Sales and purchase records	3 years
Stock and bond certificates (canceled)	7 years
Subsidiary ledgers	7 years
Tax returns	Permanent
Time cards	3 years

Fixed Assets:

- The minimum dollar amount above which expenses are capitalized is $2,000.
- Any member of the management committee can approve an expenditure for amounts of $5,000 or less if the item was already listed in the annual budget.
- Any capital expenditure exceeding $5,000 requires the approval of the president, plus all expenditures not already listed in the annual budget, regardless of the amount.

(continues)

Exhibit 14.6 *(Continued)*

- Every molding machine shall be assigned a salvage value of 25 percent of the purchase price.

Logistics:

- Any items arriving at the receiving dock without a purchase order number will be rejected.

Travel and Entertainment:

- All reimbursements require a receipt.
- Employees must show all receipts for travel advances within one week of travel, or the advance will be considered a salary advance.
- Only coach fares will be reimbursed.
- There is no movie reimbursement.
- There is no reimbursement for commuting miles.
- There is no reimbursement for lunch mileage.

---

information. It may also be helpful to include a flowchart, which is more understandable than text for some people.

- *Not reinforced.* A procedures manual does not do much good if it is immediately parked on a remote shelf in the accounting department. Instead, it should be made an integral part of all training programs and included in periodic discussions regarding the updating and improvement of key processes. Only through constant attention will the manual be used to the fullest extent.
- *Not updated.* Even the best manual will become obsolete over time, as changing circumstances alter procedures to the point where the manual no longer describes conditions as they currently exist. When this happens, no one bothers to use the manual. Accordingly, it is necessary to update the manual whenever changes are made to the underlying systems.
- *Too many procedures.* A common problem is that the manual is never released because the controller is determined to include a procedure for every conceivable activity the accounting department will ever encounter. However, the main principle to follow is that the manual must be issued soon, so it is better to issue it quickly with procedures that cover the bulk of accounting activities and address the remaining procedures at a later date. This approach gets the key information to those employees who need it the most, and does so very quickly.

Exhibit 14.7 Sample Procedure Page

Procedure: Update the annual budget

Responsibility: Controller

Steps:

1. *Expense update.* **As of mid-November,** issue each department a listing of its expenses, annualized based on actual expenses through October of the current year. The listing should include the personnel in each department and their current pay levels. Request a return date of ten days in the future for this information, which should include estimated changes in expenses.

2. *Revenue update.* **As of mid-November,** issue the sales manager a listing of revenue by month by business unit, through October of the current year. Request a return date of ten days in the future for this information, which should include estimated changes in revenues.

3. *Capital expenditure update.* **As of mid-November,** issue a form to all department heads, requesting information about the cost and timing of capital expenditures for the upcoming year. Request a return date of ten days in the future for this information.

4. *Automation update.* **As of mid-November,** issue a form to the engineering manager, requesting estimates of the timing and size of reductions in headcount in the upcoming year due to automation efforts. Request a return date of ten days in the future for this information. Be sure to compare scheduled headcount reductions to the timing of capital expenditures, since they should track closely.

5. *Update the budget model.* **This task should be completed by the end of November,** and includes the following steps:

   1. Update the numbers already listed in the budget with information received from the various managers. This may involve changing "hard-coded" dollar amounts or changing flex budget percentages. Be sure to keep a checklist of who has returned information so you can follow up with those personnel who have not returned it.

   2. Update the "Prior Year" cells on the left side of the budget model with estimated year-end balances (primarily for the balance sheet).

   3. Update the "Last Year" cells on the right side of the budget model, using annualized figures.

   4. Verify that the indirect overhead allocation percentages shown on the budgeted factory overhead page are still accurate.

   5. Verify that the Federal Insurance Contributors Act (FICA), State Unemployment Tax (SUTA), Federal Unemployment Tax (FUTA), medical, and workers' compensation amounts listed at the top of the staffing budget page are still accurate.

(continues)

Exhibit 14.7 *(Continued)*

6. Add job titles and pay levels to the staffing page as needed, along with new average pay rates based on projected pay levels made by department managers.

7. Run a depreciation report for the upcoming year, add the expected depreciation for new capital expenditures, and add this amount to the budget.

8. Revise the loan detail budget based on projected borrowings through the end of the year. Be sure to list only loan balance reductions based on principal pay-downs, not interest payments.

6. *Review the budget.* Print out the budget and circle any budgeted expenses or revenues that are significantly different from the annualized amounts for the current year (do this by comparing the last two columns on each page). Go over the questionable items with the managers who are responsible for them.

7. *Revise the budget.* Revise the budget, print it again, and review it with the president. Incorporate any additional changes.

8. *Issue the budget.* Bind the budget and issue it to the management team.

9. *Update accounting database.* Enter budget numbers into the accounting software for the upcoming year. **All tasks should be completed by mid-December.**

The single most important factor in the success of a policies and procedures manual is an active accounting manager. This person must reinforce the use of the manual with the staff so it is not simply ignored as a one-time report gathering dust on a shelf. Only through continual attention by the entire staff will it become the foundation of how all key accounting processes are completed.

     Cost: 💵💵   **Installation time:** ⏰⏰

14–9 Eliminate All Transaction Backlogs   ✔*Author's Choice*

Accounting departments get in trouble when they develop a permanent backlog of standard accounting transactions, usually in the areas of cash receipts processing, billings, and payables. When a backlog arises, the focus of the department shifts to the servicing of this backlog, to the exclusion of all other value-added activities, such as improving processes or providing better customer service. Also, backlogs tend to create piles of paperwork in which other documents can be lost, resulting in extra search time to locate needed materials.

A crucial best practice is to eliminate these backlogs, usually by allocating extra staff time to them. Once the piles are eliminated, the controller can focus on increased levels of training and process improvement in order to reduce the number of people required to keep the backlog from reoccurring. If a company has a highly variable amount of transaction volume, some backlog may reappear in periods of high activity, though this can be avoided through the careful use of the preplanned hiring of part-time workers to assist the regular staff. There is also likely to be some buildup in the backlog on a temporary basis at the end of each month and especially at the end of the fiscal year, as closing activities take priority. However, these are temporary issues whose impact on the backlog can be eliminated within a few days.

Cost: **Installation time:** 🕑 🕑

14–10 Implement Process-Centering

A major problem at many companies is the inordinate amount of time it takes to complete a process. For example, insurance companies are famous for spending many weeks to review an insurance claim and issue a payment check, when the total amount of work required is under an hour. The long time period from the beginning to the end of the process is usually due to the number of transfers between employees. For example, the insurance branch office may forward a claim to an insurance adjuster, who passes it along to a manager if the amount exceeds a set level, or who hands it off to another person who checks to see if the claim might be fraudulent or if the claimant has an unusually long history of claims, then moves the paperwork to another person who issues checks, and then returns the entire packet to the insurance branch office. Insurance is just an example—upon further investigation, it is common to find that all companies invest a shocking amount of time in moving paperwork between a multitude of employees. A related problem is that transactions can be lost when they are moved between employees. Further, it is difficult to pin blame on anyone when a transaction is improperly completed because there are so many people involved in the process. Thus, spreading work among too many people opens a virtual Pandora's box of troubles.

The solution is called *process centering*. Its underlying principle is to cluster as many work tasks for a single process as possible with a single person. By doing so, there are fewer transfers of documentation, which reduces the amount of time lost during these movements, while at the same time eliminating the risk that paperwork will be lost. Further, employees have much more complete and fulfilling jobs since they see a much larger part of the process and have a better feeling for how the entire process works. And best of all for a company, the time needed to complete transactions drops drastically, sometimes to less than 10 percent of the amount previously needed.

The main problem with process centering is employee resistance. This is a *reengineering* best practice, which means that the old process is ripped up and replaced with an entirely new workflow, which makes many employees nervous about their jobs, or if they will even have a job when the changes are complete. Accordingly, they usually are not pleased with the prospect of a new system and resist vigorously, or at least are not of any assistance. Only excellent communications and a strong commitment by top management to completing the project will make this best practice operational, given the likely level of resistance to it.

Cost: 💵💵   **Installation time:** ⏰⏰

14–11 Issue Activity Calendars to All Accounting Positions   ✔ *Author's Choice*

The bane of any accounting department is disorganization. This department, above all others, is responsible for consistently completing the same tasks, day after day and year after year, with a great deal of reliability. If the employees cannot organize themselves properly so key tasks are completed on time, the entire function can fall into disarray, resulting in payments and billings not being completed on time. Also, financial statements, the most subject to delays if there is disorganization, will be released much later than expected, possibly containing a large number of errors. Clearly, some instrument of organization must be found.

An excellent tool for straightening out the timing of accounting work is the calendar. One can create a calendar on the computer, either with a scheduling software package or an electronic spreadsheet, and load it with all of the tasks to be completed each day. An example of such a calendar is shown in Exhibit 14.8. Though some employees are naturally well-organized and will already have it in place, many others will be in desperate need of this simple organizational tool. The best way to distribute these calendar schedules is to keep the schedules for all employees in a single location, update them at the end of each month, and have a staff meeting to distribute them so the controller can emphasize all calendar changes. One can then refer to copies of all employees' calendars each day and follow up with them to ensure that they are completing the scheduled tasks.

The calendar is only one way to assist in managing the operations of the accounting department. Another excellent tool is the policy and procedure manual, which was discussed earlier in this chapter, in the "Create a Policies and Procedures Manual" section.

Cost: 💵   **Installation time:** ⏰

Monthly Calendar						
Sunday	Monday	Tuesday	Wednesday	Thursday	Friday	Saturday
		1 Issue Prior-Month Sales Figures	2 Review Receivables	3 Annual Review with A. Smith	4 Managers Meeting Back up Computers	5
6	7 Measurements Issue Financial Statements	8 Review Accounting Expenses	9 Review Receivables	10 Pizza Party	11 Managers Meeting Back up Computers	12
13	14 Measurements	15 Review Bad Debts	16 Review Receivables	17 Review Procedures	18 Managers Meeting Back up Computers	19
20	21 Measurements	22 Meet with Outsourcing Consultants	23 Review Receivables	24 Meet with Auditors	25 Managers Meeting Back up Computers	26
27	28 Measurements	29 Annual Review with J. Doctorow	30 Review Receivables	31 Go over Tasks for Issuing Next Months' Financial Statements		

Exhibit 14.8 Sample Monthly Activities Calendar

14–12   Post the Policies and Procedures Manual on the Company Intranet Site

When the accounting staff is widely scattered through many locations, it is difficult to make available to them a current version of the accounting policies and procedures manual. This can be a real problem, for the accounting department is much more procedurally driven than any other department, and operating with antiquated procedures can cause significant differences in operations between various locations. Traditionally, this problem has been addressed by creating an internal procedure-writing and publishing department that constantly updates documents, maintains a list of authorized recipients, and mails the changed documents to them. This group is expensive, and does not always result in updated manuals at outlying locations, especially if those outlying personnel take a dim view of spending their valuable time replacing pages in their procedures manuals.

A significant improvement on this method is to convert each page of the manual into an HTML or Adobe Acrobat format, so that it can be posted directly to the corporate intranet site. By doing so, there is no need to publish and distribute any more paper-based documents. In addition, an online index allows users to quickly search through the database to find the exact procedural references they need. In addition, there is no longer a need to gradually compile a lengthy list of procedure changes and then issue all of the changes at the same time; instead, a procedure writer can quickly make any change and immediately post it to the intranet site. The only problem with this approach is that all accounting personnel must have ready access to the site where the documents are posted. This requires a reasonably advanced level of networking ability within a company.

Cost: **Installation time:** 🕰 🕰

14–13 Switch to Online Reporting

In organizations that occupy a large geographical area, the accounting staff faces the chore of somehow sending financial and operational reporting information to many locations. This can mean a mass mailing once a month, or perhaps more frequently if daily or weekly reports are required. If there is some urgency to this information, overnight express mail delivery may be necessary, which is quite expensive, especially when used many times a year for many locations. Faxing this information is frequently not an allowable option, for the information being transmitted may be so sensitive that there is too great a risk that the wrong person will retrieve the information from the fax machine. Thus, sending paper reports throughout a company, and especially a large one, is a major hassle.

An effective means for eliminating the problems with paper-based reports is to switch to electronic transmission. By doing so, there is no need to send any paper documents and there is also no transmission time interval before the information is available to recipients. The only difficulty is that a few of the more formal documents, such as audited financial statements, with their accompanying footnotes and graphics, cannot be sent easily by electronic means, unless they are first scanned into an image file. However, for the bulk of all reports, this remains an effective approach.

Information can be sent electronically in either a passive or "push" mode. In the passive mode, the accounting department simply posts the information in a file and waits for employees to go to the file to scan the data. The push method involves sending information to employees by email. The push method is generally more effective, since there is no way for employees to avoid the data, unless they are in the habit of deleting their email without first reading it.

This approach can be an expensive one with a long implementation interval, but only under certain implementation approaches. It is certainly more expensive if a special file structure is created to contain the online reports, especially if the data are to be contained in a data warehouse. Even the less difficult approach of sending out reports by email requires the previous installation of a companywide email system, which can be a problem if there are many locations to be linked. However, the distribution of data is made vastly easier by the presence of the Internet; any company location can now obtain an email address from a third-party email provider at minimal cost and receive electronic transmissions through this electronic mailbox. Another alternative is to spend a moderate amount on a corporate intranet site, on which financial reports can be posted under an icon. Though an effective and easy-to-use approach, it does require access to the intranet from outlying locations. Consequently, there are implementation alternatives for all possible budgets, starting with distribution by the Internet, progressing through an intranet site, and ending with a custom-made file structure with comprehensive user access. The best approach will depend on a company's budget, existing systems, and information distribution requirements.

Cost:    Installation time: 🕐 🕐 🕐

14–14 Track Function Measurements   ✔*Author's Choice*

The role of the accounting department does not just include completing daily transactions and issuing financial statements. In addition, it must issue periodic measurements to the rest of the company that show the results of key activities. A poorly organized accounting department may issue this information only grudgingly when senior management demands it. This approach does not allow the accounting staff to derive a set of standard procedures for the collection of measurement information, nor does it build up much goodwill with the management team.

A better approach is to create a standardized set of performance criteria that the accounting staff will calculate and distribute at set intervals. An example of such a report is shown in Exhibit 14.9. By using this report, management can spot operational problems at once and correct them. Also, the controller can play a key role in determining which measurements are used; this can be a pivotal item in some situations, for other department managers may not want to have their poor performance measured and reported. Also, with a standardized set of measurements, the controller can build the measurement task into the accounting department's daily work schedule in a manner that does not interfere with other operations, while also allowing for the construction of a procedure that standardizes the calculation of each measurement (ensuring the consistency of calculations from period to period). These are all good reasons for implementing a reporting system for key corporate measurements.

Cost: 💵   Installation time: 🕐 🕐

Company Measurements (Issued on Mondays)

		Current Month							
		Week 5	Week 4	Week 3	Week 2	Week 1	Nov.	Oct.	Sep.
Cash	Available Debt (000s)	$267	$258	$242	$242	$442	$550	$500	$150
	Cash Burn Rate/Mo. (000s)	$186	$186	$186	$186	$214	$214	$182	$190
	Months Cash Available	1.4	1.4	1.3	1.3	2.1	2.6	2.7	0.8
Working Capital	Days Accounts Receivable	35	37	40	43	43	39	48	53
	Days Total Inventory	41	41	42	43	41	40	43	47
	Days Accounts Payable	40	39	38	36	37	39	33	45
Financial	Breakeven, 2-Mo. Rolling (000s)	—	—	—	—	—	$850	$839	$821
	Net Profits Before Tax (000s)	—	—	—	—	—	$228	$234	$127
Sales	Sales (weeks are cumulative) (000s)	$1,055	$792	$540	$393	$123	$1,031	$899	$1,175
	Backlog (000s)	$1,602	$1,620	$1,599	$1,498	$1,397	$1,779	$988	—
	Backlog/Sales Ratio	—	—	—	—	—	173%	110%	—
Production	Machine Utilization	67%	61%	58%	52%	44%	46%	40%	35%
	$ Not Shipped by Promise Date (000s)	$28	$29	$31	$42	$50	$37	$24	—
	% Actual Labor Hrs over Standard	8%	15%	12%	13%	22%	3%	8%	15%
	Scrap Percentage	1.6%	1.7%	1.7%	2.0%	1.2%	2.5%	1.9%	2.7%
Quality	Returns $$$ (000s)	$15	$0	$0	$0	$0	$15	$16	$14
	Returns Percentage	—	—	—	—	—	1.5%	1.8%	1.2%
Logistics	Finished Goods Inv. Accuracy, IP	68%	64%	62%	62%	36%	27%	0%	0%
	Finished Goods Inv. Accuracy, Ass'y	19%	17%	15%	0%	0%	11%	0%	0%

Exhibit 14.9 Sample Measurements Report

14–15 Use Balanced Scorecard Reporting

The typical controller only reports on the financial situation of a company. Unfortunately, financial information that is the result of many other activities that the accounting department does not normally have anything to do with. For example, profits are impacted if the customer is not satisfied (impacted by quality, pricing, and on-time delivery), if internal business processes do not function properly (impacted by such issues as machine utilization and the level of automation), and if employees are not well trained in their jobs (impacted by training and any factors leading to high employee turnover). A controller is not accustomed to reporting on any of these issues, but they all impact company profitability, the controller's primary reporting responsibility.

Robert S. Kaplan and David P. Norton have addressed this issue in their landmark book, *The Balanced Scorecard* (Harvard Business School Press, 1996). In it, they argue a strong case in favor of an entirely new method of reporting that itemizes the key factors impacting company profitability. An example of such a report is shown in Exhibit 14.10, where measurements are clustered into blocks, each one concerned with a different aspect of key success factors: financial, customer, internal business processes, and employee learning and growth. Kaplan and Norton feel that these four areas must be closely managed as a whole in order to attain truly exceptional levels of profitability.

Where does this leave a controller? This person is the one whom most of a company relies on to issue reports regularly on company status, even though those reports are only concerned with finances. Since reporting is already a part of this person's job, it only makes sense to expand the range of information covered to include those Kaplan and Norton advocate. This will require new reporting systems, as well as direction from senior management, since the exact measurements selected will require some thought by that group. In addition, the company will certainly want to see the traditional set of financial information as well, so this will be an added task for the controller—but one that management can use to track the performance of many more key functions than were previously covered by any accounting reports.

Cost: 🖘   Installation time: 🕰 🕰

14–16 Discuss Major Accounting Decisions with Auditors

All too often, a company will decide to account for a major transaction in a certain way, only to find at year-end that its auditors have an entirely different interpretation of the proper accounting, resulting in a restatement of its expected results. This problem can arise in any number of complex accounting areas, such as business combinations, intangible assets, derivatives, and revenue recognition.

ABC Company
Balanced Scorecard

Goal: To spin off enough cash flow to build new facilities and acquire competitors.

Financial:	Actual	Goal
Net Profits		22%
This Month	18.0%	
This Quarter	16.0%	
Last Year	11.0%	
F/G Turns		20
This Month	22.8	
This Quarter	17.6	
Last Year	12.0	
A/R Turns		9.0
This Month	6.9	
This Quarter	6.5	
Last Year	8.1	

Customer:	Actual	Goal
Customer Satisfaction		95%
This Month	82.0%	
This Quarter	67.0%	
Last Year	41.0%	
On-time Shipments		99%
This Month	88%	
This Quarter	75%	
Last Year	63%	

Learning and Growth:	Actual	Goal
Employee Turnover		2%
This Month*	12%	
This Quarter*	14%	
Last Year*	18%	
* All turnover figures are annualized.		
Employee Training (Hours/Year)		40
This Month*	37	
This Quarter*	35	
Last Year*	32	
* All training figures are annualized.		

Internal Business Processes:	Actual	Goal
Scrap Percentage		1.5%
This Month	2.2%	
This Quarter	2.4%	
Last Year	2.4%	
Direct Labor Percentage		10.0%
This Month	16.9%	
This Quarter	17.7%	
Last Year	15.1%	
Machine Utilization		75%
This Month	58.0%	
This Quarter	42.0%	
Last Year	76.0%	

Exhibit 14.10 Sample Balanced Scorecard

The best solution is to contact the auditors whenever such an accounting decision is being discussed internally to obtain their informal opinion regarding the proper accounting treatment. A supplemental method is for the controller to write a memo on current and forthcoming accounting issues at the end of each quarter and circulate it to the CEO, CFO, audit committee, and the audit partner for their comments. By using both techniques in combination, the accounting department keeps all relevant internal users of the financial statements aware of accounting issues and makes it much less likely that there will be any restatement surprises at the end of the fiscal year.

Cost: Installation time: 🕐 🕐

14–17 Create a Contract Terms Database   ✔ *Author's Choice*

It is a common occurrence for the accounting department to forget about the terms of various agreements other departments of a company entered into, resulting in missed billings to customers or payments to suppliers. Due to the special nature of these agreements, which fall outside of the usual accounts payable and receivable systems, it is easy for them to be forgotten. Examples of these contracts are billings for the sublease of company equipment, rebates, and maintenance agreements. The typical result of these problems is either missing revenue, because customers were not billed, or irate suppliers that were not paid. In the latter case, missing payments to suppliers may also result in the failure of key services to the company, such as failed maintenance agreements for key equipment. Thus, a lack of attention to the terms of a company's various contractual arrangements can result in lost revenues or services.

The solution is to create a database of all current contractual agreements, along with a central file containing copies of all the contracts. An example of a contract terms database is shown in Exhibit 14.11. This database lists all of the key information about each contract, including the due date on which billings or payments are supposed to occur, the termination date of the contract, the frequency with which activities are required, the amounts involved, and any extra details to clarify the nature of each transaction—in short, a brief but thorough summarization of all the activities needed to fulfill the terms of all contracts. In case there are questions about the terms of each agreement, the accounting department should maintain copies of all agreements, as well as an extra file containing any agreements that have expired in the last few years. This arrangement will quickly bring order to the administration of any contracts that are the responsibility of the accounting department.

The implication thus far has been to create a contract terms database from scratch. However, it is also possible to purchase a commercial off-the-shelf product from a number of suppliers. These systems are usually linked to a company's enterprise resource planning (ERP) or customer relationship management (CRM) software, so they can access information stored elsewhere in the company. This linkage requires a custom-built interface. Depending on the amount of contractual information to be included in the installed system, one can expect the implementation of such a system to extend from at least two months up to a year. The cost of these systems begins at about $150,000 for a small installation and can easily reach several million dollars for a large company, depending on the number of users. Some special features make this software worth the price, for example, the ability to pinpoint contract wording that may impact revenue recognition, such as

Exhibit 14.11 Sample Contract Terms Database: ABC Company
Agreements Summary

Due Date	Termination Date	Frequency	Amount	Name	Details
Last Day	7/31/11	Monthly	$90	Smith, Joseph	Lease on Pickup Truck
Mid-Aug.	Ongoing	Annual	$.01 per lb.	English Polymers	Rebate of $.01 for Every Pound Purchased in Previous 12-Month Period
After Mtg.	Ongoing	Quarterly	$250	Board of Advisors	Advisory Fee Paid to These People Immediately after Each Advisory Meeting
End of Quarter	2018	Quarterly	$12,500	Limited Partner	$50,000 pd. in Quarterly Installments, But Not to Exceed 10% of Pretax Income (Less Cost of Health Insurance) + Out-of-Pocket Expenses
None	8/31/11	Annual	$980	E-Net Cellular	Service Plan for Portable Phones
None	6/30/12	Annual	$80	Dept. of Agriculture	License Fee for Scales 1 × 2,001 lb. 12 × 50 lb. Scales
None	5/31/13	Annual	$2,700	Masterson	Annual Extended Warranty
None	5/20/11	Annual	N/A	E Prime	5% Reduction in Natural Gas Prices
None	4/1/12	Annual	$2,208	NowComm	Phone Maintenance
None	10/1/13	Monthly	$1,248	Rogers Mechanical	Building Preventive Maintenance
None	9/30/14	Monthly	$1,000	Single Source	Bill Them for Monthly Lease of Space
None	None	Quarterly	$202	Pitney Bowes	Lease on Postage Machine
None	None	Monthly	$1,150	Local Janitorial	Daily Janitorial Services
None	10/24/12	Monthly	$265	Forklift Specialists	Maintenance on 3 Forklifts
None	4/30/12	Monthly	$29,339	Dean, Struthers, Markson	Building Lease

acceptance clauses and extended payment terms. This is particularly valuable in avoiding embarrassing adjustments to the level of revenue recognized in order to be in compliance with GAAP and SEC rules.

Another feature is a warning indicator when one customer is being offered a lower price than other customers, which flags other contractual agreements in which other customers are guaranteed the lowest price offered. By spotting this problem in advance, a company can avoid having to rebate payments to other customers in order to bring the prices they paid down to the price level of the most recent customer contract.

Most of these software packages also offer a library of standard contract terms, so that a company can extract the boilerplate text it needs to construct new contracts much more quickly. By doing so, one can also ensure that the same text is used across all contracts, thereby ensuring a fair degree of uniformity.

Cost: 💵💵 **Installation time:** ⏰

14–18 Install a Knowledge Management System

Too many accounting managers rely solely upon themselves for the generation of ideas, treating their staffs simply as workers who do what they are told. This command-level management approach ignores a potentially vast amount of worker expertise. While the primary cause of this problem is the mind-set of the accounting manager, there are software systems available that can assist in collecting ideas from employees.

These systems are called knowledge management systems (KMSs). A KMS is not a glorified suggestion box (though it does have that function!). In addition to accepting suggestions, it also focuses contributors onto several key challenges identified by corporate management, establishes bulletin boards on which related comments can be posted, and keeps contributors updated with the latest posted comments. In addition, management can assign suggestions to groups of in-house experts for evaluation, score their comments, and assign approved suggestions for implementation. Thus, a KMS covers the entire workflow associated with employee suggestions, assuring that they are reviewed, approved, and implemented in a timely manner. Such systems are really designed for large organizations, and are priced accordingly (a mid-five-figure price tag is the minimum starting point).

Cost: 💵💵💵 **Installation time:** ⏰⏰

14–19 Monitor Fixed Assets with Wireless Sensors

There can be considerable uncertainty about when to replace a fixed asset, which impacts the capital allocation decision. Wireless sensors can help. These devices can monitor changes in lighting, position, temperature, humidity, incline, vibration, and pitch/roll/yaw. When configured as wireless devices that transmit from difficult-to-reach locations, they are ideal for monitoring the condition of fixed assets, especially those on the factory floor. A typical setup is for the sensor to transmit a wireless signal to a local router when it senses a significant change, which passes the data along to a computer, which, in turn, matches the data against a predetermined out-of-specification condition. If the reported condition is considered to be outside the predetermined boundary, then the computer sends a warning email to the appropriate person.

Although wireless sensors have been available for several years, the key improvement that allows for their more widespread use is the Zigbee communication protocol, which is designed for devices with low data transmission rates and low power consumption. This protocol allows sensors to run for well over a year on a single battery. Also, a recent estimate of the cost of a Zigbee-configured radio is just $1.10 (when produced in high volume), though the radio must be coupled with a sensor device that raises its total price considerably.

The wireless sensor is extremely useful for determining the exact moment when a fixed asset is failing, since the asset's temperature or level of vibration may rise by a measurable amount shortly before it fails. By monitoring these key indicators, management can determine precisely when asset replacement is needed, rather than guessing and either replacing it much too soon or waiting until it fails, precipitating a replacement crisis.

Cost: 💵💵   **Installation time:** ⏰⏰

14–20 Create an Online Tax Policy Listing

The accounting staff does not always have a clear grasp of the tax implications of various accounting transactions. Examples of these problem areas are transfer pricing, capital movements, and employee contracts and benefits. When a question arises in regard to such a problem, either it is put on hold while a question is run past the legal or tax staffs or else it is processed in ignorance of the answer— which frequently leads to a lack of consistency in the handling of transactions, and a large headache for the tax staff. These problems can be avoided by installing a clear set of tax policies online.

By itemizing the most current tax policies online, anyone in the accounting department can readily research problems and expect to find answers within a few minutes of a tax-related question being posed. If the answer is not there, then the site can also include an email linkage to the tax or legal department, so that the problem can then be properly researched and posted online for the next person who has the same problem. Also, because the posting is online, there is no need to issue a cumbersome mailing to a list of approved recipients every time a change is made to the policies; instead, the change can be readily made to the online posting, which makes it available to anyone at once. Certainly, there will be complex transactional situations that are so unique that only the advice of a trained tax person will yield the correct answer to a query. Nonetheless, the majority of tax problems can be resolved for the accounting staff by this simple means.

Cost: 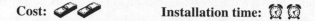 **Installation time:** 🕰 🕰

14–21 Designate a Tax Liaison for Each Government Jurisdiction

A company with multiple locations will undoubtedly have taxation issues with a variety of government entities, each of which collects taxes under a separate set of rules, forms, and timetables. The usual approach to dealing with these jurisdictions is to research problems only when contacted by one of them. This results in a crisis level of review work at the last minute, which can result in incorrect decisions regarding how to address each tax issue.

A better approach is to assign tax liaison responsibility to several members of the accounting staff (or tax staff, if this is a separate group). Each person is responsible for obtaining contact information for his or her counterpart within the assigned government. This can include establishing contact and building relations, but only if the amount of ongoing contact over tax issues warrants the level of work involved. Each liaison should know what problems the company has had in the past with the assigned jurisdiction, and be aware of any current issues over which the jurisdiction has recently contacted the company. The liaison should become the lead person for all contacts, as well as for making recommendations to management for how to deal with current tax issues (as supported by knowledgeable legal counsel, of course).

By using tax liaisons, a company can deal with tax problems in a proactive manner, and be considered a good tax "citizen" by the various government jurisdictions with which it deals on a regular basis. However, this approach is cost-effective only if there is a sufficient level of ongoing taxation issues to warrant the time commitment involved.

Cost: 💵 **Installation time:** 🕰 🕰

14–22 Assign Tax Staff to Business Units

The tax staff tends to work in a reactive mode, whereby it passes judgment on operational decisions after they have occurred. By doing so, some operational activities must be altered after they have been initiated, due to unfavorable tax results, while in other cases the tax staff must scramble to mitigate unfavorable tax situations.

These concerns can be eliminated by assigning senior members of the tax staff to the various business units as tax advisors. This is by no means full-time work; it is intended only to give each business unit manager an assigned tax contact who is available to answer taxation-related questions, as well as to review business plans for activities that may have a tax impact. This is likely to result in monthly meetings between the two parties. This approach is also a good way to develop close links between the tax department and other areas of the company, so that tax staff are considered to be helpful resources.

Cost: 💵   **Installation time:** ⏰ ⏰

14–23 Outsource Tax Form Preparation

For smaller firms, the accurate and timely preparation of tax forms is a monumental pain that frequently results in missed filing dates, incorrect payments, and penalties. The reason is that a smaller organization cannot afford the services of a full-time tax accountant, which means that incoming tax forms are routed to whomever has time to complete them. No one likes to do tax forms and so they end up at the bottom of someone's work pile, resulting in a last-minute rush to complete them, without much regard to accuracy or filing dates. Larger organizations do not have this problem, since they have specialists on staff who can organize a steady stream of tax work, resulting in accurate tax filings mailed out precisely on time and that are supported by fully documented work papers. Thus, the controller of a small company needs to find a better way to prepare tax forms.

The solution is to outsource the bulk of the tax filings to one or more suppliers, usually with a few tax returns remaining in-house. A common situation is for a company's audit firm to take over all federal and state income tax returns. These are among the most complex returns to file, and these are precisely the forms that most audit firms specialize in filing. In addition, many companies outsource their payroll so the payroll-processing suppliers will handle all of the tax return information related to payroll. This leaves local returns, which are best kept in-house—these documents are usually so specialized that suppliers do not have any experience in filing them and so are no more efficient (and much more expensive) than the accounting employees who can do the same work. Thus, there are opportunities to divest an accounting department of the majority of its tax form preparation work.

There are two factors to consider when outsourcing tax work. First, some suppliers will charge an inordinate amount to prepare a tax return. To avoid this problem, it is wise to first inquire about the hourly rates of the supplier's staff who are most likely to prepare taxes and the likely time required to complete each return. If the expected amount is too high, it may be useful to comparison-shop against the rates of other tax preparation firms. It may also be possible to institute a fixed fee for each tax return, thereby capping the expense. Second, there is some inefficiency in separating the tax filing work from the outside auditors a company already uses. The reason is that the auditor must copy the work papers and send them to the tax supplier, which is not only an extra expense, but also slower than leaving all of the work with the auditor. Despite these problems, it is a very good idea for a smaller firm to outsource the preparation of its tax returns.

Cost: 💵💵   **Installation time:** ⏰

14–24 Submit Electronic Tax Returns to the IRS

The standard procedure for a smaller company is to have a local tax professional prepare its tax returns, after which the company controller reviews the return, verifies that all pages have been attached, and mails it to the IRS. During this process, there is a risk that some attachments will be lost or misplaced, or that the entire return will be lost, either by the mail room, the Postal Service, or the IRS.

It is possible to avoid these risks with the IRS's e-filing service that allows for the electronic submission of essentially all corporate tax forms and related attachments. It also results in fast acknowledgment by the IRS of receipt. In addition, the IRS automatically checks the returns for errors and missing information, so fixes can be made immediately.

The e-filing program is mandatory for companies having assets greater than $10 million and that file more than 250 returns per year, but smaller firms can certainly file by this means as well.

A company must submit Form 8633 to apply for admission into the e-filing program, or can have an IRS-authorized e-file provider handle the submission. A number of tax-software providers have linked their systems to the IRS system, so there are multiple ways to submit tax returns.

Cost: 💵   **Installation time:** ⏰

14–25 Pay Federal Taxes Online

There are a number of taxes that a company must pay to the federal government, such as unemployment insurance, Medicare, Social Security, withheld income taxes, and corporate income taxes. Since this can involve a substantial amount of money, companies tend to wait until the last minute to deposit them, usually through the local bank. If there is no one available to go to the bank to transfer the funds to the government, or if the bank is closed for any reason, then the company will be penalized for late payments. This is a particular problem when only a few people know how to make the deposits and they are unavailable for any reason on the day when a payment is required.

These problems can be resolved by making online payments to the federal government through its free *www.eftps.gov* site. This involves creating an account with the government online through its "New Taxpayer Enrollment Form" and then waiting up to 15 days for the IRS to mail a personal identification number (PIN) number to you. Once received, a company can then request an Internet password and submit tax payments at any time of the day or night, seven days a week. The government then transfers the designated funds out of the company bank account. A printable confirmation is made available, which a company can retain as proof of payment to the government. A transaction history is also available online for all payments made within the last 120 days. It is even possible to schedule payments up to 120 days prior to a tax payment due date, so the government can automatically withdraw the required funds on a targeted date without anyone from the company having to be present. Though the implication here is that payments are only authorized through an Internet site, a company can also do this over the phone or with downloaded PC-based software that uses a dial-up modem.

Once a company's total tax remittances to the federal government exceed $200,000 per year, it *must* use this system. If a company that is required to use the system then chooses to make a manual payment with a tax coupon, it will be subject to a 10 percent penalty (though this does not apply to voluntary participants that fall below the $200,000 threshold). Also, if a company pays taxes from a variety of bank accounts, it must set up different accounts with the government for each bank account, since there is currently no way for the government to remove funds from multiple accounts through the electronic funds payment transfer system (EFTPS) system. Finally, the system cannot be used to make last-minute payments; instead, transfers must be initiated no later than the day before a tax payment is due, in order to ensure that the IRS receives it in time.

Cost: 💸   Installation time: ⏰

14–26 Subscribe to an Online Tax Information Service

Congress is constantly tinkering with the tax laws, while the IRS continues to issue a flood of interpretations in response to new tax situations. Consequently, it is extremely difficult to stay current on which changes in the tax code apply to a company's specific circumstances. Many companies solve this problem by hiring a CPA firm that specializes in taxation issues. However, the cost of this service is extremely high; moreover, the people working for the CPA firm may not be aware of ongoing operational issues at a company that may impact its tax situation.

A good alternative is to subscribe to an online tax information service, such as the CCH Internet Tax Research Network or the RIA Federal Tax Product Packages. These services allow one to conduct searches on a wide range of tax topics, including the IRS Code, executive orders, pending and enacted legislation, U.S. tax treaties, and individual tax acts. These services update their databases of tax information as soon as new information becomes available, which makes this a better source of information than CD-based products. Also, search features allow one to quickly hone in on all tax information pertaining to a specific topic.

The downside of these services is their cost, which generally falls into the range of $2,000 to $5,000 per year, depending on the scope of services purchased. Also, these subscriptions only provide information—they are no substitute for the expertise that can only be acquired through years of tax research, so a company should continue to regularly consult with its tax advisors. Thus, an online tax information service should be considered a supplement to other sources of tax information and advice, rather than a replacement.

Cost: **Installation time:** 🕰

14–27 Move Intellectual Property to an Offshore Holding Company

A company's intellectual property (IP), in the form of patents and trademarks, can be an extremely valuable resource that can generate millions of dollars in royalties from patent licensees. Given the high profit percentage on IP, a company may find that a significant proportion of its total income taxes are paid on just its IP portfolio.

A way to reduce the tax liability is to shift a company's IP to an offshore intellectual property holding company that is sited in a low-tax jurisdiction. Any earnings on the IP will then be taxed at the lower rate of the offshore jurisdiction. There are several ways to effect this transfer:

• Create a cost-sharing agreement with a holding company before IP is completed, under which international revenue rights are shifted to the holding company.

• Create an offshore research and development facility, so that IP originates in a low-tax jurisdiction.

• Shift the economic rights to the IP to the holding company, rather than the IP itself.

Of course, this strategy must include consideration of the company's ability to eventually repatriate earnings from the foreign tax jurisdiction.

Cost: 💵   **Installation time:** 🕰🕰

14–28 Create Accounting Training Teams

A key problem for accounting managers is how to determine the correct amount and type of training to require of their employees. Sending them to degree programs is too expensive and only provides relevant training for a small proportion of the time spent being trained. Shorter programs are more targeted, but are still expensive and may not directly relate to work requirements. For these reasons, many accounting managers do not allow any training, or only under very restricted circumstances. By doing so, they are limiting the skill sets of their employees and not allowing them to fulfill personal career advancement goals, which may result in increased employee turnover.

A solution is the use of internal accounting training teams. The basic process is to conduct a periodic survey of employees and job functions to determine what types of training programs are needed. A consultant or manager-level employee then creates the general course syllabus for each training program (consultants can be useful here, since managers may not have sufficient available time to work on syllabi). Each syllabus is then handed over to a group of in-house accounting staff, who become responsible for creating the details of each course, and teaching it. A manager is typically assigned to each course to oversee its development and act as a mentor.

The primary advantage of this approach is that training can be precisely tailored to a company's exact needs, throwing out all irrelevant topics that might otherwise be taught during a university-sponsored class. Because of their extreme specificity, these classes are also usually quite short, allowing employees to either fit them into daytime schedules or into abbreviated evening training sessions. Examples of training topics under this approach could be process-centering techniques, methodologies for finding cost-cutting approaches within specific transactions, and training on specific functions within the company's accounting software. Also, by bringing together trainers from all parts of the accounting organization, from administrative assistants to the CFO, the level of communication will likely improve. Finally, because all training classes are created and taught in-house, the incremental cost of classes is reduced.

Cost: 💵💵   **Installation time:** ⏰⏰

14–29 Create an Ongoing Training Program for All Accounting Personnel

The efficiency and effectiveness of an accounting department are based on many factors, but a crucial one all too many controllers ignore is training. Many accounting managers simply assume that their staffs have acquired all the knowledge they need in college and in subsequent work experience and need no further training of any kind. This belief is based on the erroneous assumption that all accounting practices are the same, no matter where accountants work, and that employees can be neatly swapped between jobs and companies with no additional training of any kind. Over the long term, this can have a major impact on the accounting staff, for the following reasons:

- *Accounting rule changes.* The accounting profession is constantly reviewing changes in how accounting transactions are completed and reported, resulting in a multitude of rule changes, especially in the area of financial reporting. Anyone who has not received formal training in these changes within the past few years must receive training in all rules updates, while those not having been trained in a decade or more will require comprehensive retraining.

- *Computer-specific knowledge.* There are many accounting software packages in use, all with their own quirks and foibles. Each of these packages requires special training before employees will fully comprehend how to use them most effectively, as well as (perhaps more importantly) what *not* to do, since some systems require expert usage to run properly.

- *Lack of management training.* Accounting is not just clerical—it requires an excellent knowledge of how to manage processes in a multitude of functional areas, frequently including employees in outlying locations. Without proper management training, there will almost certainly be gross inefficiencies and errors in the department.

- *Lack of process training.* The accounting function, above all others, deals with processes, such as the revenue cycle or the purchasing cycle. All employees in this department must have a clear knowledge of exactly how these processes work so they can process information through them most efficiently, as well as make modifications that will further increase the level of efficiency. Though some of this knowledge can be gleaned through many years of experience, it is best to cut short this interval through a training program that imparts both the fundamentals and the detailed steps involved in all key company processes.

- *Lack of training for advanced positions.* Though employees may be adequately trained in their existing jobs, this does not mean that they are in any way prepared to take over positions higher in the accounting hierarchy. Without the necessary training to prepare them for these positions, employees may become frustrated and leave for other companies willing to provide the training for more advanced and higher-paying jobs.

- *Practices that are industry-specific.* Many industries have accounting practices that are completely unique. An example of this is the gambling industry, which has an extreme orientation toward the collection, handling, and recording of cash coming from the gambling floor. In these industries, it is dangerous to bring in people from other industries without first giving them a sufficient degree of training in industry-specific accounting practices.

The types of training classes administered may vary considerably from the rote accounting topics that are covered in a traditional business college. For example, Allied-Signal includes the following topics in its accounting and finance curriculum:

- Accounting for business combinations
- Activity-based management

- Business controls
- Cash-flow management
- Coaching and career management
- Controllership
- Diversity
- E-commerce
- Financial planning and analysis
- Global finance
- Management accounting
- Mergers and acquisitions
- Six sigma
- Supply-chain management
- Taxation
- Revenue-chain management

All of these reasons sum up strongly in favor of a detailed and prolonged training program for the entire accounting department covering such areas as software, processes, new pronouncements by the Financial Accounting Standards Board (FASB), industry-specific issues, and general management training.

The best way to set up a training program is to make a list of all positions in the accounting department and determine the training strengths and weaknesses of every person occupying those positions. Then a master list of all possible training must be assembled, with the required training for each person noted on the master list. An example of such a list is shown in Exhibit 14.12, which lists the training program for a variety of software modules in an accounting software package. It is also useful to maintain a list of credit hours for continuing professional education, in case employees want to pursue or maintain professional accreditation.

The main problem with training programs is that employees usually must be forced to complete their scheduled training, since they find that there is not enough time in the midst of their other activities to fit it in. To avoid this issue, the controller should schedule a monthly review of completed training to ensure that all employees are meeting their training goals. Also, one should incorporate training goals into the targets that employees must meet each year in order to be given pay raises or bonuses. Further, the internal audit staff may also schedule an occasional review of all training records to ensure that employees are indeed completing their training work and not falsely reporting training hours that never happened. When combined, all of these measures will ensure a thorough and comprehensive training program that will improve employee knowledge, especially in regard to improving and managing systems, while also reducing the risk of employee turnover.

Cost: 💵💵   Installation time: ⏰⏰

Accounting Department Training
[Lists dates of completion for modules with 80+% scores]

	Abdullah, B.	Bronson, C.	Cavez, T.	Dingle, D.
General Ledger Account Structure				
Maintaining a chart of accounts	8/1/XX			6/15/XX
Entering a new organization	8/1/XX			
Maintaining account groups	8/1/XX		6/30/XX	6/15/XX
Using organization groups	8/1/XX		6/30/XX	
Setting up the bank master	8/1/XX		6/30/XX	
General Ledger Transaction Processing				
Entering new journal entries		12/12/XX		
Changing existing journal entries		12/12/XX		
Creating journal entry template		12/12/XX		
Using journal entry template		12/12/XX		5/29/XX
Creating recurring journal entries		12/12/XX		
Deleting a journal entry		12/12/XX		
Approving batches		12/12/XX		
Posting batches to journal entries		12/12/XX		
Using statistical journal entries				
Period close	5/31/XX			5/29/XX
Budgeting				
Budget definitions	11/30/XX			
Updating a budget	11/30/XX			
Printing a budget	11/30/XX			
Copying a budget	11/30/XX			
Product costing				
Establishing item standard costs				8/31/XX
Establishing standard costs for assemblies				8/31/XX
Inquiry screens				8/31/XX
Accumulating order costs with average actual costing				8/31/XX
Managing order costs with average actual costing			3/1/XX	8/31/XX
Managing mfg. order costs using standard costing			3/1/XX	8/31/XX
Managing purchase order costs with standard costing			3/1/XX	8/31/XX
Inventory value reporting			3/1/XX	8/31/XX
Accounts Payable Invoice Entry				
Entering an invoice			4/7/XX	
Matching an invoice to a PO receipt			4/7/XX	
Entering an invoice not associated with a PO			4/7/XX	
Tools to use for vendor inquiries			4/7/XX	
Approving an invoice for payment			4/7/XX	
Placing an invoice on hold			4/7/XX	
Taking vendor discounts			4/7/XX	
Miscellaneous disbursements			4/7/XX	
Accounts Payable Processing				
Setting up a payment run			4/9/XX	
Recording a manual payment			4/9/XX	
Voiding a payment			4/9/XX	
Tools to use in a bank reconciliation			4/9/XX	

Exhibit 14.12 Sample Master Training Schedule

14–30   Create Computer-Based Training Movies

There are several major problems with any in-house training program. It must be carefully scheduled so that the maximum number of people can attend (which means that some people will *not* be able to attend, or at least will be seriously inconvenienced). Also, an expensive trainer and training facility must be used. Furthermore, people must travel to the training site for classes, which may entail great expense. All of these problems can be avoided through the use of computer-based training movies.

A computer-based training movie is one that replicates on-screen the actions of someone who is walking through a standard set of activities, while explaining each action through a microphone. The resulting movie will show a user exactly what is being done to process a transaction while the accompanying voice recording explains what is going on. Just as is the case with a movie that is stored on a DVD, this movie format contains on-screen buttons for rewind, pause, play, and fast forward. Each movie is easily created—just plot out the steps to be followed during the movie, practice them a few times, and then press the "record" button and start recording the movie. The audio portion of the movie can be added concurrently, or at a later time.

By storing computer-based training movies at a central intranet location, a company can make it available to all employees at all company locations. Employees can download it at their leisure and review those portions about which they are uncertain. When training movies are made for a wide range of company functions, they can be set up in an index format on the intranet site, so that an entire training program can be made available to employees on a wide range of topics. The only problems with computer-based movies are that they take up a large amount of computer storage space, and that all accessing computers require audio cards and speakers. However, these are minor cost issues.

Cost: Installation time:

14–31   Implement Cross-Training for Mission-Critical Activities

There are a number of crucial accounting activities that will cause a significant amount of disturbance within a company if they are not completed on time, every time. Examples of these activities are payroll, since employees will refuse to work unless they are paid, and accounts payable, for suppliers will refuse to provide additional goods and services unless *they* are paid. In these cases and others, the greatest risk is that only one person knows how to process transactions. If that person leaves the company or is incapacitated for any reason, there can be a serious system failure that will quickly bring the entire company to a grinding halt.

The best way to avoid this dependency on a single person is to implement cross-training, using other accounting employees. By doing so, there is far less risk that mission-critical activities will not be performed in a reliable manner, which greatly reduces the chance that any key activity will not be completed on time. To do so, there should be a schedule of key activities for which there is a listing of required training elements. The controller should identify those personnel who are most qualified to act as back-ups, put them through the training regimen, and ensure that they receive continual retraining, so they can easily step into the needed jobs. A small pay hike for those employees receiving cross-training will ensure their enthusiastic participation in this system. The key factor to remember is that training alone does not make for a good back-up person— only continual hands-on practice under the direct tutelage of the person who is currently responsible for the work will ensure that this best practice will work.

The only people who ever oppose this practice are those who are currently in charge of mission-critical functions. This is because they feel more valuable if they are the only ones who can complete a task and will feel less useful if there is someone else who can also do the same work. Overcoming this problem requires a great deal of tact and diplomacy. Sometimes they continue to be hostile to the concept and must be removed to other positions while their replacements figure out the system without any support at all. These are difficult alternatives, but must be followed through if there is to be an adequate degree of cross-training in key functional areas.

Cost: **Installation time:**

Total Impact of Best Practices on General Accounting Functions

This section covers the impact of the best practices described in this chapter on the general administration of the accounting department.

Accounting processes attract most of the attention in this chapter, since there are best practices here for outsourcing some processes, using process-centering in other cases, and consolidating others. They are noted in Exhibit 14.13. The manner in which these best practices should be installed is that all outsourcing opportunities should be identified and completed first, followed by any needed consolidation of activities into the smallest number of locations. By taking these steps first, a company does not waste time reviewing existing processes that are about to be eliminated or moved elsewhere. After these tasks are completed, it is time to conduct a thorough review of all processes, increase the number of process tasks assigned to individual employees (i.e., process-centering), and then set up a continual process review system to constantly analyze them for further improvements. By taking this approach, one can achieve a remarkable improvement in the efficiency of all accounting processes.

There are also several best practices related to accounting personnel, which involve training and job standardization. They are shown in the middle of Exhibit 14.13. By implementing them all, one can not only arrive at a department that

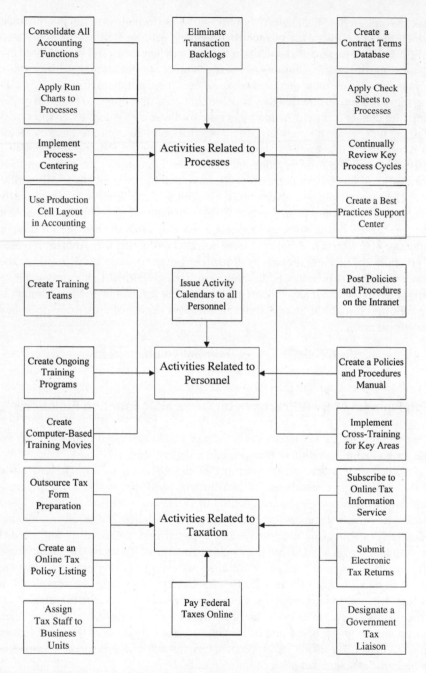

Exhibit 14.13 Impact of Best Practices on General Accounting Functions

knows exactly what to do and when to do it, but also one that experiences a much lower degree of turnover. The smaller number of employee departures is caused by the reduced level of anxiety that goes hand in hand with the fewer problems that are the end result of standardizing jobs and increasing the level of training.

Summary

This chapter covered a number of best practices that address problems in three main areas—processes, personnel, and reporting.

Many best practices covered issues in the area of accounting process, with principal recommendations covering the outsourcing of smaller functions, consolidating accounting functions, setting up a database of contract terms, as well as a knowledge management system, and focusing closely on the organization of employees around processes. These changes can bring about a major improvement in the efficiency of accounting processes.

Other best practices focused on accounting employees. A highly focused and organized training program is needed, especially when combined with cross-training for key activities, a policies and procedures manual, and a calendar of activities. These improvements will help to convert the accounting department into a highly knowledgeable and well-coordinated group.

Finally, three best practices target changes in the reporting function. One uses on-line reporting to ensure that information is disseminated as inexpensively and widely as possible, while Balanced Scorecard and function measurements are needed to determine the progress of the corporation as a whole and of individual departments, respectively, in achieving their goals. Though the reporting changes will not have an immediate impact on the efficiency of the accounting department, they will assist in informing management of companywide activities, resulting in better control over overall operations.

Chapter 15

General Ledger
Best Practices

In most of this book, the primary basis for best practices is simplification in order to achieve an enhanced level of efficiency. Though there are best practices that can streamline the general ledger in a similar manner, this is one of the rare cases where pursuing a higher degree of complexity will sometimes achieve a greater overall benefit for the entire company. The two best practices that follow this approach are restructuring the general ledger to allow for the use of activity-based costing, and using it as a data warehouse. In both cases, there are significant start-up costs and much more work for the accounting staff, but the level of information that this practice provides to the rest of the organization is greatly enhanced. Thus, there are a few situations where greater cost and complexity can be beneficial.

In addition, there are the usual streamlining actions to reduce the work needed to maintain the general ledger. These best practices include restricting the use of journal entries, automating interfaces with subsidiary ledgers, and simplifying the chart of accounts. Though all of these measures will certainly reduce the work of the general ledger accountant, one should strongly consider adding the best practices for activity-based costing and data warehousing, which will increase that person's work, because it will be so beneficial to the remainder of the company.

This chapter covers best practices for the general ledger function, as well as a series of implementation issues for each best practice, which are discussed in the next section.

Implementation Issues for General Ledger Best Practices

This section describes the general level of implementation difficulty for all of the best practices discussed in this chapter. Two levels of implementation difficulty are covered in Exhibit 15.1, which shows the general level of cost and duration to implement each best practice.

In general, the level of implementation difficulty is higher for general ledger best practices than for other functional areas because changes in this area either involve major programming work or significant alterations to the way in which

Exhibit 15.1 Summary of General Ledger Best Practices

	Best Practice	Cost	Install Time
Chart of Accounts			
15–1	Eliminate small-balance accounts	💵	🕐
15–2	Modify account code structure for storage of ABC information	💵	🕐🕐
15–3	Create alphanumeric department/subsidiary codes	💵	🕐🕐
15–4	Reduce the chart of accounts	💵	🕐🕐
15–5	Use identical chart of accounts for subsidiaries	💵💵	🕐🕐🕐
Data Warehousing			
15–6	Use data warehouse for report distribution	💵💵💵	🕐🕐🕐
15–7	Use forms/rates data warehouse for automated tax filings	💵💵💵	🕐🕐🕐
15–8	Use the general ledger as a data warehouse	💵	🕐🕐
General			
15–9	Restrict use of journal entries	💵	🕐
15–10	Avoid general ledger posting bottlenecks	💵	🕐
15–11	Have subsidiaries update their own data in the central general ledger	💵💵	🕐🕐
15–12	Prescreen construction-in-progress entries	💵	🕐
System Additions			
15–13	Construct automated interfaces to software that summarizes into the general ledger	💵💵💵	🕐🕐🕐
15–14	Create general ledger drill-down capability	💵💵💵	🕐🕐🕐
15–15	Use automated error-checking	💵💵💵	🕐🕐🕐

a company conducts its business. For example, one best practice is to switch the chart of accounts over to a structure that will allow a company to accumulate information for an activity-based costing system more easily; however, altering the chart of accounts always involves setting up new methods for collecting data, which can require major procedural changes throughout a company. In short, since the general ledger is the core data collection point in a company, alterations to it will have a ripple effect that may impact distant corners of the organization that the change initiator never anticipated.

Though many of the implementations listed in Exhibit 15.1 are described as being of long duration or expensive, many of them can still be cost-effective ways to improve the efficiency of the accounting department. However, given the potential costs, it is mandatory, in this functional area, above all others, that a controller conduct a thorough investigation and comparison of the costs and benefits associated with any best practice-related changes. An implementation should proceed only after this step has been taken.

15–1 Eliminate Small-Balance Accounts   ✔*Author's Choice*

If the general ledger accountant is in the habit of maintaining a record of all the transactions in all accounts, there can be a considerable workload in store if there are many accounts. This practice is particularly common for balance sheet accounts, where it is necessary to keep track of all asset and liability records so that they can be reviewed during the year-end audit. If there are fewer accounts, there is less maintenance work needed to update a listing of the detailed records in each account.

Accordingly, a minor and easily implemented best practice is to periodically review the balances in the balance sheet accounts and merge them into larger accounts if the current balances are quite small. This task can be included in the financial statement preparation procedure as a standard item so that someone reviews the size of accounts on a regular basis and eliminates a few as necessary. There are no downsides to this best practice since it requires minimal work, reduces the clutter in the balance sheet, and does not interfere with the proper recording of information.

Cost: **Installation time:** 🕰

15–2 Modify Account Code Structure for Storage
of ABC Information

The general ledger accountant is frequently drawn into any activity-based costing (ABC) project because of his or her knowledge of the existing account structure. This accountant is commonly asked to set up a mapping program that translates the regular chart of accounts into a different (sometimes *much* different) chart of accounts that will be used to compile information for an ABC analysis. This analysis then compiles the costs of various products or activities throughout the company, which usually results in better management decisions and a greater level of profitability. Though this sounds like a reasonable task, involvement in an ABC project requires a startlingly large amount of time, perhaps even full-time participation for a number of months. The reason for such a heavy involvement is that the existing chart of accounts rarely accumulates data in the same way that an ABC analysis requires. For example, a traditional chart of accounts stores expense information by department, whereas an ABC system needs to have this information stored by activity center (such as a machine). Thus, when an ABC system is installed, the general ledger accountant may not only expect a considerable increase in the current workload, but may even require a replacement to fill in for all previous work while the ABC project is continuing.

A possible solution to this change in workload is to alter the chart of accounts, at least in part, so that information is stored in the manner the ABC system uses. By storing information in the ABC format right away, there is no need for the general ledger accountant to spend additional time reformatting it. This can be quite a difficult best practice to implement, for several reasons. First, it requires the transfer of expense information from old accounts to new ones, as well as the alteration of all entries to the general ledger, so that all new information is redirected in a similar manner. Also, all reports derived from the general ledger must be altered so that they draw information from the new accounts instead. The greatest problem of all is that the recipients of the revised reports may not be at all pleased to find that the information they are accustomed to receiving has been substantially altered. For example, a department manager may find that there is no longer a department expense report, but instead an expense report grouped by machine. The best way around all of these difficulties is to set up automatic distributions within the general ledger so that expenses are still routed to the same accounts, but the accounts are then allocated out to a different set of ABC accounts for further ABC analysis. Unfortunately, the account allocation feature is not normally available in less expensive general ledger software packages, so this option is usually only available to larger corporations. A lesser alternative is to alter just a small portion of general ledger accounts so that they can be used for ABC work, leaving the main accounts as they are and relying on a manual conversion of data for these accounts. This approach has the advantage of not altering the existing financial reports to any significant degree, but still requires a considerable amount of work by the general ledger accountant.

Despite all of the problems with converting the general ledger format to accommodate an ABC system, this is still worthwhile in many cases. Though there is no increase in efficiency for the general ledger function (quite the contrary), there will be a rapid and smooth flow of information into the ABC system, which will result in better management decisions, which in turn will have a direct impact on the profitability of the entire organization.

Cost: 💵   **Installation time:** ⏰ ⏰

15–3 Create Alphanumeric Department/Subsidiary Codes

The usual account code structure includes a four- or five-digit code that represents the main account, a hyphen, and then a two- or three-digit code that represents a department or subsidiary. Common usage states that these department and subsidiary codes be numeric. For example, the travel expense code might be 63000, with additional department digits that look like this:

- 63000-100 = Travel expense, administration department
- 63000-200 = Travel expense, engineering department
- 63000-300 = Travel expense, sales department

Alternatively, for a "flat file" chart of accounts that contains multiple companies, the travel expense code might look like this:

- 63000-100 = Travel expense, Gerber Geriatrics
- 63000-200 = Travel expense, Highline Supplies
- 63000-300 = Travel expense, Innovative Solutions

In both cases, the person entering journal entries or transactions must know the meaning of the department or subsidiary codes, which are not entirely obvious. The accounting software may reveal the account name in a byline, but the data-entry person has to glance at the byline to see it. If the person does not verify the accuracy of her entry, then it's entirely possible that she will code the transaction into the wrong department or subsidiary. Although most companies avoid this difficulty by assigning specific expense codes to vendor files and by using prebuilt recurring journal entries, there is still a significant risk that the use of purely numeric codes will result in incorrect charges to the wrong departments or subsidiaries.

The solution is simple enough. Many accounting software packages allow for the use of alphanumeric account codes, which allow one to assign meaning to a code. Even contracting a department name into a three-digit code leaves lots of room for meaning. To use the previous example for department coding, 63000-100 becomes 63000-ADM. Unless a company employs admirals, the obvious implication is that this is the administration department. Similarly for the subsidiary coding example, the obscure 63000-300 becomes 63000-INN, which would lead a user to conclude that it involves the Innovative Solutions subsidiary.

Cost: 💵   Installation time: ⏰ ⏰

15–4 Reduce the Chart of Accounts ✔*Author's Choice*

All too many organizations are burdened with an immense chart of accounts. Instead of having a short list of accounts in which to store information—such as 100 or 200 accounts—many organizations have a convoluted and lengthy chart of accounts.

The sheer length of such a list introduces a number of problems into the general ledger function. First, it is difficult to put numbers into the same accounts consistently time after time. Instead, they are recorded in different accounts, resulting in very poor comparability of information across time. Second, it can be very difficult to train a new general ledger accountant in the use of a very complicated chart of accounts; during the training period, it is likely that the accountant will make mistakes in recording financial information into the correct accounts, resulting in inaccurate financial statements. Third, it is also more expensive to audit a long chart of accounts since the outside auditors must spend more time reviewing more accounts. Finally, writing a new report with general ledger information is quite difficult if the information is being drawn from a veritable maze of accounts. In short, a plague of problems accompanies an excessively long chart of accounts.

The solution is one that takes a fair amount of work to implement. Though it seems simple—just reduce the number of active accounts in the chart of accounts—there are ancillary issues that require additional work. One problem with reducing the chart is that users may still continue to code expenses to the old accounts, if only out of habit. To stop this from happening, the old accounts that are being retired must be blocked from further use in the computer system. Though most computer systems now have this blocking feature, it is useful to determine its presence before proceeding further with an implementation. Another issue is that when the chart is reduced, it is much more difficult to create historical reports to compare account balances to those of previous periods. For example, if five accounts are merged into one consolidated account, it is difficult to show how the balance in the new account compares to the old balances in five accounts. There is no good way around this problem, unless the existing accounting software has a reporting feature that allows old accounts to be grouped for comparison purposes. This is a particular problem if the accounts are merged in the middle of a company's reporting year so that it is not even possible to compare financial results from month to month. The best solution to this problem is to undertake major chart of account conversions only at the very beginning of a reporting year so that there is no intra-year reporting problem. Another way to resolve the problem is to fix the chart of accounts over a number of years by eliminating only a small number of accounts each year, which does not impact the comparability of accounts in any one year to any great degree. A final issue is that information may be stored in an account strictly for inclusion in a report that has some special purpose; if the account is discontinued, the report can no longer be completed, which may be a source of irritation to the report recipient. To avoid this issue, it is necessary to review all reports generated from the general ledger and determine which accounts are used to create them. If the information in these special accounts is truly indispensable, they should be left alone.

Though a number of problems have been noted that can arise when the chart of accounts is streamlined, this is still a best practice immensely worthy of consideration. It is especially useful for older companies with many departments or subsidiaries, for these have frequently accumulated a large number of stray accounts over the years that should certainly be researched and eliminated. By doing so, it is much easier to maintain the general ledger.

Cost: Installation time: 🕰 🕰

15–5   Use Identical Chart of Accounts for Subsidiaries

✔ *Author's Choice*

If a company has a number of subsidiaries, the general ledger accountant will have a much more difficult time at the end of the financial reporting period, because the results of each subsidiary must be translated into the chart of accounts structure of the corporate parent. This can involve an enormous amount of work, because the information the subsidiaries send in may be in a chart of accounts structure that is so different from the one the parent uses that it is a matter of pure guesswork by the accountant to determine the correct accounts into which the subsidiary data should be recorded. This is a particularly galling problem if the subsidiaries are in an entirely different line of business, for this means that the chart of accounts may be substantially different; thus, consolidating account numbers is more of a problem if a company acquires disparate companies, as opposed to acquiring companies that are in the same industry.

There are several variations on the same best practice that will resolve this problem, as noted in the following bullet points. They range from merely requiring the permission of the corporate parent before a subsidiary alters its chart of accounts any further to requiring the substitution of the existing chart with the one the corporate parent uses. The bullet points are listed in ascending order of conformance, with the least amount of conformance being the easiest to implement and complete conformance being the most difficult to install. The particular variation selected may be dependent on the speed with which a company is buying other companies, since a complete replacement of a chart of accounts is a major undertaking and may not be possible if the rate of acquisition is extremely rapid. The best practice options are as follows:

- *Require permission to make account changes.* It may be necessary to leave the current situation alone, perhaps because there are too many subsidiaries and too few resources available to reset the chart of accounts structure across all subsidiaries. In this situation, the easiest step is to issue a blanket order to all subsidiaries that they cannot make further changes to their charts of accounts without permission from the corporate parent—in other words, the main action is not to make the situation any worse than it already is. This is an extremely minor action to take, since it is a rare event for a company to create new accounts once the basic chart of accounts has been completed.

- *Use a written map to lay out how accounts are linked.* A more advanced level of activity, which can also incorporate the first bullet point, is to create a map that traces each account number used by every subsidiary to the corresponding account number in the corporate parent's chart of accounts. Though only a manual tool, not an automated one, this is still an important way to create consistent entries through many accounting periods. To make this approach even more effective, there should be a standardized journal entry form for each subsidiary that lists both sets of account numbers, so the general ledger accountant only has to fill in the form and enter it into the computer.

- *Have subsidiaries convert results to corporate parent's chart of accounts.* An excellent approach for organizations that do not like to impose an excessive level of control onto their subsidiaries is to let them use any account code structure that they want and just require them to make the conversion to the parent's chart of accounts when submitting period-end information. This approach is a benign one many companies use, for it avoids the effort of a complete standardization while still ensuring that the parent company receives the information it needs. It can also be completed in short order, merely requiring a visit from corporate headquarters to work with the local accounting staff to create an account code conversion table the local staff will use to submit data to the corporate parent.

- *Have subsidiaries enter their data directly into the parent's general ledger.* This approach is similar to the preceding one in that the subsidiaries can keep their own charts of accounts but must submit their reporting information in the corporate parent's format. The difference here is that the subsidiaries are given computer access to the corporate parent's general ledger, into which they are expected to enter the period-end data themselves. This approach presents the risk of someone entering incorrect information into the computer system but avoids the need for extra data-entry work by the corporate general ledger accountant. Instead, the people entering the information are the ones who know the most about it, which means that there is less likelihood of a conversion or data-entry error being made. This best practice is described in more detail later, in the section "Have Subsidiaries Update Their Own Data in the Central General Ledger."

- *Convert all subsidiaries to a common chart of accounts.* The best way to ensure complete standardization is to impose the chart of accounts of the parent onto the subsidiaries. This can involve a massive amount of work, for each accounting system must be reset to use the new accounts. This may also probably destroy all historical reporting comparisons, which must use the old account numbers. Some subsidiaries may also be in such a different line of business that the new chart of accounts is quite unsuitable for recording information, requiring the accounting staff to "shoehorn" data into accounts that do not agree exactly with the account descriptions. Many companies find this approach to be much too difficult and expensive to be worthwhile and will use one of the preceding options instead.

Thus, there is quite a range of options available for converting the chart of accounts of a subsidiary to that of the parent. The exact option taken will depend on the level of effort and resources that the parent is willing to put into this effort. Some of the easier options are quite as reliable as the most difficult, making them worthy of careful consideration when picking from the range of options presented here.

Cost: 💵💵   **Installation time:** ⏰⏰⏰

15–6 Use Data Warehouse for Report Distribution

Larger organizations, especially those with multiple locations or subsidiaries, commonly expend a great deal of time compiling and distributing reports to employees. This problem arises because each location frequently has its own general ledger, from which the information is drawn. If any of the information from multiple locations is to be combined to create summary-level reports, then either a custom interface must be built to combine the data or else it must be manually combined and inserted into a new report.

An excellent method for avoiding this trouble is to dump selected data from all of the general ledgers into a central data warehouse. This involves the use of many customized interfaces that pull the data out of outlying locations and store it into the data warehouse, so that it contains only the most current information. Then a set of reporting programs frequently (perhaps every few minutes, depending on how it would downgrade system performance) accesses the data warehouse to refresh the information stored in a set of standard reports, which in turn are made available to employees through the company intranet.

This elaborate shifting and recompiling of data results in very "fresh" data that employees can use at once, and takes the accounting department completely out of the business of repetitively compiling reports—though it may still be asked to create new reports for posting to the intranet site. A key change after this system is installed is that the accounting staff will find itself spending much more time cleaning up the data that goes into the data warehouse. The reason is that manually compiled reports give the accounting staff time to review the data and fix any obvious anomalies before they reach the user; however, this automated reporting system does not allow the accounting staff this luxury, so now its focus must shift toward ensuring that the data is always correct.

A different approach to the data warehouse is noted in the "Use the General Ledger as a Data Warehouse" section later in this chapter, where one can see that extra data can be added to an existing general ledger, rather than exporting the general ledger to a separate database. This alternative is more usable in situations where there is only one general ledger in use, and so is more applicable to smaller companies.

Cost: 💵💵💵   **Installation time:** ⏰⏰⏰

15–7 Use Forms/Rates Data Warehouse for Automated Tax Filings

Any organization that operates in a number of states will find that an inordinate number of sales and income tax returns must be filed, not to mention a plethora of lesser forms. The traditional way to meet these filing requirements is to either keep a staff of tax preparation personnel on hand or else outsource some or all of these chores to a supplier. Either approach represents a significant cost. An alternative worth exploring is to store tax rates and forms in a database that can be used to automatically prepare tax returns in conjunction with other accounting information that is stored in either a general ledger or a data warehouse.

To make this best practice operational, there must first be a common database containing all of the information that would normally be included on a tax return. This may call for some restructuring of the chart of accounts, as well as the centralization of companywide data into a data warehouse (see the preceding best practice). This is no small task, since the information needed by each state may vary slightly from the requirements of other states, calling for subtle changes in the storage of data throughout the organization that will yield the appropriate information for reporting purposes.

The next step is to obtain tax rate information and store it in a central database. This information can be manually located by accessing the tax agency Web sites of all 50 states, but is more easily obtained in electronic format from any of the national tax reporting services. This information can then be stored in the forms/rates data warehouse. An additional step is to create a separate program for each of the tax reports, so that a computer report is issued that mimics the reporting format used by each state. Then the information can be manually transferred from the computer report to a printout of the PDF file of each state's tax form. For those programming staffs with a large amount of available time, it is also possible to create a report format that exactly mirrors each state tax form and that can be printed, with all tax information enclosed within it, and immediately mailed out.

The trouble with this best practice is the exceptionally high programming cost associated with obtaining an automated solution. There are so many tax forms to be converted to a digital format that the development task is considerable. Accordingly, it is more cost-effective to determine those tax forms that share approximately the same information and to develop an automated solution for them first. Any remaining tax forms requiring special programming to automate should be reviewed on a case-by-case basis to determine if it is cost-beneficial to complete further programming work or to leave a few stray reports for the tax preparation staff to complete by hand.

Cost: 💵💵💵   Installation time: ⏰⏰⏰

15–8 Use the General Ledger as a Data Warehouse

When issuing financial reports, a controller draws all of the financial information from a single source, the general ledger. However, there are usually a number of operating statistics, such as headcount, turnover percentages, scrap, and the like that must be accumulated from a variety of sources before they can be brought together into a coherent group and inserted into the financial statements. These can be quite difficult to accumulate at the last moment and must be added manually to the financial statements since they are not stored in the general ledger, the primary source from which the statements are drawn. The reporting problem becomes worse if management is accustomed to printing financial reports on its own, for any operating statistics will not appear on them, necessitating a sudden and unscheduled accumulation of this information by the accounting staff in order to supplement the existing reports. Thus, nonfinancial data can introduce some inefficiency into the production of financial statements.

The solution is to create additional records in the general ledger for the storage of nonfinancial information. This is more commonly known as a data warehouse, since data of all kinds can be stored there. When in place, this arrangement allows a company to store all the operating data it desires in the same place as its financial data, which means that any reports accessing financial data can *automatically* include operating data as well. Since all possible information is listed on the reports, there is no need to supplement them with additional, manually compiled reports. This is a much more satisfactory state of affairs since all information and reporting is centralized.

There are some problems with changing a general ledger into a data warehouse. One is that the existing software may not allow for this arrangement; if the software is provided by a third party and regularly updated, there may be no way to alter the situation without an appeal to the supplier to include a data warehousing feature in its next update of the software. Second, the existing financial reports must be altered to include the new information that will now be stored in the general ledger. A third issue is deciding who will update the operations information and how it will be added to the general ledger. For example, if it is deemed necessary to record the monthly inventory turnover rate at each of a dozen facilities, who will collect and input this data? The answer is usually either to allow each department or facility to forward this information, have the internal audit team (which is more objective in reporting disappointing results) do it, or have the former do it with periodic reviews by the latter. It may also be possible either to give these people direct access to the statistics accounts in the general ledger so they can make these entries themselves or (best of all) to construct automated interfaces to whichever local systems are already accumulating this information.

Thus, the main problem is not having a general ledger that will accommodate the data warehousing concept; the other problems are either surmounted during the implementation or can be eliminated through automation or bringing in the assistance of the internal audit department. If these problems can be overcome, using the general ledger as a data warehouse becomes an effective way to manage and report on all kinds of key management information.

Cost: Installation time: 🕐🕐

15–9   Restrict Use of Journal Entries

Many general ledger accountants spend a large part of their time researching why journal entries have been made. This is an especially galling problem if journal entries were made by someone else, because there may be no record of why they were entered or even of who made the entry. Also, if the computer system has a *drill-down* capability for researching general ledger information in detail (see the "Create General Ledger Drill-Down Capability" section later in this chapter), an information search may end at the journal entry, with no explanation for why the entry was made. This is an uncomfortable state of affairs for a general ledger accountant, who must report back to anyone requesting information from the general ledger saying that he or she does not know the nature of an account balance. Besides being embarrassing, it also takes time to research.

An easy solution is to totally restrict the use of journal entries to the general ledger accountant. By doing so, this person can research each request for a journal entry to verify that it is valid, make sure that the correct accounts are debited and credited, and include a description with the journal entry. This approach virtually eliminates all stray or undocumented journal entries from the system. Though it should not cause any problems, it may be difficult to implement if the computer system does not allow the journal entry feature to be restricted to one person—this depends on the type of computer security system included in the software.

Restricting the use of journal entries leads to cleaner and more fully documented general ledger information that is maintained much more easily.

Cost:    Installation time: 🕐

15–10   Avoid General Ledger Posting Bottlenecks

If a company has a number of subsidiaries that forward journal entries to it for posting, this can create a bottleneck in the general ledger area, which can be a particular problem during the monthly closing process since this could become the prime bottleneck interfering with a timely close.

The potential range of solutions stretches from increasing the corporate general ledger staff to pushing these transactions down onto the accounting staffs of the subsidiaries. Here are some thoughts on how to deal with the issue:

1. Normally, it makes sense to centralize journal entries with the smallest number of general ledger accountants, since they are experts in making such entries, and can therefore minimize journal entry errors and duplications.

2. Since general ledger entries have become a bottleneck operation, there are two choices: beef up the corporate general ledger data entry capacity, or push some or all of it back onto the divisions. Here are the ramifications of each:

   ○ Adding more corporate general ledger staff requires a greater expense, and since accounting is a cost center, this approach will not go over well with the CFO if there are any viable alternatives that do not increase costs. However, this will result in greater control over the accuracy of the entries being made.

   ○ If the journal entry volume only somewhat exceeds the capacity of the general ledger staff to handle it, then consider shifting smaller, less consequential entries back onto the divisions while retaining responsibility for all remaining entries. This will require the company to open access its accounting software journal entry capability, so more people will have the ability to make entries, which will probably increase the error rate. However, by restricting the divisions to only the easier and smaller dollar-volume entries, it will be less likely for them to make erroneous entries. This is probably the best option in most situations.

   ○ If there is a general desire by the corporate accounting staff to unload the whole general ledger data entry function onto the divisions, be aware that error rates will increase, which will call for the use of more training at the division level, as well as procedures, error checking, and probably an occasional internal audit. Because of all these factors, this is a less viable option.

   Cost: 　　　　　**Installation time:**

15–11 Have Subsidiaries Update Their Own Data in the Central General Ledger

A lengthy task for any general ledger accountant who must consolidate the results of subsidiaries is to input the general ledger of each one into the general ledger of the corporate parent. This can be a lengthy and arduous task, as well as one that is easily subject to error. The typical consolidation requires a very large journal entry for each subsidiary, possibly requiring over a hundred accounts. If there is any problem with the data entry, the entire entry must be reviewed to find the mistake. If there are many subsidiaries, there are many entries to make; if there is a time crunch associated with producing financial statements, it is extremely likely that all of the data-entry work required of the general ledger accountant will be a bottleneck for the timely production of those statements.

A solution is to hand the data-entry chore over to the subsidiaries. They can be given access to the computer system of the corporate parent, as well as password access to the general ledger, and then enter their financial results directly into the computer system. The general ledger accountant thereby avoids all data-entry work related to the subsidiaries and only has to analyze his or her own data inputs to see if there are any unusual items. By having each subsidiary enter its own information, the data can be entered much more quickly, resulting in the elimination of the workflow bottleneck associated with this task. In short, a relatively simple system change can improve the efficiency of periodic corporate consolidations.

There are a few issues to consider before attempting this best practice, however. First, there must be password protection for anyone accessing the main computer system, since there is always a risk of someone hacking into the computer and destroying or accessing sensitive data. Another issue is that, by giving access to many people, the number of users accessing the system at one time may rise, which may require the purchase of additional user licenses (if the system is a third-party package that uses a licensing fee arrangement). Finally, all the new users must be trained in how to make a journal entry in the corporate computer system, which may require nothing more than an instruction sheet, but which may require travel to all locations to conduct a short training class. If all of these issues can be dealt with at minimal cost, then having subsidiaries enter their own data into the corporate general ledger can improve the efficiency of that function.

Cost:    **Installation time:** 🕐 🕐

15–12 Prescreen Construction-in-Progress Entries

A great many entries are made to construction-in-progress (CIP) accounts, because a vast number of expense items are required as part of the standard construction progress. However, the sheer volume of entries makes it an opportune area in which to park expenses that should instead be charged to the current period, rather than to a CIP account that may not commence depreciation for over a year.

To avoid this problem, prescreen CIP-related entries when they are first entered into the system. This screening process can take on one of two roles. First, it can result in items being shifted away from the CIP account and charged to expense at once, because they do not qualify under GAAP rules to be included in CIP. Second, the screening process can be used as a tracking mechanism for the entire CIP, but it shunts items to be charged to current period expenses into one subaccount, while qualified CIP expenses are stored in a separate subaccount. This latter approach has the dual advantages of ensuring that the correct costs are charged to expense within the current period, while still accumulating all costs related to a CIP.

There should be only one or a few people assigned to this gatekeeper role, because it needs to be occupied by a person with an extensive knowledge of GAAP CIP rules. If cost constraints do not allow for a person in the prescreening role, then at least have the internal audit staff conduct the same sort of examination on a spot-check basis.

Cost: 💵   **Installation time:** 🕐

15–13 Construct Automated Interfaces to Software That Summarizes into the General Ledger

A large number of transactions must be moved from subsidiary ledgers to the general ledger at the end of each accounting period. In most cases, there is some reasonable degree of integration so that this transfer of information occurs automatically. However, the majority of organizations have a few outlying ledgers that are not directly connected to the general ledger; for example, the fixed assets register or payroll. In these instances, the general ledger accountant must wade through a considerable pile of information to determine the correct amounts to shift into the general ledger. This is a time-consuming process and subject to error.

It may be possible to construct an automated interface between these outlying ledgers and the general ledger. By doing so, there is a considerable advantage in eliminating the time required to move data to the general ledger manually, particularly important if an accounting department is committed to reducing the time needed to issue financial statements. Unfortunately, because of the programming required, this can be both a difficult and expensive best practice to implement. The company's programming staff must analyze the interface requirements, design the interface, program it, and test it, all of which can add up to a cost that greatly exceeds the benefit of having the automation. The best cases in which this is still a viable option are for a large company that can afford the cost, an organization facing a very difficult manual transfer of information, or (best of all) where a third-party interface is already on the market, which can be quickly layered on top of the existing software to make the interface a reality. If any of these cases are present, then the automated interface best practice should be completed.

Cost: 💵💵💵   Installation time: 🕐 🕐 🕐

15–14 Create General Ledger Drill-Down Capability

A common problem for the general ledger accountant is the relative degree of effort required to extract information from the general ledger. For example, if someone makes an inquiry regarding the exact nature of the expenses recorded in the office supplies expense account, the accountant reviews the information listed in the general ledger, which probably shows no more than the total amount of accounts payable posted on a given day attributable to the office supplies account, then goes to the accounts payable register to obtain information about the exact invoices that were charged to office supplies, and then pulls the invoices from the filing cabinet in which they reside—all this to answer the simple request, "Give me the detail for the office supplies account." Given the number of steps involved, it is obvious that a number of information requests of this kind (which are especially common right after the financial statements are distributed) can completely overload the general ledger accountant.

Installing a drill-down capability in the general ledger software is the best way to surmount this problem. The drill-down system allows one to position the cursor on the field on the computer screen for which the user wants to find additional information; the user then presses a button, and the next most detailed level of information appears on the screen. There may be several levels of information to be accessed in this manner, allowing a user to "drill down" through the various levels until the needed information is obtained—hence the name of this best practice.

Although an obvious godsend for anyone who must research detailed information through the general ledger, this is not an easy item to install in an existing computer system. In essence, the computer programming staff must redesign large portions of the general ledger programming code so that the field in a high-level screen is automatically linked to a screen that contains more detailed information, requiring a web of cross-indexes to a multitude of screens (which may be located in other software packages) before users have a comprehensive drill-down capability. This is a major programming project, especially if the drill-down capability is given to a large number of data items, which means that there will be a large number of cross-indexes. This option is virtually impossible to implement if a company is using a third-party software package since any periodic update of the packaged software by the supplier will automatically wipe out all custom programming that the local programming staff has done since the last update was installed.

In short, the drill-down capability greatly increases a general ledger accountant's overall level of efficiency, but it requires either a large amount of internal programming time or the purchase of packaged accounting software that already contains this feature.

Cost: 💵💵💵   **Installation time:** ⏰⏰⏰

15–15 Use Automated Error-Checking

Despite the best possible training and experience, it is still possible, if not likely, for a general ledger accountant to enter incorrect information into the general ledger, or to not catch incorrect information others have entered. This information may not be caught until it appears in the preliminary financial statements, necessitating a hurried investigation and correction, which delays the completion and delivery of the statements. Given the volume of transactions summarized in the general ledger, it would take a miraculous accountant to catch all possible irregularities before they are reported for the rest of the company to see in the financial statements.

The solution is to use automated error-checking. This approach can take a variety of forms. One is that the journal entry input screen contains controls over the size of entries that are allowed or the accounts to which entries are made. For example, any entry over $1 million may be automatically rejected, as would any entry to retained earnings (though with an override by a person with the appropriate password, since sometimes these preset boundaries *will* be exceeded). Another option is for the system to allow only a preapproved set of journal entries, all with preset accounts to which changes will be allowed. All other journal entries will require a special password to enter. Yet another approach is to use a report writer to explore all of the transactions that have been entered into the general ledger, sort through the ones that exceed preset boundaries, and issue them in a report. For example, a report could extract all travel expenses of more than $5,000, or all fixed asset additions less than the minimum capitalization limit. A report can also compare all expenses to year-to-date or period-budgeted amounts and only show those exceeding their budgeted amounts. By running these reports regularly, the general ledger accountant can quickly spot those transactions that may be wrong or placed in the wrong account.

The main problem with incorporating automated error-checking into the general ledger is that many accounting software packages do not include this feature. If this is the case, the expense of programming the alterations is probably so great that it will exceed any possible benefit. In this situation, the best alternative is to use a report writer to create reports showing problems that have already been entered into the general ledger. This is a much easier alternative, since most computer systems have a report writer. In other words, if it is not possible to stop bad information from entering the general ledger, it may still be possible to spot it once it is there and subsequently make corrections.

Cost: 💵💵💵   **Installation time:** 🕐🕐🕐

Total Impact of Best Practices on the General Ledger Function

This section describes how the best practices described earlier in this chapter can be brought together as a group to achieve a more efficient general ledger function that also provides better information to management.

The best practices can be clustered into three groups: those impacting the chart of accounts, the general ledger, and the general ledger to improve the reporting of information. These clusters are shown in Exhibit 15.2. The first cluster focuses on streamlining the chart of accounts, as well as various methods for incorporating the charts of accounts of subsidiaries into those of the parent organization. These best practices focus on improving the efficiency of the general ledger function. The second cluster uses a number of techniques not only to improve the ability of the general ledger accountant to research information in the general ledger (such as with drill-down inquiries or restricting the use of journal entries), but also to reduce the amount of work needed to maintain it. In this latter category are such best practices as having subsidiaries load their own financial results into the master general ledger, using automated error-checking, and automating the interfaces with subsidiary ledgers. When coupled with the previously noted improvements to the chart of accounts, these best practices can

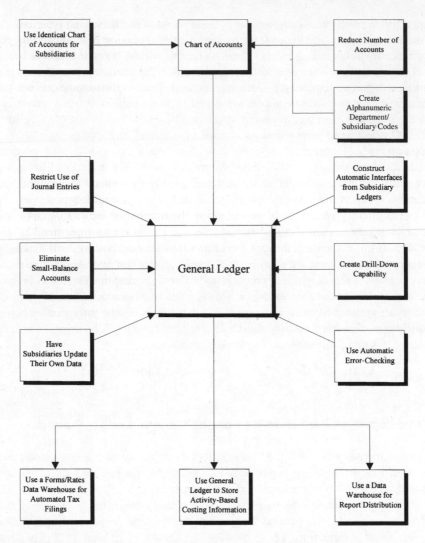

Exhibit 15.2 Impact of Best Practices on the General Ledger Function

result in a significant enhancement to the overall efficiency of the general ledger function. Finally, the third cluster of best practices actually *increases* the complexity of the general ledger, but does so in order to provide more information to other parts of the company, either by way of an activity-based costing analysis or through a data warehouse. Thus, there is a logical grouping to the best practices that may be useful in designating which clusters are implemented first.

If a controller can designate the order in which all of these best practices are implemented, it is best to work on *streamlining* the function first and adding the data warehousing and ABC functions later. Otherwise, reversing this order of implementation will result in adding complexity to a situation that is already not entirely efficient, which may result in a great deal of confusion and a complete failure to implement *any* best practices.

Summary

This chapter discussed a variety of best practices for the general ledger function. Though many of them will reduce the workload of the general ledger accountant by streamlining the workflow and reducing the number of errors that can enter into the process, a few can be both difficult and expensive to implement. Some, such as using the general ledger to support activity-based costing, will make the general ledger accountant's job more difficult, rather than less. Accordingly, for most general ledger best practices, it is necessary to ensure that there will be sufficient payback in exchange for installing a new best practice. The payback is not just greater accounting efficiency, but in a few cases the provision of better information to the rest of the company.

Chapter 16

Internal Auditing Best Practices

A traditional internal auditing department is frequently considered to be similar to the external auditors who annually review the corporate financial records, except that they also deal with operational and control issues and are more frequently found in the field. Since internal auditors are commonly hired from external audit firms, it is no surprise that they are likely to bring their old work habits with them and conduct the reviews just noted. However, as is pointed out many times in this chapter, the internal auditor's role can be viewed quite differently, switching from a systems reviewer to an active partner who can bring tremendous value to a company's business units. Thus, many of the best practices noted in this chapter focus on the revised role of auditors acting as business partners.

Another strong focus in this chapter is on the enhancement of work efficiencies within the internal audit department, which tends to suffer from continual deadline crises, unfinished paperwork, and difficulty determining which audits need to be addressed first. Examples of recommended changes involve the use of workflow software to centralize paperwork-related issues, shifting some tasks to business unit employees, and creating an auditor skills matrix.

This chapter begins with an overview of implementation issues for all of the internal auditing best practices, followed by a discussion of individual best practices, each one being presented in a separate section. The chapter finishes with a review of how these best practices will change a company's internal auditing operations.

Implementation Issues for Internal Auditing Best Practices

Most of the best practices in this chapter require very little money, since they largely involve procedural or management changes that are internal to the department. However, a number of the best practices require a modest investment of time, such as performing annual internal control assessments, creating self-audit guides, and training business unit employees on training issues. Thus, implementing these best practices will require detailed management by the internal audit manager to see when auditor time can be made available to complete the various work items. The cost and installation time required for all the best practices in this chapter are noted in Exhibit 16.1.

Exhibit 16.1 Summary of Internal Auditing Best Practices

	Best Practice	Cost	Install Time
Assisting Business Units			
16–1	Annually update an internal control assessment of each business unit	💵	🕐🕐🕐
16–2	Issue self-audit guides to business units	💵	🕐🕐
16–3	Recommend business process improvements to business units	💵	🕐🕐
16–4	Track audit results through business unit surveys	💵	🕐
16–5	Train business unit staff on control issues	💵	🕐🕐
16–6	Train new business unit managers in control issues	💵	🕐🕐
Internal Audit Management			
16–7	Avoid overauditing of internal audits	💵	🕐
16–8	Complete all internal audit work papers in the field	💵	🕐
16–9	Create a control standards manual	💵	🕐🕐
16–10	Create an online internal audit library	💵💵	🕐🕐
16–11	Create and disseminate information from a best practices database	💵	🕐🕐
16–12	Outsource the internal audit function	💵💵	🕐🕐
16–13	Schedule a portion of internal audits on a just-in-time basis	💵	🕐
16–14	Schedule internal audits based on risk	💵	🕐
16–15	Use workflow software for internal audits	💵💵💵	🕐🕐🕐
16–16	Implement continuous controls monitoring	💵💵	🕐🕐
Internal Audit Staffing			
16–17	Fill internal audit positions from operations on a rotating basis	💵💵	🕐🕐
16–18	Add specialists to audit teams	💵	🕐
16–19	Assign an auditor to be a relationship manager with each business unit	💵	🕐
16–20	Assign internal auditors to system development teams	💵	🕐
16–21	Create an auditor skills matrix	💵	🕐🕐
16–22	Use Excel for continuous auditing	💵	🕐

The glaring exception to the low-cost rule is the use of workflow software, which can easily cost well into the six figures and also require a considerable amount of time to install, which may put it out of reach of most smaller internal auditing departments.

One best practice is to outsource the internal audit department, though all the other recommendations in this chapter assume that the department will be retained. Outsourcing is only useful in those cases where a company does not feel that internal auditing is a core company function, and where it either can afford the substantially increased cost of shifting this area to an outside audit firm or where it conducts so few internal audits that it requires less than one full-time person to conduct the work.

Consequently, with few exceptions, implementing the best practices in this chapter can result in significant improvements not only in the usefulness of the internal audit department, but also in the efficiency with which it conducts its operations.

16–1 Annually Update an Internal Control Assessment of Each Business Unit

It is not uncommon for an internal audit department to continually send its auditors into the field with instructions to review whatever was done in the work papers from the year before, thereby bringing continual attention to the same risks, year after year. Though this approach certainly informs those being audited of the areas requiring strong controls, it does not account for changes in the business that may require different audit work.

An alternative is to periodically create a formal internal control assessment document, both for the entire company and for individual business units. This document points out changes in the business and how they will impact controls, as well as the status of existing controls and why those controls are needed. This document can then be sent to the senior management team to promote their understanding of emerging control issues, as well as to business unit managers, who will therefore have a greater understanding of which controls are likely to be subject to review by internal audit teams. Of particular importance to the audit manager is this document's usefulness in determining how control reviews must change from year to year in order to schedule more effective audits.

This document will require a substantial amount of time to prepare and revise, but the time investment is easily offset by the greater understanding of control issues.

Cost: 💸   Installation time: 🕐 🕐 🕐

16–2 Issue Self-Audit Guides to Business Units

Many of the best practices noted in this chapter involve the conversion of the internal audit staff from reviewers of controls to advisors who impart knowledge about business improvements. However, this shift in emphasis means that the traditional task of reviewing controls will be done much less frequently.

An alternative is to shift some of the controls review burden to the business units themselves. Though this may seem like a case of having the fox guard the henhouse, the internal audit department can still monitor business unit results at a high level to see if general operational and financial performance measures indicate a problem, and then send in a team to conduct a thorough review. In most cases, there are no serious control breakdowns, so audit tasks with lower-risk profiles can be safely assigned to business unit employees. By doing so, there is greater likelihood of audits being conducted on a regular basis, and by people who are thoroughly familiar at a detailed level with business processes, which may result in better audit work.

To make this shift of responsibilities a success, the internal audit department should construct a series of self-audit guides for the business units. These guides should briefly explain a control objective, note how specific controls are used within a process to meet that objective, and then lay out detailed auditing steps for employees to follow. The level of detail in these guides should be sufficient for employees without audit training to understand what they are doing and why it is important. The guides should be short, concise, and targeted only at specific audit objectives. Also, they must avoid any accounting language that might be confusing to a nonaccountant. When creating a self-audit guide, be sure to test it on a nonaccountant to see where points of confusion arise, so that any problems can be eliminated before the guide is released for general use. Though a great deal of work is required to create an effective self-audit guide, the effort expended will be more than offset by the eventual reduction in control review work by the audit staff.

Cost: Installation time: 🕐 🕐

16–3 Recommend Business Process Improvements to Business Units

The traditional function of the internal auditor has been to diligently root through a business unit's processes, looking for control weaknesses or evidence of fraud. If anything was found, it cast the business unit manager in a poor light. Given this sequence of events, it should be no surprise that internal auditors are not usually welcomed by joyous crowds of auditees.

A much better approach is to mix the chore of control reviews with making suggestions to the business unit managers for process improvements. The internal auditor is in an ideal position to do this, having an expert knowledge of business processes, as well as a comparative knowledge of how the same processes are handled in other parts of the company. Indeed, the internal auditor can be considered a walking encyclopedia of control process best practices. By shifting to a focus on valuable improvement recommendations, the internal auditor creates an entirely different image within the corporation of being a helpful knowledge worker who can make local managers look like stars. This is a particularly important change in focus if the internal auditor can either make additional recommendations in regard to implementation steps for process improvements or bring the local manager in contact with the in-house expert who has already completed an implementation. By taking this approach, one can not only be the source of ideas, but also assist in carrying them out in an indirect manner.

Though control reviews are still necessary to some extent in all organizations, taking this different view of the position can result in business unit managers begging the internal audit manager for more staff time to assist them with a variety of tasks.

Cost: 💸   **Installation time:** ⏰ ⏰

16–4 Track Audit Results through Business Unit Surveys
✔Author's Choice

Although auditors must sometimes issue adverse opinions about the state of process controls at a corporate business unit, this does not lead to long-lasting or friendly relations with those business units, which has ramifications in terms of cooperation from the business units when follow-up audits are conducted at a later date.

Some of these adversarial circumstances can be avoided through the use of business unit surveys in which the unit managers are given the opportunity to review audit performance in terms of their perceived relevance, value of recommendations made, accuracy of audit findings, and so on. If a survey results in excessively poor scores, the internal audit manager can meet with the unit manager to gain clarification about the issues, which may result in steps to improve auditing goals, processes, or staffing. By continually obtaining survey results and acting upon them, the internal audit department can align its mission more closely with that of the business units, resulting in greater value to the business units. This approach can also be used as an ancillary rating measure for internal audit staff performance, as well as a method for determining which unit managers need to be dealt with more carefully during upcoming audits.

The results of these surveys should be stored and tracked on a trend line for several years to gain some idea of the perceived level of performance by the department. The survey database can also be sorted by audit team, business unit, and type of audit program conducted, to see if issues continually arise in any of these three areas that require corrective action.

Cost: 💸   **Installation time:** ⏰

16–5 Train Business Unit Staff on
Control Issues   ✔*Author's Choice*

Many control problems arise because employees do not understand the impact of the improper usage of a control. They simply see it as an extra step to be followed or an inefficiency that can be overcome by altering the process. When internal auditors spot this type of problem, they usually report it to management, which must somehow find the time and resources to train employees in the proper use of the control. Since this training is not budgeted, it frequently does not occur, resulting in continuing control problems.

The internal auditor can mitigate this problem by setting aside time at the end of each audit to personally provide the necessary level of training. This will require extra time, so some padding must be added to the audit time budget to allow for training. Also, it is most helpful for the internal audit department to have a set of training guides on major topical areas prepared in advance, and readily accessible by all auditors for use. These guides should cover processes and controls in all major areas that are common to multiple business units, such as inventory transactions, order fulfillment, the purchasing process, and travel expense reporting. Though this best practice will require more auditor time than is usually the case, it helps to reduce the number of control problems that will be found during subsequent audits, and so saves audit time in the long run. It is also seen as a major benefit provided by the internal audit staff to the rest of the company.

Cost: 💵   **Installation time:** ⏰ ⏰

16–6 Train New Business Unit Managers on Control Issues

When new managers are assigned to a business unit, the last thing they want to see is an internal auditor walking in the door to conduct a review. Their experience is likely to be the uncovering of some shortfall in the control systems, resulting in a black mark against them while they are still struggling to learn the details of their jobs. In anticipation of this result, a new manager is likely to stonewall an internal auditor in hopes of avoiding any negative findings.

A more positive approach is for a senior-level internal auditor to meet with each new manager as part of the initial job training and spend a great deal of time discussing the control systems over which the manager now has responsibility. This discussion should include a hands-on review of each process step where control points are used, as well as conversations about the need for these controls, how to ensure that they are being followed, and indicators of control failures. The internal auditor can even point out other possible improvements in the manager's systems. By taking this approach, the internal auditor will be seen as a strong advisor to new managers, and one with whom a long-standing and friendly relationship can be forged that will assist in the conduct of future audits. This approach completely contravenes the more adversarial situation that typically arises between a new manager and an internal auditor.

Cost: 💵   **Installation time:** ⏰ ⏰

16–7 Avoid Overauditing of Internal Audits

Many internal audits involve the repetitive review of the same topical areas, if only because these areas are perceived to have the highest degree of financial risk to a company, and so are worthy of constant review. When internal audits are repeated on a regular basis, the managers of these audits will usually pull out the work papers from the last audit that was conducted on the same area and simply copy out the same auditing requirements. This can result in overauditing because the internal audit manager never questions why each of the tasks needs to be completed a second time. Many of the audit procedures noted in the work papers may have been intended to be one-time reviews to investigate perceived problems that have since been overcome with new control systems, rendering the original audit steps no longer valid. Given this constant tendency to copy previous audits, a nonessential audit step may have been repeated dozens of times, simply on the grounds that if it was done before, it should be done again.

A better approach is to conduct a brief, formal review of the upcoming internal audit with the internal audit team assigned to do the work. This group should review the results of the last internal audit, pore over the control chart (if any) for the area to be reviewed, and come up with a new audit plan for every engagement. By doing so, the team avoids the mindless repetition of early audit steps that are no longer valid, and concentrates on the key issues that will result in the most valuable audit results. Also, by including the entire audit team in this review, a company will find that there is much better buy-in to, and understanding of, the work being done, which may both increase employee efficiency and reduce long-term turnover in the internal audit staff.

Cost: 💵   **Installation time:** ⏰

16–8 Complete All Internal Audit Work Papers in the Field

The objective of an internal audit is to complete a report that describes any control issues found. However, one would think that, from the perspective of the internal audit team, the objective would be to move on to the next internal audit as quickly as possible. There is a preference among internal auditors to continually meet the upcoming schedule to work on the next audit, rather than to complete the one currently being conducted. This results in a long trail of incomplete audits that requires constant badgering by senior management to complete, frequently requiring weekend work by the internal audit teams. To avoid this problem, the standard procedure for all internal audits should be that the work papers be fully completed in the field before an internal audit team is allowed back to the main office or to proceed to the next audit. Work paper completion should include the clearing of all points that arose during the audit, as well as producing the draft report. If this results in delays in the completion of subsequent internal audits, then fine—it will also yield much more rapid completion of the final audit reports, which was the objective when the audits were scheduled. This point can be made to the audit teams more convincingly by issuing a small bonus for all the internal audits that are wrapped up in the field.

Cost:    Installation time: 🕐

16–9 Create a Control Standards Manual

Auditors are trained to have a good idea of which control standards should be attached to a business process. However, the managers who supervise those processes typically have no idea of which controls are involved. This can result in inadvertent changes to processes by managers who are simply trying to devise more efficient systems, which, in turn, results in adverse findings by auditors when they conduct reviews.

A reasonable solution is to create a control standards manual for use by process managers. The manual should note the internal control objectives to be met for each business process, as well as the specific procedures used to meet those objectives. The manual can also note how different control points support each other, and what happens when specific controls are removed from the process. The manual can include flowcharts of the processes, noting each control point, as well as forms used in the process. Any reports arising from a process should be noted, describing what information managers should review that can bolster the control objectives. Clearly, this can be an exceedingly dry document (except to internal auditors!), so an audit staff person should walk managers through the manual to highlight its key points. Also, whenever an audit team arrives for any type of review, it should always bring the latest version of the control standards manual, making a point of highlighting key changes to it. Only by this constant emphasis on the importance of the manual will managers take the time to review and understand it.

Cost: 🖎   Installation time: 🕐 🕐

16–10 Create an Online Internal Audit Library

An internal audit team will go on most audit engagements without a great deal of company expertise to back it up. If the team encounters an unusual problem in the field, it has no one to turn to for advice. Similarly, if it encounters a control problem, it has no way of knowing if it is an isolated issue or if it has been uncovered in other places within the company. These problems can be reduced by setting up an online internal audit library that contains records from previous completed audits, as well as who worked on them and how they can be accessed. Further, the library can hold updates on all of the most recent accounting standards, as well as cross-indexed data on problems or unusual audit scenarios encountered during other company audits. By accessing this information, audit teams can save a great deal of research time that would otherwise be spent combing through the company directory or the paper-based audit files to find the same information.

Setting up such a system requires each internal audit manager to create an electronic summary-level report on each audit as it is completed, which is then forwarded to the company webmaster for inclusion in the library. Also, accounting standards can be easily obtained from various CD-based products for posting on the online library. Be sure to obtain an accounting standards product that contains an index search capability, so that users can easily search for items of particular interest.

Cost: **Installation time:** 🕑 🕑

16–11 Create and Disseminate Information from a Best Practices Database

A large company will have many internal auditors combing through its processes in many locations and possibly on multiple continents. These auditors will build a store of knowledge about best practices that is based only on what they have seen, and which they will likely recommend to other business units as they travel throughout the company on various audit projects. Though this will result in the spread of best practices through a company over time, it is a very inefficient way to do so—knowledge will only be applicable if an auditor happens to be assigned to another business unit whose processes could benefit from that person's specific knowledge, and it will be lost when an internal auditor retires or leaves employment.

A much better way to spread the use of best practices is to store the information in a central database. It should be entered into the database as soon as an audit is completed; it can also be validated in terms of its effectiveness by specifically reviewing its results during a repeat audit at a later date. Auditors can also be given bonuses or recognition awards for any best practices they uncover and store in the database, which will have them enthusiastically rooting through business units to uncover new best practices.

Spreading information about these best practices can take several forms. The most passive approach is to simply have it available in the database, but this approach requires auditors to actively review the database in their limited spare time. A better approach is to push the information into the field through the use of newsletters and emails to the audit staff. A particularly effective approach is to email best practice information directly to those business unit managers who are most likely to use them; by doing so, the managers are more likely to contact the internal audit department with requests for assistance in installing the recommended best practices. The driving force behind the success of best practices dissemination is the use of someone who regularly reviews the best practices database for "hot" topics, and who also spends time matching best practice possibilities with various business units. In a small company, this work should be done by the internal audit manager, though a larger company may choose to assign the task to a full-time senior audit position to ensure that the company gains the most benefit from its best practices database.

Cost: **Installation time:**

16–12   Outsource the Internal Audit Function

Some organizations have their internal audit function report to the controller or chief financial officer. In these situations, the manager of the accounting function has the additional burden of selecting auditing targets, planning for audit teams to review them, managing the teams, and acting on their findings. For a larger organization, this management work can be a considerable additional burden, for there may be many auditors.

Although it is not possible to completely eliminate all management of the internal audit function, a controller or chief financial officer can outsource the function, which removes selected management tasks. For example, giving all internal audit work to an outside supplier keeps a manager from having to plan each audit or review the teams as they conduct their work. It still requires a manager to select audit targets and act on the results of the audits, but at least some activities have been eliminated. Using an outside auditor carries with it the additional advantage of reduced travel time to outlying company locations, since an audit firm with many locations can assign local staff to each company facility. Further, outside auditors are not paid if they are not working on company-specific projects, nor does a company have to pay for their ongoing training. These advantages have pushed a number of companies into the arms of outside auditors.

However, there are problems with this best practice that have raised some ire in the ranks of internal auditors. One issue is that many companies use their internal auditing departments to groom new managers for senior-level positions. This is an excellent approach, for not only does it give auditors a wide-ranging view of company operations but also it allows the managers of functions being audited to see them and to provide feedback to the human resources department regarding the wisdom of promoting them to more senior positions. Another problem is that outside auditors will sometimes assign junior staff personnel to internal audits, which allows them to charge less per hour. However, these junior personnel frequently have less experience than the internal auditors, and no experience with specific details of company operations, making them doubly inefficient. Consequently, one must carefully weigh the advantages and disadvantages of this approach before handing over the internal audit department to a supplier.

Cost: 💵💵   Installation time: ⏰⏰

16–13 Schedule Some Internal Audits on a Just-in-Time Basis   ✔ *Author's Choice*

A very common management practice is to create a schedule of all internal audits to be performed for the upcoming year. This allows the audit manager to arrange for meetings with local managers well in advance, as well as to determine the logistics of shifting auditors around the world to various company locations. It is also a common measurement tool, whereby the audit manager commits to completing a certain number of audits; subsequently, finishing all work listed on the annual schedule is used as the baseline measure of success. Unfortunately, blocking out the entire audit staff's time for a year in advance also leaves no room for audits that are requested on short notice, which typically occurs when a control emergency arises. Addressing these needs calls for a substantial reshuffling of the audit schedule.

A fine alternative is to schedule only a portion of the internal audit team's time, perhaps two-thirds, leaving the remaining time slots open. By doing so, any short-term work requests can be dealt with promptly. Not only does this give company managers the impression that the internal audit department is more responsive to their needs, but it also eliminates the need for sudden schedule changes. The only problem with this approach is that one can no longer determine the success of the internal audit department based on its ability to complete a planned set of audits.

Cost: 💵   Installation time: ⏰

16–14 Schedule Internal Audits Based on Risk

The scheduling of various areas within a company for internal audits is usually an arcane process, involving pressure from the audit committee to have a few "pet" areas investigated; during the process some department managers demand reviews of other areas, while others put forth considerable effort to avoid them, on the grounds that they take up too much staff time. The internal audit manager is caught in the midst of this maelstrom, trying to please everyone while still scheduling audits for those areas in which he or she has a feeling that some problems may lurk. A simple way to revise this scheduling process is to base all audits on the concept of risk to the company.

To schedule based on risk, a company must devise a ranking for risk levels, with number one being any potential control problem that could place the company in grave financial danger, while lower levels of risk can be assigned a lesser category. Then the internal audit manager assigns a risk ranking to each requested audit, while also conducting a review of other control areas to see if there are other areas of risk that are not currently being addressed. The upshot of this process is a clear ranking of audit reviews that is highly defensible and that will focus the bulk of company audit attention on those few key control processes that are at the most risk of causing financial trouble.

The main issue to be aware of is that the internal audit committee should formally approve of this scheduling process, so the internal audit manager can use that committee's support when telling other company managers that their requested audits will not occur quite so quickly as they would like.

Cost: **Installation time:**

16–15   Use Workflow Software for Internal Audits

Larger companies with many internal auditors face the following challenge: They have a difficult time controlling the activities of their auditors, rarely have a good knowledge of prior audits already completed, require extra travel time to return to company locations to clear hanging audit issues, and cannot readily see if the same auditing problems are cropping up in multiple parts of the company. These problems result in significant inefficiencies in work efforts.

One can resolve these problems by installing workflow software that has been tailored to the particular needs of the internal auditing environment. For example, workflow software contains forms and templates that are commonly used in most audits, allowing the staff to save time that would otherwise be spent creating work papers from scratch. In addition, information entered directly into the workflow database through these online forms can be reviewed from a central location by audit managers, thereby reducing the amount of time spent traveling to remote company locations. Further, this information is then available to *all* auditors, anywhere in the company, for immediate review.

If audit documents must be approved by multiple people, the software can send an electronic version of the documents to each person in turn, and wait for each one's approval before being sent to the next person in the approval process. It can also inform each approver of the date by which approval must be obtained. The system can also keep track of when each document was made, by whom, and when it was subsequently reviewed and approved. Reviewers can also create review notes that are attached to the electronic audit documents and that must be cleared by the audit team before the work papers will receive final approval.

Workflow software can also maintain a database of previous audit work at each company location, as well as the results of that work, so that subsequent audit teams can review the prior work to see what efforts can be avoided in the future. Of particular importance is a risk assessment by prior audit teams, so one can immediately see where the bulk of new audit work should be directed. The system can also be used to summarize audit issues across all business units, thereby giving audit managers visibility into broader risk issues that must be addressed on a continuing basis.

The initial cost of audit workflow software exceeds $100,000 (depending on the configuration and number of seat licenses) and requires significant customization and installation time.

Cost: 💵💵💵   **Installation time:** ⏰⏰⏰

16–16 Implement Continuous Controls Monitoring

Controls can be a difficult imposition on many companies. They can require extra data entry or the production of reports, which managers then review for anomalies. Also, larger firms use internal auditors to conduct laborious reviews of systems on a rotating basis. Both approaches are expensive and tend to make processes less efficient. What if there were a way to automate the monitoring of controls? There is.

Several companies have created continuous controls monitoring (CCM) solutions. These systems draw data from a number of databases and then review 100 percent of all transactions, looking for data anomalies, errors, segregation of duty issues, and possible control breaches. The systems contain tables of standard control objectives, including the areas of authorization, accuracy, completeness, validity, and segregation of duties, and contain tests to ensure that each objective is met at each step of the various transaction process flows. These tests are available for all major transactional areas, including payroll, the order-to-cash cycle, the purchase-to-payment cycle, inventory management, travel expenses, and procurement cards.

For example, a CCM will have separate tests for the proper authorization, data-entry accuracy, transaction completeness, and validity of all cash receipts. As another example, a CCM will verify that sales orders are completely filled out before being submitted for fulfillment, invoices are issued within a specified time period from order shipment, and write-offs are properly authorized.

The CCM then notifies designated employees of any problems found with browser-based reports, resulting in a highly targeted manual investigation to locate each root problem. A CCM system also makes it easier to comply with the provisions of Section 404 of the Sarbanes-Oxley Act.

Cost: 💵💵   **Installation time:** ⏰⏰

16–17 Fill Internal Audit Positions from Operations on a Rotating Basis

The problem with auditing the operations of a large company is the extremely high level of procedural complexity that must be understood in order to locate control problems. When internal auditors are hired from outside the company, they face a steep learning curve with these systems, possibly requiring well over a year to become conversant with even a limited subset of a company's systems. This not only represents an inadequate use of expensive staff, but also creates the risk that control breaches may go unobserved until new internal audit staff complete their understanding of corporate systems.

A possible solution is to fill internal audit positions from the operations divisions on a rotating basis. This approach ensures a high level of operational knowledge by auditors, so that a much higher level of audit effectiveness can be achieved at once. By rotating in new staff on a regular basis, the internal audit manager is assured of having auditors with the most current knowledge of company systems. Conversely, these employees will require training in internal audit procedures, though it typically requires less time to achieve a reasonable level of competency. There is also a risk that auditors rotated in from the ranks of the operations staff will be less inclined to bring up control problems involving the divisions from which they were hired. This risk can be reduced by creating a cooperative audit environment with the managers of audited divisions, as well as by pairing these audit staff with senior-level internal auditors who have fewer divisional affiliations.

On the whole, bringing in even a few auditors from the operations side of the business can inject a considerable level of added expertise into the internal audit department.

Cost: 💵💵   Installation time: ⏰⏰

16–18   Add Specialists to Audit Teams

A typical internal auditor has received training in a standard set of auditing functions that apply to the activities encountered in the majority of audits. However, specialized processes will be scheduled for audits from time to time for which the internal audit staff has received no training. This may arise when a business process has been specially modified or enhanced at one or a few company locations, and the internal audit staff is unfamiliar with the modifications or their impact on controls. These audits can be difficult, since the internal auditor must spend time learning the new or revised process and determining any resulting changes to the control environment.

A better approach is to invite specialists to an audit to deal with these processes. A good person to invite is someone who has personally been involved in the implementation of a particular system at a different location, and who, therefore, is an expert on the process under review. This person is particularly useful if the intent of the audit is to recommend the implementation of the system in which the person is an expert, since he or she can offer valuable implementation tips to the local management team in regard to installing the system. Once the audit is over, the audit team disbands, with the specialist returning to his or her business unit. This person may be used again at a later date, or the internal auditors can learn enough from the specialist to take that person's place on subsequent audits.

Cost: Installation time: 🕃

16–19 Assign an Auditor to Be a Relationship Manager with Each Business Unit

The internal audit department rarely has visibility into the work of individual business units. The unit managers typically revise their own systems on an ongoing basis in order to streamline processes, and never think to check with the internal audit staff for advice on these changes. Also, the internal audit department has access to a wealth of information about how other business units structure their processes, but rarely has an opportunity to relay this information to business unit managers, resulting in many lost opportunities for improvements.

Both of these issues can be avoided by assigning a senior internal auditor to the role of relationship manager with the manager of each business unit. This person is responsible for communicating regularly with an assigned manager, not only to impart improvement information but also to find out which activities at the business unit should involve the participation of the internal audit staff. For example, if a business unit is considering programming a new accounts payable system, the relationship manager can ask that an auditor be assigned to the design team to ensure that appropriate controls are built into the system. This approach is also an excellent means for improving relations between the internal audit department and the rest of the company.

Cost: 💵   Installation time: 🕃

16–20 Assign Internal Auditors to System Development Teams

When a company's systems development staff creates a new business system, either the accounting staff or the external auditors find control problems after the fact that require either significant programming changes or major modifications to other systems that must now be relied upon as secondary controls that offset the problems found. Some of these problems are so severe that entire systems must be scrapped or entirely reworked. The worst case is when a control weakness is spotted by someone who exploits it to fraudulently part a company from its assets.

Many of these control problems can be eliminated by making an internal audit person an integral part of a systems design team. By regularly reviewing the conceptual and detailed designs of new systems, internal auditors can spot potential control problems before any significant programming time has been spent on them. This not only achieves a higher level of control in new systems but also avoids the time that would otherwise be spent on correctional changes to systems at a later date. Proper use of this best practice requires the involvement of auditors with significant systems design and controls knowledge.

Cost: 🖐️   **Installation time:** ⏰

16–21 Create an Auditor Skills Matrix

Not all auditors are created equal. Some have a considerable degree of training in specific types of computer systems, others have great operational experience, while still others come from the more classical "school" of external audit firms; furthermore, some have garnered experience with particular types of business units or processes over the years. Unfortunately, these differing skill bases are sometimes ignored when assigning auditors to specific audits, resulting in mismatches of skills and required work. This in turn can result in incomplete audits or ones whose results are not sufficiently specific, detailed, or helpful to the recipient.

A solution is the creation of an auditor skills matrix. In its simplest form, this is just a collection of auditor resumes that is regularly updated after each audit. However, such a collection is not easily searched for specific skill types, and so is only useful when there are very few internal auditors on staff. A much better approach is to itemize these skills in a database that is easily searched based on key words. This allows an audit manager to punch the key requirements of an upcoming audit into the database and instantly receive back a list of those auditors most qualified to complete the work. The key issue with a skills database is that it requires constant updating, since auditor skills are constantly improving through training and new audits. Consequently, someone must be assigned the task of updating skills information on a regular basis, preferably after the completion of each audit and after auditors have completed scheduled tasks. If this updating chore is assigned to the auditors themselves, then their annual reviews should include a discussion of the updates they have loaded into the database, thereby highlighting the importance of this task.

Cost: 🖐️   **Installation time:** ⏰ ⏰

16–22 Use Excel for Continuous Auditing

Instead of waiting for an infrequent internal audit to investigate a variety of risk areas, consider a regularly scheduled investigation using Excel and data downloaded from the accounting system. Excel downloads are a staple of most accounting software, usually resulting in either preformatted spreadsheets or comma-delimited text that can be easily converted into a spreadsheet. Once in spreadsheet format, consider making the following tests:

- *Transactions during odd hours.* For all types of transactions, sort the spreadsheet based on time and date to see if anyone is accessing the system outside of regular working hours, and investigate any transactions made during those times.

- *Same data entry person for the same supplier.* For payables transactions, sort the spreadsheet by supplier name and then by the user ID of the person entering transactions. If the same person always enters payables for the same supplier, this could be a shell company owned by the data entry person.

- *Subthreshold transactions.* For payables transactions, sort in declining order by invoice totals, and investigate payments for which dollar amounts are just below the corporate approval threshold. Chances are good that some involve split payments to avoid detailed analysis by an authorized approver.

- *Late customer orders with no purchase order.* For billing transactions, first sort on overdue customer invoices, then sort the resulting subset on billings without customer purchase order numbers, and then sort this even smaller subset on orders exceeding the credit approval threshold. The result may be a small number of orders that were improperly routed around the credit department.

These are only a few suggestions for possible tests. A more company-specific approach is to periodically analyze potential risks in relation to the existing control structure and see which high-risk items are most suitable for investigation with spreadsheet analysis.

Cost: 💵   **Installation time:** ⏰

Total Impact of Best Practices on the Internal Auditing Function

Many of the best practices discussed in this chapter are noted in Exhibit 16.2, where best practices are clustered into those occurring prior to the commencement of an audit and those occurring during or after it. Best practices related to staffing, workflow management, or audit staffing are not included.

In the exhibit, it is evident that a considerable amount of work can be completed in advance, to determine the need for control assessments, as well as to provide audit teams with as much information as possible about their prospective audits. A great many changes are advocated *during* the audit, such as giving controls and self-audit training to the staff and managers of business units, and issuing process improvement recommendations to unit managers. Subsequent to the audit, the tracking of audit survey results can be used to revise the planning and staffing for future audits.

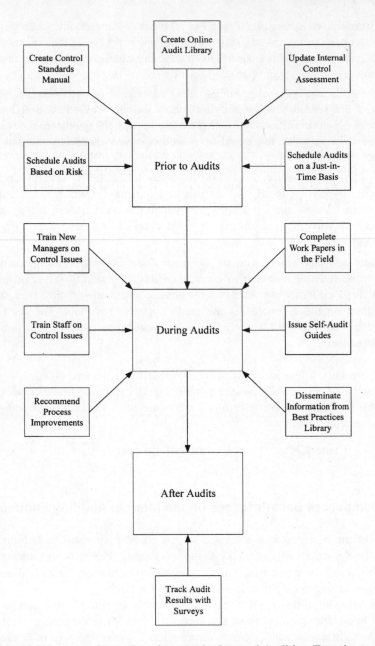

Exhibit 16.2 Impact of Best Practices on the Internal Auditing Function

Summary

The primary intent of this chapter was to recommend a shift in focus for the internal audit department, from a detailed reviewer of business processes to an enabler of process improvements. This change requires a significant attitudinal adjustment by the internal audit manager, who is may be wedded to the traditional concept of independent control reviews that tend to create adversarial or, at least, cool relations with company managers. If the recommendations made here seem to be too much of a stretch for the internal audit manager, then try just one best practice—the business unit survey—which may reveal that the rest of the company gives a lower value to the internal audit department than its manager supposes, and which may then spark further changes.

Chapter 17

Inventory Best Practices[1]

This chapter describes a variety of best practices that are focused on improving the accuracy of the existing inventory, improving inventory transactions, and reducing a company's investment in inventory. Though these improvements most directly assist other departments, such as the production, warehouse, and purchasing employees, the accounting staff is deeply interested as well. The reason is that the accuracy of the financial statements is largely driven by the accuracy of the inventory—if it is off by even a few percent, the variance flows through the cost of goods sold, resulting in a considerable amount of inaccuracy in reported profits. Even better, if the inventory investment can be reduced, the risk of incorrectly counting or valuing the inventory is also reduced.

The best practices shown in this chapter are different from those listed elsewhere in this book, in that the controller must obtain the approval and active participation of the warehouse, purchasing, and engineering managers for most of them. Without their help, such best practices as improving the bills of material, moving inventory to floor stock, and segregating customer-owned inventory will not be accomplished.

The remainder of this chapter consists of a review of implementation issues for inventory best practices, followed by a detailed discussion of each one, and ends with notes on the impact of best practices on the inventory function.

Implementation Issues for Inventory Best Practices

This section describes the levels of implementation difficulty for each of the best practices detailed in this chapter. Each one is noted in Exhibit 17.1, alongside a listing of the relative level of implementation cost and duration. Most of these best practices are not simple ones to install because they involve one or more other departments, usually warehousing, purchasing, and engineering. Whenever another manager is brought into the implementation process, the chances of success drop rapidly, since this additional person must be convinced of the efficacy of the change.

---

[1] Selected best practices in this chapter are adapted with permission from Steven M. Bragg, *Inventory Best Practices* (John Wiley & Sons, 2004).

Exhibit 17.1 Summary of Inventory Best Practices

	Best Practice	Cost	Install Time
Bill of Material Accuracy			
17–1	Audit bills of material	💵	⏰
17–2	Conduct a configuration audit	💵	⏰⏰
17–3	Modify the bills of material based on actual scrap levels	💵	⏰
17–4	Review inventory returned to the warehouse	💵	⏰
17–5	Modify the bills of material for temporary substitutions	💵	⏰
17–6	Use bills of material to find inventory made obsolete by product withdrawals	💵	⏰
Efficiency Issues			
17–7	Compare open purchase orders to current requirements	💵	⏰
17–8	Reject unplanned receipts	💵	⏰⏰
17–9	Obtain advance shipping notices for inbound deliveries	💵	⏰⏰
17–10	Eliminate the receiving function	💵💵💵	⏰⏰⏰
17–11	Use standard containers to move, store, and count inventory	💵💵	⏰⏰
17–12	Use different storage systems based on cubic transactional volume	💵💵	⏰⏰
17–13	Optimize inventory storage through periodic location changes	💵💵	⏰⏰
17–14	Eliminate the warehouse	💵💵💵	⏰⏰⏰
Inventory Accuracy			
17–15	Audit all inventory transactions	💵	⏰
17–16	Compare recorded inventory activity to on-hand inventories	💵	⏰
17–17	Eliminate the physical count process	💵	⏰⏰⏰
17–18	Cycle-count based on usage frequency	💵	⏰
17–19	Lock down the warehouse area	💵💵	⏰
17–20	Move inventory to floor stock	💵💵	⏰⏰
17–21	Segregate customer-owned inventory	💵💵	⏰⏰
17–22	Streamline the physical count process	💵	⏰
17–23	Track inventory accuracy	💵	⏰

Exhibit 17.1 *(Continued)*

	Best Practice	Cost	Install Time
Inventory Accuracy			
17–24	Train the warehouse and accounting staffs in inventory procedures	💵	⏰⏰
17–25	Initiate warehouse staff self-auditing	💵	⏰⏰
17–26	Verify that all receipts are entered in the computer at once	💵	⏰
Inventory Transactions			
17–27	Record inventory transactions with bar codes	💵💵	⏰⏰
17–28	Record inventory transactions with radio frequency communications	💵💵💵	⏰⏰
17–29	Track inventory with radio frequency identification (RFID)	💵💵	⏰⏰
17–30	Eliminate all paper from inventory transactions	💵💵	⏰⏰⏰
17–31	Eliminate all transaction backlogs	💵💵	⏰
17–32	Immediately review all negative inventory balances	💵	⏰
Inventory Reduction			
17–33	Reduce the number of products	💵	⏰⏰
17–34	Reduce the number of product options	💵	⏰⏰
17–35	Obtain direct links into customer inventory planning systems	💵💵	⏰⏰⏰
17–36	Adopt just-in-time purchasing	💵💵💵	⏰⏰⏰
17–37	Shift raw materials ownership to suppliers	💵	⏰⏰⏰
17–38	Drop ship inventory	💵	⏰⏰
17–39	Reduce safety stocks by accelerating the flow of internal information	💵💵	⏰⏰
17–40	Reduce safety stock by shrinking supplier lead times	💵	⏰⏰⏰
17–41	Reduce safety stock with risk pooling	💵	⏰⏰
17–42	Use variable safety stocks for fluctuating demand	💵	⏰
17–43	Cross-dock inventory	💵💵	⏰⏰⏰

(continues)

Exhibit 17.1 *(Continued)*

	Best Practice	*Cost*	*Install Time*
Inventory Reduction			
17–44	Use overnight delivery from a single location for selected items	💵	⏰
17–45	Focus inventory reduction efforts on high-usage items	💵	⏰⏰
17–46	Eliminate redundant part numbers	💵	⏰⏰
17–47	Standardize parts	💵	⏰⏰⏰
17–48	Identify inactive inventory in the product master file	💵	⏰

A few of the best practices noted here rarely succeed at all, though world-class companies have installed them—these are the elimination of the warehouse and the receiving function, which can only be accomplished through a time-consuming process of inventory elimination and supplier qualification. However, for those companies that are well along in accomplishing these tasks, the best practices should be considered, given the resulting reduction in costs and accounting transactions.

Most of the other best practices are relatively inexpensive to install, since they generally involve changes to procedures, which have no attendant expense. A few best practices require the installation of fencing or different bin systems, but even these expenses are not considerable, unless the warehouse in question is a very large one. The remainder of this chapter separately discusses each of the best practices shown in Exhibit 17.1.

17–1 Audit Bills of Material   ✔*Author's Choice*

Some companies use *back-flushing* as the means of recording changes to inventory. Under this methodology, inventory is taken from the warehouse without any associated picking transactions put into the computer. Then, when production is completed, the total amount of production by item is entered into the computer, and the software automatically removes the associated inventory amounts from the warehouse records, using bills of material as the basis for doing so. Though this is a simple method for keeping warehouse paperwork to a minimum, an incorrect bill of material will quickly alter the on-hand inventory balances to such an extent that inventory accuracy will plummet. In addition, the accounting department uses the bills of material to determine the cost of any finished goods; an inaccurate bill will also impact the accuracy of this costing. Thus, the accuracy of a company's bills of material impact not only the records for inventory quantities, but also their cost.

The solution that keeps bill of material errors to a minimum is an ongoing audit of them. This practice keeps inventory quantities from becoming too inaccurate in a back-flushing environment, while making the costing of finished goods more precise. To do so, a person who is knowledgeable about the contents of bills of material must be assigned to a regular review of them. Any problems must be corrected at once. To be the most effective, it is best to concentrate the efforts of the reviewer on those bills that are used the most or that are expected to be included in upcoming production runs. By focusing on those bills receiving the most usage, a company can be sure of maintaining a high degree of bill accuracy for the bulk of its products.

The only implementation difficulty is that it requires the cooperation of the engineering manager, who must assign a staff person to the reviewing process. This assistance is critical, since engineers are the ones with the best knowledge of bills of material.

Cost: 💵   **Installation time:** 🕐

17–2   Conduct a Configuration Audit

Companies can run into warranty trouble when their engineering departments design a product correction, but the engineering change never makes its way into the production process. This is also a problem when the engineering changes make it partway through the company to the purchasing department, which orders new components to match the change, but not to the production floor, which assembles products based on the old configuration. This problem leaves the warehouse manager caught in the middle, storing inventory for the new configuration that is not used by the production staff, while running out of components for the old configuration that is still being assembled. The problem is exacerbated if bills of material are not updated for the changes, so that pick lists are incorrect. From the controller's perspective, the company will experience an increase in its inventory investment, as well as a probable jump in its obsolete inventory levels.

The solution is an ongoing configuration audit, preferably right after an engineering change or a new product is released. Under a configuration audit, an engineer or internal auditor familiar with the product pulls a completed product from the manufacturing line, disassembles it, and compares it to all engineering documents related to the product, including all authorized updates. If the product accurately reflects the current design, then no further action is required. If not, one must verify the accuracy of the bill of material, pick lists presumably derived from the bill, outstanding purchase orders, and production work instructions.

This is a necessary best practice that reveals any weaknesses in the procedures used by a company to roll out new products and manufacture modifications to existing ones.

Cost: 💵   **Installation time:** 🕐🕐

17–3   Modify the Bills of Material Based on Actual Scrap Levels

The typical company relies heavily on its bills of material to determine the cost of its products. They can be used not only as a reference tool to quickly look up a cost, but also as the primary means of calculating the remaining on-hand inventory balance if back-flushing is used. Under the back-flushing concept, a company simply enters the amount of its production for the day, and the computer will automatically clear this inventory from stock, based on the amount of materials that should have been used, as noted in the bills of material. Though this approach is remarkably easy to use, given the reduced volume of paperwork, it can quickly lead to very inaccurate inventory balances if the underlying bills of material are incorrect. This is a particularly difficult problem if the true scrap level is not reflected in the bills of material. If this is the case, the amount of materials listed in each bill will be too small, resulting in an inadequate amount being back-flushed out of inventory, which leaves inventory balances too high.

The soultion is to ensure that the correct scrap levels are included in each bill of material. By doing so, the amount of material back-flushed out of the inventory will be much more accurate, resulting in a more accurate inventory, cost of goods sold, and fewer (if any) material stock-outs to interfere with production.

To add accurate scrap rates to the bills of material, there must be a scrap reporting system already in place that notes the precise quantities of scrap that occur whenever a product is produced. With this information in hand, one can easily update scrap rates with a great deal of precision. Also, access to the information in the bills of material must be severely restricted to ensure that no one but an authorized user is allowed to change the scrap rates in bills; without this security point, there is no way to ensure that the most accurate scrap rates are indeed in the computer system. In addition, there must be constant attention to the scrap rates, for they will change over time as production practices and machinery change. Without this continual review process, the existing scrap rates in the bills of material will gradually depart from actual rates. Finally, there should be a provision in the computer system for automatically changing large blocks of scrap rates in many bills of material; given the time needed to alter individual scrap line items in all existing bills, this is an extremely helpful labor-saving device to have on hand. If all of these issues are addressed, the accuracy of the bills of material should rise markedly, along with the accuracy of the inventory and cost of goods sold.

Cost: 💵   **Installation time:** ⏰

17–4   Review Inventory Returned to the Warehouse

Most organizations that produce any sort of tangible product will be familiar with this scenario: the warehouse staff uses a computer-generated picking list to pick a number of items from the shelf for use in an upcoming manufacturing order, delivers these items to the production facility, and then finds after the job is completed that a number of items are returned to the warehouse, even though the pick list it used was intended to completely use up all items picked. Any returns of this type indicate that the bills of material used to compile the pick lists are incorrect. When this happens, the bills of material are listing too high a quantity of materials; if these bills are also used to calculate the amount of items to be purchased, an excessive number of purchases are being made. From an accounting perspective, an inaccurate bill of material leads to inaccurate product costs, which results in an inaccurate finished goods valuation.

The solution is to create a procedure for closely examining the parts returned to the warehouse, in order to determine exactly which line items in the bills of material are inaccurate. This may require the assistance of the engineer who is responsible for each bill of material, since this person has the most knowledge of what is contained in each product. By making changes to the bills, one can improve the accuracy of purchases, eliminate the labor of the warehouse staff in logging parts back into the warehouse, and be assured of accurate finished goods costs.

The only problem with this procedure is that it requires the active cooperation of the warehouse manager, who will most likely try to avoid the hassle of investigating product returns and just put items back on the shelf with no further investigation. However, explaining that a proper amount of up-front investigation will lead to a smaller number of part returns in the future may sway this person to be of more assistance.

This best practice can also be used in reverse, so that any additional parts issuances to the production floor are investigated. In this situation, the quantities listed on the bills of material are too low, resulting in parts shortages that will probably lead to incomplete production runs, on the grounds that the production staff runs out of parts before completing the scheduled quantity of products.

Cost: 💸   **Installation time:** ⏰

17–5 Modify the Bills of Material for Temporary Substitutions

When a company has some excess items in stock that could be used in an existing product, the materials management staff is sometimes unwilling to use the part, because they perceive it to be so difficult to modify the bills of material and all related parts ordering systems. The result is excess parts sitting in the warehouse, representing an excessive level of inventory investment.

The solution is to create a simplified system for modifying the bills of material for temporary substitutions. To do so, there must first be a written authorization from the engineering department, specifying exactly which component is to be removed from an existing bill of material, which one is to replace it, the quantities involved, and the dates during which this change will be in effect. The materials management staff needs to be involved in the date range, since they must schedule a production run that will use up the replacement part. Finally, the person in charge of bill of material changes must make the swap in the bill of material file. Of particular concern here is that the person also reset a reorder flag for the replacement part in the item master file, so that the material requirements system does not automatically reorder the part just because it now appears to be an active part.

These steps can be reduced if the bill of material database already contains a feature allowing for the short-term swapping of parts. If this is available, the swapping procedure will be somewhat shorter.

Given the number of steps involved, temporary substitutions are not worthwhile when the swapping procedure being contemplated is for components having a small total value, since the work required to do so will offset the savings from eliminating inventory. The cost accounting staff should develop a standard transaction cost for temporary substitutions, and use this as the cutoff point below which inventory will not be substituted.

Cost: Installation time:

17–6 Use Bills of Material to Find Inventory Made Obsolete by Product Withdrawals

When the marketing department investigates the possibility of withdrawing a product from sale, it frequently does so without determining how much inventory of both the finished product and its component parts remains on hand. At most, the marketing staff concerns itself only with clearing out excess finished goods, since this can be readily identified. Those unique parts used only in the manufacture of the withdrawn product will then be left to gather dust in the warehouse, and will eventually be sold off as scrap only after a substantial amount of time has passed.

A better approach is to have the engineering department use the product's bill of material to create a list of component parts unique to that product. This typically requires a custom program and a fair amount of processing time, since the bill's components must be compared to the contents of all other active bills, including their subassemblies, to determine which parts are not used in the manufacture of any other products. Once determined, this information can be used to calculate the product withdrawal date, since it may make sense to continue manufacturing the product a bit longer in order to use up expensive stock. Engineers can also use the list to incorporate excess parts into the design of new products, if this makes sense. Worst case, the list at least brings excess parts to the attention of the purchasing department, which can work on returning them to suppliers for credit or disposing of the parts in some other manner, thereby creating shelf space in the warehouse as soon as possible for more heavily used items.

Many materials planning software packages include a "where-used" report, which fulfills this need to some extent. The report lists every product whose bill of material calls for the use of a specific component. The report may require a fair amount of investigation before one can determine which items have truly been made obsolete, since one must compare each item listed on a retired product's bill of material to the items shown on the where-used report to verify which items are not being used elsewhere and can therefore be designated as obsolete.

          Cost: **Installation time:** 🕰

17–7 Compare Open Purchase Orders to Current Requirements

Between the time when a company issues a purchase order to a supplier and the date when the ordered items arrive, several problems may arise that render the original purchase order inaccurate. First, customer orders to the company may change, resulting in a modified production schedule that no longer requires certain parts from suppliers. Second, ongoing changes in the design of company products may render some parts obsolete. Third, adjustments to recorded inventory balances through the cycle-counting process may result in a need for fewer or more parts than are currently on order. For these reasons, by the date of their arrival, the amount of goods delivered by suppliers may vary significantly from a company's needs.

    To alleviate this problem, one can design a report that should be run through the corporate materials planning system on a daily basis, comparing the amount of outstanding balances on open purchase orders to the company's needs, as listed in the material requirements portion of the company computer systems. By reviewing this report, the purchasing staff can modify the amounts listed on open purchase orders, thereby resulting in an ongoing reduction in the amount of inventory kept on hand. This report is a standard part of any material requirements planning system, but must be created as a custom report for those companies without such a system.

          Cost: 💵   **Installation time:** 🕰

17–8 Reject Unplanned Receipts   ✔*Author's Choice*

The ideal receiving scenario is when the supplier sends a message to a company's receiving department, telling it that a shipment is on its way, what is in the shipment, and when it is expected to arrive. By doing so, the receiving staff is prepared in advance to properly log in the received item and disposition it in an orderly manner. Reality is a tad less efficient. Unplanned and unidentified receipts can arrive at any time, requiring the receiving staff to set them aside for eventual identification, log-in, and disposition, which can take days and interfere with the orderly running of the receiving area. Delays can be especially long when the receiving staff has no idea who ordered something, and must conduct a Sherlock Holmes–style investigation throughout the company to identify an item's owner. Due to this delay, suppliers are more likely to encounter payment delays, while the production staff finds that necessary items are hidden amid the stack of unidentified items at the receiving dock, thereby interfering with the manufacturing process. Further, fraudulent deliveries can be received (and then billed to the company) without the company having any idea of the problem for some time, since there is no policy to reject unplanned receipts.

These problems can be overcome through the rigorous rejection of all unplanned receipts. By doing so, the receiving staff has no backlog of receipt identifications to labor through, nor is it subjected to unexpected deliveries that it may have no available labor to handle.

Though this best practice sounds simple, it is extremely difficult to implement. Success in this area requires training the entire organization to understand that only authorized purchases coming through the purchasing department will be allowed at the receiving dock. This means that a purchase order number must be assigned to every single item shipped to the company; if there is no number in evidence, the item is rejected. This is a hard lesson to learn when a rush order arrives and is rejected, potentially causing significant short-term problems in a variety of departments. Nonetheless, only a hard commitment to the rejection of unplanned receipts, coupled with strong support by senior management, can achieve this best practice. It is also easy for a company to suffer a collective relapse in this area, so management must support it consistently over the long term.

Cost: **Installation time:** 🕓 🕓

17–9 Obtain Advance Shipping Notices for Inbound Deliveries

There is a great deal of in-house activity surrounding the receipt of goods, including possible cross-docking of received items to an outbound truck, the availability of dock doors, clearing of staging space, and arranging for prompt quality assurance reviews. This is especially difficult if the warehouse manager is not aware of the exact arrival time of inbound deliveries, resulting in a bedlam of unplanned activity when a delivery arrives. Given the difficulty of planning operations against uncertain delivery arrival times, there is an inherent level of inefficiency in the receiving operation.

A good approach for introducing more planning into the receiving function is to arrange for the receipt of advance shipping notices from the inbound freight carrier. This best practice is easiest to implement with the larger third-party freight haulers, several of whom have created onboard tracking systems that monitor their progress and make this information available to customers, either by telephone, proprietary network, or the Internet (mostly the last approach). If freight is not arriving by such a carrier, one can also arrange to have the supplier contact the company by any number of communication media to notify it of the approximate arrival time of a load, as well as the contents of that load. It is also possible to obtain system-to-system transparency of this information through the use of automated electronic data interchange (EDI) transactions, but this approach is moderately expensive to set up, and so is normally used only between frequent trading partners.

The downside to this best practice is the difficulty of having minor suppliers adhere to it. They tend to arrive at unscheduled times, clogging dock doors needed for scheduled arrivals. One can mitigate this problem by leaving a small number of outlying dock doors available for the use of these suppliers, or by gradually eliminating them with the cooperation of the purchasing department. Another issue is the use of third-party freight carriers by suppliers that do not offer advance shipping notice services; the purchasing department should demand the use of specific freight carriers when it places a purchase order, thereby controlling this problem.

Cost: **Installation time:** 🕐 🕐

17–10 Eliminate the Receiving Function

The receiving function is responsible for entering receipts into the computer system, and occasionally does not do a good job in this capacity. For example, the late or inaccurate data entry of receiving information can lead to inaccurate financial statements, as well as inaccurate information for the production planning and purchasing staffs to procure and assemble materials for the production department to use.

This is an extremely difficult best practice to implement. The concept that only a relatively small number of companies have fully implemented is to fully qualify suppliers in terms of their ability to ship goods of high quality, precisely on time, and to do so directly to the production process. This requires a great deal of advance work by the purchasing staff to find suppliers that are willing to do this, as well as supplier inspections by company engineers to ensure that supplier quality standards match or exceed those of the company. Only after this work has been done can a company convert to the direct delivery of goods to the production department, bypassing the receiving area.

A final problem to overcome is how to account for receipts if there is no receiving staff. The answer is to assume that parts were received if the products in which they are used as components were built. Accordingly, production records are exploded into their component parts in the computer to determine whose parts were used, and to then pay those suppliers based on these usage records. Subsidiary problems to resolve before this payment system will work are to centralize component sourcing with one supplier per part and to eliminate all scrap from the production process. Supplier centralization is necessary because the computer system will not know which supplier to pay once it backs into the number of parts used. Similarly, there can be no scrap in the production process, or else suppliers will not be paid for the full number of parts delivered, since these parts were not included in finished products; the only alternative that will work here is to set up a scrap reporting system, from which suppliers can also be paid.

Clearly, there are a large number of major issues to overcome before the receiving department can be eliminated. Though this does result in fewer transaction errors for the accounting department to worry about, this improvement is dwarfed by the changes needed to bring it about. Accordingly, this best practice should be attempted only if there are a number of other reasons for eliminating the receiving function.

Cost: 💵💵💵   **Installation time:** 🕐 🕐 🕐

17–11 Use Standard Containers to Move, Store, and Count Inventory

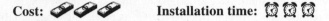

In many warehouse settings, the ideal container is the pallet. It can arrive at the receiving dock, be efficiently moved to storage with a forklift, and eventually be carried from there to the shop floor. It is also simple to count inventory when stored in pallet sizes, while many racking systems are preconfigured to hold pallets, which readily fills a warehouse's cubic volume. This excellent level of efficiency stops when pallets are broken down into cases or single items. The putaway and picking staffs must now be much more careful in recording quantities moved, while the effort required to count stock becomes much higher.

A very good best practice is the use of standard containers for these partial-pallet situations. By using a standard container size, one can more efficiently move items that might otherwise require individual piece-by-piece movement. Also, depending on how a container is set up, an inventory counter can glance at a container to determine the total quantity it contains.

Different containers will probably be needed for different types of stock, depending on the cubic volume of each one. A common approach is to fill several standard containers with the same item and pick only from the one in front. By doing so, an inventory counter can easily determine the quantities in all other filled containers and manually count only the one partial container in front. A variation on the standard container is a simple sealed plastic bag, which can be filled with a set quantity, labeled, and stapled shut. An inventory counter can determine its quantity immediately, while the usage signal (a ripped-open bag) indicates that a more careful count is in order.

The use of standard containers can be taken too far. In many situations, it is still easier to move, store, and count a partially used pallet-load without going to the sometimes-considerable effort of shifting everything into standard containers. Its best application is for small parts that would otherwise be difficult to handle and count.

Cost: 💵💵   **Installation time:** 🕐 🕐

17–12   Use Different Storage Systems Based on Cubic Transactional Volume

It can be difficult to slot items into various inventory locations around a warehouse just based on their cubic volume, since this single criterion does not reflect the amount of moves to which each one will be subject. As a result, the warehouse staff may find largely unused items slotted near the shortest access paths in the warehouse, while high-use items are parked in the rear, causing long travel times. This is a particular problem for small parts, since there are a variety of both low- and high-efficiency storage modes available for them.

A good solution is to assign storage locations based on both an item's cubic volume and number of transactions. As a result, some high-use pallets will be stored near a major picking area, while other less-used pallets will be kept in random storage along a back wall. Similarly, low-volume small parts may be stored in bins or storage drawers, while high-volume small parts will be stored in carousels from which picking can be done much more quickly. This approach can even extend to the height at which small parts are stored in fixed bins, with high-volume items stored at waist level for easy picking.

Cost: Installation time: 🕐 🕐

17–13   Optimize Inventory Storage through Periodic Location Changes

Though inventory may initially be organized to reduce the travel time of order pickers, this may change over time as different items become more or less popular. This is a particular problem for items whose sales change dramatically on a seasonal basis, or in proportion to their presence in certain catalogs or short-term sales promotions. In such cases, the picking staff may suddenly find itself traveling much farther to pick items than was the case just the day before.

A labor-intensive solution is to periodically review and revise inventory storage locations based on estimated demand patterns. This is not difficult for seasonal goods, since it is evident which items will soon experience changed levels of demand. Likewise, the imminent release of a new catalog should trigger inventory locational changes based on the contents of the catalog. On a very short-term basis, automated storage and retrieval systems can be assigned the task of completely shifting inventory overnight, so it is properly reconfigured to minimize its travel time the next day.

An advanced warehouse management system can perform this inventory review chore periodically, and can also recommend new inventory locations whenever the warehouse itself is reconfigured with new or revised storage locations. However, warehouse management systems offering this feature are extremely expensive. An alternative is to periodically bring in a consultant who can manually perform the same task; this approach can actually result in a better configuration than what is recommended by a computer since a consultant may use a larger array of configuration criteria than are built into a computer system.

Cost: **Installation time:** 🕐 🕐

17–14 Eliminate the Warehouse

The source of many accounting-related transactions is the warehouse. This department records entries for the receipt, movement, and issuance of parts to and from stock. If any of these transactions are incorrect, the inventory quantities used to derive the cost of goods sold, as well as of on-hand inventory, will be incorrect. In addition, there is probably a fair amount of obsolete inventory somewhere in the warehouse, which the accounting staff must identify and cost out. These are major issues that can seriously impact the accuracy of the financial statements.

A very difficult solution is the complete elimination of the inventory, which in turns means the elimination of the warehouse. Several world-class companies have achieved this best practice by switching to just-in-time receiving and production, which allows them to bypass all parts storage. By doing so, a company can avoid all of the transactions needed to log something in and out of the warehouse, not to mention avoiding all the staffing, space, insurance, and inventory obsolescence and damage costs that go along with having a warehouse. From the perspective of the accounting staff, this is the ultimate best practice in inventory accounting, since there is *no* inventory to account for besides the relatively minor amounts in work-in-process.

Unfortunately, this is a goal that very few companies achieve, for a variety of reasons. First, just-in-time receiving and production are very difficult concepts to fully implement, given the difficulty of changing both internal processes and the delivery systems of suppliers. Further, there may be some parts that are shipped from long distances or that are difficult to obtain, and that *must* be kept in stock. Finally, the existing inventory may take years to reduce to zero, unless a company is willing to take write-downs to eliminate some stock or return it to suppliers at a loss. Nonetheless, if a company can convert even some of its systems to just-in-time, it is possible to send received parts directly to the production facility without spending any time in the warehouse; this reduces the number of inventory transactions that can be made in error, resulting in an overall increase in the level of accounting accuracy.

Cost: 💵💵💵   **Installation time:** 🕐 🕐 🕐

17–15 Audit All Inventory Transactions

For any manufacturing organization, there are myriad transactions associated with the receipt of goods, their transfer to locations in the warehouse, and additional movement to the production floor, as well as the return of any excess items to the warehouse. Given the inordinate volume of transactions, some are bound to be done incorrectly. When this happens, the recorded quantities of inventory on hand and used will be incorrect, resulting in incorrect financial results. The problem impacts other departments, too, since inaccurate inventory volumes impact the purchasing, production, and warehouse departments.

One solution is auditing inventory transactions. By doing so, one can spot problems, research why they happened, and take action to keep the transaction errors from occurring again. For example, if an audit uncovers a lack of operator training that results in receiving not being completed in the computer, either a comprehensive or focused training session with that person, along with follow-up reviews, will eliminate the error.

Auditing can be assigned to the internal audit department. However, continual review work may be necessary, which the audit department may not have sufficient manpower to provide; the accounting department is well advised to take on this chore itself, if no other approach will work. Once the entity doing the work has been determined, the next step is to find the best way to spot transaction problems among the hundreds or thousands of inventory-related transactions that occur every month. A simple random selection of transactions will eventually discover a reasonable quantity of mistakes to review, but there are ways to improve one's chances of finding them. For example, a transaction that results in a negative inventory on-hand quantity is certainly worthy of a review, as is any transaction that takes more out of stock than is actually there. The same exception rules can be applied to transactions with inordinately large quantities. Further, transactions can be compared to the production schedule to see if any of the items received in the warehouse are scheduled to be used in production in the near future. Any of these issues are indicative of a problem and should be reviewed first. Though many of them may be valid, the odds of finding an error are greatly enhanced.

The next step in the auditing process is discovering the nature of the problem that caused the transaction error. Since the only two possibilities are systems or people problems, it is wise to assign a team with exceptional systems knowledge and people skills to this task. Since most employees will not admit to an error if they have made one, the single most important auditing skill is carefully dealing in a nonthreatening manner with the people involved in these transactions. Finally, there must be a follow-up routine established that reviews previously uncovered problems to verify that they have been fixed. Only if *all* of these steps are followed will errors in the recording of inventory-related transactions be fixed.

As several departments are involved in inventory transactions, the controller must be able to deal carefully with the managers of these other departments to ensure that the auditing process does not degrade into a situation where discovered problems are used to attack each other. Thus, interpersonal skills are critical to the success of this solution.

Cost: **Installation time:** 🕰

17–16 Compare Recorded Inventory Activity to On-Hand Inventories   ✔*Author's Choice*

Some industries deal with extremely expensive materials. In these situations, it is critical to ensure that recorded inventory levels are completely accurate, since even a small quantity variance can lead to a large impact on profitability. This is a particular concern when dealing with precious metals or gemstones, not to mention a variety of electronic components.

Many of the other best practices noted in this chapter will help to keep inventory accuracy within reasonable limits, such as auditing inventory transactions or cycle counting; but to be absolutely sure that quantities are correct, the best way is to compare recorded inventory activity to on-hand inventories. This approach varies from auditing because it assumes a 100 percent review of all transactions for selected items. Because it is a highly labor-intensive approach, one must confine it to a minimum number of especially expensive or critical inventory items.

To use this method, conduct a *daily* comparison of on-hand quantities to every transaction associated with them, such as receipts, inventory moves, scrap, production, returns from the production floor, and shipments. Of particular interest during this review process is any transaction that is not made, is made twice, is made in the wrong amount or on the wrong date, or involves the wrong part number or unit of measure. Only by conducting this complete review every day can a company determine where there are problems in the stream of transactions and fix them immediately. One should also try to spot trends in or concentrations of transaction errors, such as a number of receiving or scrap errors, which allows one to target a specific problem and fix it.

This best practice is strongly supported by those other departments that rely on accurate inventory levels, such as the warehousing, production, and purchasing departments. However, they support this because they do not have to provide the significant amount of staff time required to ensure its success. Accordingly, a controller should be extremely careful to use it only with a very small minority of the inventory items, monitor it carefully, and eliminate items from the review process as soon as it becomes apparent that there are no transactional errors occurring.

Cost: 🖊️   **Installation time:** ⏰

17–17 Eliminate the Physical Count Process

As noted in the last section, there are a variety of problems associated with having any sort of physical count at all. This section outlines how to use cycle-counts to completely avoid any physical count.

One should use cycle-counting as the primary way to eliminate the physical counting process. To do so, there are a set of carefully defined steps to follow before inventory reaches an accuracy level sufficiently high to allow one to avoid the physical count. One should read through all of the following steps and make a realistic assessment of a company's ability not only to complete them, but also to maintain the system over a long period. If it is not realistically possible, then do not run the risk of wasting up to a year of work on this project—there are other best practices in this chapter that pose a much higher chance of success. The steps are as follows:

1. *Throw out the trash.* The warehouse must first be cleaned up before spending a great deal of time on counting parts. Accordingly, trash, obsolete parts, and old supplies or tools must either be thrown out or moved to an outlying location.

2. *Identify the remainder.* The first step reduces the amount of inventory items to be reviewed for part numbers. This is now the main task—review all remaining inventory and post a part number on it.

3. *Consolidate inventory.* Once all parts are identified, cluster them together for easy counting. This takes several iterations before all inventory is completely consolidated, but do not worry about it—the main reason for consolidating at this stage is to make it easier to count and box the inventory in the next step, so a few unconsolidated items will not present a problem later on.

4. *Count and box the remainder.* Count all the inventory and then box or bag it. There should be a seal on each container, with the quantity marked on the seal, so that a glance at the container will reveal the complete quantity of the part. This is of vast benefit to cycle-counters, who can now cycle-count hundreds of items very quickly. Please note that it is not necessary at this point to correct all inventory balances in the computer, for the cycle-counters will soon take care of this problem when they methodically review the entire warehouse.

5. *Create warehouse locations.* Clearly mark every bin location. The location should include the aisle, rack, and bin number, so it is clear where an inventory item is located. This step is crucial for cycle-counting, since one cannot cycle-count if one cannot first find the part.

6. *Assign inventory to specific locations.* Go into the computer and assign a location code to every inventory item. This may require special programming to put a location field into the computer database.

7. *Create a cycle-counting report.* Create a computer report that lists all on-hand inventory, sorted by location code. The cycle-counters must have this available as their main tool for reviewing inventory.

8. *Segregate the warehouse.* Put up a fence around the warehouse and lock the gate! Now that cycle-counting is about to begin, there should be no way for nonwarehouse staff to enter the warehouse in order to take parts off the shelf.

9. *Initiate cycle-counts.* Assign cycle-counters a section of the warehouse to count. Issue them the latest cycle-counting report. They must carefully count all the items in every bin location and make corrections to the report to ensure that the computer database is correct. The warehouse manager monitors

their progress every day to ensure that they are completing their counts on time. A good initial cycle-counting frequency is to review the entire inventory six times a year; this high volume of counting can drop later, after accuracy levels increase.

10. *Audit inventory accuracy.* Audit the inventory once a week. A small sample of the total inventory is sufficient to determine its total accuracy, which should be posted for the review of the warehouse staff. It may be necessary to post accuracy by aisle, in case some sections of the warehouse are particularly prone to mistakes. If so, the best cycle-counters should be assigned to these aisles.

11. *Use a bonus program.* Reward the entire warehouse staff with a bonus at the end of each month, based on the audited accuracy of the inventory. A good measure above which bonuses should be given is 95 percent accuracy, with any item being defined as accurate if the counted quantity is within 2 percent of the amount listed in the computer (though this may not be a good measure in some industries, such as diamond processing). This is an extremely effective way to maintain the interest of the warehouse staff in the continuing accuracy of the inventory records.

Though cycle-counting will certainly allow one to avoid a physical inventory count, it is equally important to investigate why errors are occurring, not just to change inventory balances if they are wrong. If one can get to the bottom of a transaction problem and fix the underlying error, it is possible to greatly increase record accuracy and require less work by the cycle-counting staff to keep it that way.

Cost: **Installation time:** 🕰 🕰 🕰

17–18 Cycle-Count Based on Usage Frequency

The standard way to determine which inventory should be cycle-counted is to count the most expensive items the most frequently. Accountants recommend this approach, because it ensures the accuracy of the most expensive items in stock, which gives them some reasonable assurance that the inventory value they record in the financial statements is approximately correct.

The problem with this approach is that the accuracy of low-cost items is considered less important, even though the absence of those items could potentially keep an order from shipping, which negatively impacts revenue.

The solution is to base cycle-counts on the frequency of item usage, which means that an item that is used continually is counted the most frequently. This approach still satisfies accountants, because a high-cost item that does not move much will still be accurate with just a few counts per year, since very little can possibly happen to it if it just sits on a shelf. Conversely, an item that is constantly cycling in and out of the warehouse will be counted a great deal, which will hopefully ensure a high level of accuracy and therefore assist in avoiding stockouts that could halt shipments.

Creating a cycle-count sample under a frequency-of-usage approach will require a custom report from a materials planning system. To do so, accumulate the number of putaways and picks per stock keeping unit on a rolling basis over the past few months (possibly up to a year, if inventory turnover levels are low), and then create a report that is sorted in declining order by volume of total putaways and picks. This report can be used to manually select higher-frequency items for more frequent counts.

However, this approach also requires recordkeeping to ensure that high-frequency items are indeed counted more regularly than low-frequency items. An alternative is to rearrange inventory so that higher-frequency items are stored in specific aisle areas, for which an average usage frequency is calculated; then count every item in each aisle area during a single count, and track the frequency of cycle-counts for the entire block of inventory. This results in much less recordkeeping.

Cost: 💵   **Installation time:** ⏰

17–19 Lock Down the Warehouse Area   ✔ *Author's Choice*

The single most important cause of inventory inaccuracy is parts "walking out of the warehouse." This means that the physical layout of the warehouse allows anyone to wander in and take any parts they need for the production process. When this happens, there is no record that any item was taken from stock, so no one knows what is left on the shelf, or even if there is *anything* left, which renders any automated reordering system useless. From the accountant's perspective, the physical inventory count will probably be significantly different from what the accounting records show, resulting in a large negative inventory variance at the end of the year.

These problems can be eliminated by segregating the warehouse. This is done by setting up a fence around the entire storage area and locking the gate when there are no warehouse personnel on hand. In addition, there must be iron-clad rules about who has a key to this gate. If too many keys are handed out, anyone will still be able to enter the warehouse after hours. To prevent this, there should be no more than one key given to the production personnel, and then only to the most responsible person, who will faithfully mark down anything taken from the warehouse. If possible, even this should be avoided by prepositioning any needed parts outside of the warehouse for use by the production staff when the warehouse staff is not available. Further, the warehouse staff must be carefully instructed as to why no one but them is allowed in the warehouse; in addition, they should receive training in how to process inventory transactions, and then be given a bonus plan based on reaching high inventory accuracy levels. Only by taking all of these steps will there be a good chance that nonwarehouse personnel can be kept out of the warehouse and that the warehouse personnel are committed to a high level of inventory accuracy.

This best practice is always opposed by the production department, which claims that either it will be too time consuming to wait for the warehouse department to pick parts from the shelf or that they will not be able to get any parts at all if the warehouse staff is absent. The best way to allay these fears is to have all systems in place and fully functional before locking down the warehouse. By doing so, the production staff will find that there are no problems with the new system and will have no complaints left to make.

Cost: **Installation time:** 🕰

17–20 Move Inventory to Floor Stock   ✔ *Author's Choice*

The typical inventory contains an enormous number of small parts, many of which are difficult to track, are not stored in easily countable containers, and require a large amount of paperwork in proportion to their size and frequency of usage. In short, they are a pain for the warehouse staff to handle. Likewise, they represent a minor irritation for the accounting staff, since they must all be counted during the physical inventory counting process, and, because of the difficulty of counting them, they take up an inordinate amount of time. Further, they can easily represent one-third of the total number of inventory items, which is one-third more costing documentation than the accounting staff wants to track. Accordingly, it is safe to say that the smallest and most inexpensive parts in inventory are the root cause of a great deal of extra work for the employees of several departments.

A solution is to shift the small inventory items out of the warehouse and onto the shop floor, where they are treated as supplies. This approach carries the multiple benefits of requiring far less inventory handling work from the warehouse staff, fewer inventory counts during the physical inventory process, and much less inventory-costing work from the accounting staff. In addition, it brings more inventory close to the shop floor, where the production staff appreciates the readier access, as well as not having to go to the parts counter to requisition additional parts. This is one of the rare best practices greeted with universal approval by a multitude of personnel, not just those in the accounting department.

Though this step can be taken quickly, one should be mindful of the danger of issuing a quantity of expensive parts to the shop floor that may quickly disappear, resulting in a significant loss. For these few costly items, it may be better to leave them in the warehouse. Also, there must be a tracking system in place on the shop floor, whereby someone can check part bins and determine which parts to reorder. There are a variety of simple systems available that accomplish this, such as painting a reorder fill line in each storage tray, or using a two-bin system, where parts are reordered as soon as one bin is emptied. A manual reorder system is necessary for shop supplies, since items are no longer stored in the inventory database, where reordering can be done automatically, based on recorded inventory levels. Also, some of the parts being pulled from the warehouse may be listed in bills of material, which can be a problem if a company uses back-flushing. In this instance, items will be automatically withdrawn from the quantity shown in the computer system as soon as production is recorded, so the system will show negative usage of items that are no longer there. One should carefully consider and resolve all of these problems before moving parts out of inventory and into floor stock.

Cost: 💵💵   Installation time: ⏰⏰

17–21 Segregate Customer-Owned Inventory

A dangerous problem for many controllers is incorrectly valuing inventory too high because customer-owned inventory is mixed into it. This problem is especially common where customers frequently ship components to a company for inclusion in finished products. This situation arises when a customer has the rights to a proprietary product component, prefers to do some finishing work on selected components, or only wants a company to do final assembly work on its products. When any of these situations arise, the receiving staff commonly makes the mistake of recording receipts as company-owned stock and storing it alongside all other inventory in the warehouse. As a result, the inventory can be massively overvalued, leading to incorrectly reported profits.

A solution is to institute procedures and set up segregated areas that allow one to promptly identify customer-owned products at the receiving dock and shunt them immediately to the segregated area. By doing so, one can be assured of having much more accurate inventory quantities and costs. To implement this best practice, it is critical to require a purchase order on all items arriving at the receiving dock. With this procedure in place, the receiving staff can identify all receipts that the purchasing department has previously noted on a purchase order as being owned by a customer. With this information in hand, the receiving staff records the entry in the computer system and then moves the items to a separately marked-off area. This approach results in the storage of item quantity information in the computer system so the warehouse staff can easily find the parts, but at a zero cost, meaning the accounting staff does not make the mistake of increasing the amount of company-owned inventory.

The main problem with using this methodology is that the purchasing and warehousing departments must get used to issuing purchase orders for *all* items received, while also rejecting all items shipped to the company without attached purchase orders. Only by closely following these procedures can one be sure of identifying all customer-owned inventory at the point of acceptance.

Cost: Installation time: ⏰⏰

17–22 Streamline the Physical Count Process

Some companies find that they are unable to produce anything for several days while count teams perform a physical count of all on-hand inventory. When this happens, a corporation loses sales, since it cannot produce anything. In addition, the resulting inventory is not entirely accurate, since the counting process may include people who do not have a thorough knowledge of what they are counting, which results in incorrect counts and misidentified parts. Also, key people are taken away from their other work to conduct the count, resulting in little or no attention to customers for the duration of the count. Finally, the accounting staff usually stops all other work in order to devote themselves to the processing of count tags. Thus, the physical count is a highly disruptive and inaccurate process.

For those organizations that cannot entirely dispense with the physical count, it is still possible to streamline the process so that fewer resources are assigned to it, while keeping the accuracy level relatively high. The improvements are as follows:

- *Eliminate some inventory from the count with cycle-counting.* For situations where a company has just started cycle-counting (see the "Eliminate the Physical Count Process" section earlier in this chapter) but has not yet brought accuracy levels up-to a sufficiently high level, it may still be possible to concentrate the cycle-counting effort on a few key areas. By doing so, the accuracy of the inventory in these locations will be so high that there is no need to conduct a physical count.

- *Enter location code on tags.* When counters are entering information on count tags, they should also enter a location code. With this information, it is much easier for the accounting staff to later locate where a tag was used to record information, rather than wandering through the warehouse in a frustrated search for the information. This approach is even better than the common practice of tracking blocks of tags that are assigned to teams counting specific locations; though this brings a review person to the general vicinity of an inventory item, it does not precisely identify the location, which leads to lost time while someone searches for the part.

- *Enter tags directly into the computer.* It is much more efficient to directly enter tag information into the computer system, rather than entering it into an electronic spreadsheet for manual comparison to a computer-generated inventory report. This approach allows the computer to automatically issue a comparison of the counted quantities to the quantities already stored in the computer, so that one can quickly determine where there may be counting errors. Most good computer software packages contain this feature; if not, one must evaluate the cost of programming the feature into the system.

- *Identify all items in advance.* A team should review the warehouse well in advance of the physical count to spot all items that lack identifying part numbers. By researching these items and correctly marking them in advance, the counting teams do not have to address this task while also trying to count inventory, thereby shortening the counting process.

- *Only allow warehouse staff to count.* Warehouse employees have an excellent knowledge of all the parts stored in the warehouse and so are the most qualified to identify and count inventory in the most efficient manner possible. If other, less knowledgeable people are brought into the counting process, it is much more likely that there will be counting problems, resulting in wasted time at the end of the physical count, when extra counting teams must be dispatched to research potential miscounts.

- *Only conduct one count.* Do not count something more than once! Though some companies conduct a double count of all inventory items and then conduct a comparison of the two counts to spot errors, it is much easier and faster to complete a single count and compare this to the book balances already stored in the computer system. Conducting a double count adds to the time and effort needed to complete the counting process.

- *Precount the inventory.* A team should begin counting the inventory days or weeks in advance of the formal physical inventory count. This group's job is to gather inventory into single locations, count it, seal it into containers, and mark the correct quantity on the containers. By doing so, it is much easier for the physical count teams to complete their work in an efficient and accurate manner. Though this may seem like a considerable amount of advance work (it is), it results in a much shorter interval for the physical count, which allows a company to be shut down only for the briefest possible time.

When these suggestions are implemented together or individually, a company will experience significant reductions in the effort needed to complete a physical inventory, while increasing the accuracy of the resulting information.

Cost: 💵   **Installation time:** ⏰

17–23 Track Inventory Accuracy   ✔*Author's Choice*

A controller is always concerned about the accuracy of the inventory. If it is off by even a few percent at the end of the year, the annual physical count may result in a large alteration in profits that will cost the controller his or her job on the grounds that inaccurate financial statements have been issued. Furthermore, the purchasing staff cannot properly order replacement parts if it does not have an accurate idea of what is currently in stock, while the production department never knows when parts are available for current jobs. Thus, all these departments are deeply affected by the accuracy of the inventory.

The way to gain some assurance about overall levels of accuracy is to track inventory accuracy with periodic audits. By doing so, one can determine if there is an accuracy problem, resulting in further steps as outlined elsewhere in this chapter, such as locking down the warehouse and shifting inventory into the floor stock area. To review accuracy, print out a report from the computer system that shows the inventory in each warehouse location. Then an accounting person should take a sample of items from this report and verify that the items listed on it are indeed in stock in the correct quantities, and that they are stored in the correct locations. Similarly, a small sample of items should be traced from the shelf to the report to verify that all items are being tracked in the computer system. Then divide the total of all correct items by the total amount sampled to determine the accuracy percentage. For even the largest warehouse, a sample size of 30 items is usually sufficient to determine the accuracy of the entire facility. This information should be reported to management and posted for the warehouse staff to see. By showing this information to the warehouse staff and tying a series of bonus payments to it, one can be assured of an improvement in the overall level of accuracy.

There is little resistance by anyone to tracking inventory accuracy, though there are two systemic problems that may interfere with it. One is that the computer system must be able to produce a report that sorts inventory by location—if not, the auditing person cannot find items in the warehouse without a long search, turning the audit into a tedious affair that can last hours. The other problem is that the computer system must store location information for each part. If parts are scattered throughout the warehouse with no record of their precise location, it will be exceedingly labor-intensive to track down anything. If these two problems can be overcome, the auditing process becomes a simple and mechanical one that only takes an hour or so to complete.

Cost: **Installation time:** ⏰

17–24 Train the Warehouse and Accounting Staffs in Inventory Procedures

The underlying problem behind the bulk of all inventory record errors is a lack of knowledge by warehouse workers in how to process a variety of inventory transactions. As a result, cycle-counting teams waste time investigating errors; the materials planning staff must order parts on short notice due to unexplained materials shortfalls; the company incurs express delivery charges to bring in parts on short notice; and the accounting staff must record unexplained losses related to inventory adjustments.

Many of these problems can be mitigated by creating a procedures manual for all inventory transactions and by continually training both the warehouse and accounting staffs in their use. Examples of common inventory transactions are as follows:

- Back-flushing
- Consignment receipts and deliveries

- Cycle-counting adjustments
- Inventory storage in rack locations
- Issuances
- Issuances of additional parts
- Kitting
- Loaning inventory to departments
- Receiving
- Receiving customer returns
- Removing defective parts from the production process
- Returning defective parts to suppliers
- Returning stock to the warehouse from the shop floor
- Shipping completed customer orders
- Staging for shipping
- Transferring between inventory locations

It is not enough to simply create a handsome procedures manual and issue it to the staff. On the contrary, all employees involved with these transactions should go through regular refresher training, while new employees should be trained several times early in their employment and be certified by an experienced coworker as to their knowledge of the procedures. Further, any procedural change calls for a complete retraining of the entire staff on that topic. Only by enforcing the corporate commitment to training in inventory procedures can a company reduce its incidence of inventory transaction errors.

Cost: Installation time:

17–25 Initiate Warehouse Staff Self-Auditing

The bulk of all inventory recordkeeping systems still require manual data entry of inventory transactions into a computer system rather than the use of bar-code scanners or RFID to automatically track quantity and location changes. Unfortunately, it is impossible to flawlessly enter data manually, so most companies must deal with a certain amount of error investigation and correction. These errors can be traced to data entry, initial quantity miscounts, incorrect picks, or incorrect identification or recording of inventory items.

One way to reduce these errors is self-auditing within the warehouse department. The basic concept is for employees to audit each other's work, which can range from a small sample size to a 100 percent test. Obviously, this approach is only possible if there is a sufficient amount of staff time available. During peak work periods, it is probably impossible, but there may be slack time when audits can be squeezed in. Examples of inventory self-auditing include the following:

- Inventory pickers can compare each other's picked orders to the authorizing pick ticket.
- Data-entry clerks can compare input sheets to computer transaction logs.
- Cycle-counters can recount any exception conditions found by another cycle counter.
- Cycle-counters can review others' correcting entries in the inventory database.

There are two problems with self-auditing. First, it is difficult to ensure that employees are actually conducting audits. Second, there may be peer pressure to cover up mistakes. However, if the warehouse staff is partially compensated based on inventory record accuracy, there should be enough pressure amongst the group to overcome both of these problems.

Cost: Installation time: 🕰 🕰

17–26 Verify That All Receipts Are Entered in the Computer at Once

There is nothing that throws a wrench into a company's production planning and accounting more than the delayed entry of warehouse receiving into the computer system. When this happens (or rather, when it does *not* happen), the purchasing staff does not know if materials have arrived and they begin a series of frantic calls to suppliers to determine when items are to be shipped. Likewise, the production scheduling staff decide not to produce something because they do not see any receipt in the computer system. Finally, the accounting staff has a very difficult time determining what was really received at the end of the accounting period, resulting in the reporting of inaccurate inventory figures in the financial statements. All this because someone in the warehouse is slow in entering receipts.

The obvious solution is to make the warehouse staff make receiving entries as soon as the warehouse receives any parts, but the solution is not quite so simple. The underlying reason why receipts are not being entered at once is probably because the staff is too busy to do it, and so this chore waits until a slow period, perhaps at the end of the day. Thus, to make the staff enter receipts more quickly, one must find a better way to enter the receipts, one that is so simple and easy there is no excuse to delay the process. One way is to require all suppliers to attach a bar-coded sheet to all shipments, allowing the receiving staff to scan this sheet directly into the computer system, thereby recording the entry. Another approach is to restructure the receiving data-entry screen so that one only needs to enter the purchase order number on which any receipt is based. The purchase order then comes up on the screen, and the receiver quickly notes the quantity received. This latter approach is also a good way to pay customers without the extra effort of using the accounts payable staff (see Chapter 3). The latter approach carries with it the added benefit of forcing suppliers to provide only the purchase order number with their shipments—many suppliers resist having to bar code the information on their shipments. Either technique is an effective way to reduce the time needed to enter receipts, thereby eliminating a host of downstream problems.

Cost: **Installation time:** 🕑

17–27 Record Inventory Transactions
with Bar Codes   ✔ *Author's Choice*

There are many inventory transactions to record in the life of an SKU, such as receipt, storage in a bin, transfer to the shop floor, and so on. Every time these transactions are entered into the computer system, one must manually enter a transaction code, the part number being moved, and typically the location code to which it is being shifted. Each of these data items represents an opportunity for an incorrect entry, which cumulatively results in a significant reduction in the accuracy of inventory records.

Bar coding is a good, time-tested approach for improving the accuracy of inventory transactions. In brief, the warehouse staff creates a bar-coded part number for each item as it enters the warehouse and attaches the bar code to the item. It also creates preset bar code labels for each warehouse location and posts them at each location. Anyone moving stock then scans the part number bar code and the bar code for the location to which it is being shifted, and manually enters a quantity and transaction code to complete the transaction. This information is typically entered on a portable scanner that can be either placed in a cradle to upload information to the central computer system or used in real time with a built-in radio to transmit and receive transaction information.

Although this approach can significantly reduce transaction errors, there are a few problems to be aware of. First, if someone creates the wrong bar code label for an item when it first enters the warehouse, then all transactions later using that bar code will also be incorrect—a clear case of technology *increasing* the rate of transaction errors, rather than the reverse. However, one can mitigate this problem by setting the bar code printer to print not only the bar code, but also the product description and part number in English just below the bar code, so one can verify the accuracy of the bar code. Another problem is the cost of this equipment. Though a scanner can easily cost $2,000, and the rugged environment can lead to a relatively short equipment life before replacement, the reduced transaction cost can easily result in a headcount reduction in the warehouse that rapidly pays for the investment. A third problem is the time interval between a scan into a portable scanner and when its stored information is uploaded into the central computer system. If a cycle-counter were to run an inventory report after a materials handler had removed an item from stock but before the move had been recorded, she would find an error during her count, and enter a correcting transaction—resulting in another error when the original scan was finally uploaded. The best solution is to use real-time radio frequency scanning (see the following best practice) to upload transactions immediately. Finally, the warehouse staff must be carefully trained in the use of this equipment to ensure that scans are made correctly and properly uploaded. One should schedule not only training for new employees, but also refresher training for the existing staff, as well as formal training in any incremental improvements made to the system over time.

Cost: 💵💵   Installation time: ⏰⏰

17–28 Record Inventory Transactions with Radio Frequency Communications

Even if a company uses bar codes to accurately record inventory transactions, this still does not address the problem of timeliness. A person could scan a bar code into a portable device but not upload the data to a central database until the end of his shift, resulting in a significant shortfall in database accuracy. If the materials handling staff tries to solve the problem by routing their forklifts past a fixed terminal in order to enter information, they are creating longer putaway or picking routes that contribute to reduce labor efficiency. Further, if a company tries to install a warehouse management system, it will be working with transactional data that could be hours old, probably resulting in incorrect putaway or picking instructions to the staff, as well as inaccurate inventories for cycle-counters to review.

The solution is radio frequency (RF) communications. This takes the form of a handheld or truck-mounted computer, frequently integrated with a bar code scanner that communicates by radio waves with a central warehouse database. For example, a person picks a part from stock, scans the item's bar code and the location bar code from which it was taken, and enters the quantity withdrawn. The portable unit immediately transmits this information to the central database, along with a time stamp, so that the quantity in the inventory location is adjusted and a picking record is created that can be used for a delivery to either a customer or the production floor. If the database record indicates that there is not enough inventory on hand to record the withdrawal, it can even send a query back to the employee, asking for a recount of the bin's contents. Thus, one can use an RF system to verify transactions, achieve high rates of record accuracy, almost completely eliminate paper-based transactions, and have a more efficient work force.

Mechanically, an RF system begins with a transactional entry being transmitted from a portable unit, which is received by a radio transponder that routes the transaction through a network controller that essentially emulates a hardwired computer terminal. From there, the information passes along the standard company computer network to the company materials management database. Transaction verifications flow along the same route back to the portable terminal. If there are many portable units in use at one time, the radio transponder will poll the units in a looping sequence until it finds one that wants to deliver a transaction, and then it continues with the polling after receiving the transaction. An alternative approach is for the portable units to transmit transactions only when other units are not transmitting.

A significant problem with RF systems is interference caused by factory equipment. Prior to installing an RF system, one should have the supplier tour all corners of the warehouse, and anywhere else where the portable RF units may be used, to ensure that there are no "dead" zones from which transmissions cannot be made. It is also possible for a large number of portable units to cause a bottleneck on the main company network, simply because of the large volume of transactions they are initiating. This can be corrected by increasing the network throughput at whatever bottleneck is causing the problem.

Cost: Installation time:

17–29 Track Inventory with Radio Frequency Identification (RFID)

A major problem with any manually operated inventory system is the vast number of transactions required to track receipts into the warehouse, moves between bins, issuances to the shop floor, returns from the floor, scrap, and so on. Every time someone creates a transaction, there is a chance of incorrect data being entered, resulting in a cumulative variance that can be quite large by the time a stock item has wended its way through all possible transactions. Incorrect inventory information leads to a host of other problems, such as stockouts, incorrect purchasing quantities, and a seriously inaccurate cost of goods sold.

One way to avoid these transactional errors is to use the new RFID technology. Though only recently formulated,[2] the technology has already been adopted by Wal-Mart, which should ensure a rapid rollout in at least the retail part of the economy. The basic RFID concept has been around for years—attach a tiny transmitter to each product, which then sends a unique encoded product identification number to a reader device. The cost of these transmitter tags has dropped to about 10 cents, which begins to make it a cost-effective alternative for some applications. Growing use of the technology will likely reduce the cost further.

---

[2] The RFID standards can be found at *www.epcglobalinc.org*.

When a tagged inventory item passes near a reader device, the reader emits a signal, which powers up the tag, allowing it to emit its unique product identification number. In order to read a large number of tags, the reader turns on each tag in sequence, reads it, and turns off the tag, thereby preventing confusion with repetitive reads. The tag information is then logged into the inventory tracking system, indicating an inventory move past the point where the reader was located.

The most likely implementation scenario for RFID is to begin by rolling it out within the warehouse and manufacturing areas of a company, first using it to track entire pallet loads (good for receiving and inventory control transactions), and then implementing it for smaller tracking units, such as cases (good for picking, cycle counts, and shipment transactions) or even individual items (most applicable for WIP inventory or retail applications). This implementation approach allows for a gradually increasing investment in the technology as a company gradually learns about its applicability.

A major advantage of RFID is its ability to provide inventory count information without any manual transaction keypunching. This eliminates the need for manual receiving, inventory move, and issuance transactions. It can also provide real-time information about the precise location of all inventory, which can assist with locating missing inventory, arranging cycle counts, and auditing stock. If issued to suppliers, this information tells them precisely how much inventory is currently on hand, so they can more accurately determine when to deliver more stock to the company.

One problem with RFID is the possibility of radio interference, which can be a major problem in heavy manufacturing environments. As a general rule, if wiring into the warehouse and shop area must already be shielded in order to ensure proper data transmission, then RFID may not work. If this potential exists, then be sure to conduct extensive transmission testing in all areas where inventory may be tracked to ensure that radio interference will not be an issue. Another problem is that certain products, such as steel or fluids, obviously cannot be tagged.

An additional problem is that RFID is simply too new. Few case studies have been made, so it is difficult to determine what other problems will arise.

Cost: 💵💵   **Installation time:** ⏰ ⏰

17–30 Eliminate All Paper from Inventory Transactions

Every time someone handles a piece of paper listing an inventory transaction, there is a chance of losing the paper, misconstruing its contents, or transcribing it back into the computer system with an error. This problem is especially prevalent in the handling of inventory, since there is a potential for a paper-based transaction at every step in the handling of inventory—receiving, quality assurance, putaway, moves, picking, scrap, shipping, and so on.

The best solution is the complete avoidance of paper documents for all inventory transactions. This can be done through best practices already noted—bar coding and radio frequency identification. As an example of how one can use these technologies to avoid paper-based transactions, one can use a bar-coded scanner to record the receipt of an incoming item, scan the bar code again when the item is put away, scan it yet again when picked, and scan it one last time upon either shipment or delivery to the shop floor. As an alternative to bar coding, a radio frequency identification system requires no scanning at all—a radio chip attached to each pallet, case, or item transmits its location to receiving stations as it moves about the company premises. These technologies have the added benefit of requiring much less or no employee labor, so they can concentrate on their primary tasks and have no opportunity to incorrectly record a transaction.

The downside of all these alternatives to paper-based transactions is their cost. Virtually all alternatives require an investment in the real-time updating of inventory records. However, one should compare this added investment to the cost of correcting transactional errors related to the use of paper, which frequently reveals that paper avoidance is a very cost-effective policy.

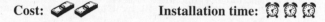

Cost: **Installation time:**

17–31 Eliminate All Transaction Backlogs

The warehouse staff gets into serious trouble when it develops a permanent backlog of inventory transactions, usually in the areas of receiving, moves between bin locations, picking, and receipts from the shop floor back into the warehouse. When a backlog arises, inventory records are not being updated on time, rendering inaccurate the reports used by cycle-counters to verify inventory quantities and locations. If cycle-counters use these inaccurate reports, they will undoubtedly find differences between the inventory database and their physical counts, and will make entries into the computer system to eliminate the differences—which will not improve the record accuracy situation once any unentered transactions are included in the inventory database. Thus, a transaction backlog results in permanent inventory record inaccuracy. Further, transaction backlogs tend to create piles of paperwork in which other documents can be lost, resulting in extra search time to locate needed materials.

A crucial best practice is to eliminate these backlogs, usually by allocating extra staff time to do them. Once the piles of paperwork are eliminated, the warehouse manager can focus on increasing levels of training and process improvement to reduce the number of people required to keep the backlog from recurring. Real-time, online data entry using wireless bar-coded scanners is an excellent method for having forklift operators update inventory move transactions on the fly, so there is no paperwork for anyone to keypunch at a later date. One can also use real-time entry of receipts at the receiving dock by having a computer terminal stationed there. The main point is to make transaction entries at the time of initial occurrence as easy as possible, so there is no need for the warehouse staff to delay the data-entry task.

If the warehouse has a highly variable amount of transaction volume, some backlog may reappear in periods of high activity, though this can be avoided through the careful use of the preplanned hiring of part-time workers to assist the regular staff.

Cost: **Installation time:** ⏰

17–32 Immediately Review All Negative Inventory Balances

The impact of a variety of transactional problems can result in the computer system reporting a negative inventory balance. Source problems could include the presence of a transaction backlog where offsetting entries have not yet been made, incorrect cycle counts, improper counts at the receiving stage, picks from stock without an update to the inventory records, and so on. Whatever the cause, negative balances are a clear indicator of inadequate warehouse management, and show that the inventory database cannot be reliably used for materials planning, much less inventory valuation.

The solution is to immediately investigate all negative inventory balances. Investigation means not just correcting the book balance to match the on-hand balance, but also reviewing all underlying transactions to find the reason for the negative balance and following through to ensure that the problem does not happen again. One should create a procedure for spotting negative balances right away. Also, include in the daily warehouse activity list a requirement to print an inventory report sorted in ascending order by quantity on hand, so negative balances appear at the top of the report. Also, since cycle-counters should have expertise in resolving inventory problems, have them correct and investigate the negative balances as part of their daily cycle-counting routines.

Cost: 💵   **Installation time:** ⏰

17–33 Reduce the Number of Products

The sales department loves to shower customers with a broad range of products to fit every possible need. A company can certainly maximize its sales by doing so. The problem is that it is not maximizing its profits. With an enormous range of product offerings comes a massive investment in finished goods inventory, since many of the products will sell only occasionally but must still be stocked against the possibility of an order. Further, raw materials and subassemblies must be stocked in case more products are needed. In addition, the rates of obsolescence will be higher with more products, since some products will almost certainly be overproduced and will languish in the warehouse for years.

The solution is a periodic planned review of the entire range of product offerings, with the intent of eliminating the slow-moving items. The accounting staff must be heavily involved in this effort, reporting on sales trends, inventory investment, and direct profits by product. The sales department will resist the reduction on the grounds that sales will be lost, so the company should involve senior management in the process in order to enforce the decision to eliminate products.

The primary downside to this best practice is the initial reduction in earnings caused by inventory write-offs when it is first implemented, since a number of products may require pruning.

Cost: 💵   **Installation time:** ⏰ ⏰

17–34 Reduce the Number of Product Options   ✔*Author's Choice*

Design engineers like to offer a wide range of product options from which customers can choose. The assumption is that customers will perceive a company to have a high degree of customer service by offering products in a multitude of variations. The trouble with this approach is the considerable expansion in the number of subassemblies and items that must be kept in stock to deal with the full range of possible variations in product configurations. In many cases, specific configurations are ordered so rarely that inventory must be stored for long periods prior to use; the odds of eventual obsolescence due to nonuse are also high.

The solution is to offer customers a greatly reduced set of product options. One can then reduce the number of inventory items kept in stock to those used on a small number of basic offerings. This approach does not mean that customers are offered only a "bare-bones" product—on the contrary, a fully loaded product is quite acceptable, but the number of variations from that fully loaded model must be kept low in order to avoid retaining inventory for rarely ordered features. Customer satisfaction levels will still remain high as long as they can choose from a clustered set of features offering them the choice of minimal extras at a low price, many features at a high price, and just one or two variations between these two extremes.

Cost: 💵   **Installation time:** ⏰ ⏰

17–35 Obtain Direct Links into Customer Inventory Planning Systems

The purchasing department usually places orders based on the requirements output by a material requirements planning (MRP) system. Although this output may appear to be precise, it is still driven by an estimate of what someone in the sales department thinks customers are most likely to purchase. Consequently, despite the appearance of a great deal of precision in the types and quantities of parts ordered, the purchasing staff's efforts may still result in excess inventory or shortages.

A solution is to actively pursue direct system linkages with the inventory planning systems of customers. By doing so, one can eliminate all estimates from the planning process and avoid considerable amounts of excess quantities for some inventory items and shortages for others.

The problem is getting customers to agree to reveal their demand information. This can be achieved by suggesting some type of shared cost savings, or by promising long-term fixed pricing, and so on—the inducement must be sufficient to attract the customer's attention, while at the same time not being too expensive for the company. Another approach is to offer the customer free software with which it can more easily place orders to the company, which yields a less efficient manual linkage to the customer. Given the time required to achieve direct customer linkages, this best practice is usually only cost-effective for the largest customers.

Cost: 💵💵   **Installation time:** 🕐🕐🕐

17–36 Adopt Just-in-Time Purchasing

A core inventory reduction problem is a company's reliance on a demand forecast, which inherently introduces a risk of demand inaccuracy based on the perceptions of the people creating the forecast.

The only way to eliminate inventory fluctuations based on an inaccurate forecast is to eliminate the forecast. This requires the complete reorientation of the purchasing (and manufacturing) system from one that pushes materials through the production process based on a forecast, to one that pulls items from production based on actual customer orders. Under this demand-pull approach, when a new customer order is received, the manufacturing operation is authorized to build exactly enough units to fill the order, which in turn requires an order to a supplier for the exact amount of materials needed to fill the company's purchasing requirement.

This is an advanced best practice requiring the completion of the following activities prior to its implementation:

1. *Certify supplier quality levels.* It makes no sense for suppliers to deliver shoddy goods directly to the production department, so every supplier's production process must be certified in advance.

2. *Communicate materials needs to suppliers.* Suppliers need to know exactly when materials are needed, so the company must find a way to communicate this information to them. A sound approach is to allow them on-line access to the company's materials planning database.

3. *Alter the accounts payable process.* If suppliers bypass the receiving department, there will be no receiving documents from which to authorize a pay-

ment. Instead, the accounts payable staff must be trained to make payments based on scheduled deliveries, as shown in the materials planning system.

4. *Arrange for limited storage facilities near the production process.* If there is no room for inventory near the production department, the area will be choked with inventory deliveries. It is better to arrange for sufficient inventory storage in strategic locations, and show suppliers exactly where their deliveries are to be made.

5. *Arrange for small, frequent supplier deliveries.* Storage near the production floor is likely to be limited, so suppliers must be able to make small-quantity deliveries to avoid overburdening the storage areas. This will call for frequent deliveries in order to avoid stockouts.

One must first address all five of these activities before just-in-time purchasing can be successfully implemented, so the implementation period can be quite long. Also, some suppliers will never pass the quality certification process, which requires their replacement with better suppliers or a more limited receiving function to handle their deliveries.

Cost: 💵💵💵   **Installation time:** ⏰⏰⏰

17–37 Shift Raw Materials Ownership to Suppliers

The raw materials portion of a company's inventory can consume a major part of its working capital investment, money that could otherwise be used for other activities. Also, the occasional purchase of excessive quantities of stock will eventually result in a large proportion of the inventory being obsolete. Manufacturing companies will find that these are particularly large problems that have a major impact not only on cash flow but also on profits.

One way to mitigate the adverse effect of raw materials inventory is to shift its ownership to suppliers. Under this scenario, suppliers deliver goods to the company in whatever quantities they want, above a designated minimum, as long as they do not exceed the physical storage area set aside for their use. The company logs these items out of the storage area when it uses them and pays the supplier for the amounts used. This has the obvious impact of eliminating a company's investment in raw materials, and shifts the burden of obsolescence to the supplier. In exchange, the supplier obtains a single-source contract with the company, ensuring itself of sales for at least one year and possibly for several, and using a pricing schedule that both parties have agreed to in advance. In addition, the supplier can park extra inventory at the customer location, thereby avoiding the cost of just-in-time deliveries.

Unfortunately, there are several problems with this best practice that limit its practical application. First, it is generally limited to nearby suppliers that can regularly monitor stocking levels at the company location. Second, the company must be willing to share its material requirements information with suppliers. Third, the company must be willing to sole source large portions of its inventory. Fourth, any custom parts made or obtained by the supplier will ultimately be paid for by the company, even if it never uses them, since the supplier has no other means for liquidating the stock. Fifth, the company is responsible for any inventory discrepancies, since these problems typically arise through the lack of knowledge of inventory-tracking procedures by its own staff. Within these restrictions, many companies with large raw material inventories will find that the prospective elimination of at least some of their inventory investment is well worth the effort.

Cost: Installation time: 🕰 🕰 🕰

17–38 Drop Ship Inventory

A typical set of inventory transactions involves receiving items, moving them to a quality review area, checking them, moving them again to main storage, picking them for an order, assembling and packaging the order, and shipping it. Not only does this process require a large number of transactions, any of which could be made in error, but it also involves a great many "touches" of the inventory, increasing the odds of product damage.

In situations where a company is purchasing a finished product from a supplier, turning around and selling it to a customer, there is a possibility of using drop shipping. Under this approach, the supplier ships the product directly to the customer, bypassing the company's warehouse entirely. By doing so, all of the transactions and risks of product damage just noted are eliminated. This is the ultimate approach to storing inventory—there is nothing to store. It is an especially attractive option for large items, which would otherwise require special handling and take up considerable space within the warehouse.

Unfortunately, drop shipping is an option only in the minority of situations. Many suppliers are unwilling to ship directly to customers, especially if shipment sizes are smaller than full pallets; issuing small shipments increases a supplier's costs, so the company may have to accept a supplier price increase in exchange for this service. Another problem is the need for new procedures to handle drop shipments. The accounting department must be trained to accept a shipment notification from the supplier, so it can issue an invoice to customers and also have a control point in place for verifying if no shipment notification has been received. Further, the company may not want the customer to know the name of the supplier, since the customer could theoretically purchase the product at a lower price directly from the supplier.

Cost: Installation time: 🕰 🕰

17–39 Reduce Safety Stocks by Accelerating the Flow of Internal Information

A typical reordering scenario is for the warehouse manager to forward to the purchasing department a daily list of items requiring reordering. This goes by intercompany mail to the purchasing department, which places it in the department inbound work queue. After some time passes, the request reaches the top of the stack, and a purchasing person confirms the need for the item, obtains supervisory approval, and then mails a purchase order to a supplier. The total lag caused by all these activities and wait times can easily exceed a week; during this time, the inventory level continues to decline, possibly resulting in a stockout before the delivery arrives from the supplier. When this problem goes on for some time, the purchasing staff starts to lengthen the item lead times in its database, forcing the company to order sooner and sooner. The result is long lead times for many items, requiring extremely long time horizons for product forecasting, which becomes inherently more difficult when stretched further into the future.

To avoid longer lead times caused by internal communications problems, we must shrink the time required to notify suppliers of new purchasing requirements. This can involve a number of system improvements, such as having a computerized materials planning database automatically issue purchase orders to suppliers without human intervention, based on the production plan and existing stock levels, and transmitting the purchase orders by e-mail to avoid mail float. If such an advanced solution is not possible, then one can fax purchase orders to suppliers, require less supervisory approval of purchase orders, employ runners to move reorder requests more quickly within a company, and use extra staff to eliminate the queue of purchasing requests in the purchasing department.

The variety of improvement possibilities will require the active cooperation of the purchasing manager, since all the changes impact his or her area of responsibility. If there is resistance, then a senior manager must intervene to require implementation of the improvements.

Cost: 🖙🖙   Installation time: ⏰ ⏰

17–40 Reduce Safety Stock by Shrinking Supplier Lead Times

A company goes to great lengths to reduce its internal lead times by a variety of just-in-time techniques, but it tends to accept the lead times handed to it by suppliers. These lead times are frequently not even based on the supplier's actual production capabilities but are simply the lead times announced by the salesperson with whom a company deals. The result is long lead times, which a company deals with by investing in excessively large safety stocks.

The purchasing department can shorten supplier lead times by including a reduced delivery time in its request for quotes. By specifying short lead times up front, a supplier realizes that this is an important criterion for a company, and must commit to it before there will even be any discussion of orders. This can have an added benefit for suppliers, since by being forced to revamp their internal processes to improve their lead times they will now have a new basis on which to compete.

Sometimes an even simpler approach to reducing lead times may have a positive impact—specify the exact date *and time* of expected receipt on the purchase order. By making it clear that the company has a high expectation of receipt within a very narrow time frame, suppliers become more aware of the importance of this issue.

This best practice does not mean that one should force impossibly short lead times on suppliers, just that lead time should be a prime focus of discussion with suppliers, rather than being blindly accepted by the company.

Cost: 💵   **Installation time:** ⏰ ⏰ ⏰

17–41 Reduce Safety Stock with Risk Pooling

Risk pooling is the concept that safety stock levels can be reduced for parts that are used in a large number of products because fluctuations in the demand levels of parent products will offset each other, resulting in a lower safety stock level.

For example, engineers are usually instructed to use common parts in more than one product, so that fewer total parts can be stocked (another inventory reduction technique). A useful side benefit of this approach is that the fluctuations in the demand levels of a single part by multiple parent products will offset each other. This results in a smaller standard deviation in usage levels for a part having multiple sources of demand, as opposed to the usage deviation for parts with fewer sources of demand.

In order to reduce safety stock levels for parts having multiple sources of demand, use a simple trial-and-error approach of determining the actual stockout level of these items over a rolling three-month period and gradually reducing the in-stock balance until the mandated service level is reached. For these items, the safety stock level will likely be substantially below the average corporate safety stock level.

Cost: 💵   **Installation time:** ⏰ ⏰

17–42 Use Variable Safety Stocks for Fluctuating Demand

Most materials planning systems include a feature that calculates an adequate safety stock level based on parts usage levels and supplier lead times. If a company experiences a steady level of demand, this approach will yield reliable safety stocks. However, what if demand fluctuates to a high degree, as is the case for seasonal sales? When this occurs, safety stocks calculated during a low-demand period will result in repeated stockouts, while safety stocks calculated during a high-demand period will result in an excessive inventory investment. Even the midway approach of using a safety stock level based on the average level of demand satisfies no one—still some stockouts during high-usage periods, and still too much inventory during low-usage periods.

The solution is to obtain materials planning software that allows for variable safety stocks. These systems automatically reset safety stock levels as forecasted demand levels change, so the conflicting objectives of minimal stockouts and minimal inventory levels are both balanced. If the existing system does not contain this feature, the software development staff may be able to program it into the existing system.

A low-budget approach is to schedule a quarterly review of safety stocks, focusing on those impacting the largest dollar value of inventory, and manually adjust safety stocks at that time. Since the materials management staff rarely has time for such a review, be sure to examine only the highest-investment safety stocks, so the review results in a significant impact on inventory investment and stockout levels in exchange for the minimum amount of staff review time.

Cost: **Installation time:** 🕐

17–43 Cross-Dock Inventory

As noted under the "Drop Ship Inventory" best practice, there are a great many inventory transactions and physical moves required if an item is brought into a warehouse, stored, retrieved, and shipped. All these moves introduce the possibility of creating an incorrect transaction or damaging items. Though the drop shipping approach completely eliminates this problem, it is not always possible to do so, either because suppliers refuse to ship direct, container sizes must be reconfigured prior to final delivery, or items from multiple suppliers must be combined into a single shipment.

If drop shipping is not possible, cross-docking may be an alternative. Under this approach, items arrive at the receiving dock and are immediately shifted across to a shipping dock for immediate delivery. By doing so, the only inventory transactions are for receiving and shipping, while the only inventory move is from one dock to another. There is no quality review, putaway, or picking transaction at all. Because of these missing transactions, the use of warehouse staff is kept to a minimum.

To make cross-docking work, inbound deliveries must have a high enough level of product quality to eliminate the quality assurance review, which would otherwise create a potential delay in the delivery of shipments to customers. Also, there must be excellent control over the timing of inbound deliveries, so the warehouse manager knows exactly when items will arrive. This is especially critical when some parts of a customer order must still be picked, since the picking transaction should be completed just prior to the arrival of a delivery containing the remaining items in a customer order. Further, the computerized warehouse management system must be sufficiently sophisticated to tell the receiving staff that items are to be cross-docked, and the number of the shipping dock to which items must be shifted for delivery. Finally, this approach requires a number of docks, since trailers may have to be kept on-site longer than normal while loads are accumulated from several inbound deliveries.

Cost: 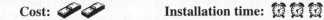   Installation time: 🕐🕐🕐

17–44 Use Overnight Delivery from a Single Location for Selected Items

It makes a great deal of sense to store most types of inventory in distribution warehouses strategically located in a company's primary markets or near major customers. By doing so, one can more easily ship products to customers on short notice. However, this approach does not work well for the minority of products having uncertain demand levels. It is impossible for material planners to estimate how much of these items to stock in each distribution warehouse, so they face the alternatives of frequent stockouts or the expense of an excessive inventory investment (especially for those items having a high unit cost).

An inexpensive best practice that resolves this issue is to retain high-value items with uncertain demand levels in a central warehouse, and use overnight delivery services to ship them to customers when needed. By doing so, material planners can store a large quantity of the items in one location, rather than in several. The cost of overnight delivery services is usually minor in comparison to the saved inventory investment. However, this best practice works less well for bulkier items, since express delivery expenses rise dramatically with the size of the shipment. Consequently, one should conduct a cost-benefit analysis to determine the maximum item size beyond which it is impractical to ship items from a central location.

It may also be necessary to alter the customer order system, so that orders placed for items retained in the central storage facility are automatically flagged and forwarded to that location for immediate shipment.

Cost: Installation time: 🕐

17–45 Focus Inventory Reduction Efforts on High-Usage Items   ✔*Author's Choice*

When the directive is handed down to reduce the total company investment in inventory, the materials management staff tends to throw up its hands in dismay and tackle the directive for all the thousands of items in stock. The result is a pitiful effort on a per-unit basis, since the materials management staff can devote only a minor amount of time to this goal. Due to the broad scope of its efforts, the company's inventory investment may not decline at all.

A solution is to focus their attention only on the reduction of high-usage items. There are several reasons for doing so. First, by definition, slow-moving items are not going anywhere soon, so the materials management staff would have to wait a long time before the natural ongoing usage of these items will bring about any sort of reduction. Conversely, the turnover speed of high-usage items will cause a rapid inventory reduction in short order. Second, high-usage items represent a small portion of the total items in stock, so the staff can focus on reducing the quantity of far fewer items, resulting in both more attention to fewer items and plenty of leftover time for the staff to complete other tasks.

Cost: 💵   Installation time: ⏰ ⏰

17–46 Eliminate Redundant Part Numbers   ✔ *Author's Choice*

When a company consolidates multiple locations in an effort to streamline its engineering and purchasing functions, a common problem is the discovery of duplicate part numbers, since each location has assigned a different part number to the same part. Part duplication is also common when many new products are being launched at the same time, since multiple engineers are needed at the same time for design work, and they may not be aware of part designations being made by their counterparts. It also occurs when a company switches to a new supplier, since the person assigning part numbers may not be aware of existing designations. Whatever the reason may be, redundant part numbers typically result in a considerable increase in the amount of on-hand inventory.

The key task in eliminating redundant part numbers is finding these parts. There are several methods for doing so. One is to simply ask the warehouse staff's cycle-counters, who have the best knowledge of what parts are currently on hand. Though this approach will highlight some duplicates, it will not spot everything—cycle-counters are frequently assigned to specific warehouse aisles and so have no knowledge of what lies elsewhere in the warehouse. Also, they frequently count sealed containers and have no idea of their contents.

Another possibility is to audit a sample of the inventory, deliberately looking for duplicate parts. This will eventually spot some duplicates, but is more effective when the warehouse is organized by part type, so one can conduct 100 percent audits of selected bins and aisles.

Yet another approach is to assign meanings to part numbers, so that certain letters or numbers in each part number refer to a type of part. By using this approach, one can review certain ranges of part numbers for duplicates. Though this approach initially appears attractive, it can quickly become unwieldy if a company must renumber all the parts of an acquired company to match its internal numbering system. Also, unless very carefully laid out, a part numbering scheme can run out of space for new parts. Further, one must run the part numbering task through a single person or small group who are responsible for assigning "smart" part numbers, which can become a bottleneck. Thus, despite its initial attractiveness, this approach is not heavily used.

Whichever of the preceding approaches is used, there are several additional implementation steps to follow once duplicate parts are found. One must assign a single part number to all parts found in the warehouse with other part numbers, alter the related quantity information in the inventory database, designate the old part numbers in the item master file as inactive, adjust any outstanding purchase orders using the old part numbers, modify bills of material to include only the single remaining part number, and also alter any engineering drawings to reflect the changed number. Thus, a great many steps are required to ensure that more inventory items using the duplicate part numbers are not inadvertently ordered as replacements.

Cost: 💸   **Installation time:** 🕑 🕑

17–47 Standardize Parts   ✔*Author's Choice*

Though one can certainly use the steps just noted in the "Eliminate Redundant Part Numbers" best practice to reduce the number of items in the inventory, this still does not eliminate those similar, but still slightly different, parts designed to be used in different products. The engineering department has probably created a series of products without regard to the components used in preceding designs, so fittings, fasteners, and other items are used in slightly varying sizes across a range of products. The result is an ever-growing list of components, each one varying just enough from other items to require separate stocking.

A long-term solution is to standardize parts across multiple products, thereby greatly reducing the number of items in stock. The key ingredient in this best practice is to require approval of all new components by the engineering manager, whose performance is judged partially on his or her ability to keep the number of parts at a minimum. By requiring engineers to go through a tough review before being allowed to use new parts, they will be much more inclined to design existing stocks into new designs. A useful tool in the identification of commonly used parts is the matrix bill of material; this format displays the components of similar products in a side-by-side format, so that visual comparisons can be more easily made.

The concept can be taken further by reviewing the on-hand components list and winnowing out those for which there is clear duplication in similar components. By reducing the approved parts list in this manner, the number of components used in new products can bc gradually reduced. Further, the engineering manager can gradually eliminate the use of redundant parts in existing products by using engineering change notices to eliminate some components from use. This last step is the most difficult, since one must alter work instructions and the bill of material, as well as dispose of excess parts. The easier approach by far is to limit engineers to a specific parts list and design parts standardization into new products.

An ideal time to implement a parts standardization program is following an acquisition, since an obvious synergy is to standardize parts for both organizations. Another project initiation trigger is the implementation of a material requirements planning (MRP) system, since MRP reports make it much easier to review bills of material in a matrix format for similar parts. Finally, parts standardization can be implemented as part of a new product phase-in, which may be triggered by the scheduled end of a product life cycle, a change in suppliers, engineering change orders, or product upgrades due to safety or feature enhancement issues.

Cost: **Installation time:** 🕑 🕑 🕑

17–48 Identify Inactive Inventory in the Product Master File

There are few things more frustrating than for someone to disposition obsolete inventory, only to find that more inventory is then ordered, requiring additional effort to disposition once again. This typically happens when the company's automatic reordering system notices that the inventory balance for this item has dropped to zero, and sends a message to the purchasing department, asking for a new purchase to bring the inventory balance up to some predetermined minimum.

The obvious best practice is to reset the product's activity flag in the product master file to "obsolete," "inactive," or some similar code. This not only tells the system to stop buying more inventory, but also makes it impossible for the purchasing staff to create a purchase order through the computer system. The main problem is getting the person responsible for rendering inventory obsolete to remember to reset the flag. This can be accomplished by noting the deactivation step in bold on the written inventory deactivation procedure. However, if the person doing this work ignores the procedure, it may be necessary to include a pop-up reminder in the inventory software code that appears whenever an inventory balance is set to zero. Another alternative is to modify the software to automatically alter the product master file whenever an obsolescence code is used as part of a transaction to write down inventory.

Cost: **Installation time:** 🕑

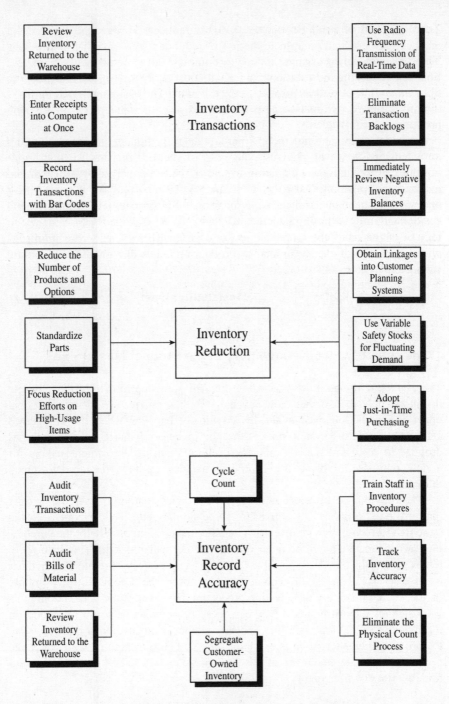

Exhibit 17.2 Impact of Best Practices on the Inventory Function

Total Impact of Best Practices on the Inventory Function

The impact of the best practices described in this chapter on the inventory function is a considerable increase in the accuracy and speed of inventory information, as well as a reduced investment in inventory. They are not designed to directly improve the functions of the warehouse, since this book only deals with accounting improvements. Nonetheless, it would be surprising if the warehouse personnel were not to experience a much easier existence if they had certain knowledge of the exact quantities and locations of all parts. As for the accounting staff, improved inventory accuracy leads to much less concern about the accuracy of the inventory and cost-of-goods-sold figures noted in the balance sheet and income statement, respectively. Further, the purchasing staff have a much easier time ordering parts, since they have much better knowledge of the accuracy of the on-hand inventory balances and no longer need to make a trip to the warehouse to verify this information. Finally, the production department will no longer experience parts shortages due to inaccurate inventory balances, resulting in the timely completion of more production runs. Thus, the best practices shown graphically in Exhibit 17.2 are unique among the best practices listed in this book in that their beneficial impact spreads far beyond the accounting department.

Summary

This chapter covered many best practices that improve the accuracy of the inventory database and the speed with which transactions are recorded. By doing so, the accounting department can be assured of much better accuracy in the inventory valuation figures it records in the financial statements, which has the related benefit of reducing any chance of error in the reported level of profitability. Also, a number of best practices should shrink the amount of on-hand inventory, which reduces the risk that inaccurate inventory information will have a significant impact on reported financial results.

Unfortunately, the bulk of the best practices noted here are ones that must be implemented and maintained by the warehouse and engineering departments, which means that the controller cannot use any direct authority to ensure their completion and use. Instead, this is a case where active persuasion is the key component of the implementation effort on the part of the controller.

For more information about inventory best practices, please refer to Bragg, *Inventory Best Practices* (John Wiley & Sons, 2004).

Chapter 18

Payroll Best Practices[1]

The payroll function involves a large clerical workload occurring shortly before and at the end of each pay period. For example, the typical payroll department collects time cards, calculates the amount due, checks with supervisors regarding questionable time cards, subtracts deductions of various kinds, cuts the checks, issues them, and reconciles any differences when employees bring in their paychecks with questions. After this frenetic time period, there is little for the department to do—until the end of the next pay period arrives. This highly predictable surge and drop in the payroll staff's workload can be a difficult one for a controller to manage because it requires either large amounts of overtime by the payroll staff during the heaviest work periods or else a redistribution of the accounting department staff to assist in the effort from time to time. It is best to avoid the problems associated with periodic strains on the staffing of the accounting department by examining each step of the payroll process and streamlining it to reduce the overall workload. This chapter contains a number of best practices that assist in doing so.

Another problem with the payroll function is that it is very error-prone. For example, it is easy to miss a pay raise, a vacation accrual, or a deduction. Every time this happens, an employee will arrive with questions he or she wants answered on the spot, which seriously impairs the efficiency of the department. In addition, these problems create concern on the part of employees that their paychecks are not being correctly calculated, which causes them to review pay data even more carefully, which in turn brings even more employees to the payroll department, requesting investigation of their real or imagined payroll problems. Thus, payroll errors not only require valuable time to fix, but also bring about a decline in employee confidence in the accounting department. This chapter contains several best practices that will reduce or eliminate many payroll errors.

Though this chapter reveals many techniques for *reducing* the workload and error rate of the payroll staff, there are no methods for entirely sidestepping the process, as is the case in the accounts payable area, so most of the best practices described here are incremental in nature. Nonetheless, cost reductions can be substantial. Data-entry errors, in particular, can be substantially reduced, along with the cost of payment distribution. The cost of employee data maintenance will also decline, as well as the cost of calculating pay. The net result of the changes outlined in this chapter can reduce overall payroll costs by as much as

---

[1] Selected best practices in this chapter were adapted with permission from Steven M. Bragg, *Payroll Best Practices* (John Wiley & Sons, 2005).

one-third. The remainder of this chapter describes the implementation problems associated with each best practice, followed by a description of each one.

Implementation Issues for Payroll Best Practices

For the reader to understand which of these best practices is the right one for a specific situation, it is useful to review Exhibit 18.1. This table lists a number of key implementation issues for each best practice. It notes the likely cost and duration of implementation, which is of concern to those companies that may have a short time and cost budget for improvements. The table is an effective approach for quickly determining which projects to work on and which ones to avoid.

A danger of using Exhibit 18.1 to pick only the easiest best practices is that these are primarily "quick hits" that will generally have a relatively small impact on the overall level of efficiency of the payroll function. Accordingly, it is important to insert changes requiring greater implementation effort and that have a correspondingly higher payback. For example, adding direct deposit is an easy and popular improvement, but a more fundamental change that requires much persuasion and more time to implement is reducing the number of payroll cycles. Creating a mix of both easy and difficult projects is key to showing continuing successes, while working toward greater levels of efficiency over the long term.

Exhibit 18.1 Summary of Payroll Best Practices

Best Practice	Cost	Install Time
Employee Deductions		
18–1 Disallow prepayments	💵	⏰
18–2 Create employee self-service for payroll changes	💵💵	⏰⏰
18–3 Minimize payroll deductions	💵	⏰
18–4 Prohibit deductions for employee purchases	💵	⏰
Employee Forms		
18–5 Post forms on an intranet site	💵	⏰⏰
Employee Time Tracking		
18–6 Avoid job costing through the payroll system	💵	⏰
18–7 Switch to salaried positions	💵	⏰⏰
18–8 Use computerized time clocks	💵💵	⏰⏰

Exhibit 18.1 *(Continued)*

Best Practice	Cost	Install Time
Employee Time Tracking		
18–9 Use biometric time clocks	💵💵	⏰⏰
18–10 Track time with mobile phones	💵💵	⏰⏰
18–11 Install additional time clocks	💵💵	⏰⏰
Payments to Employees		
18–12 Issue electronic W-2 forms to employees	💵	⏰⏰
18–13 Post payroll remittances on company intranet	💵💵💵	⏰⏰⏰
18–14 Only allow online payroll remittance viewing if employees use direct deposit	💵	⏰
18–15 Transfer payroll to debit cards	💵	⏰⏰
18–16 Use direct deposit	💵	⏰
Payroll Management		
18–17 Automate vacation accruals	💵	⏰
18–18 Consolidate payroll systems	💵💵💵	⏰⏰⏰
18–19 Create a payroll call center for employees	💵💵💵	⏰⏰
18–20 Eliminate personal leave days	💵	⏰
18–21 Improve unemployment claim administration	💵	⏰⏰
18–22 Link payroll changes to employee events	💵💵💵	⏰⏰⏰
18–23 Install manager self-service	💵💵💵	⏰⏰⏰
18–24 Link the 401(k) plan to the payroll system	💵💵	⏰⏰⏰
18–25 Link the payroll and human resources databases	💵💵💵	⏰⏰⏰
18–26 Minimize payroll cycles	💵	⏰⏰⏰
18–27 Electronically verify employee I-9 information	💵	⏰
18–28 Outsource employment verifications	💵	⏰
18–29 Outsource the payroll function	💵	⏰⏰
18–30 Use Web-based payroll outsourcing	💵	⏰⏰
18–31 Post FAQs answers and issue a payroll orientation brochure	💵	⏰

The reader should use Exhibit 18.1 to select the best practices listed in the remainder of this chapter that most closely match specific company requirements.

18–1 Disallow Prepayments

Many employees do not have the monetary resources to see them through until the next payday. Their solution is to request a pay advance, which is repaid at the time of the next payday. It is a humane gesture on the part of the payroll manager to comply with such requests, but it plays havoc with the efficiency of the payroll department. Whenever such a request is made, the payroll staff must manually calculate the taxes to take out of the payment, then manually cut a check and have it signed. However, the inefficiencies are not yet over! In addition, the staff must manually enter the pay advance in the computer system so that the amount is deducted from the next paycheck. For larger advances, it may be necessary to make deductions over several paychecks, which requires even more work. Clearly, paycheck prepayments do not help the efficiency of the payroll department. This is a particularly large problem in companies where a large proportion of the employees are paid at or near the minimum wage, since these people may not receive enough money to meet their needs.

The solution is to create a rule that no paycheck prepayments will be handed out, which effectively ends the extra processing required of the payroll personnel. The trouble with this rule is that a needy employee can usually present such a good case for a pay advance that exceptions will be made, which grinds away at the rule over time until it is completely ignored. Other managers will assist in tearing down the rule by complaining that they will lose good employees if advances are not provided to them. The best possible way to stand firm with the rule is for a company to form an association with a local lending institution that specializes in short-term loans. Then, if an employee requests an advance, he or she can be directed to the lending institution, which will arrange for an interest-bearing loan to the employee. When this arrangement exists, usually employees tighten their budgets rather than pay the extra interest charged for use of the lender's money. This improves employee finances while increasing the processing efficiency of the payroll staff. In short, this best practice involves two steps: prohibiting pay advances, while at the same time arranging for alternative financing for employees.

Cost: Installation time: 🕰

18–2 Create Employee Self-Service for Payroll Changes

Employees always have some sort of data change they want to make in the payroll system, such as changes to their direct deposit, withholding, address, name, and marital status information. The payroll staff must make all of these changes, as well as the inevitable corrections caused by errors in data entry. For example, when an employee first wants to set up direct deposit, she forwards this information to the payroll staff, who inputs it into whatever payroll software is in use. If the employee forwards incorrect information or it is incorrectly keypunched into the system, it is rejected and must be dealt with again during the next payroll cycle. In addition, employees may switch bank accounts or want to split deposits into multiple accounts—all of which require additional work by the payroll staff. Depending on the number of employees, these types of changes can represent a significant ongoing effort.

The latest advance in the area of self-service is for payroll outsourcing companies to manage self-service Web sites on behalf of their clients, who merely provide a link to these sites from their intranet sites. ADP provides this service, and estimates that a customized site can be operational in as little as 30 days. The ADP site allows the payroll manager to upload a variety of employee-centric documents, such as the employee manual, company phone directory, payroll forms, and news releases. In addition to these basic functions, the site also allows employees to access their pay statements and W-2 forms, view their earnings history, check their remaining vacation time, see performance reviews, view their 401(k) plan balances, and verify their benefits elections. However, the range of services offered varies considerably, as does the implementation time period. Advanced features found on a few employee self-service systems allow staff to request time off, swap shifts with other employees, submit work availability periods, bid on shifts, and request overtime.

An alternative is to construct this type of portal for an in-house legacy payroll system, but the programming effort required is so substantial that a company must have a considerable number of employees to make it worthwhile. An alternative would be to install a self-service module if a company uses commercial off-the-shelf payroll software that already provides this functionality.

For example, employees can alter the bank routing and account numbers used for the direct deposit of their pay into bank accounts, or change the amounts split between deposits to their savings and checking accounts. They could also use this approach to process requests for additional W-2 forms, or to download files containing the employee manual or other relevant personnel information. Further, they can register for company training classes, update emergency contact information, and make time-off requests.

A cautionary note regarding employee self-service is that direct-deposit prenotes should always be used when employees are allowed to enter their own direct deposit information through a self-service portal. Some companies have eliminated the prenote function when their own payroll staff enters direct-deposit information, on the grounds that a data entry professional will rarely make data-entry mistakes. However, this is not the case for employees who enter personal information, so prenoting should be used to ensure that account information has been correctly entered.

Cost: 💵💵   **Installation time:** ⏰ ⏰

18–3 Minimize Payroll Deductions

A company can offer a large number of benefits to its employees, many of which require some sort of deduction from payroll. For example, a company can set up deductions for employee medical, dental, life, and supplemental life insurance, as well as cafeteria plan deductions for medical insurance or child care payments and 401(k) deductions. If there are many employees and many deduction types, the payroll staff can be snowed under at payroll processing time by the volume of changes continually occurring in this area. Also, whenever there is a change in the underlying cost of insurance provided to the company, the company commonly passes along some portion of these costs to the employees, resulting in a massive updating of deductions for all employees who take that particular type of insurance. This not only takes time away from other, more value-added accounting tasks, but also is subject to error, so that adjustments must later be made to correct the errors, which requires even more staff time.

There are several ways to address this problem. One is to eliminate the employee-paid portion of some types of insurance. For example, if the cost to the company for monthly dental insurance is $20 per employee, and the related deduction is only $2 per person, management can elect to pay for the entire cost, rather than burden the accounting staff with tracking this trivial sum. Another alternative is to eliminate certain types of benefits, such as supplemental life insurance or 401(k) loans, in order to eliminate the related deductions. Yet another alternative is to create a policy that limits employee changes to any benefit plans, so they can only make a small number of changes per year. This eliminates the continual changing of deduction amounts in favor of just a few large bursts of activity at prescheduled times during the year. A very good alternative is to create a benefit package for all employees that requires a single deduction of the same amount for everyone, or for a group (such as one deduction for single employees and another for employees with families); employees can then pick and choose the exact amount of each type of benefit they want within the boundaries of each benefit package, without altering the amount of the underlying deduction. This last alternative has the unique advantage of consolidating all deductions into a single item, which is much simpler to administer. Any of these approaches to the problem will reduce the number or timing of deduction changes, thereby reducing the workload of the payroll staff.

Cost: 🖾   **Installation time:** 🕰

18–4 Prohibit Deductions for
Employee Purchases

Many companies allow their employees to use corporate discounts to buy products through them. For example, a company may have obtained a large discount on furniture from a supplier. Its employees buy at the discounted rate and then have the deductions subtracted from their paychecks in convenient installments. Some employees make excessive use of this benefit, purchasing all kinds of supplies through the company; accordingly, it is common to see a very small minority of employees making up the bulk of these purchases. The problem for the payroll staff is that it must keep track of the total amount that each employee owes the company and gradually deduct the amount owed from successive paychecks. If an employee has multiple purchases, the payroll staff must constantly recalculate the amount to be deducted. Depending on the number of employees taking advantage of purchases through the company, this can have a measurable impact on the efficiency of the payroll department.

The apparently easy solution is to prohibit purchases. By doing so, all the extra paperwork associated with employee purchases is immediately swept away. Though a good best practice for most companies to implement, this is one that should first be cleared with senior management. The reason is that some employees may be so accustomed to purchasing through the company that they will be rudely surprised by the change, which may be something that management wants to avoid (especially if valuable employees are impacted). Also, some companies have valid reasons for allowing employee purchases. The most common situation is when employees buy products that are meant to be used at work, such as work boots or tools. In these cases, the reasons in favor of maintaining a purchasing program may outweigh the reduced efficiency of the payroll department. A possible alternative approach that will still eliminate payroll deductions is to still allow employee purchases, but on condition that either the purchases are billed straight to them, or that the employees pay the company in full as soon as the goods are received.

In short, eliminating employee purchases that require deductions is a simple best practice to implement, though there are employee relations issues that may keep it from being implemented.

Cost: 💵   **Installation time:** ⏰

18–5 Post Forms on an Intranet Site   ✔ *Author's Choice*

Employees frequently come to the accounting department to ask for any of the variety of forms required for changes to their payroll status, such as the IRS's W-4 form, address changes, cafeteria plan sign-up or change forms, and so on. These constant interruptions interfere with the orderly flow of accounting work, especially when the department runs out of a form and must scramble to replenish its supplies.

This problem is neatly solved by converting all forms to Adobe Acrobat's PDF format and posting them on a company intranet site for downloading by all employees. By using this approach, no one ever has to approach the accounting staff for the latest copy of a form. Also, employees can download the required form from anywhere, rather than waiting until they are near the accounting location to physically pick one up. Further, the accounting staff can regularly update the PDF forms on the intranet site, so there is no risk of someone using an old and outmoded form.

Converting a regular form to PDF format is simple. First, purchase the Acrobat software from Adobe's Web site and install it. Then access a form in whatever software package it was originally constructed, and print it to Distiller, which will now appear on the list of printers. There are no other steps—your PDF format is complete! The IRS also uses the PDF format for its forms, which can be downloaded from the *www.irs.gov* site and posted to the company intranet site.

Cost:    Installation time:

18–6   Avoid Job Costing through the Payroll System

Some controllers have elaborate cost accounting systems set up that accumulate a variety of costs from many sources, sometimes to be used for activity-based costing and, more frequently, for job costing. One of these costs is labor, which is sometimes accumulated through the payroll system. When this is done, employees use lengthy time cards where they record the time spent on many activities during the day, resulting in vastly longer payroll records than would otherwise be the case. This is a problem when the payroll staff is asked to sort through and add up all of the job-costing records, since this increases the workload of the payroll personnel by an order of magnitude. In addition, the payroll staff may be asked to enter the job-costing information that it has just compiled into the job-costing database, which is yet another task that gets in the way of processing the payroll.

The solution is to not allow job costing to be merged into the payroll function, thereby allowing the payroll staff to vastly reduce the amount of work it must complete, as well as shrink the number of opportunities for calculation errors. However, this step may meet with opposition from those people who need the job-costing records. There are several ways to avoid conflict over the issue. One is to analyze who is charging time to various projects or activities and see if the proportions of time charged vary significantly over time; if they do not, there is no reason to continue tracking job-costing information for hours worked. Another possibility is to split the functions so the payroll staff collects its payroll data independently of job-costing data collection, which can be handled by someone else. Either possibility will keep the job-costing function from interfering with the orderly collection of payroll information.

Cost: Installation time:

18–7   Switch to Salaried Positions

When processing payroll, it is evident that the labor required to process the payroll for a salaried person is significantly lower than the labor needed to process payroll for an hourly employee. The reason is that there is no change in the payroll data from period to period for a salaried person, whereas the number of hours worked must be recomputed for an hourly employee every time the payroll is processed. Therefore, it is reasonable to try to shift as many employees as possible over to salaried positions from hourly ones in order to reduce the labor of calculating payroll.

Implementing this best practice can be a significant problem. One issue is that it is not under the control of the accounting department—it is up to the managers of other departments to switch people over to salaried positions, so the controller must rely on persuasion of other managers to make the concept a reality. Another problem is that this best practice may be opposed by unions. They prefer to keep the employees they represent on hourly pay, since this gives employees the opportunity to earn overtime. If a union has a strong presence in a company, this will almost certainly keep a company from switching people to salaried positions for at least those employees represented by the union. Finally, there may be legal issues that interfere with conversion. There are frequently regulations at the state level that prohibit converting employees to salaried positions, with the main determining criterion being that a salaried person must be able to act with minimal supervision—this situation will vary by state, depending on local laws. All of these issues can impede the implementation of a complete conversion of employees to salaried pay.

Cost: **Installation time:** 🕑 🕑

18–8 Use Computerized Time Clocks

The single most labor-intensive task in the payroll area is calculating hours worked for hourly employees. To do so, an accounting clerk must collect all the employee time cards for the most recently completed payroll period, manually add up the hours listed on the cards, and research missing hours with supervisors. This is a lengthy process and usually has a very high error rate, due to the large percentage of missing start or stop times on most time cards. The errors are usually found by employees as soon as they are paid, resulting in a loud and (sometimes) boisterous visit to the payroll department, demanding an immediate adjustment to the paid amount with a manual paycheck.

One solution is to install a computerized time clock. This is a clock that requires an employee to "swipe" an employee-specific plastic card through the clock. The card is encoded with an employee-identifying number, using either a bar code or a magnetic stripe. Once the swipe occurs, the clock automatically stores the date and time, and downloads this data upon request to the payroll department's computer, where special software automatically calculates hours worked and highlights any problems for additional research (such as missed swipes). Many such clocks can be installed throughout a large facility, or at outlying locations, so that employees can conveniently record their time, no matter where they may be. The more advanced clocks also track the time periods when employees are supposed to arrive and leave, and require a supervisor's password for card swipes outside of that time period—this feature allows for greater control over employee work hours. Many of these systems also issue absence reports, so that supervisors can easily tell who has not shown up for work. Thus, an automated time clock eliminates much low-end clerical work, while at the same time providing new management tools for supervisors.

Before purchasing a bar-coded time clock, it is important to recognize its limitations, of which the most important is cost. This clock usually costs $2,000 to $3,000, or can be leased for several hundred dollars per month. In addition, outlying time clocks that must download their information to a computer at a distant location require their own phone lines, which represents an additional monthly payment to the phone company. There may also be a fee for using the software on the central computer that summarizes all the incoming payroll information. Given these costs, it is most common for bar-coded time clocks to be used only where there are so many hourly employees in a company that there is a significant time savings in the payroll department resulting from their installation.

A key flaw of the computerized time clock is that employees can use each other's cards to clock themselves in, resulting in payments for time worked to employees who may not have even been on the premises. To avoid this problem, one can install an Internet camera next to the clock that snaps an image for every card swipe made and stores it for easy access by the payroll staff. The information can be stored for a few weeks in this manner until there is no need for the information, and then written over. By using this approach, employees will be much less inclined to clock in or out for their buddies, while the payroll staff will have ready evidence of improper card swipes. The main problem with this approach is the difficulty of linking information from the card swipe to the image created by the camera, so one can tell what information was entered into the system by each person.

Cost: **Installation time:** 🕰 🕰

18–9 Use Biometric Time Clocks

The computerized time clocks noted in the previous best practice represent a wonderful improvement in the speed and accuracy with which employee time data can be collected. However, it suffers from an integrity flaw—that employees can use each other's badges to enter and exit from the payroll system. This means that some employees may be paid for hours when they were never really on-site at all.

An alternative is the biometric time clock. It requires an employee to place his or her hand on a sensor, which matches its size and shape to the dimensions already recorded for that person in a central database. The time entered into the terminal will then be recorded against the payroll file of the person whose hand was just measured. Thus, only employees who are on-site can have payroll hours credited to them. These systems have a secondary benefit, which is that no one needs an employee badge or pass key; these tend to be lost or damaged over time, and so represent a minor headache for the accounting or human resources staffs, who must track them. In a biometric monitoring environment, all an employee needs is a hand.

An objection sometimes raised by employees about biometric time clocks is that there may be a risk of employees passing bacteria to each other, since everyone is touching the same sensor pad on the clock. The clock manufacturers reduce the risk of bacteria transmission by incorporating antimicrobial materials into the sensor pad that reduce bacteria levels. To further allay fears about this issue, have the janitorial staff include biometric clock disinfecting in its standard cleaning list. Also, make hand sanitizers available near each clock.

Cost: **Installation time:**

18–10 Track Time with Mobile Phones

When employees are occupied with off-site service jobs, such as copier repair, security monitoring, or landscaping work, it is quite difficult to track the exact amount of time they spend on each job. Instead, they tend to wait until they are back in the office and then jot down their billable time from memory. Also, if they are paid based on their billable hours, this introduces a great deal of uncertainty into the determination of their payroll hours. The use of a Web-based timekeeping system is not a good solution, since it requires Web access and a computer, which are not always available to this type of employee.

The solution is to incorporate a timekeeping system into a GPS-enabled cell phone. Under this approach, a company acquires a cell phone and associated Nextel service contract for each employee, and then signs up for the WorkTrack service (accessible through *www.worktrack.com*). For a small monthly fee, this service allows employees to punch their job start and stop times directly into the phone, which transmits this information as a text message that the payroll staff can access through a simple Web browser. There is no other hardware or software required, since the text messages are sent to WorkTrack, which handles the reformatting of the resulting data for access through the Web. The system also allows the payroll staff to download standard time reports, as well as track employee locations on a map (which is useful for determining which people to send to another customer location). The system can also be used to push text messaging information back to users through the cell phones.

By using this approach, employees no longer have to manually complete timesheets, while the payroll staff can summarize payroll data more rapidly and the billing staff can issue invoices to customers within minutes of a job being completed in the field.

Cost: 　　　　　　　　　　Installation time: 　

18–11 Install Additional Time Clocks

When a company elects to install electronic time clocks, as advocated previously in this chapter, it may make the mistake of installing too few clocks because of the high cost of the equipment. This creates two problems. First, employees may queue up in front of each clock during check-out times. In anticipation of waiting in the queue, employees may leave their workstations slightly early. In addition, if a time clock is positioned too far away from their workstations, they may also stop working early in order to be in front of the nearest time clock at check-out time. Although these issues may only be a few minutes per person, it becomes a much larger issue when multiplied by many employees, over all of the business days in a year.

The obvious solution is to add more time clocks. However, this does not necessarily call for the profligate purchase and installation of a vast quantity of additional clocks. The original decision not to install more clocks may have been driven by such problems as not having electrical power in a distant location, not wanting to install a clock outdoors, or not wanting to string network cable to a prospective clock location. These issues may be more important than the price of a time clock. Consequently, adding time clocks involves a close review of the total cost of installation and will probably result in a gradual rollout, as management evaluates how the cost of each installation is offset by the savings in labor for those people who use the clock.

Cost: 　　　　　　　　　　Installation time: 　

18–12 Issue Electronic W-2 Forms to Employees

A large company can experience some difficulty in issuing W-2 forms to its employees if they are distributed over a wide area. The mailing cost of this distribution can also be quite expensive, especially if the employer wants proof of receipt, which calls for the use of more expensive overnight delivery services. This problem can be avoided by issuing electronic W-2 forms to employees, thereby avoiding all related postage costs.

The IRS has issued specific regulations for the use of electronic W-2 forms. First, employees must give their consent to the receipt of an electronic W-2 form, and do so electronically, thereby showing proof that they are capable of receiving the electronic format in which the W-2 form will be sent. Second, the W-2 forms must contain all standard information that would normally be found on a paper W-2 form. Third, employees must be notified that the forms have been posted on a Web site for their access, and give them instructions on how to access the information. Finally, the access must be maintained through October 15 of the year following the calendar year to which they relate.

These regulations are not difficult to meet, and the use of a central Web site for storage of the information also allows the employer to determine precisely which W-2 forms have been accessed. However, it is likely that some employees who either have minimal access to computers or who are not computer literate will not access their W-2 forms in this manner, requiring a last-minute distribution of W-2 forms to anyone who has not accessed their electronic copies. Also, paper-based W-2 forms must still be issued to any employees who left the company prior to the end of the calendar year. Thus, this best practice will likely result in only a partial electronic distribution of W-2 forms.

Cost: 🖋️   **Installation time:** ⏰⏰

18–13 Post Payroll Remittances on Company Intranet

A company can post payroll remittances on a company intranet site. To ensure that employees access their pay information in a timely manner, a schedule of posting dates should be listed in the employee manual or a memo. This approach is popular with those employees having Web access, since they can access payroll information from anywhere—at work, at home, or on the road. It has the additional advantage of providing employees with pay information for any time period they want; an employee just selects from a list of previous pay dates to view the details for that paycheck.

Although an elegant solution to the issue of getting payroll information into the hands of employees in a cost-effective manner, this approach also presents the following challenges:

- *Account security.* Each employee must be issued a user ID and password, and the intranet site must have high-quality security to prevent hackers from accessing key payroll information.
- *General employee access.* Though it is technically up to the employees to find their own access to the intranet site, the company should recognize that some employees do not have access of any kind, and provide terminals and printers at company locations to resolve this need.
- *Posting from payroll system.* The process of posting to the intranet site should be an automated one, and so will likely require a custom interface from the payroll system.

- *Outsourced payroll*. If a third-party supplier processes payroll, it will be difficult to obtain a data feed that can be posted to the intranet site. However, some payroll suppliers now offer feeds into their own Web-based systems where employees can access this information.

This approach also overcomes the problem of having to send a paper remittance to terminated employees, since anyone can access the Web site, even those who have not been employees for a long time.

Cost: 💵💵💵   Installation time: ⏰⏰⏰

18–14 Only Allow Online Payroll Remittance Viewing if Employees Use Direct Deposit

Some employees have a strong preference for being handed an actual paycheck, walking it to a bank, and cashing it themselves, no matter how many inducements a company dangles before them to use direct deposit. Thus, there is always a small percentage of employees for whom the company must create a different paycheck-handling process.

A subtle inducement to make them switch to direct deposit is to implement an online payroll remittance system (as noted in the previous best practice), but to allow viewing of the information only if an employee has also enrolled in the direct deposit program. Given the increasing dependence of society on access to electronic information, it is entirely possible that this added benefit will persuade a few more employees to make the switch to direct deposit. The lure will be especially great if additional features are added to the online payroll remittance program, such as allowing the viewing of multiple years of payroll information and access to an online W-2 form.

Cost: 💵   Installation time: ⏰

18–15 Transfer Payroll to Debit Cards

Some companies employ people who, for whatever reason, either are unable to set up personal bank accounts or do not choose to. In these cases, they must take their paychecks to a check-cashing service, which charges them a high fee to convert the check into cash. Also, employees will be carrying large amounts of cash just after cashing their checks, which increases their risk of theft. They also run the risk of losing their paychecks prior to cashing them. Thus, the lack of a bank account poses serious problems for a company's employees.

A good solution to this problem is to set up a payroll debit card for any employees requesting one, and then shift payroll funds directly into the card. This allows employees to pull any amount of cash they need from an ATM, rather than the entire amount at one time from a check-cashing service. The card can also be used like a credit card, so there is little need to make purchases with cash. Further, the fee to convert to cash at an ATM is much lower than the fee charged by a check-cashing service. There is also less risk of theft through the card, since it is protected by a personal identification number (PIN). Employees will also receive a monthly statement showing their account activity, which they can use to get a better idea of their spending habits.

Payroll cards are superior to direct deposit in the following respects:

- *First payment is electronic*. When paying an employee through direct deposit, the first payment to a new employee is with a check, since the bank wants to prenote the first direct deposit transaction. This is not the case for a payroll card, where the first payment can be issued electronically.

- *Data collection*. Direct deposit requires the employer to collect bank routing and account number information from employees, which may be incorrect or difficult to obtain. This is not needed for payroll cards, since the employer creates each account.

- *Account lockdown*. Employees sometimes shut down their bank accounts and forget to inform the company that direct-deposit payments must now be sent to a new location. Since the employer controls the payroll card account, employees cannot shut down the account.

- *Termination pay*. Terminated employees can be paid within one day through a payroll card, and there is no need for them to come back to the office to pick up a final check.

- *Information security*. Unlike direct deposit, an employer does not need to retain personal banking information for payroll cards, since it is setting up all accounts.

- *Additional cards*. Some card providers will issue extra payroll cards to other family members, which allows them to withdraw funds in other cities; this keeps the wage earner from paying wire transfer fees to send money to other family members.

- *Pay routing*. Some card providers now allow card users to automatically route incoming funds to personal bank accounts, though there is a one-day delay in the funds transfer.

Here are some additional considerations regarding the setup of a payroll debit card program:

- Employees should not have to pay a withdrawal fee when they extract funds from an ATM (in some states, it is illegal to require employees to pay such a fee as part of their payroll payments). Accordingly, either have the company pay the ATM fee or have the paycard supplier specify in its contract which

ATMs will offer free services to employees. It is also possible to set up an on-site company-owned ATM, which ensures that ATM fees will be free.

- Paycard issuers can impose a blizzard of fees, such as fees for an excessive number of paycard transactions, card replacements, a "load fee" (when a card is funded), and a monthly fee. First, be sure than none of these fees are charged to employees, only the company. Second, write limitations into the contract on increases in these fees, as well as the exclusion of as-yet unspecified fees. Also, it is helpful to model the full cost of all fees, using reasonable estimates of card usage, in order to determine which paycard program is the most economical.

- Some paycard issuers are not banks, so funds issued to paycards maintained by them could be lost if the issuer goes out of business. Instead, provide your employees with some extra security by using only paycards issued by a bank, which carries FDIC insurance on funds deposited with it.

- The way to access cash from a payroll debit card is to obtain it through an ATM, but since ATMs only issue cash in denominations of $20, this presents a problem for card balances of less than $20. One option is to see if the provider will issue a check to employees for such residual balances, or if convenience checks are provided to employees so they can extract this balance themselves.

Cost: Installation time: 🕰 🕰

18–16 Use Direct Deposit

A major task for the payroll staff is to issue paychecks to employees. This task can be subdivided into several subsidiary steps. First, the checks must be printed—though it seems easy, it is all too common for the check run to fail, resulting in the manual cancellation of the first batch of checks, followed by a new print run. Next, the checks must be signed by an authorized check-signer, who may have questions about payment amounts, which may require additional investigation. After that, the checks must be stuffed into envelopes and then sorted by supervisor (since supervisors generally hand out checks to their employees). The checks are then distributed, usually with the exception of a few checks that will be held for those employees who are not currently on-site for later pick-up. Finally, the person in charge of the bank reconciliation must track those checks that have not been cashed and follow up with employees to get them to cash their checks—there are usually a few employees who prefer to cash checks only when they need the money, surprising though this may seem. In short, there are a startlingly large number of steps involved in issuing payroll checks to employees. How can one eliminate this work?

The solution is to pay by direct deposit. This best practice involves issuing payments directly to employee bank accounts. Besides avoiding some of the steps involved with issuing paychecks, it carries the additional advantage of putting money in employee bank accounts at once, so that those employees who are off-site on payday do not worry about how they will receive their money—it will appear in their checking accounts automatically, with no effort on their part.

Implementing direct deposit can be somewhat more difficult than one may first realize. It requires an ability to transfer payment information to the company's bank in the correct direct-deposit format, which the bank uses to shift money to employee bank accounts. This information transfer can be accomplished either by purchasing an add-on to a company's in-house payroll software or by paying extra to a payroll outsourcing company to provide the service; either way, there is an expense associated with starting up the service. Also, it can be difficult to get all employees to switch over to direct deposit. Though the benefits to employees may seem obvious, there will be a large proportion of employees who prefer to cash their own checks, or who do not possess bank accounts. To get around this problem, a company can either force all employees to accept direct deposit, or only do so with new employees, with existing employees being allowed to still take paper checks. If employees are forced to accept direct deposit, the company can make the issue less onerous by working with a local bank to provide a free bank account to each employee. Also, there will be the inevitable start-up problems for the first few weeks, resulting in some direct deposits not going through to employees on time. These issues mean that it may take quite some time to convert a large proportion of employee payments over to direct deposit. To monitor progress, consider creating a direct-deposit usage percentage and including it in the standard monthly reporting package. This keeps the issue in front of management. All of these issues make implementing direct deposit somewhat more difficult and expensive than would first appear to be the case.

Another issue with direct deposit is prenotification. This is the prior validation of an employee's bank account information before an actual payroll payment is made into that person's account, to see if there are any errors in the account information. Engaging in the prenotification process delays the implementation of direct deposit by one pay period, which means that a new employee always receives one pay check before switching to direct deposit. A company can sometimes choose not to prenote, which eliminates the employee waiting period but which also increases the possibility that a payment will be rejected. It is possible to reduce the risk of a rejection by other means than prenotification, such as by contacting an employee's bank directly to verify account information.

Besides implementation issues, there are a few other problems to consider before using direct deposit. One is the fee charged by the bank or payroll service to do it—a common charge is $1 to make a direct deposit to each employee's account, which can add up if there are many employees and frequent pay periods (e.g., once a week). Also, some paper-based form of notification must still be sent to employees so that they know the details of what they have been paid. This means that using direct deposit does not eliminate the steps of printing, envelope stuffing, or check distribution (though there is no need to sign the pay notifications or hold them for stray employees, nor is there any further trouble with tracking payroll checks that have not been cashed). Finally, most companies find that they end up with a dual system—some employees take direct deposit and some go with paper checks—so that they have a *more* complicated system with two forms of payment. However, do not let all these problems shoot down an initiative to use direct deposit. If one follows through on it properly, then most or all employees can still be converted to it over the long term. Despite its disadvantages, direct deposit can be a clear advantage to both the accounting department and employees, if properly implemented.

Cost: Installation time: 🕐

18–17 Automate Vacation Accruals

A topic that is of considerable interest to employees is how much vacation time they have left. In most companies, this information is kept manually by the payroll staff, so employees troop down to the payroll department once a month (and more frequently in the prime summer vacation months!) to see how much vacation time they have left to use. When employees are constantly coming in to ascertain this information, it is a major interruption to the payroll staff, because it happens at all times of the day, never allowing them to settle down into a comfortable work routine.

A simple solution is to include the vacation accrual in employee paychecks. The information appears on the payroll stub, and shows the annual amount of accrued vacation, net of any used time. By feeding this information to employees in every paycheck, there is no need for them to inquire about it in the payroll office, eliminating a major hindrance. However, there are several points to consider before automating vacation accruals. The first one is that the payroll system must be equipped with a vacation accrual calculation option. If not, the software must be modified with custom programming to allow for the calculation and presentation of this information, which may cost more to implement than the projected efficiency savings. Another problem is that the accrual system must be set up properly for each employee when it is originally installed. This start-up problem is caused by having employees with different numbers of days of vacation allowed per year, as well as some with carryover vacation from the previous year. If this information is not accurately reflected in the automated vacation accrual system when it is implemented, employees will hasten to the payroll area to correct this problem at once. Another issue is that the accruals must be adjusted over time to reflect changes. For example, an employee may switch from two to three weeks of allowed vacation at the fifth anniversary of his or her hiring. The payroll department must have a schedule of when this person's vacation accrual amount changes to the three-week level, or the employee will come in and complain about it. If these problems can be overcome, using vacation accruals becomes a relatively simple means of improving the efficiency of the payroll department.

Cost: 💵   **Installation time:** ⏰

18–18 Consolidate Payroll Systems   ✔*Author's Choice*

A company that grows by acquisition is likely to have a number of payroll systems— one for each company that it has acquired. This situation may also arise for highly decentralized companies that allow each company location to set up its own payroll system. Though this approach does allow each location to process payroll in accordance with its own rules and payment periods, while also allowing for local maintenance of employee records, there are several serious problems that can be solved by the consolidation of all these systems into a single, centralized payroll system.

One problem with having many payroll systems is that employee payroll records cannot be shifted through a company when an employee is transferred to a new location. Instead, the employee is listed as having been terminated in the payroll system of the location that he or she is leaving and is then listed as a new hire in the payroll system of the new location. By constantly reentering an employee as a new hire, it is impossible to track the dates and amounts of pay raises; the same problem arises for the human resources staff, who cannot track eligibility dates for medical insurance or vesting periods for pension plans. In addition, every time employee data is reentered into a different payroll system, there is a risk of data inaccuracies that may result in such embarrassments as wrong pay rates or mailing checks to the wrong address. Also, a company cannot easily group data for companywide payroll reporting purposes. Finally, if an employee switches among multiple payroll systems, there is a chance that the corporate entity as a whole will pay an excessive amount of payroll taxes. For all these reasons, it is common practice to consolidate payroll systems into a single, centralized location that operates with a single payroll database.

Before embarking on such a consolidation, one must consider the costs of implementation. One is that a consolidation of many payroll systems may require an expensive new software package that runs on a large computer, which entails extra capital and software maintenance costs. In addition, there is probably a significant cost associated with converting the data from the disparate databases into the new consolidated one. In addition, there may be extra time needed to test the tax rates for all company locations, in order to avoid penalties for improper tax withholdings and submissions. Finally, the timing of the implementation is of some importance. Many companies prefer to make the conversion on the first day of the new year so there is no need to enter detailed pay information into the system for the prior year to issue year-end payroll tax reports to the government. The cost of consolidating payroll systems is considerable and must be carefully analyzed before the decision to convert is reached.

Switching from many payroll systems to a single one is an excellent best practice to implement, with many long-term benefits. However, due to the conversion cost, it is important to weigh the costs and benefits of the project and to insert the project into a company's capital budget only when the funds are definitely available.

Cost: 💵💵💵   **Installation time:** ⏰⏰⏰

18–19 Create a Payroll Call Center for Employees

When employees have payroll questions, they typically call anyone they know in the payroll department, or whoever is listed in the company directory. In either case, this can cause disruption for payroll people who may be trying to meet deadlines for other tasks. A possible solution is to create a call center that is expressly targeted at resolving employee payroll issues.

Having a payroll call center does not mean that a specific group of employees are simply given new titles as customer service representatives—far from it. A true call center requires the following items:

- *Advanced training and senior personnel.* If a call center is staffed with new employees who have minimal knowledge of payroll systems, then callers will quickly stop using the call center. Instead, call center employees should have considerable prior payroll experience and be subjected to detailed training on topics that callers are most likely to bring up. Having such a high-quality team gives callers confidence that their questions will be correctly answered, which increases employee usage of the call center.

- *Metrics tracking.* A system should track the total handling time required to resolve an employee request, as well as the percentage of requests that are resolved on the first call. These two metrics are used to determine the efficiency (handling time) and effectiveness (first call resolution) of the call center.

- *Call-routing software.* For high-volume call centers, a call-routing system places callers in a queue and routes them to the first available call center representative.

- *Case tracking.* If a call cannot be resolved on the first contact, then a case tracking system should be used to describe the issue and assign a tracking number to it.

- *Workflow management.* This system is tied to the case tracking system, and monitors the progress of resolution of all open cases. It should also escalate to a manager any cases that have not been resolved within a predetermined time period.

To set up this best practice, it may be necessary to remove payroll phone numbers from the company directory in favor of a single phone number for the call center. This will route callers away from payroll staff, which no longer deals with employee support issues.

    This solution may appear to be overkill for a smaller company. If so, consider adding additional functionality to the call center so that it also handles additional requests for information. For example, the human resources department could combine with the payroll department to support a call center that also provides benefits-related information. Another option is an extremely small call center of one person, with a designated backup person. All of the software used in a larger call center can still be used, so that callers are put in a queue and metrics collected on call durations, topics addressed, and resolutions.

        Cost: 💵💵💵   **Installation time:** ⏰⏰

18–20 Eliminate Personal Leave Days

A common task for the payroll staff is to either manually or automatically track the vacation time employees earn and use. Depending on the level of automation, this task can require some portion of staff time every week on an ongoing basis. Some companies then take the additional step of accruing and tracking the usage of personal leave days, which are essentially the same thing as vacation time, but tracked under a different name. By having both vacation and personal leave days, the payroll staff is reduced to tracking data in both categories, which doubles the work required to simply track vacation time.

    A reasonable, and easily implemented, best practice is to convert personal leave days into vacation days and eliminate the extra category of time off. By doing so, the payroll staff can cut in half the time it devotes to analyzing employee vacation time. The only resistance to this change usually comes from the human resources department, which likes to offer a variety of benefits to match those other companies offer; for example, if a competitor offers personal leave days, then so should the company. Though only a matter of semantics, this can cause a problem when implementing the simpler system.

        Cost: 💵   **Installation time:** ⏰

18–21 Improve Unemployment Claim Administration

If there is no human resources department, then the payroll staff will likely receive unemployment claims from the local state government for any employees who have left the company. A busy payroll staff has little time to contest unemployment claims, and so generally experiences a high failure rate when it does so. The result is some amount of spurious unemployment claims being granted, which increases the unemployment tax rate that a company pays.

The best way to deal with unemployment claims is first to understand the types of scenarios under which claims will be denied, so that the payroll staff does not focus undue attention on contesting claims that will automatically be granted to a former employee. For example, a discharge for misconduct will still result in unemployment payments if an employee was let go due to inefficiency, ordinary negligence, or good-faith errors in judgment. Conversely, an unemployment claim should be contested if a discharge for misconduct was based on theft, willful damage of company property, alcoholic consumption on the premises, fighting with other employees, or falsifying expense vouchers. It is important to document these differences so the payroll staff does not waste time contesting claims that will be settled in favor of former employees.

A second step is to fully document employee departures so there is plenty of documentary evidence that can be used to contest a claim. This includes the use of written warnings and exit interviews. This documentation must extend to responses made to the state claims officer. Such responses should be well-considered, fully documented, and submitted well within the timeline set by the claims officer. Also, if the claims officer calls for a meeting, then the payroll manager should bring witnesses with firsthand knowledge of the situation.

In nearly all cases, it will be immediately apparent when a claim will be settled in an employee's favor, so the payroll manager should be very selective in contesting only those claims for which the company can present a cogent case and for which there is complete documentary evidence to support its position. Given the time required to respond to unemployment claims, this is the best way to cost-effectively manage unemployment claims.

Cost: Installation time: 🕑 🕑

18–22 Link Payroll Changes to Employee Events

There are many payroll changes that must be made when certain events occur in an employee file. Many of these changes are never made, because either the payroll staff is so busy with the standard, daily processing of information that it has no time to address them or the payroll staff does not possess enough knowledge to link the payroll changes to the employee events. For example, when an employee is married, this should trigger a change in that person's W-4 form, so the amount of taxes withheld will reflect those for a married person. Automation can create many of these linkages. Here are some examples:

- As soon as an employee reaches the age of 55, the system issues a notification to the pension manager to calculate the person's potential pension, while also notifying the employee of his or her pension eligibility. These notifications can be by letter, but a linkage between the payroll system and the email system would result in more immediate notification.

- As soon as an employee has been with a company for 90 days, his or her period of probation has been completed. The system should then automatically include the employee in the company's dental, medical, and disability plans, and include deductions for these amounts in the person's paycheck. Similarly, the system can automatically enroll the employee in the company's 401(k) plan and enter the deductions in the payroll system. Since these pay changes should not be a surprise to the employee, the system should also generate a message to the employee, detailing the changes made and their net payroll impact.

- When a company is informed of an employee's marriage, the computer system generates a notice to the employee that a new W-4 form should be filled out, while also sending a new benefit enrollment form, in case the employee wishes to add benefits for the spouse or any children. Finally, a notification message can ask the employee if he or she wants to change the beneficiary's name on the pension plan to that of the spouse.

- When an employee notifies the company of an address change, the system automatically notifies all related payroll and benefit suppliers of the change, such as the 401(k) plan administrator and health insurance provider.

- When a new employee is hired, the system sends a message to the purchasing department, asking that business cards be ordered for the employee. Another message goes to the information systems department, requesting that the appropriate levels of system security be set up for the new hire. Yet another message goes to the training department, asking that a training plan be set up for the new employee.

Many of these workflow features are available on high-end accounting and human resources software packages. However, this software costs more than a million dollars in most cases, and so is well beyond the purchasing capability of many smaller companies. An alternative is to customize an existing software package to include these features, but the work required will be expensive. Accordingly, these changes should only be contemplated if there are many employees, since this would result in a sufficient volume of savings to justify the added expense.

Cost: 💵💵💵   Installation time: ⏰⏰⏰

18–23 Install Manager Self-Service

A considerable amount of payroll staff time is occupied by the setup and deletion of employees from the payroll database, as well as by the recording of payroll events, such as employee pay raises, transfers, and employee leave situations. Usually, a local manager fills out paperwork pertaining to these events and forwards it to the payroll department, which keypunches the information into the payroll system. This workflow can result in lost or delayed paperwork as well as incorrect data entry. If the events being entered pertain to employee pay raises, an error is also likely to result in boisterous contacts by the affected employee.

An elegant solution is to create an intranet portal through which local managers can enter all of this information themselves, with no need for any data entry by the payroll staff. Since most managers have access to a computer terminal already, there is generally no need to acquire additional computer hardware.

The efficiency improvement resulting from this best practice for the payroll staff is obvious. However, in order to prevent them from immediately converting to error-correction mode for all the errors being made by local managers through the new payroll intranet site, there are a number of enhancements to consider when building the site:

- *Install data limit checkers.* Managers may inadvertently enter incorrect information that is patently false, such as a $1,000,000 salary, by not entering a decimal place. The data-entry system can include a number of data limit checkers that will automatically reject data unless they fall within a tight parameter range.

- *Require transaction-specific approvals.* If a manager wants to give an employee an inordinately large pay raise, the system should bring this raise to the attention of the payroll staff or an upper-level manager, who must approve it before the payroll database is updated with the new information.

- *Issue warnings to affected departments.* When a manager enters an employee termination into the computer system, this should trigger a message to the human resources department, who may want to conduct an exit interview. Similarly, the 401(k) plan administrator needs to know about the termination in order to send plan termination documents to the former employee; the same goes for the health plan administrator, who must mail out a packet of COBRA information. A number of similar notifications are needed at the point of initial hire.

Thus, the manager data-entry system is not really a simple interface. It must review input data, issue notifications and warnings, and generally take over the roll of an experienced payroll clerk to ensure that employee transition data is correctly handled throughout the company.

A manager self-service system can go beyond the more basic data-entry tasks just noted. In addition, the system can also report to a manager which staff members are currently clocked in or out, and can also send alerts when an employee comes in late or leaves early, or when employee work hours violate a predetermined set of disciplinary criteria. It may also have reporting functions, such as an analysis of absentee trends by employee. An advanced system may also track leave requests and eligibility under the Family and Medical Leave Act.

Given the complexity of the manager self-service system, it is generally best to roll out only one function at a time, not only to ensure that sufficient system checking is conducted, but also to give managers sufficient time to train on each function and become used to its mode of operation.

Cost: 💵💵💵   **Installation time:** ⏰⏰⏰

18–24 Link the 401(k) Plan to the Payroll System

A common activity for the payroll staff is to take the 401(k) deduction information from the payroll records as soon as each payroll cycle is completed, enter it into a separate database for 401(k) deductions, copy this information onto a compact disc, and send it to the company's 401(k) administration supplier, who uses it to determine the investment levels of all employees, as well as for discrimination testing. This can be a lengthy data-entry process if there are many employees, and it is certainly not a value-added activity when the core task is simply moving data from one database to another one.

The best way to avoid retyping 401(k) payroll deductions is to link the payroll system directly into a 401(k) plan. This is done by outsourcing the payroll processing function to a supplier that also offers a 401(k) plan. A good example of this is Automated Data Processing (ADP), which offers linkages to a number of well-known mutual funds through its payroll system. When a company uses ADP's payroll and 401(k) services, a payroll department can record a 401(k) payroll deduction for an employee just once and ADP will then take the deduction and automatically move it into a 401(k) fund, with no additional bookkeeping required from the payroll staff. For those companies with many employees, this can represent a significant reduction in the workload of the payroll staff.

There are two problems with this best practice. One is that a company must first outsource its payroll function to a supplier that offers 401(k) administration services, which the company controller may not be willing to do (see the "Outsource the Payroll Function" section later in this chapter). The second problem is converting to the new 401(k) plan. To do so, all employees in the old plan must be moved to the new plan. The associated paperwork may be great enough to not make the transition worthwhile; also, the old 401(k) administrator may require a separation fee if the company is terminating its services inside of a minimum time interval, which may involve a small penalty payment. These issues should be considered before switching to a centralized payroll and 401(k) processing system.

Cost: 💵💵   **Installation time:** ⏰⏰⏰

18–25 Link the Payroll and Human Resources Databases

The payroll database shares many data elements with the human resources database. Unfortunately, these two databases are usually maintained by different departments—accounting for the first and human resources for the second. Consequently, any employee who makes a change to one database, such as an address field in the payroll system, must then contact the human resources department to have the same information entered again for other purposes, such as benefits administration or a pension plan. Thus, there is an obvious inefficiency for the employee who must go to two departments for changes, while the accounting and human resources staffs also duplicate each other's data-entry efforts.

The obvious best practice here is to tie the two databases together. This can be done by purchasing a software package that automatically consolidates the two databases into a single one, but the considerable cost of buying and implementing an entirely new software package will grossly exceed the cost savings obtained by consolidating the data. A less costly approach is to create an interface between the two systems that automatically stores changes made to each database and updates the other one as a daily batch program. Creating this interface can still be expensive, since it involves a reasonable amount of customized programming work. Consequently, consolidating the payroll and human resources databases is an expensive proposition and is usually done only when both computer systems are being brought together for more reasons than a simple reduction in data-entry work.

Cost: 💵💵💵   Installation time: ⏰⏰⏰

18–26 Minimize Payroll Cycles   ✔*Author's Choice*

Many payroll departments are fully occupied with processing some kind of payroll every week and possibly even several times in one week. This situation arises when different groups of employees are paid for different time periods. For example, hourly employees may be paid every week, whereas salaried employees may be paid twice a month. In addition, the employees of acquired companies may be paid in accordance with the pay periods that were in existence prior to their acquisition. Processing multiple payroll cycles eats up most of the free time of the payroll staff, leaving it with little room for cleaning up paperwork or researching improvements to its basic operations.

An excellent solution is to consolidate the payroll cycles into a single, companywide cycle. By doing so, the payroll staff no longer have to spend extra time on additional payroll processing, nor do they have to worry about the different pay rules that may apply to each processing period—everyone is treated exactly the same. To make payroll processing even more efficient, it is useful to lengthen the payroll cycles. For example, a payroll department that processes weekly payrolls must run the payroll 52 times a year, whereas one that processes monthly payrolls only does so 12 times a year, which eliminates 75 percent of the processing that the first department must handle. These changes represent an enormous reduction in the payroll-processing time the accounting staff requires.

However, reducing the number of payroll cycles may engender a considerable number of objections by employees. The main complaint is that they have structured their spending habits around the old pay system. For example, employees who currently receive a paycheck every week may have a great deal of difficulty in adjusting their spending to a paycheck that only arrives once a month. If a company were to make a switch from a short to a long pay cycle, it is extremely likely that the payroll staff will be deluged with requests for pay advances well before the next paycheck is due for release, which will require a large effort to handle. To overcome this problem, many companies only lengthen their pay cycles incrementally, usually to once every two weeks or twice a month, and make it clear to employees that pay advances *will* be granted for a limited transition period. By making these incremental changes, a company can keep the level of employee discontent to a minimum.

Another implementation point is to make sure that the rest of the management team is supportive of the length of the new payroll cycle. They must buy into the program because all of their employees will be impacted by the change. If they receive an inordinate volume of complaints from their employees about this issue, they may argue against the change; if enough of them do that, this best practice may never succeed.

In short, consolidating and lengthening payroll cycles is an excellent method for making a significant improvement to the efficiency of the payroll staff, but it must be done with the full approval of the management team and with adequate forewarning of all company employees.

Cost: 💵   **Installation time:** ⏰ ⏰ ⏰

18–27 Electronically Verify Employee I-9 Information

It is becoming increasingly difficult for employers to maintain a legal workforce. Immigration authorities have become more active in tracking down and removing illegal aliens. Now the federal government has supplied a tool for verifying a new hire's citizenship information as provided by them on the Form I-9.

The tool is called E-Verify, and it is accessed through the Internet, on the U.S. Citizenship and Immigration Services Web site (*www.uscis.gov*). It is operated by the Department of Homeland Security (DHS) in partnership with the Social Security Administration (SSA), and is a free resource that employers can use to verify the Social Security numbers of their employees. It also includes a photo screening tool that allows an employer to check the photo on a new hire's Employment Authorization Document or Permanent Resident Card (green card) against a large database of images stored in the DHS immigration databases.

The employer can initiate a query on the system only after an employee accepts an offer of employment and has completed the Form I-9. The employer must initiate the query no later than the end of three business days after the new hire's actual start date. The results of a verification through the system normally take just a few seconds. If the information presented does not match the government's databases, then the employer will be asked to review the accuracy of the information just entered. Upon any reentry of information, the system will either authorize employment, issue a tentative nonconfirmation, or state that DHS verification is in process. The DHS verification in process message means that the SSA match is correct but does not match the DHS information (which requires additional time for a government review). If there is a tentative nonconfirmation, then the employer must notify the new hire of the situation. The new hire can resolve the issue by calling the USCIS or by going to any Social Security Administration field office. If the issue is not resolved or the new hire does not contact the government for resolution, then the case is considered to be a final nonconfirmation and the employer can then terminate employment.

A company can register for E-Verify at *e-verify.uscis.gov/enroll,* after which a signatory authority for the company must sign a memorandum of understanding. An employer can also authorize a designated agent to register on its behalf, which would happen if the employer chooses to outsource this task to a third party.

The system is voluntary for employers but is required for federal government employers and contractors having federal contracts greater than $100,000. Some state governments also require employers in their states to use the system.

Cost: Installation time:

18–28 Outsource Employment Verifications

Companies with a large number of employees will find that their payroll departments are constantly burdened with employment verification requests for both current and previous employees. This can be a considerable chore, and one that cannot wait, since employees need these verifications in order to qualify for car loans, mortgages, apartment leases, and so on.

A solution to this labor-intensive activity is to have a third party handle all employment verifications with both automated voice response and Internet access. The largest provider of this service is The Work Number, which is a service of the TALX Corporation. Using this service, employers send employee information to The Work Number's central database in either flat file or XML format. Then, when an outside party wants to verify employment information, they enter the employee's social security number and the five-digit employer code (which is accessible on The Work Number's Web site at *www.theworknumber.com*). If they also want salary information, then the employee must use their PIN number to create a salary key code (either through the Web site or over the phone), which is good for a one-time access of their salary information.

The Work Number gives employers access to webManager, which is an on-line site on which they can see metrics for verification information, including verifications by the Web versus the phone, and for verifications of active versus inactive employee records.

By taking this approach, employers can eliminate all employment verification work, while also speeding up the verification process for their employees and ensuring that the information provided is as accurate as possible.

Cost: 💵   **Installation time:** ⏰

18–29 Outsource the Payroll Function   *✔Author's Choice*

A typical in-house payroll department has many concerns. Besides the task of issuing paychecks, it may have to do so for many company locations, where tax rates differ, employees are paid on different dates, and tax payments must be made to state governments by different means (e.g., direct deposit, bank deposit, or mail), and W-2 forms must be issued to all employees at the beginning of each year. Of all these issues, the one carrying the heaviest price for failure is a government tax deposit—missing such a payment by just one day can carry a large penalty that rapidly accumulates in size. All of these problems and costs can be avoided by handing over some or all portions of the payroll function to an outside supplier.

Payroll is one of the most commonly outsourced company functions. There are several good reasons for this. First, a supplier will undertake to pay all payroll taxes without troubling the company. The savings from avoiding government penalties for late tax payments will, in some cases, pay for the entire cost of the payroll supplier! In addition, the supplier can usually process payroll for all company locations; several suppliers have locations in all major cities, so they can handle paycheck deliveries to nearly any location. Other smaller suppliers get around not having multiple locations by sending checks to company locations with overnight delivery services—either approach works well. Another advantage is that nearly all payroll suppliers can deposit payments directly into employee bank accounts, which is something that many in-house payroll systems, especially the smaller ones, are incapable of performing. In addition, the time-consuming task of stuffing checks into envelopes is one that suppliers will handle, thereby freeing up the internal staff for less mundane work. A typical supplier also provides a wide array of reports, usually including a report-writing package that can address any special reporting needs. Once again, many smaller in-house payroll systems lack a report-writing package, so this can be a real benefit. If these advantages are not enough, one must also remember that payroll suppliers are staffed with a large team of experts who can answer payroll questions over the phone, provide specialized or standard training classes, or visit company locations for hands-on consulting. The wide array of benefits has convinced thousands of companies to switch to an outsourced payroll solution.

However, before jumping on the outsourcing bandwagon, one must consider a few reasons for not using a payroll supplier. One is that outsourcing is generally more expensive than an in-house solution, because the supplier must spend funds on marketing its services and make a profit—two items that an in-house payroll staff does not have to include in its budget. A supplier will usually sell its services to a company by offering an apparently cheap deal with a small set of baseline services, and then charge high fees for add-on services, such as direct deposit, check stuffing, early check deliveries, report-writing software, and extra human resources additions to the payroll software. As long as a company is well aware of these extra fees and budgets them into its initial cost-benefit calculations, there should be no surprises later on, as more supplier services are added and fees continue to rise. Another problem is that the payroll database cannot be linked to a company's other computer systems. Since a company's payroll data are usually located in a mainframe computer at an off-site supplier location, it is nearly impossible to create an interface that will allow for user access to payroll data. The best alternative (though a poor one) is to either keypunch the most important data into a company payroll database from payroll reports printed by the supplier or to download data from the supplier's computer. Because of this missing database linkage, a number of larger companies prefer to keep their payroll-processing work in-house.

In short, there are many good reasons for a company to outsource its payroll function to a qualified supplier. The only companies that should not do so are those that are either highly sensitive to the cost of payroll processing or those that must link their payroll data to other computer databases.

Cost: 💵   **Installation time:** ⏰ ⏰

18–30 Use Web-Based Payroll Outsourcing

Payroll processing has been the most common accounting function to outsource for many years. However, it suffers from several deficiencies, such as having to send information to the payroll supplier only on certain days, or (if the amount of information is minimal) waiting for a supplier representative to call, so that the information can be conveyed over the phone. In addition, any information that is verbally conveyed to the supplier runs the risk of being incorrect, since an additional person is involved in data entry. Yet another problem is that the supplier will typically run the payroll in a batch-processing run that evening, and then deliver the completed payroll to the company one or two days later, which is the earliest point at which the accounting staff knows the exact amount of its payroll liability, which it needs for cash management purposes.

To get around these problems, one can process payroll over the Internet. This involves accessing a supplier's Web site, entering payroll and time card information on the spot, and gaining access to fully processed payroll information immediately. This approach also allows one to enter payroll information at any time of the day or night, and to avoid additional data-entry problems caused by the use of an extra data-entry person by the supplier.

A particularly fine benefit to this approach is the lack of any software that must be installed on a computer in the accounting department. This software is needed for traditional outsourced payroll processing, where the data entry is conducted by an accounting clerk into a local computer, and then uploaded to the supplier through a modem. This software may be incompatible with other operating or application software on the computer, generally requires that the computer be reserved for payroll use (since it contains sensitive information), must be updated as the supplier issues new software versions, and costs money—payroll suppliers will charge several hundred dollars to give participating companies the "privilege" of using it.

The main downside to Web-based payroll processing is that it can be difficult to access or process if there is a poor Internet connection. Also, as is the case for any outsourced payroll, the payroll information is kept separate from other accounting information in the company's central database, so it is difficult to combine payroll information with other types of information for reporting purposes.

Cost: Installation time:

18–31 Post FAQs Answers and Issue a Payroll Orientation Brochure

Payroll departments spend a great deal of time answering employee questions about their pay. According to some surveys, this involves at least one-third of all department time! Though most of the questions are simple enough ones to answer, when they are multiplied by the number of employees in the company, it is easy to see how the payroll staff can spend so much time just responding to queries.

If the payroll staff could compile a list of the most commonly asked questions by employees, it would not be an especially long list—perhaps just 10 or 20 questions for a basic payroll system, and maybe twice that amount if they also handle benefits through the payroll system. Given the high proportion of questions dealing with a limited number of issues, this is an ideal area in which to create answers to frequently asked questions (FAQs) and post them on a company intranet site. Employees can then be directed to the FAQs list, and asked to address the payroll staff regarding only the more complex questions. Sample FAQs and their answers are as follows:

- **If I am on direct deposit, at what time of day on payday will my pay be deposited in my checking account?**

  Your pay will be available in your checking account as of 8 A.M. on payday.

- **If payday falls on a weekend, when am I paid?**

  If payday falls on a weekend, you will be paid as of the first business day prior to that weekend.

- **Can I get an advance on my next paycheck?**

  No. The company policy is to never issue pay advances under any circumstances.

- **If I resign from the company, when will I be paid my final paycheck?**

  If you voluntarily leave the company, you will be paid as part of the next regularly scheduled payroll.

- **How much unused vacation time can I roll forward into next year?**

  You can roll 40 hours forward. For exceptional cases, you must apply to your department manager for a waiver.

Though these FAQs can also be listed in the employee manual, employees do not always refer to that document. By also presenting them on the intranet site (which employees tend to access more frequently, especially if it is a rich, multifunction site), there is a much greater chance that employees will access the FAQs instead of the payroll staff.

The preceding list of frequently asked questions and their related answers will address the bulk of the payroll questions that employees are likely to have. However, some questions involving process flow require a more comprehensive response, which can be addressed with a payroll orientation brochure. For example, the brochure can graphically describe the steps involved in entering hours worked into a company time clock, or how to apply for vacation time.

The use of both FAQs answers and an orientation brochure forms an excellent knowledge base for employees to fully understand the corporate payroll system.

Cost: **Installation time:** 🕃

Total Impact of Best Practices on the Payroll Function

This section selects many of the preceding best practices and merges them into a sample payroll department, in order to show the overall impact of best practices on the payroll function. Not all of the best practices are shown here because some are mutually exclusive. Though the solution presented would work well for most companies, a careful controller should review *all* of the best practices presented in this section and modify the payroll system discussed in this section, thereby arriving at a system that fits the particular needs of his or her company more exactly.

When selecting those best practices from the previous list in order to construct a more efficient system, it rapidly becomes apparent that the overall trend of the best practices is to streamline the existing payroll system by paring away unnecessary functions. Accordingly, this section notes a number of tasks that can be completely dispensed with. These items are noted down the left side of Exhibit 18.2 with a line through them, denoting processes that have been eliminated from the payroll processing system.

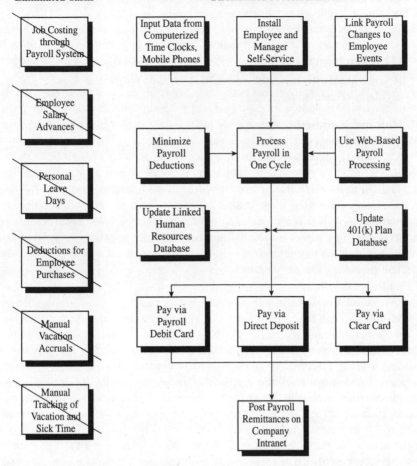

Eliminated Tasks

Job Costing through Payroll System

Employee Salary Advances

Personal Leave Days

Deductions for Employee Purchases

Manual Vacation Accruals

Manual Tracking of Vacation and Sick Time

Streamlined Process Flow

Input Data from Computerized Time Clocks, Mobile Phones

Install Employee and Manager Self-Service

Link Payroll Changes to Employee Events

Minimize Payroll Deductions

Process Payroll in One Cycle

Use Web-Based Payroll Processing

Update Linked Human Resources Database

Update 401(k) Plan Database

Pay via Payroll Debit Card

Pay via Direct Deposit

Pay via Clear Card

Post Payroll Remittances on Company Intranet

Exhibit 18.2 A Modified Payroll System

As noted in Exhibit 18.2, a fully streamlined payroll function should avoid any additional tracking time for job costing, avoid special entries for employee advances, not include additional calculations for personal leave days, eliminate deductions for employee purchases, and avoid manual vacation accruals, as well as the manual tracking of vacation and sick time—in short, one must strip this function down to the single key task of calculating employee pay, which is what it was originally intended to do.

Even the simple task of calculating pay can be further reduced so that more automation and fewer paychecks keep the amount of manual intervention to a minimum. As noted in Exhibit 18.2, a computerized time clock can be used to avoid the manual entry of employee time cards, while employees and managers can be allowed direct access to the payroll database so they can enter a variety of information on their own. Once payroll processing is completed, the payroll system can be automatically linked to the human resources and 401(k) databases, which further reduces the work needed to update multiple databases. Additional automation includes issuing direct-deposit payments or payments to payroll debit cards, as well as online access to pay information. All of these extra levels of automation reduce the labor of the payroll staff to a bare minimum.

An additional improvement is to consolidate all of the diverse payrolls that a company may have into a single payroll processing run that covers the pay of all employees, which avoids having the payroll staff get bogged down in constant payroll calculations, check printings, and distributions. A further enhancement is to stretch out the time between payroll processing runs by changing the payroll frequency from as low as once a week to possibly as long as once a month. These steps will keep the payroll staff from spending all its time processing payroll data.

The sum total of all these changes can transform an overwhelmed payroll department into one that focuses on a minimal number of tasks, handles far fewer transactions, experiences a minimal number of errors requiring correction, and probably needs fewer employees—in short, one arrives at a low-cost and very efficient payroll processing engine.

Summary

This chapter primarily dealt with a variety of techniques for streamlining an existing payroll system. The key improvement concepts are the use of automated timekeeping systems, shifting some of the data-entry burden to employees and managers, reducing the number of payroll cycles, and issuing electronic payments. These changes leave the payroll staff in a monitoring role, which varies substantially from its existing data-entry orientation. Though few companies would implement all of the best practices listed in this chapter, given the variations in how payroll is processed in some industries, there are still many techniques listed here that a payroll manager should strongly consider installing.

Some of the best practices noted in this chapter work to the detriment of employees. For example, in order to streamline the payroll function, a company may do away with employee purchases and payroll advances, since these require extra monitoring work from the payroll staff. However, if a company is in an industry or geographical region where qualified employees are in short supply, it may be a reasonable decision by the management team to allow these inefficiencies to continue, rather than run the risk of losing employees over such minor streamlining changes. Because of the impact on employees of many payroll best practices, it is wise to consult with senior management prior to making any significant changes and not to be surprised if the decision handed back is to retain the status quo, despite higher levels of inefficiency.

For more information about payroll best practices, please refer to Bragg, *Payroll Best Practices* (John Wiley & Sons, 2005).

Summary of Best Practices

Chapter 3: Accounts Payable Best Practices

Approvals

3–1   Pay based on receiving approval only

3–2   Reduce required approvals

3–3   Use negative assurance for invoice approvals

Credit Cards

3–4   Use procurement cards

3–5   Use a ghost card

3–6   Negotiate procurement card rebates

Documents

3–7   Route all invoices directly to accounts payable

3–8   Split payables processing based on discounts

3–9   Adopt a standard invoice numbering convention

3–10   Automate three-way matching

3–11   Digitize accounts payable documents

3–12   Directly enter receipts into computer

3–13   Fax transmission of accounts payable documents

3–14   Have suppliers include their supplier numbers on invoices

3–15   Receive billings through electronic data interchange

3–16   Request that suppliers enter invoices through a Web site

3–17   Shift incoming billings to an EDI data-entry supplier

Expense Reports

3–18   Audit expense reports

3–19   Automate expense reporting

3–20   Eliminate cash advances for employee travel

3–21   Link corporate travel policies to an automated expense reporting system

Management

Payments

Purchasing

Suppliers

Chapter 4: Billing Best Practices

Invoice Delivery

4–1   Avoid missed billings

4–2   Add carrier route codes to billing addresses

4–3   Mark envelopes with "address correction requested"

4–4   Do early billing of recurring invoices

4–5   Issue electronic invoices through the Internet

4–6   Issue single, summarized invoices each period

4–7   Print separate invoices for each line item

4–8   Transmit transactions via electronic data interchange

Invoice Error Checking

4–9   Enhance the invoice layout

4–10 Add receipt signature to invoice

4–11 Automatically check errors during invoice data entry

4–12 Proofread invoices

4–13 Have delivery person create the invoice

4–14 Computerize the shipping log

4–15 Track exceptions between the shipping log and invoice register

Invoicing Efficiency

4–16 Eliminate month-end statements

4–17 Reduce number of parts in multipart invoices

4–18 Replace intercompany invoicing with operating transactions

4–19 Improve shipping charge revenue

Chapter 5: Budgeting Best Practices

Budget Assumptions

5–1   Link the budget to key business drivers

5–2   Clearly define all assumptions

5–3   Clearly define all capacity levels

5–4   Establish project ranking criteria

5–5   Apply throughput analysis to capital budgeting

5–6   Establish the upper limit of available funding

5–7   Identify step-costing change points

5–8   Budget for attrition

Budget Models

5–9   Budget by groups of staff positions
5–10 Create a summarized budget model for use by upper management
5–11 Include a working capital analysis
5–12 Use activity-based budgeting
5–13 Incorporate target costing into the budgeting process
5–14 Link a bonus sliding scale to the budget
5–15 Use flex budgeting
5–16 Incorporate risk analysis into budget modeling

Budget Management

5–17 Automatically link the budget to purchase orders
5–18 Issue a budget procedure and timetable
5–19 Preload budget line items
5–20 Adopt two-stage capital budgeting
5–21 Purchase budgeting and planning software
5–22 Reduce the number of accounts
5–23 Revise budgets on a quarterly basis
5–24 Simplify the budget model
5–25 Use online budget updating

Chapter 6: Cash Management Best Practices

6–1   Access bank account information on the Internet
6–2   Automatically apply cash
6–3   Avoid delays in check posting
6–4   Collect receivables through lockboxes
6–5   Install remote deposit capture
6–6   Consolidate bank accounts
6–7   Implement physical cash sweeping
6–8   Implement notional pooling
6–9   Implement controlled disbursements
6–10 Negotiate faster deposited-check availability
6–11 Open zero-balance accounts
6–12 Shift money with electronic funds transfer

Chapter 7: Collections Best Practices

Collection Management

Collection Systems

Chapter 8: Credit Best Practices

8–1   Create a credit policy

8–2   Modify the credit policy based on product margins

8–3   Modify the credit policy based on changing economic conditions

8–4   Modify the credit policy based on potential product obsolescence

8–5   Centralize credit risk analysis

8–6   Preapprove customer credit

8–7   Subscribe to a credit report database

8–8   Create an internal credit scoring system

8–9   Modify credit application terms to favor the company

8–10   Create a credit application guidebook

8–11   Create standardized credit level determination system

8–12   Require a new credit application if customers have not ordered in some time

8–13   Review the credit levels of all customers who stop taking cash discounts

8–14   Call new customers and explain credit terms

8–15   Issue a payment procedure to customers

8–16   Join an industry credit group

8–17   Refer a potential customer to a distributor

8–18   Require intercorporate guarantees

8–19   Obtain check verification and guarantee coverage

8–20   Obtain credit insurance

8–21   Obtain an export credit guarantee

8–22   Shorten the terms of sale

8–23   Insist on lien rights

Chapter 9: Commissions Best Practices

Commission Calculations

9–1   Automatically calculate commissions in the computer system

9–2   Calculate final commissions from actual data

9–3   Construct a standard commission terms table

9–4   Periodically issue a summary of commission rates

9–5   Simplify the commission structure

Commission Payments

9–6   Include commission payments in payroll payments

9–7   Lengthen the interval between commission payments

9–8   Only pay commissions from cash received

9–9   Periodically audit commissions paid

Training

14–28   Create accounting training teams

14–29   Create an ongoing training program for all accounting personnel

14–30   Create computer-based training movies

14–31   Implement cross-training for mission-critical activities

Chapter 15: General Ledger Best Practices

Chart of Accounts

15–1   Eliminate small-balance accounts

15–2   Modify account code structure for storage of ABC information

15–3   Create alphanumeric department/subsidiary codes

15–4   Reduce the chart of accounts

15–5   Use identical chart of accounts for subsidiaries

Data Warehousing

15–6   Use data warehouse for report distribution

15–7   Use forms/rates data warehouse for automated tax filings

15–8   Use the general ledger as a data warehouse

General

15–9   Restrict use of journal entries

15–10   Avoid general ledger posting bottlenecks

15–11   Have subsidiaries update their own data in the central general ledger

15–12   Prescreen construction-in-progess entries

System Additions

15–13   Construct automated interfaces to software that summarizes into the general ledger

15–14   Create general ledger drill-down capability

15–15   Use automated error-checking

Chapter 16: Internal Auditing Best Practices

Assisting Business Units

16–1   Annually update an internal control assessment of each business unit

16–2   Issue self-audit guides to business units

16–3   Recommend business process improvements to business units

16–4   Track audit results through business unit surveys

Index